Shakespeare after Mass Media

EDITED BY
RICHARD BURT

INDIANAPOLIS MARION CO.
PUBLIC LIBRARY

palgrave .

SHAKESPEARE AFTER MASS MEDIA
Copyright © Richard Burt, 2002.
All rights reserved. No part of this book may be used or reproduced in any
manner whatsoever without written permission except in the case of brief
quotations embodied in critical articles or reviews.

First published 2002 by PALGRAVE™
175 Fifth Avenue, New York, N.Y. 10010 and
Houndmills, Basingstoke, Hampshire, England RG21 6XS.
Companies and representatives throughout the world.

PALGRAVE is the new global publishing imprint of St. Martin's Press LLC
Scholarly and Reference Division and Palgrave Publishers Ltd. (formerly
Macmillan Press Ltd.).

ISBN 0-312-29453-0 (cloth)
ISBN 0-312-29454-9 (paperback)

Library of Congress Cataloging-in-Publication Data
Shakespeare after mass media : edited by Richard Burt.
    p.   cm.
  Includes bibliographical references and index.
  ISBN 0–312–29454–9
  1. Shakespeare, William, 1564–1616—Criticism and interpretation—
History—20th century. 2. Shakespeare, William, 1564–1616—
Adaptations—History and criticism. 3. Shakespeare, William,
1564–1616—Film and video adaptations. 4. Shakespeare, William,
1564–1616—Stage history—1950- 5. Mass media and literature.
I. Burt, Richard, 1954-

PR2970. S49   2002
822.3'3—dc21   2001036203

Design by Letra Libre, Inc.

First edition: January 2002
10 9 8 7 6 5 4 3 2 1

Printed in the United States of America.

For Laurie Osborne,
as extraordinary a friend and colleague
as she is a scholar and teacher

CONTENTS

LIST OF ILLUSTRATIONS

CONTRIBUTORS

Editor

RICHARD BURT is Professor of English at the University of Massachusetts, Amherst and the author of *Unspeakable ShaXXXspeares: Queer Theory and American Kiddie Culture, Licensed by Authority: Ben Jonson and the Discourses of Censorship,* and numerous articles on topics such as the erotics of pedagogy, the celebrity intellectual, Renaissance drama, Shakespeare and film, and museum censorship. He is the editor of *The Administration of Aesthetics: Censorship, Political Criticism, and the Public Sphere,* and co-editor of *Shakespeare, the Movie, II: Popularizing the Plays on Film, TV, and Video* (forthcoming), *Shakespeare, the Movie: Popularizing the Plays on Film, TV, and Video,* and *Enclosure Acts: Sexuality, Property, and Culture in Early Modern England.* Burt has also taught as a Fulbright Scholar at the Free University and Humboldt University in Berlin, Germany, and is currently writing two books, *Ever Afterlives: Fashioning the Renaissance on Film and Video* and, with his wife Betsy, *Dumb Love: A Loser's Guide.*

> email: burt@english.umass.edu
> website: http://www.richardburt.com

Essayists

STEPHEN M. BUHLER is Associate Professor of English at the University of Nebraska-Lincoln. He has published several articles on Shakespeare, Spenser, and Milton, many with an emphasis on engagements between literary culture and the performing arts. He is the author of *Shakespeare in the Cinema: Ocular Proof.*

> email: smb@unlserve.unl.edu

MARK THORNTON BURNETT is Reader in English at the Queen's University of Belfast. He is the author of *Masters and Servants in English Renaissance Drama and Culture: Authority and Obedience,* the editor of *The Complete Plays of Christopher Marlowe* and *The Complete Poems of Christopher Marlowe,* and the co-editor of *New Essays on Hamlet, Shakespeare and Ireland: History, Politics, Culture* and *Shakespeare, Film, Fin de Siecle*. He is currently completing *Constructing "Monsters" in Shakespearean Drama and Early Modern Culture*.

email: Mark.Burnett@Queens-Belfast.AC.UK

CRAIG DIONNE is Associate Professor of English at Eastern Michigan University, where he teaches Shakespeare, Renaissance Literature and Theory. Editor of the *Journal of Narrative Theory* for three years, and now director of the graduate program in English Literature at EMU, Dionne is co-editor with David Shumway of the anthology *Disciplining English* and has published essays in Shakespeare in popular culture, Elizabethan underworld, and pedagogy.

email: eng_dionne@ONLINE.EMICH.EDU

PETER S. DONALDSON is Professor of Literature at M.I.T. and director of the Shakespeare Electronic Archive. He is author of *Machiavelli and Mystery of State, Shakespearean Films / Shakespearean Directors* and of a series of multimedia essays on Shakespeare on film including "Digital Archives and Sibylline Sentences: *The Tempest* and the 'End of Books.'"

email: psdlit@mit.edu

DONALD K. HEDRICK is Professor of English at Kansas State University and founding director of the Program in Cultural Studies there. He has taught at Cornell University, Colgate University, and Amherst College, and has published articles on architecture, drama, cultural studies, Shakespeare, and film. He is co-editor with Bryan Reynolds of *Shakespeare Without Class: Misappropriations of Cultural Capital* and is currently working on a project on valuation and entertainment in the early modern period and a project on movie trailers.

email: hedrick@ksu.edu

DIANA E. HENDERSON, Associate Professor of Literature at M.I.T., is the author of *Passion Made Public: Elizabethan Lyric, Gender, and Performance* and numerous articles, including essays on early modern drama, poetry, and domestic culture, Shakespeare on film, James Joyce, and Virginia Woolf. Her current book manuscript is entitled *Uneasy Collaborations: Shakespeare across Time and Media*.

email: dianah@mit.edu

JOSH HEUMAN is a doctoral candidate in Media and Cultural Studies at the University of Wisconsin-Madison. His dissertation examines relationships between projects of cultural regulation and discourses of communication and citizenship.

email: jmheuman@students.wisc.edu

D. J. HOPKINS is a doctoral candidate in the U.C. Irvine / U.C. San Diego Joint Ph.D. Program in Theatre and Drama. Most recently, he published an article on Charles L. Mee's radical appropriations of classic texts. Hopkins works as a professional dramaturg and holds an M.F.A. in dramaturgy from U.C. San Diego.

email: dhopkins@ucsd.edu

DOUGLAS LANIER is Associate Professor of English and Director of English graduate studies at the University of New Hampshire. He has published articles on Shakespeare, Marston, Jonson, Milton, the Jacobean masque, and literature pedagogy in a number of journals and collections. His most recent publication is an essay on the cultural politics of Branagh's *Hamlet* in *Spectacular Shakespeare: Critical Theory and Popular Cinema*, edited by Lisa Starks and Courtney Lehmann. He is currently at work on a book about Shakespeare and modern popular culture forthcoming from Oxford Univ. Press.

email: doug.lanier@unh.edu

LAURIE OSBORNE is Associate Professor of English at Colby College. She has published *The Trick of Singularity: Twelfth Night and the Performance Editions* as well as several essays on Renaissance audiences and Shakespeare in film and popular culture. Her forthcoming work includes "Cutting Up Characters in Trevor Nunn's *Twelfth Night*" in *Shakespeare, Cinema, Spectacle: Critical Theory and Film Practice*, edited by Courtney Lehmann and Lisa Starks, and an essay on pedagogy entitled "Shakespeare and the Construction of Character."

email: leosborn@colby.edu

BRYAN REYNOLDS is Associate Professor of Drama at the University of California, Irvine. His book, *Becoming Criminal: Transversal Theater and Cultural Dissidence in Early Modern England* is forthcoming from the Johns Hopkins University Press, and a book on acting and transversality is under contact with Palgrave. He has published articles on the work of Shakespeare, Cixous, de Certeau, Dekker, Deleuze, Foucault, Guattari, Rousseau, Middleton, Polanski, and Robert Wilson.

email: breynold@e4e.oac.uci.edu
website: http://www.bryanreynolds.com

FRAN TEAGUE is Professor of English at the University of Georgia. Her books include *The Curious History of "Bartholomew Fair," Shakespeare's Speaking Properties*, and *Bathsua Makin, Woman of Learning*. She has edited *Acting Funny* and published articles on performance theory and history as well as on early women writers.

email: fteague@arches.uga.edu

website: http://www.arches.uga.edu/~fteague

HELEN M. WHALL is Associate Professor of English at Holy Cross College and the author of *Didactic Method in Five Tudor Dramas* and an editorial consultant for the 1993 edition of *Bartlett's Quotations*. She is now an associate editor of *Interfaces*, "an international journal of *Word and Image*," and she has served as associate editor for *Theatre Journal*. She has published articles on Saint Paul and Shakespeare's comedies and on *Hamlet* and the manner of the miniature.

email: hwhall@att.net

TO E- OR NOT TO E-?

Disposing of Schlockspeare in the Age of Digital Media

RICHARD BURT

Schlockspeare?

On the cover of the December 2000 issue of *Time Digital* devoted to electronic publishing, Shakespeare stands clutching a copy of *Hamlet* and, with eyebrows arched, eyes wide open, and lips pursed, peers intently over the shoulder of a young woman at the e-book she is holding. The woman smiles in amusement at the reader.

Perhaps unsurprisingly, Shakespeare here represents the printed book, literacy, and literature. The *Time Digital* cover replays a familiar modernist scenario of the twentieth century in which art is gendered masculine and new technologies feminine. As Andreas Huyssen (1986) has shown, modernism defined itself in large part by displacing its fears about technology and the commodity form onto women represented as sexually voracious, and the woman's open book, contrasting with Shakespeare's closed book, places her in the line of vamps who haunted modernism.[1] The feminization of print culture by electronic media signaled by the woman reader registers a possible threat to Shakespeare, whose male gaze is decentered away from the knowing woman by her sexier e-book. Is he just another dead white male, soon to be obsolete? Or will he be able to catch up to this new, feminine medium?

One anachronistic element of the *Time Digital* cover complicates, however, any quick conclusion that Shakespeare is on the conservative, male, probably out-of-it, anti-e-media side. That element is the copy of *Hamlet* that Shakespeare holds, not a quarto but a pseudo Everyman's Library edition marked as upscale by the fact that it is hardcover and by the bookmark

I.1. Shakespeare looking over e-media

ribbon hanging down from it. Shakespeare's copy of *Hamlet* is not an original, contemporary edition but a simulacrum of a modern commodity presumably accessible in the present to likely readers of *Time Digital*. So Shakespeare and art are already on the side of modern mass media, not apart from it, yet not wholly identified with it either. As a result, Shakespeare's cultural authority is perhaps less clear. Whereas in the twentieth century, adaptations of the plays helped legitimate new media such as film at its very inception, radio in the 1930s, and television in the 1950s, it now appears that electronic publishing may confer legitimacy on Shakespeare rather than the reverse. The cover also exemplifies a tendency in recent accounts of communications technologies to distort the differences between past and future: Shakespeare as trope for print culture misrecognizes the pervasive presence of Shakespeare in visual culture, most notably film. It has become a cliché to say that Shakespeare would be a Hollywood screenwriter were he alive today.

Given that what many have heralded as an electronic revolution is in a state of infancy (the present moment has been compared to the Model T era of cars), and given that Shakespeare and academia have only just begun to go digital it would be foolish to try to assess what the impact of the new media on Shakespeare and Shakespeare criticism will be.[2] There are already signs of its impact, however, which suggest, in my view, a need to reorient the study of Shakespeare and mass media. Shakespeare's relationship to mass media has been interpreted one of two ways, either as the democratization of high culture through low media, Orson Welles being a central figure in this regard, or as the dumbing down and debasement of Shakespeare for the masses. Both of these have to do with exclusion of some readers, viewers, and theatergoers from access to Shakespeare: in the view of avowedly progressive critics such as Lawrence Levine (1989), Alan Sinfield (1992), and Michael Anderegg (1999), among others, exclusion is a bad thing foisted on the lower working poor by the higher dominant elites, often with the help of the colluding bourgeoisie; in the view of avowedly conservative critics such as Allan Bloom (1989), exclusion is a good thing, necessary to preserve civilization against the barbarian hordes.

Despite their differences, progressive and conservative critics making these interpretations share a low estimate of mass culture. Though often used interchangeably with popular culture, mass culture is typically defined as culture imposed on "the people" whereas popular culture is culture made by "the people." Richard Halpern, for example, defines mass culture as "a set of global conditions reorganizing the totality of cultural production and consumption in modern culture rather than a specific class culture. Mass culture is not the expression of the masses; it is, rather, the sum of the conditions that produce the historically unprecedented phenomenon of massification and that reorganize the relations of different class cultures as they had developed during the nineteenth century"(1997, 54).

Critics typically condemn mass culture as repetitive, mechanical, alienating, conformist, and dehumanizing, and it is thus hardly surprising that Shakespeareans follow progressive cultural critics by invariably replacing the term "mass culture" with the term "popular culture" (Williams 1976, 199; Hebidge 1979; Ross 1989; Strinati 1995; Penley 1977; Frecerro 1999), substituting a bottom-up receiver as active fan model for the top-down receiver as passive dupe model in earlier ideology critiques of what Theodor Adorno and Max Horkheimer called "the culture industry" (1972; 1991). "The people" are thus said to be reproducers if not producers of their own culture. The task of the critic is to "intervene" in the present political and pedagogical scene by locating contradictions in the "texts" of popular culture, to show that the dominant culture has to include dissident voices in order to maintain its own always incomplete, and thus always contestable, hegemony (Ross 1989; Freccero 2000). In addition to doing a close reading, the critic points out the material conditions of exploitation, appropriation, reception, and exclusion that made the cultural artifact possible. And in attending to popular culture, the critic also takes on the role of public intellectual and gains greater cultural legitimation and wider public access (Berubé 1994).

Like conservative Shakespeareans, progressive Shakespeareans tend to dismiss and denigrate mass culture as such. In his fine book, *Orson Welles, Shakespeare, and Popular Culture*, Michael Anderegg writes, for example,

> What made the culture of the nineteenth century America—including the plays of Shakespeare—at all "popular" was the interaction between production and reception, actor and audience, speaker and listener. By definition, of course, radio, recordings, television, the movies, and all other forms of mass communication are antithetical to such a relationship. Not only is there no genuine interaction between sender and receiver, but there is precious little interaction among the various receivers themselves. The whole notion of popular culture, when the term is used in a positive sense, nearly ceases to have meaning in the twentieth century. For most people most of the time, the consumption of culture is an individual, private experience. Without attempting to make an absolute distinction, it might be suggested that . . . a production of Shakespeare in front of an audience of two hundred is (or can be) popular culture; a television transmission of a Time-Life BBC Shakespeare play viewed by five million people . . . can in no way be thought of as popular in this sense. (1999, 165–67)

In Anderegg's idealizing, nostalgic narrative of Welles's career, mass culture has effectively made popular culture impossible. This rather nostalgic account of popular culture is not only self-defeating but quite conservative in its implications. From the 1950s, in sociological works like Fredric Wertham's *Seduction of the Innocent: The Influence of Comics on Today's Youth*, to the 1990s in pop-psych works like Mary Pipher's *Reviving Ophelia* and William Pollack's *Real Boys' Voices*, mass culture has been regarded as a threat to the moral development of young people.[3] Anderegg's account, though opposed to this moralistic view nevertheless converges with it: mass culture is now a threat to literature and to academics who teach it.

Some Shakespeareans have been willing to concede that Shakespeare's plays were always part of mass culture. As Michael Bristol writes, for example: "The complexity of the plays might . . . be described not as an artistic achievement but rather as a shrewd strategy to curry favour with as many sectors as possible within a complex multi-cultural market. This would suggest that a Shakespearean work is in effect an industrial rather than an individual product and that its specific form of appearance is in some fundamental way motivated and sanctioned by an ethos of business success. Shakespeare would then be seen as something more like a modern corporate logo or trademark rather than the specific name of an exceptional individual or creative genius. . . . Shakespeare and his contemporaries . . . organized institutions that constitute the ancestry of the modern culture industry "(1996, 5; 50–51). Yet Bristol's neo-Frankfurt school account of mass culture is even more conservative than Anderegg's. Bristol valorizes traditional hierarchies of print over visual culture, literature over other cultural forms. He laments "the devolution of public cultural authority from print to animated film to television," and he bemoans the way that "the impoverishment of [the institution of literature] coincides with opportunities for capital accumulation in larger but more fragmented cultural markets where hyperactivity and distraction are preferred to the more difficult pleasures of traditional literature" (1996, 233). In both Anderegg's and Bristol's accounts, we have a familiar binary opposition between mass culture, distraction, and passive consumerism, on the one hand, and literature, difficulty, and active involvement, on the other.

As editor of this volume, I have preferred the terms "mass media" and "mass culture" over "popular culture" in order to question the rather simply drawn binary oppositions on which narratives of Shakespeare and mass media have been constructed. What these interpretations of Shakespeare and mass culture have failed to recognize is that Shakespeare's reproduction in mass culture is not identical with greater public access, whether or not the form Shakespeare takes in a given medium or subgenre is thought to be intelligent or stupid. In fact, one of the main reasons no one has probably ever before edited an anthology on Shakespeare and mass media, apart from film, is that Shakespeare (both as an icon and as cited text) comes up in so many media and so often that it is impossible to archive all the examples. Shakespeare appears frequently nearly wherever one looks: in images like the one on the cover of *Time Digital;* political cartoons on the editorial pages of newspapers; comic books; popular music lyrics; musicals; detective fiction; theme parks; romance novels; hardcore pornography; advertising; cigar brands; science fiction; board games; gift wrapping paper; greeting cards; shopping bags; T-shirts; beer labels; rubber duck bath toys (http://www.celebriducks.com/shakespeare); Internet websites; business management guides; and so on.

Many of these examples remain known to a handful of people. In contrast to the Academy Award winning *Shakespeare in Love* (dir. John Madden,

I.2. Shakespeare's *Macbeth* in the flesh (Courtesy VCA Films)

Jr., 1998), few academics will have heard of romance novels like Malia Martin's *Much Ado About Love* (Shakespeare turns out to be Queen Elizabeth's daughter) or hardcore porn adaptations such as *A Midsummer Night's Cream* (dir. Stuart Canterbury, 2000) and the even more obscure Hungarian gay porn *Midsummer's Night Dream* (dir. Steve Cadro, 2000), the futuristic *Macbeth* porno spin-off *In the Flesh* (dir. Stuart Canterbury, 1999), or porn adaptations of *Romeo and Juliet* such as *West Side* (dir. Ren Savant, 2000) and *Shakespeare Revealed* (dir. Ren Savant, 2000).[4] Perhaps even fewer academics know of the gay porn novel *Shakespeare's Boy* (1991) by Casimir Dukhaz. And doubtless very few viewers of Michael Almereyda's mainstream film *Hamlet* (2000) will recognize clips taken from the classic porn film *Deep Throat* (dir. Gerard Damiano, 1972) in Hamlet's deep inside Denmark film within a film, "The Mousetrap: A Movie." Surely, there are many similar examples no one has ever archived or ever will.[5]

I prefer the terms mass culture and mass media to popular culture in order to foreground the extent to which Shakespeare's heterogeneous cultural presence often cannot be recuperated as so many examples of resistance to hegemony and cultural imperialism. Yet even if all of the examples of Shakespeare were to be archived, some critics might shrug their shoulders and ask, "So what? If they aren't politically transgressive or subversive, aren't these examples merely trivial and ephemeral, mere taglines and cliches without serious critical import except insofar as they testify to Shakespeare's cultural capital or his universality? Don't they amount to schlock and nothing more?" To be sure, one could attempt to defend the study of arcane examples on the same political grounds many progressive cultural critics have defended the study of popular culture, namely, that they have some transgressive, protopolitical meaning to be interpreted by the critic/fan. Given the importance of reading popular culture in relation to and in terms of print culture (movies and other visual media are read as "texts") and high culture, Shakespeare's presence in mass culture could be regarded as a key site for critical "intervention" and pedagogy.

This defense is not one I wish to adopt. Most instances of Shakespeare in mass media do not have sufficient hermeneutic density to qualify as politically transgressive (see Burt 1999, 12–24).[6] I think they do have value, however, in suggesting a different way of thinking about Shakespeare and mass media, one that focuses on both communications technologies as obsolete, ephemeral, dated, and schlocky, and on the personal collection rather than on the politics of exclusion and public access.[7] The figure for the critic here is not the protopolitical revolutionary fan and member of a techno-youth culture nor the common reader, but the melancholic loser who, because of what some critics would call his or her "interpretive community," (Fish 1980) happens to be both a reader of Shakespeare and a reader / viewer of media and subgenres in which Shakespeare is adapted and cited.[8] In titling this book, *Shakespeare After Mass Media,* I do not mean to suggest that Shakespeare ever existed prior to mass media and mass culture. I mean to suggest, rather, that electronic and digital mass media, along with shifts in the global political landscape after the end of the Cold War and the development of transnational, global capitalism, have begun to transform the ways in which we attend to Shakespeare and conceptualize him and his writings both in criticism and in the classroom. I think it is therefore necessary to theorize what I call "Schlockspeare" rather than laugh it off, dismiss it as trivial, and doing so means a wholesale rethinking of some of the central assumptions enabling cultural studies to conceptualize all cultural practices as written "texts." In particular, Shakespeare's cultural authority, appropriation, and adaptation in print, cinematic, and digital communications technologies may usefully be theorized in terms of loss: new technologies are always about speed, and therefore are always already about belatedness and obsolescence. Quick-Time video players, for example, will soon be to more advanced media what the daguerreotype is to film shot in digital.

Except for a few well-known films, the media and subgenres discussed by contributors in this collection may be regarded as marginal not because they and their readers are devalued and excluded by the dominant culture, but because of the accidental and particular interests some readers, viewers, or listeners happen to have.[9] I don't mean to imply that there is a consensus among the contributors about preferring the terms "mass media" and "mass culture" to "popular culture" or about the terms in which mass media should be viewed. There isn't. And I concede that there are many aspects of mass media and many media not covered here. In an ideal world, this collection would include essays on Shakespeare and television, CD-ROMs, pop music, editorial cartoons, Indian and other post-colonial mass cultures, the Internet, detective fiction, children 's literature, among others.[10] Yet however inclusive this volume might be, total coverage would be impossible to achieve simply because no one person or body of persons can be sure to know all the references, and sheer description of the material would be of little use or critical interest. What the contributions assembled here do share is a common interest in theorizing mass media in relation to schlock, or what I am calling "Schlockspeare": mass media as trash, kitsch, obsolete, trivial, obscure, unknown, forgotten, unarchived, beyond the usual academic purview. How is Shakespeare adapted in these media? How does Shakespeare's cultural authority play out in these media? How do they bear on academic constructions of his authority? These are some of the questions the contributions hope to open up.

The chapters fall into two parts, with "Part One: Questions of Shakespeare's Cultural Authority: Theories, Issues and Instances" engaging theoretical issues involving Shakespeare's cultural authority, and "Part Two: Histories of Shakespeare's Appropriation: Case Studies" engaging particular examples of Shakespeare's appropriation and adaptation. Part One begins with several chapters addressing schlock in relation to marketing forces. In "Bardguides of the New Universe: Niche Marketing and the Cultural Logic of Late Shakespeareanism," Donald K. Hedrick pursues schlock in terms of Shakespeare's citation and transformation in advertising and business-management training manuals. "Late Shakespeareanism," the discursive field increasingly responsible for Shakespeare's artistic production after the triumph of the mass media, constitutes the logic of niche marketing for target audiences. While this logic was significantly present in the early modern entertainment industry as evidenced in Shakespeare's acute awareness of its implications (in addresses to the audience, representations of commerce), what is distinctive and consequential now, Hedrick maintains, is the postmodern consumer mode of "no fashion, only fashions." Evidence of this logic reaching its completion is the recursive phenomenon of the market now itself becoming just another niche and swallowing itself up, evidenced in the sudden flourishing of corporate management guides explicitly based on Shakespeare's business wisdom, guides that through readings of the plays reveal at the same time the moral and political fault lines of a corporate-driven culture.

From a complementary critical perspective, Peter Donaldson in his essay "In Fair Verona:" Media, Spectacle, and Performance in *William Shakespeare's Romeo + Juliet*. Donaldson discusses advertising, mass media, and religious and queer kitsch and reads Luhrmann's 1996 adaptation as an updating of Shakespeare's play for an age of media convergence. In Luhrmann's surreal Verona, media are so ubiquitous and so interrelated that the boundary between events and their unending replication becomes lost as fetishized image replaces reality in what Guy Debord called the regime of "the Spectacle" and later theorists termed hyperreality. Replacing the "airy word" as the cause of the feud, the reign of integrated media is opposed, uneasily but poignantly, by vestiges of older forms—spontaneous youth improvisation, theater, festival—that persist at the margins of the late capitalist urban space. In portraying the youth culture of his Verona, Luhrmann's neopunk and high drag style derives, the essay argues, from the iconography and practices of the Sydney Gay and Lesbian Mardi Gras, and continues existing traditions of "Antipodean camp" in its reappropriation of fetishized religious icons and symbols. The focus on marketing is followed up by Mark Burnett in "'We are the makers of manners': The Branagh Phenomenon," understands the *auteur's* Shakespeare films in terms of a trajectory from classic adaptation to ironic, populist appropriation. In particular, Burnett argues that Branagh's singularity resides in the ways in which he has both generated, and been shaped by, a more amorphous and even anti-bardolatrous conception of the Schlocks-pearean. Taking up the form of the personal memoir, Diana E. Henderson discusses a different kind of market and marketing in "Shakespeare: The Theme Park." Henderson examines the transformations of Shakespeare in theme parks like Busch Gardens and the reconstructed Globe in London. In her view, overemphasis on the distinctions between "legitimate" and "illegit-imate" treatment of Shakespeare—in terms of (im)proper locales, "content," audience desires, and analytic emphases—obscures the resemblances and shifts in Shakespeare/Schlockspeare's cultural work over time, as media em-phases and consumer habits likewise shift.

Laurie Osborne, Josh Heuman and Richard Burt, and Craig Dionne pur-sue questions of Shakespeare's cultural authority and value in romance nov-els, comics, and the science fiction show *Star Trek* (and its spin-offs), respectively. In "Harlequin Presents: That '70s Shakespeare and Beyond," Osborne shows that the almost self-defined kitsch of Harlequin serials makes Shakespeare disposable. At the same time, "Schlockspeare" evolves in these forms as the forms themselves carve out audiences and relative status. So there is trash Shakespeare and there is trash Shakespeare that attempts to distinguish itself from trash Shakespeare. In their chapter "Suggested for Mature Readers?: Deconstructing Shakespearean Value in Comic Books," Heuman and Burt examine the manifold ways in which comic-book editors and writers have defined their cultural value against other, "trashier" comics and their more or less "mature" readers by citing Shakespeare and invoking his authority as an icon. Exclusion is perhaps built into the competitive ways in which comic books establish their value.

Craig Dionne theorizes Shakespeare's cultural authority through mass media in terms of quotation. In "The Shatnerification of Shakespeare: *Star Trek* and the Commonplace Tradition," Dionne argues that in *Star Trek* ci-tations of various plays and sonnets, we can see some of the many ways in which a nonacademic tradition of citing Shakespeare runs parallel and even overlaps with the academic tradition. Rather than regarding the long history of editing Shakespeare's "purple passages" as one that is limited, in terms of textuality and influence, to the stage, or alternatively, seeing the history of allusions and references to Shakespeare in popular culture as being influ-enced from the top down—where famous stage productions influence film and other mixed media allusions to the plays—Dionne proposes that the rel-atively unexamined practice of "commonplacing" Shakespeare's writing in famous quotation handbooks and manuals can be written as a "bottom up" history, where one particular mass-market industry shapes an entire range of middle-brow literacy practices that, in turn, shape the expectations of a mass readership generally and actually influence how film and stage productions of his plays will be directed and produced.

In Part Two, we turn to a variety of case studies of Shakespeare's appropriation and adaptation in mass media. In his chapter "WSHX: Shakespeare and American Radio," Douglas Lanier examines the relationship between Shakespeare and radio drama, both as a media form, which he argues has some affinities to Shakespeare's largely language-driven drama, and as a culture industry. Lanier's point is that formal rather than institutional questions have tended to shape discussion of Shakespeare on radio (what little discussion there has been). The radio industry developed under different institutional models in different nations, some of which—notably the state-sponsored BBC in Britain—have protected radio Shakespeare from having to accommodate the demands of the commercial marketplace. Shakespeare on American radio, he observes, provides a useful case study—and a model for later mass media like TV—of how Shakespeare might be adapted to the characteristic idioms and genres of popular entertainment programming. He contrasts the early years of radio, when it seemed "proper" Shakespeare might find a home on the American airwaves, and the later years, when it became apparent that for all its formal affiliation with the theater (primarily its reliance on language), American radio used Shakespeare largely as a highbrow foil to define itself as a "popular medium."

Fran Teague and Stephen M. Buhler take up Shakespeare's citation in music in their respective essays, "Shakespeare, Beard of Avon" and "Reviving Juliet, Repackaging Romeo: Transformations of Character in Pop and Post-Pop Music." It is hardly surprising that *Romeo and Juliet* occupies a special position of importance in both the musical and the pop song. If American culture has generally seen the reduction of Shakespeare to a few plays, as Lawrence Levine argues, then the quintessentially American forms of the musical and the pop lyric are places we can see this reduction happening acutely. In her chapter, Fran Teague looks at Broadway musicals based on Shakespeare, arguing that Shakespeare serves as a beard that permits the show to get on with what it really wants to do by misdirection. Because American musicals were often opposed to the legit theater, citing Shakespeare allowed variety-theater performers simultaneously to claim Shakespeare as their own and reject him as alien to the popular stage. Although mass culture renders such pop culture distinctions between variety and legit theater meaningless, certain characteristics survive from the earlier tradition. Stephen M. Buhler traces the impact of market forces, pedagogical strategies, and youth culture on the depiction of the characters Romeo and Juliet in pop and pop-reactive music. His essay proposes that several songs that reflect changing notions about these characters function as instances of both mass and popular culture—of both exploitation and authenticity, whether configured either as fan-based or authorial. The newly and renewed "sincere" Romeo and "assertive" Juliet are two emblems of a larger, recent cultural definition of adolescence: the importance attached to that age helps to explain why *Romeo and Juliet* is one of the few Shakespearean works that remains widely known.

D. J. Hopkins and Bryan Reynolds turn to mass media and theatrical performance in their chapter "The Making of Authorships: Transversal Navigation in the Wake of *Hamlet,* Robert Wilson, Wolfgang Wiens, and Shakespace." Hopkins and Reynolds explore the relationship between text and performance, using Robert Wilson's radical appropriation of *Hamlet* as a paradigm of contemporary Shakespearean stage discourse. A study in the investigative-expansive methodology of transversal theory, their article positions Wilson and his collaborators in relation to a Shakespearean author-function. Reynolds and Hopkins argue that theater is a provisional site of representational authority, not unrelated to the stagey stigma surrounding Shakespeare's "bad" quartos. And returning to the question of quotation engaged by Dionne, Helen Whall examines in her chapter "Bartlett's Evolving Shakespeare" the ways in which *Bartlett's Book of Familiar Quotations* has for over 150 years appropriated Shakespeare in ways that reflect the vagaries of editing and the disappearing line between popular and mass culture.

In his chapter, "Shakespeare and the Holocaust: "Julie Taymor's *Titus* is Beautiful, or, Shakesploi Meets (the) Camp," Richard Burt returns explicitly to the phenomenon of Schlockspeare. Burt reads Taymor's film as a failed neoconservative response to a perceived excess of violence in contemporary mass media such as video games. Taymor both embraces the Holocaust and the horror film (*Silence of the Lambs,* in particular) to recode Shakespeare's tragedy and hero and attempts to elevate her own Shakespeare film above more overtly schlocky horror films and cinematic adaptations of *Titus Andronicus.*

Shakesbites

I think it is worth asking what happens if we view Shakespeare and mass media from the perspective of obsolescence and loss and begin to theorize "Schlockspeare" from the perspective of what I call "loser criticism" (Burt 1999). For one thing, it means that the failure to attend to many, often arcane examples is not merely a matter of practical difficulty but of a constitutive blindness. What critics implicitly tend to cordon off from legitimate academic study is a field of Shakespeare citations and replays that threatens the coherence of their critical practice.[11] That coherence depends on a firm boundary being in place between Shakespeare adaptations and citations that can be regarded as dialogical and hermeneutic and those that are postdialogical and posthermeneutic. Whereas the former can be assigned a meaning and hence be read as political or protopolitical, the latter do not have a meaning and hence appear to be if not outside politics at least lacking in political-use value. Shakespeare is subsumed under the category of reproductions, with the plays being one site and Shakespeare's reputation and Shakespeareana being others, what has been called "the Shakespeare myth" (Holderness 1988), "Bardbiz" (Hawkes 1992), "Big-time Shakespeare" (Bristol 1994), the "Shakespeare trade" (Hodgdon 1998), and the "Bawdy Bard" (Keevak 2001). In these accounts, Shakespeare's identity and his cultural capital remain intact. As Terry Eagleton writes, "Shakespeare is the quintessential commodity, at once ever new and consolingly recognizable, always different and eternally the same, a magnificent feat of self-identity persisting through the most bizarre diversions and variations" (1988, 206).[12]

In my view, however, it is precisely the boundary between hermeneutic and post-hermeneutic examples of Shakespeare in mass media that is increasingly less clear, and existing accounts of Shakespeare adaptations have not theorized the difference, assuming that all adaptations are dialogical and hermeneutic (Novy 1998; Desmet 1999; Hedrick and Reynold 2000). When the notion of an authoritative, stable, authentic original Shakespeare canon is widely regarded as the invention of eighteenth-century editors, where and how would one draw the line? What would the criteria be? Consider the highly acclaimed *The Donkey Show: A Midsummer Night's Disco*, an adaptation that substitutes for the text of Shakespeare's comedy the lyrics and music of a series of brilliantly timed 1970s disco hits including Alicia Bridges's "I Love the Night Life" (Tytania to Oberon), Thelma Houston's "Don't Leave Me This Way" (Helen to Dimitri), and Stephanie Mills's "I Never Knew Love Like This Before" (Helen, Dimitri, Mia, Sander) among others. Flower juice becomes angel dust and Puck becomes Rollerina, a skater who hung out at Studio 54 during its cocaine-inspired heyday. Is *The Donkey Show*'s relation to *A Midsummer Night's Dream* hermeneutic or post-hermeneutic? Hard to say. I would argue that the self-identity Eagleton attributes to Shakespeare as a commodity is no longer there, if it ever was. When Shakespeare is invoked by the documentary *The Filth and the Fury* (dir. Julien Temple, 2000) in highly mediated fashion through footage of Laurence Olivier's *Richard III*, itself inspired by Disney's *Snow White*, which inspired Johnny Rotten, what counts now as essentially, characteristically Shakespearean? Again it is hard to say, particularly, when the Shakespeare canon itself is becoming enlarged and fragmented (see Burt 2000).

Another way of making this point is to say that the distinction between serious performances and criticism of Shakespeare, on the one hand, and a tradition dating from the end of the nineteenth century of citing famous "purple passages" from the plays rather than the plays in their entirety (see Levine 1988, 16–45; Evans 1989; Uricchio and Pearson 1993, 74–81; Anderegg 1999, 46–47; 164), on the other, has become blurred. The purple passage tradition, recently continued in books such as Frederic Talbott's *Shakespeare on Leadership: Timeless Wisdom for Daily Challenges* and the anonymous collections *William Shakespeare Quotations* (anon [a] 1997), *Shakespeare on Love: Quotations from the Plays and Poems* (1991), and *Shakespeare in Love: The Love Poetry of Shakespeare* (anon [b] 1998), has often been deplored and mocked for taking passages of the plays and poems out of context or into a context that trivializes them. I would argue, however, that academic Shakespeare criticism increasingly resembles the purple passage tradition as it relies more and more on film and other visual media and fragments the plays into "Shakesbites" and what are effectively trailers.[13] A related distinction between works produced for adult and child readers of Shakespeare is also breaking down. The 1990s and millennium saw the publication both of a series of books for adults on Shakespeare that position them as uneducated children such as *Shakespeare for Idiots* (1999), *Shakespeare for Dummies* (1999), and *Shakespeare for Beginners* (1997) and a series of books for children that essentially repackage the same information for younger readers, along with novels for young readers about Shakespeare, including a "Shakespeare Can Be Fun Series" in which *Hamlet for Kids* is introduced by Kenneth Branagh. (See also Aagesen 1999; Alikiki 1999; Bender 1999; Blackwood 1998 and 2000; Burdett 2000, Cooper 1999; Ganeri 1999; Langley 2000; Stanley 1992).[14] And in a fine essay on the use of the film clip as a movie trailer, Laurie Osborne (2002) suggests along complementary lines that a distinction between what I would call "Shakespeare, the movie" and "Shakespeare, the trailer" is also breaking down. Showing clips from films students generally have not seen rather than showing the entire films, the classroom professor functions, Osborne points out, much like a voice-over narrator in a movie trailer, rearranging scenes into sound bites for student consumption. Critiques of Shakespeare's citation and adaptation in mass media based on the politics of exclusion and appropriation rest on exclusions of their own.

Schlock and Schlockspeare are thus not meant as derogatory terms. I use them to draw attention, rather, to a central category of epistemic exclusion and, as such, also a category of dismissal based on a variety of criteria (quality, interest, endurance, seriousness, topicality). Although my focus here is on the exclusion of schlock from academic consideration, and more generally the archive, exclusion may be extended to cover attempts to popularize Shakespeare in mass media as well. Consider, for example, what may well be the end of Kenneth Branagh's celebrated efforts to popularize Shakespeare's plays in nontheatrical media. It has been widely reported that after the financially disastrous film of the heavily cut *Love's Labour's Lost* as Broadway musical, Branagh has decided to scrap plans for two more Shakespeare films: *As You Like It*, to have been set in a Japanese tea garden, and *Macbeth*, in which the tragic hero was to be a Wall Street broker. If these reports are true, they suggest that mainstream cinematic Shakespeare adaptations can fail at the box office if they are regarded by journalists and filmgoers as being either too Schlockspearean or not Schlockspearean enough. (The romantic comedy *Shakespeare in Love* may have been a success precisely because it kept a safe distance from Shakespeare's plays, which appeared recontextualized and only in brief citations and performance excerpts.)[15] Branagh's efforts to popularize Shakespeare via film, including an appearance in a trailer for Lloyd Kaufman's openly trashy, "sexploitation" film, *Tromeo and Juliet* (1996), and in a CD-ROM video game based on his 1996 film of *Hamlet* entitled *Hamlet: A Murder Mystery* (the player becomes Hamlet and "saves" Ophelia, Rosencrantz and Guildenstern, and Gertrude), evidently foundered not only on distribution problems (Kaufman's film was really a cult film that screened only in a few cities and the *Hamlet* CD-ROM is still very hard to find) but also on cultural and marketing pressures that required him both to uphold and to deconstruct an opposition between the Shakespearean and the Schlockspearean. Branagh might well be considered the heir not only to Laurence Olivier but even more to Orson Welles, Branagh being yet another box-office loser unable consistently to reconcile "high" art and "low" mass media. It would not be entirely surprising to find Branagh, like Oliver and Welles before him, ending up doing television commercials for everyday products like camera film and wine. Insofar as Branagh's case is representative, it instructs us that popularization cannot be fully assimilated to the canonically Shakespearean (the recuperated, academically viable "high art"), just as it cannot fully be elided with the apocryphally Schlockspearean either (mass media-driven ephemera of the trivial and discardable). Schlockspeare has always run deeply alongside Shakespeare—a feature of mass media Shakespeare that we can discover perhaps throughout its history, at least, I would argue, as far back as the nineteenth-century performance editions of Shakespeare's plays.

Some critics might nevertheless want to salvage an avowedly (and in my view overly narrow) political critique of exclusion (focused on the absence of representation of a disenfranchised, subordinate or subaltern group or on its denial of access to Shakespeare). One can easily imagine an argument for using education and electronic media as a means of updating the means of cultural reproduction and for seeing in the deconstruction of Shakespeare's identity and the boundary separating the hermeneutic and the posthermeneutic as a good thing if it diminishes Shakespeare's cultural authority or disrupts hegemonic constructions of Shakespeare (Holderness 1987; Taylor 1994; Cartmell 2000). In these terms, Schlockspeare would predictably be either embraced as a transgressive form of dissidence or dismissed as being yet another even more insidious means by which a subversive critique of Shakespeare is contained (by transforming Shakespeare into yet another commodity).

Yet political critiques of Shakespeare and mass media focused on the exclusion of a given minority or subordinate group are arguably themselves already obsolete. As Bill Readings maintains in *The University in Ruins,* the argument that the canon was really a white male canon that excluded the writings and art of women and minorities depended for its force on culture itself being a central point of reference. That center no longer exists, according to Readings, as what he calls the University of Culture has been replaced by the corporate University of Excellence. Culture has been "dereferentialized," and hence no longer means anything because it includes everything: "The so-called center, the nation state, is now merely a virtual point that organizes subjectivities within the global flow of capital; it is not a site to be occupied. Hence everyone seems to be culturally excluded, while at the same time almost everyone is included within the global flow of capital" (111). This is not to say that the conservative groups who in the past controlled the cultural center, Readings points out, have simply disappeared but that the right "feel the emptiness of the cultural power they hold. The cultural right is not rebelling against its exclusion from the center, but against the exclusion of the center, its reduction" (114). What Readings calls "the relentless self-marginalization" of both left and right is "a self-blinding, a refusal to recognize that the stakes in the game have changed, that the center actually does not speak, that the privileged position of enunciation is not that of the subject who participates in culture" (114–15).

The obsolescence of the critique of exclusion is compounded by two related factors. First, the Internet has decentered academic authority insofar as nonacademic Shakespeare sites have as much authority as academic ones and academic ones are not located on university and college campuses. Any attempt to oppose serious education to silly popularization ("edutainment" and "infotainment") will be deeply troubled by increasingly mediatized classrooms, now often sites for the use of new, electronic communications technologies. Second, Shakespeare critics (and humanities faculty in general) are rapidly shrinking in number as universities and colleges have become, cinematically speaking, the equivalent of *Academics in the Mist,* game preserves for the endangered species of the humanities professor (see Traub 2000). Taken together, these developments call into question the print-centered culture as text and critic as rewriter models prevalent in Shakespeare criticism and in cultural studies since the 1980s. Identified with reading rather than channel and website surfing, cultural critics may already resemble the stereotypical, sexist image of the reader as sterile woman present in Donna Reed's portrayal of Mary Hatch as a spinster, nerdy librarian (what she would have been if George Bailey had never lived and thus never married her) in *It's a Wonderful life* (dir. Frank Capra, 1946) or Marion the librarian (Shirley Jones) in *The Music Man* (dir. Morton DaCosta, 1962).[16] Yet more recent moves to acknowledge the primacy of visual over literary culture, especially for students, don't have any more currency, since visual media, too, are constantly updated or forgotten (like printed books being displaced by e-books, celluloid film stock may soon be entirely displaced by digital film).

Attending to Shakespeare and mass media in terms of Schlockspeare opens up not only a different way of thinking about Shakespeare and communications technologies but of thinking about academic legitimation and academic labor in general. Instead of greater accountability and access to the public and more rationalized, I would say industrialized, forms of labor, Shakespeareans and cultural critics might consider framing what we do in terms of archaism, obsolescence, data-dandyism, and hyperunproductivity.

E-race-ing Shakespeare

To clarify some of the consequences of the contrast I have drawn between an older, now naive criticism focused on popular culture as a means by which subordinate groups can voice their oppositional response to their exclusion and exploitation under capitalism versus "loser criticism" and mass culture as technologies of obsolescence and loss, between "Shakespeares" and what I call "ShaXXXspeares," "Shakesploitation" and "Schlockspeare," I would like to turn from considerations of electronic publication and digitalization to three film comedies. *Free Enterprise* (dir. Robert Meyer Burnett), *Bamboozled*, (dir. Spike Lee, 2000), and *Scary Movie* (dir. Keenen Ivory Wayans, 2000) all pose the question of Shakespeare and the exclusion of African Americans from cultural representation. All three films involve incidental references to Shakespeare and link Shakespeare to African Americans. These films participate in a larger development in African American mass culture dating back to the 1980s, namely, the greater visibility and market share for representations of black people, which nevertheless, in the view of some critics, exclude and oppress them. As Carla Freccero writes, "Black culture has now become a commodity like any other, one that does not, by and large, profit African Americans. This commodification, by managing race relations, increases possibilities for control as well" (1999, 16). And Michelle Wallace (1992) and bell hooks (1990 and 1992) have similarly criticized the capacity of mainstream mass media to represent African Americans.

Left out of this critique has been any consideration of the regular citation of Shakespeare by African American mass culture and in mainstream white culture representing African Americans including, among others, *Shaft in Africa* (dir. John Guillermin, 1973), a rap version of *Hamlet* in *Renaissance Man* (dir. Penny Marshall, 1994); a comic citation of the theme song from Franco Zefferelli's *Romeo and Juliet* (1968) during a parody of the balcony scene in *Waiting to Exhale* (dir. Forrest Whitaker, 1995); an anonymous black man on the street interviewed in *Looking for Richard* (dir. Al Pacino, 1996); a Busta Rhymes vs. William Shakespeare episode of MTV Celebrity Deathmatch (1999); a black Juliet and Montague clan in the martial arts action picture *Romeo Must Die* (dir. Andrzej Bartkowiak, 2000); *West Side* (dir. Ren Savant, 2001), an interracial porn adaptation of *Romeo and Juliet;* and a hip-hop adaptation of *Romeo and Juliet* called *Rome and Jewels.*(Roca 2000)[17] In examining *Free Enterprise, Bamboozled,* and *Scary Movie,* one could argue that Shakespeare functions effectively as a means of excluding blacks from representation or including them only in terms of stereotypical roles and images, primarily the entertainer. This would involve attending to the fact that *Free Enterprise* is written and directed by a white man, and *Bamboozled* and *Scary Movie* by black men. One could point out that Lee and Wayans, unlike Robert Meyer Burnett, pointedly engage questions of race-based exclusion. While I think this critique can be made, I also think it makes no difference. At the center of each film is a loser character or characters who trump concerns about identity politics, exclusion, cultural property and expropriation, and authenticity. Moreover, all three films thematize audience reception and involve a self-conscious and self-defeating use of parody in which Shakespeare functions in different ways to foreground race rather than to erase race, thereby calling into question the efficacy of signifying, mimicry, and parodic resignification as theorized, respectively, by Henry Louis Gates, Jr. (1988), Homi Bhaba (1986), and Judith Butler (1990). Access to Shakespeare and racial visibility do not in themselves remedy the present disenfranchisement of African Americans.

Heavily indebted to the far superior film *My Favorite Year* (dir. Richard Benjamin, 1982) and drawing on *The Player* (dir. Robert Altman, 1992) and *Swingers* (dir. Doug Liman, 1996), *Free Enterprise* tells the story of two loser male friends named Mark (Eric McCormack) and Robert (Rafer Wiegel). Mark is a screenwriter with money but no girlfriends, and Robert is a film editor who is broke but a pick-up artist. Both men are twenty nine and have been fans of the original *Star Trek* television series since they were children.[18] They happen to meet the series star, William Shatner, who plays himself, in a bookstore, and, over drinks, he pitches his idea for a screenplay:

SHATNER: It's a musical version of *Julius Caesar.* I got it all worked out. I want
   to do the complete text, you know, like Branagh did with *Hamlet?*
MARK: Won't that be a little long?
Shatner: Well, there'll be three intermissions.
ROBERT: Who do you see starring in it?

SHATNER: Well, I'll play Julius Caesar. (Pauses.) And I'll play all the other parts too. I'll play, uh, Cassius with a beard, and uh, Lucius with a long robe, and Trebonius a hat, and a full suit of armor for Marc Antony.
MARK: So you'll play all the parts?
SHATNER: Well, I can't play Calpurnia (laughs). I thought I'd get Sharon Stone for that.
MARK: She actually could be difficult to get.
SHATNER: Then we'll get Heather Locklear. I know her.
MARK: If you play both Caesar and Brutus, won't you have to stab yourself in the back?
SHATNER: (pauses, then smiles) I've done it before. Can't you see it? William Shakespeare's and William Shatner's *Julius Caesar.*

After Shatner leaves, Mark and Robert go off to play pool, and Robert comments in despair, "A musical *Julius Caesar.* Possibly the worst idea since new Coke." Robert adds that Shatner is "a loon." Like Peter O'Toole in *My Favorite Year,* Shatner is an over-the-hill heavy drinker who disappoints his younger fans.

The original *Star Trek* had a fairly self-conscious commitment to multiculturalism, the original series having an alien, a black woman communications officer, and an Asian Lieutenant (see Penley 1997). Some of the *Star Trek* movies and all three of the later television series, *Star Trek: The Next Generation, Deep Space Nine,* and *Star Trek Voyager* have gone beyond the tokenist representation of minorities in the original series, putting a woman captain in charge (*Voyager*), having black men as admirals (*Star Trek VI: The Undiscovered Country* [dir. Nicolas Meyer, 1992]), and so on (see Penley 1997). True to what some critics would regard as a *faux* multicultural tradition, *Free Enterprise* includes a black friend of Mark and Robert (he buys a copy of *Putney Swope*), and Shatner performs "No Tears for Caesar" as the "Artist Formerly Known as Shatner" with the Rated R, an African American rap group who backed up Shakespeare-citing Tupac Shakur before he was murdered, as his accompaniment. Like nearly all of the plot developments in this awful film, the move from *Julius Caesar* musical to *Julius Caesar* rap music video is handled clumsily. Shatner merely runs into the Rated-R by accident, and then inexplicably shows up with them at the final scene (Mark's birthday party) to perform "No Tears for Caesar," a rap montage of lines from Antony's funeral oration ending with Caesar's "et tu Brute?" Despite a few rap effects such as scratching (the record is spun in reverse so the needle skips back, and the track repeats), so that "No Tears" makes Shatner sound as if he is stuttering "No tear . . . tear tear . . . tear tears . . . for Caesar, No tear . . . tear tear . . . tear tears . . . for Caesar," Shatner's style is the same as it ever was. Shatner's lame attempt to adapt Shakespeare marks him as a loser.

One could easily mount a critique of the film's appropriation of black mass culture for white, patriarchal purposes. Unlike Shatner, the lead black singer is incomprehensible (not only to a white audience unfamiliar with ghetto slang but to all viewers because the recording is so bad). The unnamed black friend is not present at the birthday party, and everyone there besides the rapper is white. Racial difference is visible only indirectly in a green alien girl who comes out of a birthday cake and dances with Robert. One could conclude, then, that *Free Enterprise* is a throwback to the original television series in which cultural imperialism masqueraded as political progress (women and minorities were represented, but always as obedient role models in subordinate positions).

Yet to do so would be to ignore the way that Shakespeare is not enlivened or authenticated through the rappers. Shatner's version and the faux MTV video editing produce a song that it is incoherent either as rap or as Shakespeare. Moreover, Shakespeare does not redeem the white characters from loserdom. This is most obvious in the case of Shatner, who is not a Shakespearean actor. It is even more the case in the writers of the film. They seem simply to have stumbled onto Shakespeare. Anyone familiar with Shatner's career, all four *Star Trek* television series and several *Star Trek* movies, knows that many of the episodes and films cite Shakespeare or are based on Shakespeare's plays. And when he was still doing the original *Star Trek* series, Shatner recorded an awful album called *The Transformed Man* by "William Shatner Captain of Star Trek" with Shatner talking, in his inimitably bad overacting style, the lyrics to covers of songs like "Lucy in the Sky with Diamonds" and "It Was a Very Good Year" alternating with his readings of famous passages from various Shakespeare plays, including *Henry V, Hamlet,* and *Romeo and Juliet.* The number of *Star Trek, Star Trek: The Next Generation, Deep Space Nine,* and *Star Trek Voyager* episodes and movies citing or adapting Shakespeare is too long to list here.[19] Far from being serious trekkies or slash rewriters of *Star Trek* (they are totally unfamiliar with Star Trek fandom), the writer and director (who name the two lead characters after themselves) show themselves to be total geeks whose wanna-be nerdiness is in direct proportion to their massive overestimation of their truly meager creative abilities. Instead of comic parody, the "No Tears for Caesar" video and the film itself are major embarrassments.[20]

Unlike the obnoxiously smug *Free Enterprise, Bamboozled* (dir. Spike Lee, 2000) is a direct expression of its director's critique of the racism of American film and mass media. After his pitch for a *Cosby Show*-like series which would show middle-class blacks in non-stereotypical terms is shot down by the white management at the network, Pierre Delacroix (Damon Wayans), a Harvard-educated, African American television producer, decides to produce a variety show based on older minstrel shows. He intends to make the show so offensive that the white viewers will see how racist the (white) media are when (mis)representing African Americans. Shakespeare is cited briefly in the film. A man named Honeycutt (Thomas Jefferson Byrd), auditioning for a deliberately racial minstrel show, says he knows some Shakespeare, and when asked by Delacroix to do a passage, recites Hamlet's "To be or not to be" soliloquy in homey fashion: "To be or not to be? That is the motherfucking question, or some shit like that." Delacroix asks Honeycutt if he knows anything else besides Shakespeare, and, in response, Honeycutt offers up a song called "Niggers Is Beautiful." Delacroix is delighted upon hearing it since its offensiveness is exactly what he is after, and Delacroix casts Honeycutt as the show's emcee on the spot. In a funny and angry film satirizing the exclusion of African Americans from roles except those that confirm a long and embarrassing history of representing them through racist stereotypes, citing Shakespeare, in contrast to satirizing black face, does not signify racist exclusion. (Lee is apparently unaware of the many minstrel show parodies of plays by Shakespeare, *Othello* chief among them. See Browne 1960; MacDonald 1994; and Collins 1996.)

Moreover, Lee himself becomes a loser auteur, deriving his plot from Mel Brooks's *The Producers* (1968) (just like Bialystock's [Zero Mostel] and Leo Bloom's [Wilder] musical "Springtime for Hitler," Delacroix's show is a massive success despite his intention that it fail) and making Delacroix a collector of past mass-produced racist figurines of black people. Delacroix's reluctant assistant, Sloan Hopkins (Jada Pinkett), gives Delacroix one such figurine, a "Happy Nigger Bank," as a present along with a museum curator-like commentary on it, and Delacroix thereafter becomes a collector. As if he were both Delacroix and Hopkins, Lee ends his film with extremely maudlin music playing over his own collection of brief clips from films and cartoons in which a black character appears through a heavily racist lens. What Lee disavows is his own melancholic investment in this culture and the African Americans who performed in it. Lee tries to salvage the failure of parody (white and black audience members all come dressed in black face to see the show live in a television studio) by turning the narrative into a tragedy of black-on-black violence (Mantan, his black killers, and Delacroix are all gunned down), but fails miserably, in my view. What emerges is really a nostalgia for earlier leaders like Malcolm X (a clip from Lee's film *Malcolm X* [1992] is shown). The rap group the Mau Maus is itself a parody of earlier militant groups like the Black Panthers. Similarly, Delacroix's father is a locus of nostalgia. He is a loser stand-up comic who has stuck to his guns but failed in Hollywood and so is reduced to playing small clubs. The problem for Lee is that there is no authentic African American identity outside of and prior to parody.

If parody fails in *Bamboozled* to create a different kind of reception of African Americans beyond the limited, often demeaning roles to which they are typically confined by largely white-owned and managed film and television studios, it fails even more clearly in the politically incorrect and rather dumb film *Scary Movie*. Keenen Wayans directly takes up the topic of the exclusion of black characters in Hollywood horror films: a parodic episode in which a black couple, Ray (Shawn Wayans) and Brenda (Regina Hall), decide to go to a movie together replies directly to the introductory scene of the already self-parodying *Scream 2* (dir. Wes Craven, 1997). (The title of the *Scream 2* DVD chapter for this introduction is "Scary Movie.") In *Scream 2*, a black couple, Maureen (Jada Pinkett) and Phil (Omar Epps), stand in line to buy tickets, and Maureen voices a complaint about the film they are about to see, *Stab!*: "I'm gonna tell you what I think it is, OK? It's a dumb ass white movie about dumb ass white girls getting their dumb asses cut the fuck up. . . . The entire genre is historical for excluding the African American element." Phil replies, "Where'd you get your Ph.D. in black cinema, Sista Souljah?" "From *Entertainment Tonight*," she replies in turn. When they watch the movie, Maureen continues to be outspoken, talking back to it and telling the blonde woman on screen (Heather Graham) not to "go in there." *Scream 2* guts, so to speak, the force of its own critique by immediately killing off the black couple. After telling Maureen to be quiet, Phil goes to the bathroom where he is murdered by the disguised killer, who shoves a knife into his head. During a scary part, Maureen grabs the killer, thinking he is Phil, and telling him that if she were the character on the screen, she'd know how to escape. He silently nods "yes" to all her questions. She also accurately predicts the woman character's death on the screen. Yet, we know, of course, that she herself is ironically just about to be killed by the killer, and we're right. She is.

In *Scary Movie*, the corresponding black couple go to see *Shakespeare in Love*, first seen by us on a movie theater marquee, and then in clips in the theater the couple enters, just as *Stab!* was seen in *Scream 2*. The plot of the *Scream 2* episode is replayed, this time in humorous fashion. For example, Ray, who is gay but seems to be the last one to know it, goes off to the bathroom, enters a stall, and hearing some voices in the next stall, lowers his head to what is a glory hole and looks in it. An erect, white penis goes through it briefly and quickly withdraws, but Ray doesn't see it. He puts his ear to the hole, and then the erect penis literally goes through one of Ray's ears and out the other, killing him (though he appears alive later in the film). To be sure, Wayans departs from *Scream 2* in accentuating the difference between the all-white audience's silent response to the film and Brenda's practice of talking back. Yet Wayans also exaggerates the ironic distance between the way we read the film and the way Brenda reads it. In this case, Brenda mistakes the genre of the film she is watching, reading the balcony scene in which Shakespeare (Joseph Fiennes) meets Viola de Lessups (Gwyneth Paltrow) (itself a parody of the balcony scene in *Romeo and Juliet*, of course) as if it were a horror movie. She shouts "Uh, uh. Don't go in there!" as Shakespeare climbs up the vine, and then screams after the Nurse (Imelda Stuanton) comes to the window and screams upon seeing Shakespeare, who then screams in turn and falls down. Referring to Viola, Brenda says "She's not a man" as Shakespeare unwinds the white bandage Viola used to flatten her breasts so she would look like a boy.

Before the movie starts, Brenda refuses Ray's offer of popcorn, taking out "some chicken" instead, and she disregards the request on the screen to "please observe silence." Members of the all-white audience attempt to "shush" Brenda, but she is defiant, saying "shush back at you" to one, and filming one guy with her digital camcorder. The murderer, dressed in costume, sits downs next to Brenda and soon takes out a knife and places it on his lap. Like Maureen, she assumes he is her boyfriend, Ray, telling the murderer, "This movie is good! Hey baby, you came back just in time. She's about to get it on with Shake-uh-speare. He found out she's a girl." Brenda then gets a call on her cell phone, and when she objects to people telling her to shut up by telling them that "they don't even stay together in the end, " a white guy sitting next to the murderer picks up the knife in disgust and stabs her. Brenda gets up to leave, but several other white people in the audience high-five each other after stabbing her too. As she makes it to the aisle, other people get up and either stab her or hit her with things including a baseball bat while saying, "This is for *Halloween!* You ruined *Shindler's List!* For *The Fugitive!* For all Jackie Chan movies! This is for ruining *Big Moma's House!*" Finally, Brenda makes it to the stage, and, again like Maureen, gurgles in front of the movie screen, before collapsing, dead.

So what sense does it make that *Shakespeare in Love* is cited in *Scary Movie?* *Shakespeare in Love* is there partly, no doubt, because it was such a successful film and won so many Academy Awards. Also, Shakespeare is not entirely foreign to the horror genre. *Romeo and Juliet* is cited, for example, in *The Rage: Carrie 2* (dir. Katt Shea, 1999). Kevin Williamson, the screenwriter for *Scream 2*, does have (all-white) characters mention Ophelia, Romeo, and Juliet in *Teaching Mrs. Tingle*, a film he wrote and directed. And Roman Polanski made *Macbeth* after making horror films like *Rosemary's Baby*. However it got into *Scary Movie*, the result is that *Shakespeare in Love* compounds the element of parody in Wayans's film: *Scary Movie* parodies a scene in the parodic *Scream 2* and uses a scene from *Shakespeare in Love* that parodies *Romeo and Juliet*. *Scary Movie* also implies a parallel between the black couple, Ray and Brenda, and the white couple, Shakespeare and Viola de Lessups, that foregrounds the way desire errs. Ray's gay tendencies and disavowal of his homosexuality roughly parallels the homo-eroticism of Viola's cross-dressing, and the error Shakespeare makes in fail-ing to recognize Viola in drag roughly parallels Brenda's misreading of her boyfriend as straight and of John Madden's romantic comedy as a horror movie. Perhaps the similarity between Brenda and Viola/Juliet elevates the woman's death to tragic status, making her into a rebellious, Juliet-like fig-ure white people just don't understand; or perhaps the similarity pokes fun at Shakespeare and is meant as a kind of aesthetic incorrectness (as in, "Shakespeare ain't all that"). *Scary Movie* takes the license to be as nasty and as silly as it wants to be. Perhaps. What I find most interesting about the film, however, is that absolutely everything is parodied. Whereas for Spike Lee angry critique drives a parody that fails and turns unconvincingly to tragedy, here even that angry critique is only one among many stock ele-ments of the horror genre to be parodied.

Far from making a difference in terms of a critique of the exclusion and in-visibility, then, the racial identity of the director makes no difference. Delacroix is a loser like Shatner and a collector like Shatner 's fans; and audiences repre-sented in all three films remain obtuse to this critique. In *Free Enterprise,* the au-dience is content to dance and party on to an incoherent rap song; in *Bamboozled,* black and white audience members show up in black face, equally appreciative of the show; and in the *Scary Movie* episode, the difference between white and black modes of viewing allows for a critique of Brenda as much as it does of the white audience who kills her (the comedy of the scene places the film's audience on the side of the murderous white audience).

If Bill Readings is right about culture no longer having a reference and occupying the center, and if critical interventions addressed at the exclusion or marginalization of subordinate groups from the cultural center are there-fore useless as such, some might want to return to "real" politics outside the University. Yet any such return would meet the same problem. The political landscape is decentered such that older political oppositions no longer seem recognizable. As Slavoj Žižek points out:

> Insofar as today's moderate Left, from Blair to Clinton, fully accepts this de-politicization [of the economy], we are witnessing a strange reversal of roles; the only serious political force which constitutes to question the unrestrained rule of the market is the populist extreme Right (Buchanan in the USA; Le Pen in France). . . . We are therefore approaching a situation in which the ex-treme Right openly says what the moderate Left secretly thinks, but doesn't dare say in public (the necessity to curb the freedom of Capital). . . . So, again, it is as if the roles are reversed today: Leftists support a strong State as the last guarantee of social and civil liberties against Capital; while Rightists demonize the State and its apparatuses as the ultimate terror machine. (2000, 355; 356)

What, then, is the point of writing about Shakespeare and mass media under the rubric of communications technologies as obsolescence and loss? My answer, which no doubt will strike some as bizarre, is that Schlockspeare (etc.) is a new way of commodifying Shakespeare, one that enables Shakespeareans to position our market value as archaic, obsolete, useless, unproductive, without it being recuperated as a Kantian aesthetics (purpose without a purpose) since schlock is subaesthetic. What tends to pass for political criticism now is, at least in my view, itself routinized, conformist, canned, and predictable. From the perspective of an Adorno, it represents so much more commodified thought rather than a critique of commodification, which is to say that it is not really thought at all. What I am proposing through the conceptualization of Shakespeare as Schlockspeare is a different mode of criticism, what I characterize as paradoxical hyperunproductivity. I hope readers will find the possibility engaging enough not to mind reading a volume of chapters that take as one of their shared concerns the possible obsolescence and uselessness not only of mass media citations and adaptations of Shakespeare but of Shakespeare criticism as well.

Notes

I would like to thank Laurie Osborne and Mark Burnett for their astute comments on earlier drafts of this chapter, and Judith Haber for the opportunity to present a version of it to the English Department at Tufts University. I would also like to thank Douglas Lanier and Fran Teague for their helpful suggestions for organizing the chapters in this book.

1. On technology and gender, see also de Lauretis 1987.
2. For a tempered and astute analysis of electronic publishing and academic scholarship, see Darnton 1999.
3. Mary Pipher writes: "As I looked at the culture that girls enter as they come of age, I was struck by what a girl poisoning culture it was. The more I looked around, the more I listened to today's music, watched television and movies and looked at sexist advertising, the more convinced I became that we are on the wrong path with our daughters. . . . With puberty, girls crash into junk culture. (1994, 12; 131). She lauds Hillary Rodham Clinton and Tipper Gore for "sounding the alarm" (13). Pollack cites Pipher approvingly and extends her analysis of Ophelia (20) into a parallel analysis of Hamlet. The difference between 1950s and 1990s attacks on mass culture is that in the '90s Shakespeare is exempted from mass culture.
4. I will discuss these porno adaptations and others in Burt 2003. My thanks to David Linton for alerting me to *Midsummer Night's Dream* and for sending me a copy of it. The topic of Shakespeare pornography has received attention in the Field Notes section of *Lingua Franca* (See Hearst, 2000).
5. Rothwell and Meltzer write "Still another sub-species of the Shakespeare on screen genre lies in the appropriation of bits, pieces, and segments of

Shakespeare by the scenarists for popular television shows. Difficult to track down because they are not listed separately in the television guides, and therefore not fully covered in this volume, are Shakespeare episodes in commercial programs like *Cheers* and *Star Trek*." (1990, 16).

6. There are no doubt exceptions. For example, two South African scientists, Dr. Frances Thackeray and Professor Nick van der Merwe, have claimed that Shakespeare smoked dope. See Dunn 2000.

7. I theorize further what I call "Shakesploitation" in Burt 2001 and "Schlock-speare" in Burt 2002.

8. For more on the fan versus the loser, see Burt 1999.

9. I theorize the accident in Burt 2002.

10. For reasons of space, timing, and/or to avoid having chapters focused on the same medium, I was unable to include fine essays on some of these topics by Allies, Castaldo, Folkerth, Linton, Perret, and Riddens.

11. For an example see Cartmell 2000.

12. And along somewhat different lines, Bristol distinguishes between Shakespeare as commodity and essential Shakespeare: "Like any product of the culture industry, Shakespeare as a commodity is more often than not trivial and inconsequential. Even in the most vitiated and meretricious presentations, however, the semantic potential of Shakespeare's works can 'break through' into a 'more intense and fuller life.' The possibility of breaking through is what makes Shakespeare essential" (1996, 117).

13. See also Harries 2000 for a fascinating analysis of scare quotes from Shakespeare in the writings of Marx and Keynes. For a brilliant analysis of the film clip as trailer, see Osborne 2002.

14. A corresponding development is the fragmentation of children readers into smaller and smaller groupings.

15. The story received a lot of coverage in the U.K. See Allen 2001, John 2001, Lister 2001, and MacEntee 2001. In a "Chat" interview on February 15, 2001 Branagh denied the rumors: "What I hope to do this summer is to have a private workshop on [*Macbeth*] with some actors to work on the screen adaptation. And I hope towards the end of next year we will get to film it. Once again, the media seem to have made up my mind for me. Reports of my premature retirement are grossly exaggerated." See http://www.homeworkhigh.com.

16. For a wonderful account of the way Shakespeare has been read as feminine in American mass culture, see Dionne 1995.

17. Apart from these examples and the casting of black actors in mainstream adaptations of Shakespeare's plays, others include a black character named Miles Pope (Lenny Henry) who wants to play Othello in *True Identity* (dir. Charles Lane, Jr., 1991); a black Don Pedro (Denzel Washington) in Kenneth Branagh's *Much Ado About Nothing* (1993); a black Voltemand (Don Warington) in his *Hamlet* (1996); and two black actors in his *Love's Labour's Lost* (2000, Carmen Ejogo as Maria and Adrian Lester as Dumaine); Harold Perrineau, Jr. as Mercutio in Baz Luhrmann's *William*

Shakespeare's Romeo + Juliet (1996) and as Caliban in a television adaptation of *The Tempest* set in the Civil War South called *The Tempest* (dir. Jack Bender, 1998); Daryl Mitchell as an English Literature high school teacher (Mr. Morgan) in *10 Things I Hate about You* (dir. Gil Junger, 1999); Harry J. Lennix as Aaron in *Titus* (dir. Julie Taymor, 1999); black hip hop star Aaliyah as a Juliet character in *Romeo Must Die* (dir. Andrzej Bartkowiak, 2000); a black character named Larry Banks (Tygh Runyan) who mentions Shakespeare in *AntiTrust* (dir. Peter Howitt, II, 2001); *O* (dir. Tim Blake Nelson, 2001); *Othello* (dir. Geoffrey Sax, 2001); and *Rome and Jewels*, a rap musical about Romeo and Juliet, and *A Bombitty of Errors*, a rap musical version of *The Comedy of Errors* performed in New York by four white college students. Also, there was a skit on an episode of the Fox Network 1980s series *In Living Color*, episodes of which Keenen Ivory Wayans appeared in and wrote, about a black man named Anton (Damon Wayans) panhandling on a New York subway. The premise is that the guy is not simply a beggar but will entertain for handouts. He is so terrible that people give him money just so he will stop and go away. At one point, Anton begins to quote Hamlet's "To be or not to be?" soliloquy but only gets the first line right. The second comes out garbled. And I only saw the last few minutes, but a sitcom that ended at 7 P.M. EST on Wednesday, 20 September 2000 had two black male characters doing a scene from a high school production of *Hamlet*. One is helping the other, who just got a call on his cell phone, remember his line, saying quietly "to thine own self be true." And the other actor says, with a big smile on his face, "To thy cell phone be true." Both men are dressed in period costumes. On *Good Morning America* (ABC Network) at about 8:40–45 A.M. EST, September 18, 2000, there was an interview with a white guy who had quit his lucrative job to become a teacher in New York City's "toughest schools." He was surrounded by his students, all black, and a girl on his right held a copy of a children's version of *Romeo and Juliet* with "William Shakespeare" written in large letters across the top. She and the book were prominently visible during most of the interview. Only the white teacher spoke. (This teacher was representative of many similar people in the story, almost all white, who responded to a call for teachers placed by the [surprise, white] superintendent of NYC schools.) The students looked to be about twelve years old. See Burt 1999 and Burt 2002 for further discussion of many examples not given above, and see Royster 1999 for other examples, some of which I find unconvincing as putative citations of Shakespeare, however.

18. For the film's website, go to: http://www.freeent.com/index.shtml.
19. For a partial list, see Burt 1999.
20. Only recently has Shatner managed to make his own acting inability into something really funny in a series of Priceline.com television commercials in *MTV Unplugged*-format that ran during 2000. Shatner talks covers of songs such as "The Age of Aquarius" and "Convoy." (Fortunately for him, Shatner, who does not use the service, sold off most of his stock in the company

before it plummeted over 64 percent in value by late 2000.) See http://cb-snews.com/now/story/0,1597,235342–412,00.shtml.

Works Cited

Aagesen, Colleen and Margie Blumberg. 1999. *Shakespeare for Kids: His Life and Times.* Chicago: Chicago Review Press.

Adorno, Theodor and Max Horkheimer. 1972. *The Dialectic of Enlightenment.* Trans. by John Cumming. New York: Herder & Herder.

Adorno, Theodor. 1991. *The Culture Industry: Selected Essays on Mass Culture.* Ed. by J. M. Bernstein. New York and London: Routledge.

Allen, Richard. 2001. "Branagh Shelves Two New Films as 'Bard Boom' Ends." *The Evening Standard* (London). January 31: 4.

Alikiki. 1999. *William Shakespeare and the Globe.* New York: HarperCollins.

Allies, Jennifer. Unpublished. "'Mr. William Shakespeare and the Internet': A Study in Bard Management."

Anderegg, Michael. 1999. *Orson Welles, Shakespeare and Popular Culture.* New York: Columbia Univ. Press.

Anderson, Jack. 2000. "Romeo Is on the Streets. But Where's Juliet?" September 28, section E: 5.

Anon(a). 1997. *William Shakespeare Quotations.* Norwich: Jarrold.

Anon(b). *Shakespeare in Love: The Love Poetry of Shakespeare.* New York: Miramax Books/Hyperion.

Anon(c). 2001. "Parting from Bard Is Such Sweet Sorrow for Branagh." February 1. http://www.belfasttelegraph.com/today/feb01/News/kenn.ncml.

Babha, Homi K. 1986. "Signs Taken for Wonders: Questions of Ambivalence and Authority under a Tree Outside Delhi, May 1817." In *"Race," Writing, and Difference.* Ed. by Henry Louis Gates, Jr. Chicago: Univ. of Chicago Press, 163–84.

Bender, Michael. *All the World's a Stage: William Shakespeare, a Pop-Up Biography.* San Francisco: Chronicle Books.

Berubé, Michael. 1994. *Public Access: Literary Theory and American Cultural Politics.* London: Verso.

Blackwood, Gary L. 2000. *Shakespeare's Scribe.* New York: Dutton Books.

———. 1998. *The Shakespeare Stealer.* London: Puffin Books.

Bloom, Alan. 1987. *The Closing of the American Mind.* New York: Simon & Schuster.

Boose, Lynda E. and Richard Burt. 1997. "Totally Clueless: Shakespeare Goes Hollywood in the 1990s." In *Shakespeare, the Movie: Popularizing on Film, TV, and Video.* Ed. by Lynda E. Boose and Richard Burt. New York: Routledge, 8–22.

Bristol, Michael. 1997. *Big-Time Shakespeare.* New York and London: Routledge.

Browne, Ray B. 1960. "Shakespeare in American Vaudeville and Negro Minstrelsy." *American Quarterly.* 12: 374–91.

Burdett, Lois. 2000. *Hamlet for Kids.* New York: Firefly Books.

Burt, Richard. [1998]1999. *Unspeakable ShaXXXspeares: Queer Theory and American Kiddie Culture.* 2nd ed. New York: St. Martin's Press.

————.2000. "*Shakespeare in Love* and the End of the Shakespearean: Academic and Mass Culture Constructions of Literary Authorship." In *Shakespeare, Film, Fin-de-Siecle*. Ed. by Mark Burnett and Ramona Wray. London: Macmillan, 203–31.

————. 2001. "T(e)en Things I Hate About Girlene Shakesploitation Flicks in the Late 1990s, or, Not So Fast Times at Shakespeare High." In *Spectacular Shakespeare: Critical Theory and Popular Cinema*. Ed. by Lisa Starks and Courtney Lehmann. NJ: Farleigh Dickinson Univ. Press, 205–232.

————. 2002. "Slammin' Shakespeare In Acc(id)ents Yet Unknown: Liveness, Cinem(edi)a, and Racial Dis-integration." Ed. by Barbara Hodgdon. Forthcoming in *Shakespeare Quarterly* 53: 2 (Summer). Special issue on Shakespeare and film.

————. 2003. "Bardcore: Liveness and the Tactile Technologies of Unspeakable ShaXXXsporns." Forthcoming in *Shakespeare, the Movie II: Popularizing the Plays on Film, TV, and Video*. 2nd. rev. and expanded ed. Ed. by Richard Burt and Lynda Boose. New York and London: Routledge Press.

Butler, Judith P. 1990. *Gender Trouble: Feminism and the Subversion of Identity*. New York: Routledge.

Castaldo, Annalisa. Unpublished. "'No more yielding than a dream': The Construction of Shakespeare in *The Sandman*."

Cartmell, Deborah. 2000. *Interpreting Shakespeare on Screen*. New York: St. Martin's Press.

Collins, Kris. 1996. "White Washing the Black-A-Moor: Othello, Negro Minstrelsy and Parodies of Blackness." *Journal of American Culture* 19 (Fall): 87–102.

Cooper, Susan. 1999. *King of Shadows*. New York: Margaret K. McElrerry Books.

Darnton, Robert. 1999. "The New Age of the Book." *New York Review of Books*. March 18. http://www.nybooks.com/nyrev/WWWarchdisplay.cgi?19990318005F.

de Lauretis, Teresa. 1987. *Technologies of Gender: Essays on Theory, Film, and Fiction*.Bloomington: Indiana Univ. Press.

Desmet, Cristy and Robert Sawyer, eds. 2000. *Shakespeare and Appropriation*. New York and London: Routledge.

Dionne, Craig. 1995. "Shakespeare in Popular Culture: Gender and High-Brow Culture in America." *Genre* 38 (Winter): 385–412.

Doyle, John and Ray Lischner. 1999. *Shakespeare for Dummies*. New York: IDG Books.

Dunn, Alan. 2000. "The Bard and Dope: Was this such Stuff as Dreams Were Made on?" *Independent on Sunday*. November 5. http://www.independent.co.uk/sindy/sindy.html

Eagelton, Terry. 1988. "Afterword." In *The Shakespeare Myth*. Ed. by Graham Holderness. Manchester, U.K.: Manchester Univ. Press.

Evans, Malcolm. 1989. *Signifying Nothing: Truth's True Contents in Shakespeare's Text*. London: Harvester Wheatsheaf.

Fish, Stanley. 1980. *Is There a Text in This Class? The Authority of Interpretive Communities*. Cambridge, MA: Harvard Univ. Press.

Folkerth, Wes. Unpublished. "Roll Over Shakespeare: Bardolatry Meets Beatlemania in the Spring of 1964."

Frecerro, Carla. 1999. *Popular Culture: An Introduction.* New York: New York Univ. Press.

Ganeri, Anita. 1999. *The Young Person's Guide to Shakespeare.* London: Pavilion Books.

Gates, Jr., Henry Louis. 1988. *The Signifying Monkey: A Theory of Afro-American Literary Criticism.* New York: Oxford Univ. Press.

Halpern, Richard. 1997. "That Shakespeherian Mob: Mass Culture and the Literary Public Sphere." In *Shakespeare Among the Moderns.* Ithaca, NY: Cornell University Press, 51–113.

Harries, Martin. 2000. *Scare Quotes from Shakespeare: Marx, Keynes, and the Language of Reenchantment.* Stanford, CA: Stanford Univ. Press.

Hawkes, Terence. 1992. "Bardbiz." In *Meaning by Shakespeare.* New York and London: Routledge, 141–53.

Hearst, Andrew. 2001. "The Pound of Flesh." *Lingua Franca.* September, 11: 6, 8–9.

Hebidge, Dick. 1979. *Sub-Culture: The Meaning of Style.* London: Methuen.

Hedrick, Don and Bryan Reynolds, eds. 2000. *Shakespeare Without Class: Misappropriations of Cultural Capital.* New York: Palgrave.

Hodgson, Barbara. 1999. *The Shakespeare Trade: Performances and Appropriations.* Philadelphia: Univ. of Pennsylvania Press.

Holderness, Graham. 1994. "Radical Potentiality and Institutional Closure: Shakespeare in Film and Television." In Dollimore and Sinfield 1994, 206–225.

———. ed. 1988. *The Shakespeare Myth.* Manchester, U.K.: Manchester Univ. Press.

hooks, bell. 1992. *Black Looks: Race and Representation.* Boston: South End Press.

———. 1990. *Yearning: Race, Gender, and Cultural Politics.* Boston: South End Press.

Howard, Jean and Scott Shershow, eds. 2000. *Marxist Shakespeares.* London: Routledge.

Huyssen, Andreas. 1986. *After the Great Divide: Modernism, Mass Culture, Postmodernism.* Bloomington: Indiana Univ. Press.

Johns, Ian. 2001. "Liked that? Then Try This . . . Movies with Literary Inspiration." *Times* (London), February 1, features.

Keevak, Michael. 2001. *Sexual Shakespeare.* Detroit: Wayne State Univ. Press.

Langley, Andrew. 2000. *Treasure Chests: Shakespeare and the Elizabethan Age.* London: Quarto Children's Books.

Levine, Lawrence. 1988. *Highbrow/Lowbrow: The Emergence of Cultural Hierarchy in America.* Cambridge MA: Harvard Univ. Press.

Linton, David. Unpublished essay. "Shakespeare in Heat: Two Pornographic Adaptations of *A Midsummer Night's Dream.*"

Lister, David. 2001. "Is This a Slump We See before Us? Ken Calls Off New Shakespeare." *The Independent* (London), January 31, 76: 84.

MacDonald, Joyce. 1994. "Acting Black: *Othello, Othello* Burlesques, and the Performance of Blackness." *Theatre Journal* 46: 231–249.

Martin, Malia. 2000. *Much Ado About Love.* New York: Avon Romance.

Mcentee, John. 2001. "Ken's Labour's Lost on the Bard." *The Express* (London). January 30: 39.

Midgette, Anne. 2000. "The Bard's Hip-Hop Foot Soldier: Choreographer Rennie Harris Blends Shakespeare With Rap in a Modern Take on *Romeo and Juliet.*" *Los Angeles Times.* September 17: 7.

Novy, Marianne, ed. 1999. *Transforming Shakespeare: Contemporary Women's Re-Visions in Literature and Performance*. New York: St. Martin's Press.

Osborne, Laurie. 1999. "Romancing the Bard." In *Shakespeare and Appropriation*. Edited by Christy Desmet and Robert Sawyer. New York: Routledge.

————2000. "Sweet, Savage Shakespeare." In *Shakespeare Without Class*. Edited by Don Hedrick and Bryan Reynolds. New York: St. Martin's Press.

————. 2002. "Clip Art: Theorizing the Shakespearean Film Clip." Special issue on Shakespeare and film. Ed. by Barbara Hodgdon. Forthcoming in *Shakespeare Quarterly*, 53: 2 (Summer).

Penley, Constance. 1997. *NASA / Trek: Popular Science in America*. London: Verso.

Pipher, Mary. 1994. *Reviving Ophelia: Saving the Lives of Adolescent Girls*. New York: Ballantine Books.

Perret, Marion. Unpublished. "Speaking Pictures: How Comics Books Challenge Critical Thinking."

Pollack, William S. With Todd Shuster. 2000. *Real Boys' Voices*. New York: Random House.

Readings, Bill. 1997. *The University in Ruins*. Cambridge, MA: Harvard Univ. Press.

Riddens, Geoffrey. Unpublished. "Dreadful Trade! Shakespeare and Advertising."

Roca, Octavio. 2000. "Where Art Thou, Juliet?: Hip-Hop Romeo Lacks a Leading Lady." *San Francisco Chronicle*. August 13, C7.

Ross, Andrew. 1989. *No Respect: Intellectuals and Popular Culture*. New York: Routledge.

Rothwell, Kenneth and Fracoise Meltzer. 1990. *Shakespeare on Screen. An International Filmography and Videography*. New York and London : Neal-Schuman Publishers.

Royster, Francesca. 1999. "Cleopatra as Diva: African-American Women and Shakespearean Tactics." In Novy, ed. 1999, 103–125.

Rozakis, Laurie. 1999. *The Complete Idiot's Guide to Shakespeare*. New York: Alpha Books.

Sinfield, Alan. 1992. *Faultlines: Cultural Materialism and the Politics of Dissident Reading*. Berkeley: Univ. of California Press.

Stanley, Dane and Peter Vennema. 1992. *Bard of Avon: The Story of William Shakespeare*. New York: Morrow Junior Books.

Strinati, Dominic. 1995. *An Introduction to Theories of Popular Culture*. New York and London: Routledge.

Talbott, Frederic. 1994. *Shakespeare on Leadership—Timeless Wisdom for Daily Challenges*. Thomas Nelson Publishers.

Taylor, Gary. 1994. "Bardicide." In *Shakespeare and Cultural Traditions: The Selected Proceedings of the International Shakespeare Association World Congress, Tokyo, 1991*. Ed. by Tetsuo Kishi, Roger Pringle, and Stanley Wells. Newark: Univ. of Delaware Press, 333–49.

Toropov, Brandon. 1997. *Shakespeare for Beginners*. New York: Writers and Readers Publishing.

Traub, James. 2000. "On Line U." *New York Times Sunday Magazine*. November 19. http://www.nytimes.com/library/magazine/home/20001119mag-onlineu.html.

Uricchio, William and Roberta E. Pearson. 1993. *Reframing Culture: The Case of the Vitagraph Quality Films.* Princeton: Princeton Univ. Press.

Wallace, Michelle. 1990. *Invisibility Blues.* London: Verso.

Weiberg, George, ed. 1991. *Shakespeare on Love: Quotations from the Plays and Poems.* New York: St. Martin's Press.

Wertham, Fredric. 1954. *Seduction of the Innocent: The Influence of Comics on Today's Youth.* New York: Rinehart.

Williams, Raymond. 1976. *Keywords: A Vocabulary of Culture and Society.* London: Fontana.

Žižek, Slavoj. 2000. *The Ticklish Subject: The Absent Centre of Political Ontology.* London: Verso.

Films and Videos Cited

Bartkowak, Andrezj, dir. 2000. *Romeo Must Die.* USA. Warner Bros. Sound, col., 115 mins. DVD edition.

Burnett, Robert Meyer, dir. 1999. *Free Enterprise.* USA. Mindfire. Sound, col., 109 mins. DVD edition.

Cadro, Steve, dir. 2000. *Midsummer's Night Dream.* Hungary. Cadro Films. Sound, col., 90 mins. Video.

Canterbury. Stuart, dir. *In the Flesh.* USA. VCA Films. Sound, col., 110 mins. DVD edition.

———. 2000. *A Midsummer Night's Cream.* USA. Adam & Eve Productions. Sound, col., 90 mins. DVD edition.

Capra, Frank, dir. 1946. *It's a Wonderful Life.* USA. New Live Films. Sound, col., 130 mins.

DaCosta, Morton, dir.1962. *The Music Man.* USA. Liberty Films. Sound, col., 130 mins.

Lee, Spike, dir. 2000. *Bamboozled.* USA. New Line Films. Sound, col.,135 mins.

Madden, Jr. John. 1998. *Shakespeare in Love.* USA. Miramax. Sound, col., 118 mins.

Pacino, Al, dir. 1996. *Looking for Richard.* USA. Twentieth Century Fox. Sound, col., 118 mins.

Savant, Ren, dir. *West Side.* USA. Dream Team. Sound, col., 180 mins. DVD edition.

———. 2000. *Shakespeare Revealed.* USA. Vivid. Sound, col., 96 mins. DVD edition.

Wayans, Keene, dir. 2000. *Scary Movie.* USA. Dimension Films. Sound, col., 88 Mins. DVD edition.

Whitakker, Forrest, dir. 1995. *Waiting to Exhale.* USA. Twentieth Century Fox. Sound, col., 126 mins. DVD edition.

PART ONE

QUESTIONS OF SHAKESPEARE'S CULTURAL AUTHORITY

Theories, Issues, and Instances

CHAPTER I

BARDGUIDES OF THE NEW UNIVERSE

Niche Marketing and the Cultural Logic
of Late Shakespeareanism

DONALD K. HEDRICK

Market Segmentation for Dummies

A recent *New Yorker* cover cartoon by the amazing Roz Chast (November 22, 1999) shows an urban newspaper kiosk whose vendor is surrounded by a display of current magazines for sale. Reading the titles posted in this dauntingly large spread, however, one encounters a succession of geometrically expanding specializations: *Reader's Digest Digest, Celebrity Surgery, Staten Island Poetry Journal, Home Dentist, Tinfoil Crafts, Plastic Wrap Crafts, Wanna-bes, Has-beens, Vegan Surfer,* to the magazine with the ultimate contemporary identification, *Loser.* The joke about increasingly narrow and esoteric magazines is at the same time an insightful play on my subject here—niche marketing. Here I want to consider the state of Shakespeare, at the present historical moment in an explosion of film adaptations and other interest, with respect to the phenomenon (or fiction) of the "mass market" in what is something like a "postmodern consumerism" of niche marketing, where the "old hierarchies are becoming obsolete," where there is "no fashion, only fashions" (Featherstone 1991, 110–11), style is manufactured with planned or "progressive" obsolescence (Ewen 1988, 244, 249–51), and where we are in the era of "demassification" and "the end of mass culture" (Toffler, Denning, cited in Agnew 1993, 38). I want to begin to describe how this market phenomenon helps account for central features of what I will term "late Shakespeareanism"—a cultural phenomenon I make analogous to the "late capitalism" of left economic analysis (Mandel

1975) but one without, for most Shakespeareans at least, that term's implicit hope of decay and implosion. That is, we watch anxiously rather than hopefully as a gigantic phenomenon disappears, the supernova becoming a black hole, the ultimate niche.

Shakespeare's own awareness of this contemporary logic, I wish to show, is useful in understanding what happens to him after the introduction of the mass market proper. What happens in its contemporary evolution, however, is distinctive and consequential, as niche marketing reaches a radical completion as a "mode of consumption" turning back on itself, as the commercial itself becomes just another niche within the field. I want to explore, later in the essay, this new market context as it appears in an exemplary appropriation of Shakespeare—recent guides to corporate management that adopt the words, characters, and lessons of corporate wisdom supposedly found in several Shakespearean plays. Overall, I trace the final resting place of a demassified imaginary in a new version of the "universalism" usually discredited by contemporary theory, and describe in some detail the way that envisioning Shakespeare as master CEO symptomatically reveals the ethical and political fault lines of a corporate-driven culture.

Chast's comic version of market targeting and segmentation has found a darker resonance in the recent hearings of the Federal Trade Commission regarding the discovery of documents from the advertising side of the film industry. These documents reveal the explicit strategies of marketing campaigns and devices specifically aimed at young people who are, in fact, too young to be allowed to see the movies or games being promoted. Federal Trade Commission Chair Robert Pitofsky, finding some 80 percent of violent movies thus covertly marketed, points out that this is at the very least a deceptive practice, given that the industry by its own self-regulation regards these films as inappropriate for the young.[1]

Presumably, marketing Shakespeare as entertainment does not have such nefarious circumstances attached to it, at least not so directly, though Shakespeare is perhaps ever protected by the equivalent of the Elizabethan "benefit of clergy," by which quoting scripture could save a felon's neck. Nevertheless, the history of this marketing may reflect something of the ways in which marketing itself has historically tended to shift. Applying the broad categories of sociologist Richard Tedlow (1996), one might perceive that the development of marketing tends to fall in something like his three developmental stages, from Fragmentation to Unification to Segmentation. While I would not press the model too confidently into an overview of the history of marketing Shakespeare, a rough trajectory of this sort may nevertheless be seen from the early modern period to the present: the identification of the reading portion of the public by Shakespeare's actor friends Heminges and Condell, who urge us to buy the Folio they have posthumously compiled of his works, and to "read" it; then the later elevation of Shakespeare into National Poet and book, exemplary of all Britain herself (Dobson, 1992); then the more demographic and psychological and cultural divisions of the modern period. The latter would seem to begin with the cutting off of the "lowbrow" Shakespeare for the sake of the imagined "highbrow" one (the history of the late-nineteenth century and modern eras recounted by Levine [1988]), and continue with further segmentation within the twentieth century, namely, an "academic" Shakespeare associated with the highbrow. This new "official territory" is regarded in turn as something against which to rebel or resist in an alternative way, a "Shakespace" available for socially creative or "transversal" movements across "subjective territory" (Hedrick and Reynolds 2000, 8–10). The shift to the non- or even antiacademic is illustrated in niche terms by the inevitable publication of *Shakespeare for Dummies* (1999), the ostensibly nonacademic bardguide, which actually does what academic introductions have always done (language tips, character complexity, "themes"), but for a target audience that eschews "academic" identity. Added to this range of imaginary and real niches are the pop and subpop versions, from teen-exploitation to gay and lesbian "Shakespeare porn." This is the realm explored by Richard Burt's study of the current dissemination of Shakespeare into niches hitherto unimaginable or taboo, a study relegating Shakespeareans into a niche of "losers" resigned to their "loser criticism" (Burt, 1999), although the notion of "loser" is at the same time transvalued into positive terms, itself a new niche status.

"'Tis ten to one this play cannot please all that are here":
Early Modern Market Research and Those "Delightful Little Niches"

Resisting a premature historicization of niche marketing that would limit it to the modern or contemporary eras, however, one might acknowledge the niche as represented in the fledgling entertainment industry itself. There we find it in Shakespeare's own awareness of market segmentation starting its trajectory toward cultural centrality after the mass media. We can, moreover, expose the structure of late Shakespeareanism by way of attention to the outlines of market segmentation evident in the early modern period. Indeed, a short survey of Shakespeare's addresses to the audience in his epilogues reveals not only the operation of segmentation but an awareness of the implicit trajectory of its development, a logic of niche marketing as well as a logic of the evolution of niche marketing. The earliest of epilogues in which we see this, Puck's address to the audience of *A Midsummer Night's Dream*, combines Tedlow's Fragmentation and Unification stages. Moving as it does from the singular you of address to the plural, Puck invites "you" to "think . . . That you have but slumb'red here" at the start of the speech, but concludes by wishing "good night unto you all" at the end (5.1.425; 436). Thus, individual fantasy is replaced by collective fantasy, the latter mode crucial for a fully aware marketing that would enable the advertising strategies for a truly *mass* market—a first stage of the developmental story.

Division rather than unification is, however, suggested by the curious concluding lines of another early comedy, as the Armado actor ends *Love's Labour's Lost*, "You that way; we this way" (5.2.931). Whether the line, as various readers speculate, refers to the winter and spring groups of the final song, to the men and women characters, or to the actors and the audience, in any case the corresponding market fantasy is one of division, constituting an appeal that perhaps befits this play's experimental exercise in unresolved romantic comedy by which "Jack hath not Jill" (5.2.875). In the later epilogues, moreover, we see a continuing awareness toward and a development of sophistication about the division or bifurcation of an audience, here considered not so much as an emblem of theoretical authority but rather as the embodiment of potential market success. Thus, the Rosalind/boy actor in his "conjuring" speech comically divides the audience at once by gender—"and I'll begin with the women." Tautologically wishing them to like as much of the play as they like—a *reductio ad absurdum* of low-pressure sales—the actor's next sales pitch, delivered to the men, is even more absurd: he "charges" them, not to like the play, but somewhat more cryptically, "that between you and the women the play may please" (*Epilogue* 11–17). What is striking in market terms is not only the awareness of segmentation but the *promotion* of a segmentation producing emulation—liking what someone else likes—in accord with the production of envy constituting the heart of the advertising system. The complexity of this appears as well in the epilogue to *Henry IV, Part Two* another bravado tip of the hat to the women of the audience, in a comic denial and elevation of the battle of the sexes: "all the gentlewomen here have forgiven me; if the gentlemen will not, then the gentlemen do not agree with the gentlewomen, which was never seen in such an assembly" (Epilogue 22–25).

The awareness of marketing and segmentation becomes most self-conscious, however, in a later epilogue in *Henry VIII*, which directly announces its intent in market terms if not actual accounting terms, right from the start: "'Tis ten to one this play can never please / All that are here" (Epilogue 1–2). The epilogue, moreover, rejects the unification ambition from the start and, in Jonsonian fashion, anticipates the uncollected segments of taste: those who "come to take their ease, / And sleep an act or two" but who are annoyed when waked by the trumpets, or those who want city comedy and are disappointed at the lack of wit. Again relying on segmentation by gender, the epilogue also acknowledges the *interaction* of those segments, claiming that the play's approval rests only in the "merciful construction of good women." This curious phrase refers, it seems, to the men's comic vulnerability in wanting to please (as the play attempted to please but failed) the women by going along with them: "If they [the women] smile / And say 'twill do, I know, within a while / All the best men are ours; for 'tis ill hap / If they hold when their ladies bid 'em clap" (11–14). The men's desire here *multiplies* the understated or marginal approval of the women (i.e., their curt "'twill do") in a way that escalates the overall success of the play. From such a striking awareness of subtle market dynamics we might also ask whether or not in addition to or even apart from the reader response ideal of Stanley Fish's "interpretive communities," or even the current attention to the *ideological* function of the women audiences, we should consider their more specifically *market* function.[2] What would it mean, for instance, if we were to follow the logic of these epilogues by considering the role of female spectators, however much they happen to have been in the minority in Shakespeare's audience, as something like Shakespeare's actual or desired *fan base?* Too, what does it mean to think of a market segmentation involving coalition or *negotiation* with such a base? The idea in this instance hardly corresponds to what might otherwise be thought of as being "protofeminist" about Shakespeare: if Shakespeare's epilogue reflects actual business awareness, he is thinking along the lines of the happily coercive marketers to children who strategize to get children to demand their products from parents, children constituting the "delightful little niches" of a child-centered U.S. culture. If so, this might account for much of the history of feminist ambivalence about Shakespeare. Such considerations, in any case, follow necessarily from niche logic rather than from text- or linguistic-based "audience response," and hence constitute a far more complex and sophisticated relation to a nonunitary public sphere.

Understanding the place of Shakespeare in a contemporary consumer culture requires further attention to the relevant genealogy of consumerism. Accordingly, one would need to acknowledge the role of the eighteenth century as the preindustrial era that might even be regarded as a "consumer revolution" (Campbell 1987, 8; McKendrick 1982, 5). Or, even more ambitiously, the traditional marxist concept of mode or "means of production" might be theorized to have been replaced by "means of consumption" with the construction of a corresponding "subject of value" (Smith 1997, 47). What is interesting in this epochal shift for purposes of the present essay is the creation of a formation seemingly paradoxical or contradictory, namely, an opulence—sometimes argued to be the foundation of capitalism itself (Sombart 1967)—available not merely to one class but to *all* classes. If the origin of niche marketing, therefore, has much to do with what one writer in 1771 paradoxically termed "UNIVERSAL luxury," what is experienced is the making widely popular of what was designatedly nonpopular, a version of the aspiring practice of "distinction" explored in French contexts by Bourdieu. Here the British figure is the pottery king Josiah Wedgwood, who perfected a market campaign in the same way he perfected his product (McKendrick 1982,108), in order to disseminate this presumed "luxury" (luxury status maintained, in fact, by a later refusal to lower prices more competitively) worldwide, with products, from dog bowls to crucifixes, aimed at every group. By the present moment, moreover, this product had eventually located a Shakespeare niche, in upscale pottery plates bearing scenes from Shakespeare, as studied by Barbara Hodgdon (1998, 234). While I do not know an origin for the term *niche* as used in this sense, it is noteworthy that Wedgwood once employed the term in a literal and revealing way when he began globally marketing his pottery: after observing in Turkey how the wall niches of their household architecture, traditionally used to hold pots of perfume, might be used instead for a line of Turkish-style ceramics, he ruminated, "Let who will take the Sultanas if I could get at these delightful little niches, & furnish them, is all I covet in Turkey at present" (cited in McKendrick et al. 1982, 27–28). Such desires fueled Wedgwood's stated ambition to become "Vase Maker General to the Universe."

Whose universe is it, anyway? It may be, as I want to suggest here, that the notion of the universe has expanded with the "consumer revolution" into something, to use the marketing term describing the proliferation of target audiences in the Chast cartoon, comparable to market "shelf space." While the unpacking of the purportedly universal has been the larger project of the critical and theoretical revolution of the end of the millennium, it may be that Shakespeare *is* in fact universal, as he was claimed to have been when Jonson called him in the Folio dedication, "not for an age but for all time." That is, he is universal, as the cliché has it—only universality is not now what it used to be.

In the period of the industrial revolution of the end of the nineteenth century the targeting of markets in advertising, always present to some extent as we see from the early modern examples, began fully to inhabit the territory of the niche market as first explored by the Elizabethan theater, corresponding to a specialization of market practices generally. In the 1860s, for example, businessman did their own advertisements, but by the 1890s there were specialized ad professionals, and by 1910 businesses typically commissioned advertisers (Laird 1998, 3–4).[3] At the same time, after the 1890s, though most advertisers still aimed at relatively broad audiences, they began to address specific classes of people, and even the trade literature began, for instance, to discuss the "feminine eye" of women consumers (Laird 1998, 285). Perhaps it is only coincidental that the late nineteenth century was also the time when Shakespeare found his own niche as an academic object of study in the schools (but what is coincidence?).

Again, while these large-scale shifts occur unevenly over time and place, they occur repeatedly. Shifts to niche marketing, however, while associated with progress are not invariably associated with success. The Chast cartoon's humor depends on our recognition that at some point the segmentation or rather extreme fractalization of target groups would simply dissolve or implode, the group becoming tinier and tinier until a readership of one (at which point the price of a single magazine would have to be high enough to keep the entire enterprise going). A memorable case of uneven segmentation history is the joint history of marketing of Pepsi and Coca-Cola. Pepsi, which tried segmentation through competitive pricing in the 1930s, and "psychographic" segmentation in the '40s (campaigns to "Be Sociable"), and then by the 1950s using ads that shifted from the product to the context in which the product was consumed, eventually hit pay dirt with a youth-directed campaign of the 1980s, the "Pepsi Generation" (Tedlow 1996, 7). Coke's segmentation response in 1985, however, failed, as they tried to introduce new lines such as "New Coke," producing an uproar, failing in part because Coke's brand identity had always been one of a timeless universalism (since the 1890s), an identity undercut by the new strategy. In effect, in the Coke-Pepsi competition we have a model for the war of universalisms against one another. Shakespeare may be seen as the Coke of the aesthetic world, historically depending for his success on one special brand of timelessness, not to mention his indefinable secret ingredient (see Michael Bristol on Shakespeare's presumed value "outside" the market, 1996), but whose ultimate value is in no way logically dependent on that brand. There is nothing timeless about his price, as the flexibility of late Shakespeareanism may demonstrate, for if subjected now to the transformations of niche marketing, Shakespeare will become, in ways that remain to be seen, more and more our Pepsi instead of our Coke,[4] a soda-change affecting everything from pedagogy and canonization to the place of Shakespeare in the public sphere.

Once again, as in the phenomenon of segmentation itself, Shakespeare's uncanny explorations of the practical economics of his own time, to the extent to which he pushes and perverts their systems (like the comic antisystematicity of Roz Chast), are remarkably prescient about the relatively unpredictable ways that the phenomenon or system of segmentation itself is subject to transformation. Now, however, fragmentation and unification may thus suddenly shift places, the segment can swallow up the whole, or the whole become the segment. As a logic of the end or black hole, the limiting case is much like Shakespeare's image of the "universal wolf," his figure of a radical appetite that, as Ulysses describes, ends up making a "universal prey, / And last eat up himself" (*Troilus and Cressida*, 1.3.121–24). Regarded by Hugh Grady as Shakespeare's anticipation of *reification* (Grady 1996), this image of the "universal wolf" also describes what Colin Campbell in his study of the history of consumerism regards as the epochal shift between kinds of consumption, "traditional versus modern hedonism" (Campbell 1987, 58). The latter, a Romantic-based ethic of dynamically generating new wants, shifts the activity of consumption to a "mentalistic" hedonism not of pleasure-seeking through a product's purchase or use, but through imaginative pleasure-seeking emphasizing novelty and insatiability (Campbell 1987, 89), a view like that of Jean Baudrillard's world of sign-consumption. If so, the future of Shakespeare's use lies less in the marketing of Shakespeare as a valued *commodity* (an axiom far more fundamental to literary studies than the narrower issue of canonicity) than in his marketing as a valued *consumption practice,* as the current boom in Shakespeare would seem to affirm.

As it happens, the revolutionary transformation of segmentation itself constitutes the comic theme and structure of Shakespeare's most densely packed study of business and market practices, the brothel scenes of *Pericles.* While the brothel to which the captured heroine Marina is brought and sold might at first seem to invite a reading as symptomatic of "nascent capitalism," the scenes actually make clear that the economic model of this business is a rather old-fashioned artisanship: the brothelkeepers are concerned about the scarcity of goods (BAWD: "We have but poor three [creatures]"); about their quality ("and they with continual action are even as good as rotten"); about improvement of the stock (PANDER: Therefore let's have fresh ones, whate'er we pay for them"); with an explicit guild-like business philosophy that requires good products and, more importantly, *conscience,* in order to achieve success (PANDER: If there be not a conscience to be us'd in every trade, we shall never prosper," *Pericles,* 4.2.7–11). While Shakespeare is, of course, ironic about this particular sort of "conscience" (they go on to pride themselves on raising infant bastards, who grow up however into the same occupation), Marina's novel purity and conscience clearly disrupt the traditional ways of sex work. The typical practices of these brothel-owners signal an earlier phase of commodity production that focuses on product more than on desire creation, since desire and sexual need in this business are traditionally (but mistakenly, as it turns out) taken for granted. As their mode of production is old-fashioned, so is their advertising, depending on the "crying" of the wares: they advertise that they have acquired a new virgin in a manner that assumes their audience to be fragmented consumers united by a single desire for a single offering. Thus the Bawd bawdily tells the horrified Marina that she will "taste gentlemen of all fashions" (4.2.78), and, though making a special point of targeting youth ("tell me, how dost thou find the inclination of the people, especially of the younger sort" 4.2.96–97), Boult tells her that his enticing description of the new virgin will work, as it did on one Frenchman, for *all* nationalities: "Well, if we had of every nation a traveller, we should lodge them with this sign" (4.2.113–145). For this old-fashioned sales team, unification of the so-inclined predominates over fragmentation.

The transformation that Marina accomplishes by righteously refusing to sell herself is portrayed comically, with the first two customers so turned off by hearing "divinity preached there" by her, that one even swears off "rutting forever" (5.4. 4–9). What proceeds to happen to the niche of rutting young men, through a kind of market crash of the brothel, is noteworthy in its focus on the market as a system. When the governor Lysimachus, the brothel's next customer, also confronts the power of Marina in her long speeches about her chastity, he is transformed even more radically—not to abstinence but to active virtue. This newly produced virtue in turn assumes at once another *monetary* form: namely, he pays her for the use of the moving words she gave ("I did not think / Thou could'st have spoke so well") instead of paying for her body, that is, he pays for what he describes as the wetting of his "foul thoughts" by her tears, and goes on to announce that, having originally intended to pay a gold piece for her virginity, he will now pay twenty for her honesty (4.6.402–03).

The consumer revolution, which happens right under our noses in these paired scenes, is not merely the destruction of a market but the substitution of one market for a different, more profitable one. The former just happens to sell vice and the latter virtue, in the characteristic moral indifference often noted by Marx in his explanations of exchange-value. That this picture of a market turnaround is really not a moralist argument of the triumph of virtue over vice, or of the replacement in the moral niche of prostitution by chastity, is evident in that the scene doesn't stop with Lysimachus's moral reformation. All is swallowed up by monetary transformation, the continuing narrative motif of these scenes, as Lysimachus explicitly makes Marina more profitable than her keepers, with a profit of twenty times as much. Nor does this "moral" stop there, for Lysimachus out of nowhere suddenly offers her even more ("Hold, here's more gold" 4.6.113) in a monetary *jouissance* of good-hearted benevolence. After he exits and the outraged brothel-keepers now brutally threaten to rape Marina to keep her in her place, this reward then becomes the very source of money by which Marina is able to protect herself as well as to buy them off, thereby backing up her admonition to Boult that he should find another line of work, any line of work, however ignoble, rather than continue brothel-keeping (MARINA: "Here's gold for thee" 4.6.181). Here Shakespeare portrays something like Josiah Wedgwood's entrepreneurial fantasy of niche as *replacement*, hence anticipating contemporary niche logic, since Marina goes on to propose that the owners could go round the city to find maidens who could all work at her new industry, who could "sing, weave, sew, and dance" (4.6.183) as she does. Here the Marina- project intends to drive prostitution out of business, replacing it with an alternative form of what was there in the first place, namely, entertainment, but this time targeting the newly produced niche of reformed rutters. The capitalist market is, as Shakespeare here and others elsewhere have observed, not so much competitive as anticompetitive, seeking the actual destruction of the opposition, as one learns from marketing manuals themselves, seen today in the concept of "predatory marketing" (See Beemer 1997). As Axelrod's management guide using another Elizabethan mentor, *Elizabeth I CEO*, succinctly summarizes, "Know the 'enemy' (your competition)" (Axelrod 2000, xiii). From Shakespeare's scenes in *Pericles*, therefore, we might imagine yet another magazine to add to the Chast cartoon's collection: *Formerly Horny Guy.*

Niche Marketing Marketing: Sucking Up (to) Shakespeare

While Shakespeare, as we have seen, anticipates the revolution of consumerism in his representations of business, it is not until the contemporary era and the hegemony of mass media that we see niche marketing become radically productive. Symptomatic of a historical shift to "modes of consumption," we thus arrive at a postmodern moment in which business or the market itself becomes just another niche, the moment in which Shakespeare is discovered to be, as in the present essay itself, a consultant for business practices. The connection of Shakespeare to contemporary business has been made recently in the arts, through films that interestingly enough select *Hamlet* as the play with charged significance for business, specifically for the corporate realm. The dead-pan Finnish film *Hamlet Goes Business* (dir. Aki Kaurismaki, 1987) influenced in turn the recent *Hamlet* with Ethan Hawke (dir. Michael Almereyda, 2000, who directed a noncorporate vampire movie before this). These films, directed at and appealing to audiences with an anti-business or even with an academic disposition, do not fall, however, within the more surprising and innovative phenomenon of Shakespeare's deliberate incorporation into the business sphere. The more recent niche practice may be exemplified by the recent, somewhat controversial partnership (controversial for some businessfolk, it seems) of Shakespeare's Globe Theatre in London with the Cranfield School of Management, a collaboration whereby plays such as *Henry V* and even *Hamlet* are studied by M.B.A. students for their management lessons, even though the value of studying the character Hamlet is questionable for some businessmen (Rowe 1999).

Turning now to this recent area of market penetration, we find a new Shakespeare made over as a corporate trainer, carrying further the historical Shakespeare's own project of self-elevation into the community of "gentlemen" with a coat of arms. This new universe continually expands, with the proliferation, even as this essay is being written, of books purporting to give "counsel" (an old word) from the Bard. Jay Shafritz's *Shakespeare on Management: Wise Counsel from the Bard* (New York: Harper 1992), recently issued in paperback, is the first and perhaps least culturally remarkable of these bardguides. Here, the appropriation of cultural capital in this collection of Shakespearean passages of advice about everything from "dressing for success" to "presentation techniques" is generally assumed to be direct and unproblematic, conferring classic status on the borrowing itself; hence the dust jacket describes the book as a "time-tested classic that belongs on every well-read executive's bookshelf," although the introduction uses the same phrases applied to Shakespeare to his "time-tested and truly class executive philosophy" (xiii), the Bard become a super CEO. Here, the traditionally compulsory Shakespeare-quotation of the upwardly mobile aspirants to taste is replaced by the same aspiration for the upwardly mobile business executive, supplementing the "use-value" of the sayings for everyday life, here everyday business life. The new axiom becomes that the citation of the classic confers classic status on the citer. Not entirely tongue-in-cheek, its introduction announces that Shakespeare's "contributions to the theory of management and administration have been all but ignored" (xi), and announces the time-saving feature of saving busy executives from having to read the plays themselves (xii). A shortcut to culture, the book even has the practical advantage of providing "Shakespeare's words . . . to add tone, importance, and especially wit to your memorandums and memos" (xiii). Someone will, without giving the present author credit, undoubtedly produce and market some software to enable busy wit-challenged executives to do this more easily without requiring a book.

In its fault lines, however, the book manifests an allegiance as well to what I term the "enduring immorality" of the Bard. This more Machiavellian component furnishes such chapters as "Getting Even," "Staff Popinjays," "Marrying the Boss's Daughter," and "Fat Versus Thin Employees." Occasionally, the position is only accidentally maintained, as in the unintentionally comic moment when the book adopts lines from the Captain, assigned at the end of *King Lear* to carry out the hangings of the king and his daughter, describing to Edmund his willingness to do *anything*, to just do it, as it were: "I cannot draw a cart, nor eat dried oats, / If it be man's work, I'll do it." (5.3.38–39). Citing this as an example not of a cold-blooded, murderous lackeyism but, astonishingly, of Shakespeare's sympathetic attitude toward work and workers, Shafritz proclaims it represents Shakespeare's view of the "essential nobility of all work" (143). Right. Like other works to be considered here, the new niche is specifically those upwardly striving on the corporate ladder or, as the guide based on Elizabeth I's practices rather than Shakespeare's characters would have it: "this book is not directed at just *anyone*. It is aimed specifically at the leaders of today, the builders and would be builders of contemporary empires" (Axelrod 2000, xii).

Shakespeare on Management thus reflects the time-honored practice of appropriating Shakespeare in the form of the pithy epithets we now think of as soundbites, often wrenched from their context as in this lurid example. Two additional revealing and more sophisticated corporate management guides, however, go well beyond the forms of conventional wisdom into the murkier realms of interpretation and the culture of business, and thus deserve additional attention to the way they fit, or fail to fit, Shakespeare into business in a contemporary way.

The subtitled "Bard's Guide" to business by Norman Augustine and Kenneth Adelman, *Shakespeare in Charge: The Bard's Guide to Leading and Succeeding on the Business Stage* (New York: Hyperion, 1999) gives us a full expression of the transformations of consumption appropriate to late Shakespeareanism. Not only has the "market" now become in this latest stage of marketing a niche in itself, the whole swallowed up by the part as in the other management books, but this book represents a new "business" Shakespeare that has subsumed everything from pragmatic how-to's of social interaction to the deeper cultural contradictions of capitalist industry itself. [5] Here, the fault lines of the work reveal themselves most when the market itself enters the transversal space of the Shakespearean niche or "Shakespace" (Hedrick and Reynolds 2000) potentially becoming what it is not and even revealing the "enduring immorality" I have elsewhere argued is implicit, I have found, in most ethical treatments of Shakespeare (Hedrick, 2000).

The book is cleverly structured not as a set of sayings on topics, a la *Shakespeare on Management*, but rather in academic fashion with play-specific coverage, chapter-by-chapter, in the mock format of a dramatic work itself (once again shaking up the otherwise fixed boundaries between Shakespeare and used or appropriated Shakespeare. After an introduction fashioned as a "Prologue," each of the five chapters is listed as an "Act," furnishing an interpretation of one play organized around a summary of the topic at hand (cutely latinized as "Dramatis Executivus Summarius); a Prologue and several scenes that summarize the play in business terms and with business anecdotes, and concluding with several "Acting Lessons" which review the applied wisdom in executive and business terms. The book becomes, through this clever structure, not merely an encyclopedia or catalogue but a *creative* work itself, hence a Shakespace that, as we will see, is both inside and outside the realm of business, simultaneously liminal and vanguard. Throughout, the assumption seems to be, moreover, that the "business stage" of the book's subtitle is like the monarch being "set upon a stage" for Elizabeth, and that the audience here, as in other current books on

Shakespeare and business, is directed at the CEO, established or aspiring. The new CEO of the new universe of today will find in Shakespeare not merely wise sayings but an actual space of social creativity; like Henry V he will himself become a virtual playwright and inventor, as the king does when with macho bravado he boasts to Katherine of France that "we are the makers of manners, Kate" (*Henry V,* 5.2.270–71).

The first chapter, "On Leadership," for instance, covers *Henry V,* the type who figures in "contemporary corporate success stories," who is praised for his "true grit, grand strategizing, sheer competence, dogged perseverance, and creativity" (2). Explored here are Shakespeare's "keen insight into group dynamics" among the nobles gathered on the battlefield at Agincourt (11), his confidence in assuming victory in the Crispin's Day speech (12), and other qualities specific to the narrative. The application is not uncritical or pat, however, as some of Henry's actions, like the supposedly bluffing threat to destroy the town of Harfleur, are regarded as limited in value. The moralized narrative is interwoven with anecdotes, some brief and some more extended, about contemporary business successes: Virgin Atlantic (illustrating Henry's quick resolve in an exec's "snappy" decision to buy a single 747 and jump into the market [19]); Burton snowboards (illustrating Henry's bravery through its owner's own addiction to the risky sport, now commanding 45 percent of the market [21]); or Amazon.com (illustrating Henry's clear vision in its founder's quitting his job to drive west in a station wagon with his family and set up a business designed to speed up consumer access to information products [25]).

While these boosterish applications seem casually if not rather arbitrarily derived (often, in fact, relying on illustrating citations not from *Henry V* but from other plays where necessary), the fault lines of the work become more evident in illustrating perhaps what the authors do not wish their CEO Shakespeare to illustrate. Thus, they initially concede that the very basis of their opening act on leadership is not really Shakespearean but rather an anomaly: "Oddly enough, Henry V is one of the Bard's few kings who is good and does well" (2). Offhandedly undermining the purportedly moral implications of their good counsel, we see the logic of this qualification, the suspicion of a lack of honor at the heart of the enterprise, in the assurances of the final "acting lesson" that ultimately the executive world requires honor, or "Do what honor would thee do," as the Chorus of *Henry V* intones (34). Honor, in what for Shakespeare would probably be decidedly Machiavellian terms, however, is primarily "spotless reputation" (citing Mowbray from *Richard II* [35]). The extended anecdote provided to illustrate "honor" is one not so much about the executive's honor but rather about the accounting fraud in her company that forced her into a crisis of reorganization from which she eventually prevailed (37). Such stories, based not on the older model of rags-to-riches but on the newer one of bankruptcy-to-riches, exemplify the pluck and determination of the newly valorized realm of corporate survivordom, of course, but they perforce make us continually aware in this counsel of practices viewed not as endemic but as external to the good business bard guide.

Human nature in these lessons is made business-sized, as they praise Shakespeare's fascination with the "depths and complications of human relationships: boss to subordinate, colleague to colleague, lawyer to client, customer to salesperson, parent to child, and friend to friend" (xiii). Only fleetingly or less intentionally, however, do they push through to the market implications of their observation that Shakespeare also observes "the darker side of human nature—greed, overreaching ambition, ravaging jealousy, dishonesty," viewing them entirely as outside their niche, as the external dangers that can "undermine or even destroy a business" (xiii) as Shakespeare understood well.

Nor is there anything particularly dark in the ruthlessness, for instance, of studies of corporate layoffs and downsizings, as we learn from the lesson of the CEO of Pak Mail Centers of America. This executive returns to success after his company's losses, by closing his fifty weakest stores, "following the prescription of the gardener in *Richard II:* 'superfluous branches we lop away, that bearing boughs may live'" (23). Richard's lesson, and the quotation, are repeated later in the book in Lesson Ten of the chapter on crisis management, a chapter whose unironic epigraph is actually Polonius's "To thine own self be true," urging, with a Polonius-like dissociation of moralism from Machiavellianism, that executives must "feel that" their company's position is "the right and honorable one" (203). The chapter recounts the story of a decline in GM sales and quality, at the same time it "suffered strikes" at two major plants, followed by a rescue by a "hero in the situation," G. Richard Wagoner, Jr., who "took the direct approach by cutting a thousand jobs," lopping away "superfluous branches, etc." with the happy result that "analysts are becoming excited about the company again" (205), citing a source who noted how "comfortable" the analysts now are (206), analysts as the occluded actual audience in the corporate theater.

Never apparently having seen either Michael Moore's devastating satirical documentary on GM plant closings, *Roger and Me,* or even the provocative *Time* magazine cover of black and white, police-style "mug shots" of America's downsizing "corporate killers," the voice here is the remarkably direct voice of corporate and capitalist ideology, ever attentive to the happiness of economic analysts. By no means reductive or simpleminded in their analysis (as the occasional smug tone of my analysis itself might imply) the authors readily adopt the New Critical virtues of complexity and ambiguity as easily as they are evoked by literary critics. In one case, for instance, Lepidus is analyzed, the figure in the triumvirate in *Julius Caeser* who is dismissed by Antony as a "slight, unmeritable man / Meet to be sent on errands" (4.1 12–13). Like traditional "ambiguous" readings of character that emphasize the multiplicity of positive and negative views, the book concludes ambiguously about the scene: either Antony is a *bad* manager who "fails to discuss the performance review" with the employee Lepidus, or else a *good* manager "who treats Lepidus like a contingency worker, his chops needed only for a particular project and thus not worth developing for long-term employment" (96). Rather than adjudicate the application in one direction as opposed to the other, both are suspended in signification, remaining available for the flexible accumulation of cultural authority needed for contingent, occasional, or local uses. The Bard becomes a hyper-CEO by virtue of this flexibility of meaning.

Downsizing Hamlet

As the shift in the field of Shakespeare production after mass media is newly determined by the shift to niche marketing and modes of consumption, so Shakespeare's newly constructed entrepreneurial expertise now creates a completion of the logic of niche marketing. The market itself become another niche, Shakespeare's own authority in it becomes symptomatic. The new apotheosis of ruthlessness in the name of the national religion of business achieves its highest mode in *Shakespeare in Charge's* deliberately against-the-grain reading of *Hamlet,* in its concluding chapter on crisis management. In this chapter the cultural and philosophical authority of Shakespeare continually asserted at the usual level of the quotation seems mysteriously to drop out at the level of plot and character—the Bard implicitly, it seems, no longer our best guide. Hamlet, as he is also for many critics and for the generation of criticism from which the authors most likely borrow, is clearly the problem. Or rather, he is not a problem, interpretively, since he seems to be so clearly a bad "crisis manager" dealing with the crisis of the ghost, one who "fails to take control and *act*" but rather "struggles and reacts." The tragic figure becomes, in short, a "case study on how *not* to handle a crisis." Where the guide takes its even more revealing turn, however, is in the corresponding identification of Claudius as Hamlet's opposite in business terms, that is, as one who is exemplary in every way: appointing a "crisis team," devising a "tight action plan," constantly keeping "his stakeholders (his wife and subjects) in mind" and, with a business tip of the hand outside itself, "most of all, he thinks creatively" (168). Where the moral sympathy goes, moreover, is the contrast between Hamlet, who kills without feeling, and Claudius, who "at least feels terrible about it" (170). His "motivating" manipulation of Laertes is "another of Shakespeare's magnificent depictions of a successful business meeting" (178). In effect, the tragic ending of the play is largely erased in order to keep Claudius's corporate standing: "while Claudius's crimes are deplorable . . . there is still much to be learned from his crisis-management skills" (180).

All in all, the new universalism of this niche bardguide requires that business itself, be viewed not as an institution developing over time or as changing and unstable in its relation to exploitation but as timeless—at least when Shakespeare's cultural authority conjoins with it. Not only do people not change, as one understood from the cliches of the old universalism, but business does not. As the authors proclaim revealingly from the start of their bardguide, "The essence of business is thus remarkably constant" (xii).

Equally remarkable and even more revealing in the thoroughness and complexity of its discussions of Shakespeare's works is the recent *Power Plays: Shakespeare's Lessons in Leadership and Management,* by John O. Whitney and Tina Packer (New York: Simon & Schuster, 2000). Another collaboration of business with the humanities, one coauthor, Whitney, is a professor at Columbia Business School, a former Harvard faculty member, a CEO and director at various "publicly held companies," and an "expert on corporate transformations and turnarounds" (dust jacket). Based on the course he teaches after having wanted to teach it for the fifty years since he "fell in love" with Shakespeare in college, Whitney introduced the course just as others had been introducing the Machiavelli course for business majors at Columbia University. Students praise his course as the most influential of their two years at the school, one noting the niche circumstance that "a literature professor could never bring it off" (Herring 1998, 8). These credentials of the imagination for the businessman form a marketing chiasmus with the business credentials of imaginative Tina Packer, the founder, president, and artistic director of the performance group Shakespeare & Company in Lenox, Massachusetts. Indeed, her creative credentials assumed, the trial-by-fire business credentials turn out to be once again the contemporary ritualization of corporate authenticity, willingness to fire or to downsize without letting conscience make one a coward. Thus, as Whitney describes his own failure of will when he was once involved in a corporate "turnaround" where he, as in the dilemma of Henry IV, had "two Worcesters" who wanted his job," failing to fire them (for reasons of their connections and power) after "my spies reported," they had badmouthed him to others (66). The artist Tina Packer, however, during her third year of running "Shakespeare & Company," found herself in a management crisis of tight money, unwieldy reliance on volunteerism, and a personnel mess, so that eventually she "decided to put us out of the misery and fired everyone—even those I wasn't paying," and thus starting over with a clean slate for the company (66–67).

The rhetorical position of Whitney is *a fortiori,* that is, if a sensitive, creative, female artist can carry this ruthlessness off, what could someone like *you* manage to do? The lesson of Shakespeare, like that of late Shakespeareanism in the new corporate world, is ultimately a lesson of *will.* Here is the bardguides' dream of the creative niche swallowed up by the larger world of the market, refusing to have the status of niche that the marketing of the bardguide would itself seem logically to imply. Rather than simply admire, say, Hal's rejection of Falstaff as a necessary layoff, the book more open-mindedly imagines a business utopia (often in conflict with its *Realpolitik*) by which such creative characters are *used* productively. Thus, a chapter "Banish Not Your Jack Falstaff" ends with tips on "Managing Your Mavericks" by listening, using their creativity, and not stopping their ideas before carefully judging them (257). Of course, again the ritual test of authenticity is, as ever, in firing, with the approving anecdote of a CEO talking to his wife about her plans for the day: "I'm playing bridge with Gloria today," she said. "That's interesting," said Bud. "I'm planning to fire her husband this morning" (254).

In such instances as these, the corporate bardguide *Power Plays* reveals its political fault lines through its very thoroughgoingness in pushing to their logical conclusion the interpretations of both Shakespeare and the corporate world. Rather than resting on the comfortable platitudes of "to thine own self be true," it turns business ruthlessness transversally into a philosophically corrosive medium, thus onto business itself. Paradoxically, despite their resistance to all things Hamlet, the authors find themselves again and again, Hamlet-like, turning to questions, rather than answers, temporarily paralyzed by the self-reflexivity of their guide through corporate purgatory. No longer merely rhetorical, the authors more undecidedly and open-endedly (if not indecisively) wonder, "When is deception acceptable?" (215). "What ever happened to Truth in Advertising?" (225), they rant, at such a point not considering business as timeless but rather condemning the marketing world as one subject to historical change and even moral and social decay. In this late Shakespearean moral chaos, however, they are following the wild new corporate management strategies of the postmodern moment of chaos (see Peters 1987), they advise, "Uncertainty and Risk—Make Them Your Friends" (276).

Yet, the status of this business world becomes one of paradise lost; for all the targeted marketing of the era of late Shakespeareanism, they note that all we have left now is advertising that "no one believes in any more" (226), the innocence of the fallen world of business now replaced by a new one of untruth and complete dissociation from the public to which it is directed. With common truths dropping out along with commonality, all that is left is an audience cynicism to match that of the marketers.

This public, moreover, is only problematically viewed as democratic, for everything in business seems to rule against it. *Power Plays* is at least on occasion ruthlessly honest, in fact, in observing what virtually no U.S. political candidate or leader now would dare say openly in the public sphere: namely, that business, even when its executives avoid "imperial" styles of leadership condemned in some manuals, is profoundly and ultimately *antidemocratic.* As one of their section titles announces without apology (*without apology* constituting the latest tone of corporate ideology), "Democracy, No; Meritocracy, Yes" (113), or as another does, "Corporations Are Not Democracies" (42). When, after the idealized business lessons continually undermined by their philosophizing, and remarkably by the explicit rejection of religion in a section "Does Religion Have the Answer?" (197), they claim that "Shakespeare could not escape the market system" (200), by "Shakespeare" they mean themselves, and us. The question of what the universe is, or who owns it, may now be answered comfortably. The niche of business is the new universe. The public sphere is now coterminous with the market.

Instead of parroting "To thine own self be true" as the portable wisdom of the Bard, Whitney and Packer remarkably explore the dramatic circumstances of the quotation, just as any contemporary literary critic would do, by noting Polonius's discrepancy between his maxims and his actions. Going much further than this, in order to incorporate the ambiguity into the new, ambiguous religion of the corporate world, they further stipulate what they call the "Polonius paradox" to explain Polonius's contradiction, not in terms of an idiosyncratic personality but instead philosophically, as the contradiction inherent throughout the world. Thus, Polonius, for them, exemplifies Shakespeare's view of the complexity of this new universe, as explained in an entire chapter entitled, "Polonius's Paradox: Choices and Consequences for Man Alone and Man in Society" (187). In its secular philosophizing *Power Plays* even daringly concludes in one section that "religion alone has . . . not been able to solve [the Polonius paradox]" (198), implicitly rejecting the current coalition of business and right-wing fundamentalism which drives a good deal of the conservative Restoration experienced in the United States.

If Polonius is curiously elevated to accidental corporate philosopher, Hamlet, again, is the quintessential corporate loser and negative exemplar of corporate *de casibus* tragedy. In chapter 11 "To Be or Not to Be: It's Up to You. *Hamlet's* Fatal Flaws," we find the authors' lessons on fatally flawed corporate strategies, with Hamlet "failing on all counts" the authors' axiom: "An effective strategy is grounded in a set of realistic beliefs and expectations about our external worlds that helps us know what to do and how to do it, while making certain that we have the resources and will to

carry it out" (260). With a catalogue of stories of actual, grandiose corporate initiatives either dropped or never carried through, the book even
manages in its corporate imaginary to associate its tragic protagonist with
the most radical and disruptive phenomenon of the late capitalist corporate universe, namely corporate layoffs and downsizing. The new world of
downsizing has, it seems, managed to produce, of all the Shakespearean
characters possible, a welter of virtual Hamlets and a new version of the
old *melancholia:* "The downsizing of the past two decades has thrust many
brilliant, thoughtful, perceptive people in a strange world" (267). While
some apparently have downsized their princely ambitions by taking jobs in
"smaller companies" or "working from their homes, answering their own
phones," others remind us of Hamlet proper, whose combined attributes
of *vacillation, paralysis, bravado, intransigence, impatience, hand-wringing,
breast-beating and rage,* and *withdrawal and flight,* are each given separate
sections of the chapter with contemporary business anecdotes illustrating
each corporate sin. An even more ominous parallel is drawn about these
brilliant types, when it is noted in passing that of these Hamlets "a few
dream of revenge." Thus, the niche of Elizabethan stage violence becomes
subsumed within the seemingly "natural" universe of contemporary workplace violence. Perhaps the lessons of the chapter are reduced to a single
image, however, in the cover and frontispiece illustration of *Power Plays.*
There we see globalization wittily portrayed as an executive boardroom
table in the shape of a globe, with four Elizabethan-costumed CEOs sit
ting around it in corporate *habitus.* The four, Shakespeare, Queen Elizabeth, a generic king (probably Henry V), and, finally, Hamlet, seem to
present the new stock characters of the corporate stage, each in a characteristic posture and with an emblematic prop: Shakespeare, to whom the
others are all attentive, is making an emphatic point with an outstretched
finger and raising a shrewd eyebrow, his prop a calculator; Elizabeth is
poised and alert with report in one hand, quill poised in the other (taking
minutes, perhaps?); King Whatever leans forward over his notes and lap-
top; while Hamlet, his fingers and thumb propped pensively on his chin,
seems less involved, his telltale notes reading only "To Be? Or Not To
Be?"—the prototype of the nonproductive dreamer. Even villains, after all,
get things done.

I conclude this consideration of the significance of the corporate
bardguide with a final note on one other lesser luminary in the field, Paul
Corrigan's *Shakespeare on Management: Leadership Lessons for Today's Managers* (1999). Corrigan's bardguide uncannily and unintentionally reproduces one of the funnier gags from the satirical theatrical group, *The
Reduced Shakespeare Company,* at the same time instructively representing
the logic of late Shakespeareanism. One might remember the comedy

troupe's dumbfounded realization at the conclusion of their *Complete Works of Shakespeare, Abridged* show when, after the increasingly absurd race through the canon, it hits everyone at once that—duh—they completely forgot *Hamlet*. What is to be done? As we have seen in the other management manuals, as the niche market for Shakespeare begins to take over the shelf-space of the whole universe, the niche swallowing up the whole, the play *Hamlet* and its "hero" appear on the scene, as the ghost come to tell us that all is not well in the corporate kingdom, that business's hectic turn to the humanities partly marks a rottenness growing at its ever more self-indulgent and ruthless core, and even to hint at the alternative of revenge. Corrigan's book manages to solve the problem by simple exclusion from major consideration: in the entire book, the play is mentioned only once in passing (noting that like *Lear* it concludes with a stage full of dead bodies), its hero only once (in a discussion of the appeal of Stoppard's *Rosencrantz and Guildenstern are Dead* directed to those of us not lucky enough to be in a leadership role). *Hamlet* is subsumed into another Shakespearean niche, imagined otherwise than the corporate setting of the recent Almereyda film version of the play.

If *Hamlet*, manditorily forgotten under central European communism, functioned for dissidents as a disturber of the official peace (See Stříbny, 2000), perhaps it might in the current epoch function as a specter, risen from the early modern anticipations of the present moment, capable of disturbing the lazily reptilian complacency of the corporation. Smuggled into the business niche like a renegade Division of Human Resources, it might even constitute our last best hope within a corporate culture with no apparent exit. Jacques Derrida's *Specters of Marx* (1994), notwithstanding the overwrought elegance of his puffery for lapsed or wounded marxists in need of encouragement (or is it Will?), may have a point.

Notes

1. As it happens, my own exploration of this industry two years ago, as I was engaged in a project on movie trailers, accidentally touched on this area when I was able to interview the head of the trade organization for the movie advertising business. While the woman was congenial and welcoming, she politely but firmly indicated that she would not be able to discuss or reveal any of the marketing research practices of the trade. She thus short-circuited any inquiry into any practices, including some possibly controversial ones to which my contacts in the industry had obliquely hinted, practices now exposed in legislators' criticism of Hollywood now taking the form of its demonization by an alliance of right-wing social conservatism and protective neoliberalism.

2. A segmented and targeted audience is also implied in an epilogue here omitted, that from *The Two Noble Kinsmen*, which anticipates the audience response that "No man smile?" by concluding, "Gentlemen, good night" (*Epil.*
4, 18). But the example is not on all fours with the others, since it fails to
acknowledge the women at all. From my perspective this omission, unchar-
acteristic of Shakespeare, may be yet another of the formal characteristics
that cast doubt if not suspicion on the claims for Shakespeare's coauthorship,
not my subject here.

3. The market logic of this is not bound to a single historical period, I might
note, since we may see the same profession in the history of movie trailers,
which were originally tied to the directors and studios producing the movies
but which eventually broke off into an industry of their own by the late
1960s.

4. A local subtext of this transformation is the deal cut by the Pepsi Corporation with my university to have exclusive marketing of soft drinks on
campus in exchange for a considerable donation to the university and its
library of a million dollars in the first year of exclusivity. Immediately
after this deal they replaced the 55 cent cans in all vending machines with
one dollar bottles, presumably thereby recouping much of their "donation" over time. Now, the state division and traditional rivalry of its major
universities is replicated as a market segmentation, of Coke U. (University of Kansas) vs. Pepsi U. (Kansas State University). My own proposal
to receive some consideration for wearing a monogrammed Pepsi jacket
to classes was politely rejected by the regional promotion executives of the
company, who urged me to wear the jacket proudly anyway, without
compensation.

5. Richard Burt tells me that a commercial for *Shakespeare in Charge* precedes
the video of *Shakespeare in Love*, a film which of course locates Shakespeare
in a capitalist theatrical marketplace.

Works Cited

Agnew, Jean-Christophe. 1993. "Coming Up for Air: Consumer Culture in Historical Perspective." In *Consumption and the World of Goods.* Ed. by John Brewer and
Roy Porter. London and New York: Routledge, 19–39.

Augustine, Norman, and Kenneth Adelman. 1999. *Shakespeare in Charge: The Bard's
Guide to Leading and Succeeding on the Business Stage.* New York: Hyperion.

Axelrod, Alan. 2000. *Elizabeth I CEO: Strategic Lessons from the Leader Who Built a
Empire.* New York: Prentice Hall.

Beemer, C. Britt. 1997. *Predatory Marketing: What Everyone in Business Needs to
Know to Win Today's Consumer.* New York: William Morrow.

Bristol, Michael. 1996. *Big-Time Shakespeare.* New York and London: Routledge.

Burt, Richard. [1998]1999. *Unspeakable ShaXXXpeares: Queer Theory and American
Kiddie Culture.* 2nd ed. New York: St. Martin's Press.

Campbell, Colin. 1987. *The Romantic Ethic and the Spirit of Modern Consumerism.* New York and Oxford: Blackwell.

Corrigan, Paul. 1999. *Shakespeare on Management: Leadership Lessons for Today's Managers.* London: Kogan Page.

Derrida, Jacques. 1994. *Specters of Marx: The State of the Debt, the Work of Mourning, and the New International.* New York and London: Routledge.

Dobson, Michael. 1992. *The Making of the National Poet: Shakespeare, Adaptation and Authorship: 1660–1769.* New York and London: Oxford Univ. Press.

Ewen, Stuart. 1984. *All-Consuming Images: The Politics of Style in Contemporary Culture.* New York: HarperCollins.

Featherstone, Mike. 1991. *Consumer Culture and Postmodernism.* London: SAGE.

Grady, Hugh. 1996. *Shakespeare's Universal Wolf: Studies in Early Modern Reification.* New York and London: Oxford Univ. Press.

Hedrick, Donald. 2000. "Shakespeare's Enduring Immorality: The Ethical and the Performative Turns, or Toward a Transversal Pedagogy." In *Shakespeare Without Class: Misappropriations of Cultural Capital.* Ed. by Donald Hedrick, and Bryan Reynolds. New York and London: Palgrave, 241–74.

Hedrick, Donald, and Bryan Reynolds. 2000. "Shakespace and Transversal Theory." In *Shakespeare Without Class: Misappropriations of Cultural Capital,* ed. Donald Hedrick and Bryan Reynolds. New York and London: Palgrave, 3–47.

Herring, Hubert B. 1998. "To Teach, Perchance to Manage," *New York Times,* December 6, Sec. 3: 8.

Hodgdon, Barbara. 1998. *The Shakespeare Trade: Performances and Appropriations.* Philadelphia: Univ. of Pennsylvania Press.

Laird, Pamela Walker. 1998. *Advertising Progress: American Business and the Rise of Consumer Marketing.* Baltimore and London: Johns Hopkins Univ. Press.

Levine, Lawrence. 1988. *Highbrow/Lowbrow: The Emergence of Cultural Hierarchy in America.* Cambridge, Massachusetts: Harvard Univ. Press.

Mandel, Ernest. 1975. *Late Capitalism.* London and Atlantic Highlands, New Jersey: Humanities Press.

McKendrick, Neil, John Brewer, and J. H. Plumb. 1982. *The Birth of a Consumer Society: The Commercialization of Eighteenth-century England.* London: Europa Publications.

Peters, Tom. 1987. *Thriving on Chaos: Handbook for a Management Revolution.* New York: Harper & Row.

Rowe, Michael. 1999. "Music and Theater Enter the Business Curriculum." *International Herald Tribune,* November 15, 1999.

Shafritz, Jay M. 1999. *Shakespeare on Management: Wise Business Counsel from the Bard.* New York: HarperCollins.

Shakespeare, William. 1974. *The Riverside Shakespeare.* Ed. by G. Blakemore Evans. Boston: Houghton Mifflin.

Smith, Paul. 1997. *Millennial Dreams: Contemporary Culture and Capital in the North.* New York and London: Verso.

Sombart, Werner. [1913]1967. *Luxury and Capitalism.* Ann Arbor: Univ. of Michigan Press.

Stříbrny, Zdenek. 2000. *Shakespeare and Eastern Europe.* Oxford, England, and New York: Oxford Univ. Press.

Tedlow, Richard S. 1996. *New and Improved: The Story of Mass Marketing in America.* Boston: Harvard Business School Press.

Whitney, John O., and Tina Packer. 2000. *Power Plays: Shakespeare's Lessons in Leadership and Management.* New York: Simon and Schuster.

CHAPTER 2

"IN FAIR VERONA"

Media, Spectacle, and Performance in
William Shakespeare's Romeo + Juliet

PETER S. DONALDSON

Shakespeare Media Allegories

Shakespeare's plays are endlessly metatheatrical, commenting on the theater and its practices often and in many different ways. There are plays within plays, explicit comparisons of life to the stage, scenes in which playhouse audience and players onstage seem to merge, and perhaps thousands of more fleeting moments that refer directly or through metaphor or double meaning to stagecraft or performance. But if, as Michael Goldman once wrote, there is *always* a play within a play in Shakespeare (Goldman 1972), it is nonetheless true that some plays reflect on their medium in such a sustained way that they can be read as allegories of theater, exploring the paradoxes of performance and representation as in *A Midsummer Night's Dream*, calling attention to historical change in theater practices (as Hamlet does when he laments the success of the new all-boys companies), and even, as in *The Tempest*, imagining the end of all theater, when something called "the . . . globe," at once playhouse and cosmos, will dissolve without a trace.

Shakespeare film adaptations are also often self-referential, either in the simple sense of alluding to performance simply by following the metatheatrical text of the play, or in ways that invoke the special properties of the cinematic medium. All of Welles's Shakespeare films are rich in such metacinematic moments, as is Peter Brook's *King Lear*, in which antirealist techniques such as anachronistic black and white and violations of the conventions of space-time continuity are used not only to portray the king's increasing isolation and madness, but also to create a cinematic equivalent to the play's suggestion that we are watching "not Lear" but "Lear's shadow" or simulacrum. Brook plays, too, on the difference between the simultaneous presence of audience and performers in the theater, and the numbing absences that cinema can invoke in the hands of a skilled director. Facing the camera in a poignant close-up, Brook's Lear offer his hand to "us," the film audience, as he does to the dead Cordelia, without the possibility of response.

While not unique in its metacinematic concerns, Laurence Olivier's *Henry V* differs from these films in several respects that make it a significant precursor of a number of more recent Shakespeare films and a useful starting point for my interpretation of the 1996 Bazmark production, *William Shakespeare's Romeo + Juliet*. First, Olivier's film is concerned with a wide range of media, not only the stage (the film begins on a reconstructed model of the Globe) and the cinema, but with pictorial media, basing its scenes in the French court on *Les tres riches heures de Duc de Berri*, and with its own status as a kind of broadcast to the nation, alluding, in various ways, to its origins in the radio broadcasts of the Crispin's Day speech that Olivier made for the War Ministry (Donaldson, 1999). Second, the film attempts a kind of historical media allegory, suggesting, quite intentionally on the evidence of Olivier's published memoirs, that the techniques of modern epic cinema fulfill and perfect the representational ambitions of theater, making good the chorus's wish for " a muse of fire" that could bring real horses and battles before the spectators. And, just as modern media fulfill the hopes of earlier techniques of representation, so, it is implied, the England of 1944, nearing triumph over despotism, inherits both the war-like spirit and the humane civilization of the era of Shakespeare.

A number of recent Shakespeare films also make media history and media transition a part of their message. Jean-Luc Godard's *King Lear* (1987) takes place in a surreal future society in which Shakespeare's text has been lost and is reconstructed as oral history, while a mad inventor (Godard himself) attempts to reinvent cinema by illuminating tiny toy dinosaurs in a darkened cardboard box using fairground sparklers. Peter Greenaway's *Prospero's Books* (1994) imagines Prospero writing the text of *The Tempest*, stages the destruction and recovery of the First Folio, and associates Prospero's rejection of his magic books with the replacement of conventional cinema by digital multimedia. Richard Loncraine's *Richard III* (1996) explores a range of media forms, including still photography, silent black-and-white film, and recorded as well as amplified live sound in its characterization of Richard as a modern, media-reliant, Hitler-like tyrant, urging upon us questions of media complicity in the creation of contemporary regimes of death. These films—to which one might add Michael Almereyda's bleak, techno-logically inflected film noir *Hamlet* (1999) in which Hamlet produces with digital editing *The Mousetrap: A Movie*—are less celebratory, more critical and apocalyptic than Laurence Olivier's war-time epic, *Henry V* (1944), but, like Olivier's film, they span a range of media and offer an implicit (if somewhat fantastical) history of media in transition. As makers of media allegory, these filmmakers take Shakespeare as their precursor and predecessor, rewriting metatheatricality as cross-media self-consciousness.

Baz Luhrmann's film belongs with this group of Shakespeare films that make creative use of the present ferment in communications technologies and representational practices not only to attempt new interpretations of the plays but to explore our own rapidly shifting media landscape. His *Romeo + Juliet* is perhaps the most media-saturated of all Shakespeare films yet produced, with televisions on the beach and in the pool halls of its contemporary "Verona," and a kaleidoscopic succession of video, newspaper, and news magazine coverage replicating the details of the Capulet-Montague feud, all adding, as the slogan on a gas station sign proclaims, "more fuel to the fire" of the urban culture of violence that destroys the lovers.

While the film's attention to media, especially to "the media" (broadcast and print news media) is obvious, the idea of associating Luhrmann's work with that of Olivier or Godard may well be questioned. When *Cineaste* solicited comments from a number of Shakespeare film directors for a recent print symposium, *Romeo + Juliet* was easily the most controversial film mentioned, provoking negative comments even from innovators like Peter Hall and Franco Zeffirelli. Zeffirelli was particularly harsh:

> The Luhrmann film didn't update the play, it just made a big joke out of it. But apparently the pseudo-culture of young people today wouldn't have digested the play unless you dressed it up that way, with all those fun and games. (Brook et al. 1998, 54)

Other critics have been equally severe, especially in regard to the film's allegedly inept handling of Shakespeare's verse or "language." The characters sound, in this line of critique, as if they were reading from a script. In contrast, academic critics, notably Timothy Murray (1997), Barbara Hodgdon (1999), and William Worthen (1998) have praised the film for its blend of popular culture, mass media savvy, and theoretical sophistication. Worthen, for example, reads the film's sometimes awkward handling of verse as well as its visual excess as elements of a "citational" strategy, Luhrmann's acknowledgments that a contemporary work is not and cannot offer us an authentic or original Shakespeare. Like all performances for which there is a script, *Romeo + Juliet* quotes or cites its text. But in Brechtian fashion this particular performance draws attention to the fact of citation, to its distance from the text and from Shakespeare. Its bold and dissonant namings and labelings—a title that claims literal Shakespearean authorship and then immediately explodes the claim of authenticity by gross anachronism; a "Verona" that is not Verona but a phantasmatic double of Los Angeles; "swords" that are not swords but 9mm pistols engraved with that brand name—help direct our attention to the gulf that separates text and performance.

The citational strategies of the film are central, I would argue, not only to the distinctions the film makes between Shakespeare's "original" and its surrogation in contemporary performance, but also to its success and power as media allegory and critique, for Luhrmann's unsettling juxtapositions place us at a distance not only from Shakespeare, but from the seductions of the high-style media-intensive culture the film evokes and might otherwise seem to revel in. Luhrmann depicts a world saturated by image, where mass media and corporate power have triumphed even more decisively (if such a thing is possible) than in real life. But while this system is portrayed with immense energy and even delight, it is also presented as cause of the tragic action. The out-of-control media culture of Verona is the film's equivalent for the Capulet-Montague conflict in the play, Luhrmann's extrapolation of the text's insight that the violence of the feud, ("bred of an airy word") is self-replicating and meaningless. Rather than constituting an endorsement of media culture, Luhrmann's presentation of "Verona" as a society in which fetishized image and capitalism constitute a unified and nearly unopposable system is a critique, convergent with several of the more radical strands of contemporary media theory such as those articulated by Guy Debord and the Situationists in the 1960s (Debord [1967]1994. See also Crary 1989 and Sadler 1998). The Situationist legacy continues today in both an activist strain, represented by Kalle Lasn and the editors of *Adbusters,* and a more theoretical one represented by Umberto Eco and Jean Baudrillard, who use the term "hyperreality" for the supersession of reality by media image which Debord had named "the spectacle." While *Romeo + Juliet* resonates with both earlier and later versions of this tradition, I will more often draw on the earlier formulations in glossing the film—in part because, like the Situationists, Luhrmann is concerned to show how traces of earlier, more popular and participatory cultural practices—such as an impromptu drag performance—survive at the margins of late-capitalist, media-saturated cities. "Fair Verona" has a past that is more theatrical, closer to Shakespeare than its mass-media present: traditions of live performance, improvisation, and festival persist and at times challenge the reign of what Debord called "the spectacle." But such challenges do not prevail and the feud—linked in the film to the domination of media image over life—continues. In what follows I fill in some of the details of this sketch of the film's shape, reading Baz Luhrmann's energetic and innovative work as an allegory of life in the age of media spectacle.

Origins: The Myth of Autochthonous Television

The whole of life of those societies in which modern conditions of production prevail presents itself as an immense accumulation of spectacles. All that once was directly lived has become mere representation. (Debord [1967]1994, 12)

Whereas Olivier's prologue is spoken on the stage of the Globe, Luhrmann's is presented as a news broadcast that we watch on a 1970s television set, decontextualized by its placement at the center of an otherwise black film screen. Old-time TV, not Elizabethan London, is the point of origin. At first the TV screen is dark like the filmic image that frames it, and then the channel switches, audibly clicking as if the dial were turned by an invisible hand, or turned by itself in mystic anticipation of the later technology of infrared remote control. Visual static appears, followed by the image of an African American anchorwoman. As she delivers the opening lines of the Prologue in the tones of contemporary reportage, a slow zoom brings the set nearer until it fills a substantial proportion of the screen. As the Prologue ends, here as in the play, by announcing the "two hours traffic of *our* stage," coverage "goes live," and we are pulled toward and through the television screen, like a spaceship entering a time warp, into an urban landscape which seems to be inside the set or on the other side of the screen.

In this and in a variety of other ways that follow, Luhrmann suggests that the boundary between reality and its media representations is shaky or nonexistent. The city we see is shaped, even created, by the broadcast. What we see on screen is a fantasy version of Los Angeles, but bold title cards name it, impossibly, "Fair Verona," writing Shakespeare's setting over a surreal version of our own world in the manner of Godard's *King Lear*. As in more conventional establishing sequences, we are first shown the city's center, dominated by a cathedral tower topped by a grand modernist statue of Mary, hands rigidly outstretched, ringed by news or police helicopters. (The production team called this the "Church of the Traffic Warden.") An even larger freestanding statue of Christ matches and balances the cathedral, on the same axis. Twin, featureless corporate office towers of the Capulet and Montague corporations flank the main thoroughfare which runs between the statues. As is increasingly the case in the opening sequence of contemporary film, the establishing sequence shows us not only the landmarks, but the media that define the space: mediascape as well as landscape. The rapid zoom sequences that bring us in toward the center and out again to a wider view traverse not only the urban grid but a broad range of media representations of it, shifting, in successive shots, from video to newsprint and glossy newsmagazine photo versions of Jesus and Mary as well as to the 35mm cinematic images of these sculptures that in a conventional film would signal the "real" space and time of the narrative. In this blazingly rapid and protean sequence the real cannot be easily identified among its mediated representations. It appears (if at all) as one option in an integrated media spectrum. While it has become a commonplace that media coverage often influences or provokes the events that are covered, the Capulet-Montague conflict is a media-generated event in a far more literal sense. The film suggests, at least at the start, that there is nothing "before" or "outside" television. In Jean Baudrillard's terms, media simulacrum takes precedence over reality: "the map engenders the territory " (1983, 2).

When the credit/prologue sequence has ended, the film adheres somewhat more closely to narrative and spatio-temporal continuity, but unpredictable frame rates, hallucinatory sequences, and the omnipresence of surreal advertising slogans and video displays continue to convey a sense of unreality even as we follow the familiar story of Romeo and Juliet. Media are ubiquitous, including not only television receivers, but an array of surveillance technologies. A huge bank of closed circuit monitors cover every part of the Capulet mansion, including the swimming pool in which the "balcony" scene is enacted; floodlights mounted on police helicopters illuminate dark corners of the city; the high-powered binoculars in police helicopters and the telescopic rifle and pistol sights attached to the guns carried by the rival clans as well as by the police also bring distant sights near, reinforcing the cross-media video zooms of the opening sequences and bringing to the surface the root metaphor of television as real-time *Fernsehen*, distant sight. To borrow a phrase from Benjamin's classic essay, "The Work of Art in the Age of Mechanical Reproduction" (Benjamin [1936]1969) the film brings everything in the city "very near, very fast." Magnification, replication, and dissemination are instantaneous.

For contemporary theorists of the hyperreal, the replication of images extends beyond the cheap reproductions of works of art that Benjamin had in mind to broadcast images and even to urban architecture, where the vogue for repeatable, modular forms signals the replacement of competition by its simulacrum. Baudrillard, not entirely fancifully, reads changes in the New York skyline as indicative of this shift. In the era of individual competition, the landscape was dominated by skyscrapers each reaching higher than the last—the Chrysler Building, the Empire State Building. In the age of late capitalism, global corporations and the hyperreal, the featureless twin rectangular solids of the World Trade Center dominated, until their destruction on September 11, 2001. "Why are there two towers" he asks (Baudrillard 1993, 135–36), and answers that their twinning is a warrant of the power to generate identical forms. In the film, the twin corporate headquarters of the Montague and Capulet families, identical except for their surmounting signs, function in the construction of the hyperreal in a similar way. The text of

Romeo and Juliet itself emphasizes binaries and suggests twinning, providing a textual anchor for this postmodern *motif:* there are "*two* households" ("both alike"); a "*pair*" of lovers have sprung from the generative but "fatal loins" (whatever parts of the body these are, they certainly come in pairs) of "*two* foes" (four parents are needed, but the strict binarism continues, perhaps to suggest at the outset that the polar oppositions of the feud, as arbitrary as they may be, will prove decisive, perhaps to suggest that, in a sense, Romeo and Juliet are nearly twins). In the film, even the prologue itself is doubled: spoken once by the newscaster, then in voice-over by the Friar. Then it is repeated again in fragmentary form on monitors that are part of the narrative sequences. The phrase "two households," repeated many times in the doubled prologue film, is also the framing motif of the play. In the play the reasons for the conflict between the houses are arbitrary and superficial, the political meaning of the Guelph and Ghibelline conflict that divides these families in Dante having long been forgotten or ignored by the time of Da Porto's *Istoria* ([1530]1831), the earliest source that tells the story of the lovers. In contemporary versions of the story of Romeo and Juliet, the feud tends to be repoliticized, as in *West Side Story.* In Luhrmann's postmodern Verona, the feud is ethnically tinged as well but the appearance of conflict between these corporate families is a mask for a deeper alliance of interest and the daily violence in the streets is simply one of the ways in which a highly unified and all but unopposable system conducts its normal business.

Religious Imagery:
Appropriation and Détournement

For the Situationists, television was especially important as a means by which the image culture of the spectacle could penetrate into the home. The January 1963 issue of the *Internationale Situationiste,* for example, focuses on the intrusion of the spectacle into domestic space, and is illustrated by an image of a television set displaying the message "le spectacle a la masion ce soir" [The spectacle—at home tonight]. As a powerful agent for extending the reach of false consciousness into the recesses and corners of personal life, television was thus, in a sense, the successor to the ideological role assigned to religion in Marx and Feuerbach. In fact, Debord's manifesto, the *Society of the Spectacle* uses a quotation from Feuerbach's *Essence of Christianity* as its epigraph:

> For the present age, which prefers the sign to the thing signified, the copy to the original, representation to reality, the appearance to the essence, *illusion* only is sacred, *truth* profane. Nay, sacredness is held to be enhanced in proportion as truth decreases and illusion increases, so that the highest degree of

illusion is held to be the highest degree of sacredness. (Debord 1994[1967], citing Feuerbach, *L'essor du Christianisme*, 2nd ed.)

In Debord's terms, "the spectacle is the material reconstruction of the religious illusion and its heir" (17–18). While religion plays a more complex role in Luhrmann's film than simply as a vehicle for false consciousness, as in the line of ideological theory that connects Marx, Feuerbach, and the Situationists, the many "sacred" spaces and objects in *Romeo + Juliet* illustrate Feuerbach's thesis. Mass-produced religious images closely parallel other media messages in ubiquity, and are presented as instances of the power of the media to saturate the city with false consciousness.

The central cathedral, the locus of "the highest degree of sacredness" in Verona, seems at times to be a broadcast tower, and as in many "real-life" newscasts, this downtown landmark serves as a dual symbol of the city and of the evening news. Further, the monumental statue of the Virgin that surmounts the building is itself a media icon, reproduced across the range of media the film presents. Religious images are not merely a subset of mass-produced or broadcast image, however—they embody the power of the spectacle to penetrate the most intimate recesses of personal life. Literally hundreds of crosses are shown on screen in the course of the film, in all sizes and styles. They are worn around the neck, shaved into the backs of heads, tattooed on the body, printed on shirts, engraved on gunstocks, mounted on dashboards. They are shown in absurd proliferation in every public and domestic space, many of them internally illuminated by neon light. In creating the Christian hyperreal of Verona Beach's cathedral, the art director, Catherine Martin, brought so many images into the sacristy of the Church of the Sagrada Corazon de Maria in Mexico City (where the film was shot) that the real priest became suspicious of mockery, and she had to "explain" that they were necessary to portray the faith and customs of another time (Luhrmann 1996; see Modenessi 1998).

Though this explanation is disingenuous (the film does not recreate a period environment), mass-produced and *faux* mass-produced religious images are indeed used in the film for something more than mockery of religious kitsch and popular Latin Catholicism. Rather, such images play a role in the artistic and political strategy Debord called *détournement*, the appropriation of the motifs of the spectacle by its adversaries (Debord and Jorn 1959; Marcus 1989, 168ff.). Luhrmann's style at once unmasks the role of religious symbol as commodified and fetishized brand name and badge, and also constructs dynamic sequences in which such symbols are appropriated in ways that derive from punk or Gothic *détournements* or are even restored to something like their "original" significations, as symbols of love, compassion, or tolerance.

One of the most characteristic instances of the spiraling of religious signification in the film involves the "+" in the film title. Worthen understands it as an instance of citationality or distancing of performance from originating text. It is certainly that—marking classic "high culture" text with the informal typography of playground romance and youth culture graffiti. But it is also a cross, and its introduction on screen places it at the center of the complex contestation over the meaning of the Christian cross that the film explores.

In the credit sequence, the title *Romeo + Juliet* is first seen in white block lettering against a black background, the two names connected by a plus sign that is a miniature, fiery red Gothic cross, very like those seen in the literature and on the websites of the "Goth" subculture of today. The sign thus is a *détournement* of Shakespeare title as signifier of official culture and of Christian symbol.

In the context of the sequence in which it first appears, this "+" is seen also as a compression of the violence of the streets into the tiny space between the names of the lovers. The sequence begins with a cross of one kind at the center of the screen—the crosshairs of a telescopic pistol sight tracking a victim in a car (whose jerky frame-by-frame movement evokes the Zapruder footage of the Kennedy assassination). As the bullet strikes the passenger in the open car, there is a match cut to the falling body, spiraling through space, its twisting limbs momentarily taking a cruciform shape. Then the body is replaced in a split second by the red Gothic cross, shown full screen only for several frames before it "zooms" down into the miniscule red plus sign in the title. Though seen only briefly here, the red Gothic cross is a central image for and of the film, and was reproduced in publicity materials, posters, and in digital form on the pages of the film's website. In its "full size" instantiations, the red cross that forms the "+" sign is illuminated by the flickering reflections of candlelight, relating it both to Goth subculture as well as to the supersaturated religiosity of the Capulet tomb, Juliet's bedroom, and other spaces of the sacred in the film, where candle, pulsing strobe, and neon lights flicker on the surface of countless icons, crosses and statuary. Further, as the red cross replaces the falling body, the dark outline of the falling human body *also* zooms down, diminishing almost to a point, as it morphs into the tiny ampersand ("&") at the center of the cross. The dynamic replacement of wounded body by a typographic symbol within another symbol suggests endless replication, a *mise-en-abyme* of reinscription and resignification—but it also suggests that any cross (any coupling or copula) is marked with the trace of the suffering human body and is thus also a crucifix. In a sense, the complex cross of the title is a dynamic visual equivalent for the deathmark in the text, inspired by the Prologue's reference to the "fearful passage" of a "deathmarked love."

Such complex patterns of reinscription are frequent in *Romeo + Juliet*. A second example is the way in which the meaning of the lines referring to the star-crossed lovers who "take their life" from the loins of foes is shifted or *detourné* by another typographical choice. A title card with an initial "t" in the shape of a runic cross appears as Pete Postlethwaite reads the line on the soundtrack in a way that brings to the surface the suggestion of suicide latent in the line. This potential meaning is enacted in the play's final scene, but few productions enable us to hear it in the Prologue, where "take their life" refers to the birth of the lovers (albeit from "fatal" loins). Because the prologue is read twice—once on the evening news and once in a solemn and more compassionate voice-over—the conventional meaning, as well as the deeper proleptic meaning that fuses birth and suicide, are both presented. In this case, Luhrmann's repetitions and complex overlays of significance restore possibilities of meaning that an attentive reading of the text can amply support.

A third example of the spiral of religious signification typical of the film is offered by the interpretation of the line "Turn thee, Benvolio, look upon thy death." In speaking these lines, Tybalt opens his jacket to reveal his pistols. In Shakespeare's text, the line is already intertextual, an echo of the scene in Marlowe's *Tamburlaine* in which the conqueror commands his captives to behold their imminent death, seated on his sword-point. But in Luhrmann's version, as Tybalt shows his holstered pistols he also makes visible another of the film's ubiquitous Christian symbols, the image of Jesus and the sacred heart imprinted on his T-shirt. Read one way, this sacred image is debased by its appropriation as youth gang brand, while from another perspective, that of Marxian critique, the juxtaposition of the gun and the image of Jesus merely reveals the ideological function religion normally plays. However Luhrmann's postmodern sensibility does not allow either of these meanings to be final ones, for the image of Christ and the sacred heart undergoes further development in the film, in which its potential as a symbol of compassion is in part restored. The friar's hallucinatory image—which prompts him to find ways to turn the "household rancor to pure love" is identical to the image on Tybalt's shirt, and it also appears on Romeo's shirt as he moves decisively (but ironically and very temporarily) from the world of the feud to commitment to Christian love. Each of these uses of the image are themselves complex, their ironies balancing the trust that the lovers and the friar place in them, but they cannot be contained within the limits of ideological critique. Further, what is shown on Tybalt's shirt is not simply an image of the sacred heart, but an image of Jesus *displaying* it, this *ostentatio,* or unveiling, mirroring and complicating Tybalt's gesture, which now can be read as a revelation of the symbols of compassion as well as a display of the instruments of death. Furthermore, even the pistols and rifles in the film are doubly or triply marked, "turned" in signification, since they are decorated with religious images and, in one of the most remarked upon citational strategies of the film, bear brand names drawn from Shakespeare's text ("Sword," "Dagger," "Longsword"), reminding us, with campy exuberance, of the early modern props they substitute for and overwrite.

These complexities create a spiraling of reference, in which the religious symbolism of the film can be (indeed, must be) understood in relation to multiple frameworks. Cross and sacred heart are inherited Christian images, but they are also signs of the domination of the spectacle, their ubiquity and plenitude a sign of its power. They are also appropriated as badges of the youth culture (cf. Hebdige 1979), where they oscillate in meaning, marking the gangs' attempt to distinguish themselves from the dominant corporate/media culture of the adult Capulets and Montagues as well as their participation in and victimization by that culture. Beyond these frames, the plenitude as well as the contested status of religious icons function not only to create the world of the film, but as markers of the signature visual style of Baz Luhrmann and Bazmark Productions. This style—strong, intrusive, copious, witty, appropriative, allusive—attempts to fill the screen with icons, logos, turned images of all sorts, and so, in a sense, to out-spectacle the spectacle.

So that if, in *Romeo + Juliet*, religion has become (or is shown to have always been) a fetish or brand logo, it is never only that. There is always another turn in signification by which appropriated or corrupted tokens regain some of their force as signifiers of fidelity, compassion, charity, and seriousness. The Friar sees a huge image of a wreathed heart in the sky as he hatches the fatal plan of turning the rancor of the feud to love through the marriage of Romeo and Juliet, the Friar is inspired by the huge image of a wreathed heart in the sky. But any sense that this is a divine vision is qualified by the fact that this image is an exact but greatly magnified replica of the one printed on his gaudy tropical shirt. We see the moment as excessive, an index of the Friar's semi-stoned wackiness, perhaps as a hallucination induced by the helpful weeds and flowers he has been distilling—but it also conveys what the director considered the film's central message—one of compassion and tolerance in the face of the labeling of differing religions, ethnic groups, and sexual communities as enemies because of "a brand name that someone made up in the dark ages" (anon. 1997). The cross and the sacred heart are in one sense, prominent among those Medieval trademarks, in another sense they stand for values the film affirms and for a style of citational but passionate reappropriation not only characteristic of youth subcultures, but of Luhrmann himself who often wears a large Gothic cross, as in victory photographs taken during the successful Paul Keating campaign for prime minister of Australia, for which the Bazmark group managed events and image-creation.

La Dérive: The Place of the Stage

If *détournement* is one mode of resistance to media, another is called "*la dérive*," goalless and spontaneous walking in the city. Deriving, perhaps, from the persona of the hypersensitive urban stroller in Baudelaire and other

Symbolist poets, it is the urban radical's equivalent to geomancy, involving cultivation of sensitivity to energies and traces of an urban experience prior to or resistant to the regime of the spectacle (Debord and Jorn 1959; Marcus, 1989, 168ff). To apply Baudrillard's metaphor, one might think of this practice as the search for the tattered map of the real in the hyperreal urban grid that has all but effaced it.

In Luhrmann's film, Romeo's *dérive* is associated with Sycamore Grove, the part of Verona Beach that is actually adjacent to the beach and distinct in style and pace from downtown, where the feud takes place and corporate towers and monumental Christian architecture dominates. Though the filming for these sequences was done in Vera Cruz, this locale in its contrast to the city center evokes the relationship between Venice Beach and downtown Los Angeles. It is a run-down area devoted to the cheap amusements of a former era—rusty merry-go-rounds turn in the wind, the seedy pool hall (labeled "The Globe Theater") is located here, and the landscape is dominated by the contrast between the grandeur of the ocean, sand, and sky and a large ruined arch that stands on the beach. This is where Romeo's "early walking" takes place, and he is first seen looking at the sea and writing lines of verse in a small notebook with a pen. Luhrmann takes Romeo's poetic side seriously, restoring an aspect of the character often lost in productions that see only the empty imitation of the conventions of courtly love in the pre-Juliet Romeo. The production commentary makes clear that the ruin is the central proscenium arch of a decayed cinema palace, it's "fourth wall" destroyed and open to the sky, as if the building had been blown open by ordinance from a battleship. Yet, because the building has a stage under the arch and a few broken seats remain of the city side, it also evokes theater, and in fact it is used as a stage for improvised performances by the Montague gang. Impromptu theater and cinema thus merge: they are both aspects of the city's past, this place a site for fragmentary and improvised alternatives to the powerful media-intensive culture of the center. The world of the film is thus postcinematic as well as post-theatrical. Sycamore Grove provides a hint of history at odds with the counter-myth of the televisual origin of the city, and in the history of the production it competes with television as point of origin, since it was the originating image of Luhrmann's design, imagined and built as a model two full years before shooting began in Mexico City (Luhrmann 1996).

Though the theater is in ruins, it provides a setting for Romeo's withdrawal and his attempt to separate himself from the violence of the feud and a location for the wild improvisations of Mercutio and the Montague boys, who watch his performances from the few seats that remain on the city-side of the structure. "The place of the stage" to use Steven Mullaney's term, is indeed marginal or liminal in Verona, and allows a free space for satire and poetry, slower rhythms, older media.

"In habito di ninfa:"
Drag Performance from Da Porto to the Sydney Mardi Gras

At night, the meditative space of the ruined stage is transformed into a site for alternative drag performance, as Romeo is joined there by the Montague boys before the Capulet ball. Mercutio, an African American in a resplendent platinum wig, sequined bra, and miniskirt, is introduced to the audience in full drag, screeching onto the beach in his low-rider, producing purloined invitations from between his legs as he vamps on the stage to the lyrics "just another lost and lonely wife." Some reviewers objected to the drag sequence and its sequel at the ball, but it has a long history, for even before Shakespeare conceived Juliet, the Nurse, and Lady Capulet as drag roles for his transvestite theater, Romeo had appeared in the very earliest rescension of the story, Da Porto's in drag at the Capulet ball—"in habito di ninfa." What a nymph might wear might be little enough, less perhaps than Mercutio's short skirt in the Luhrmann film, but prose narrative can afford to be imprecise in a way that stage and film cannot. In the second edition, perhaps out of a modesty that would increase as the story made its way through more puritanical hands, from Belleforest and Boiastuau to Shakespeare's immediate sources in Painter and Brooke, the phrase is altered to "in habito di donna" (Da Porto, [1530]1831). Though Shakespeare did not know Da Porto, intermediate texts—Bandello, Boiastuau, Painter, Brooke—retain traces of Da Porto's design, emphasizing Romeo's beauty. Bellini's concert opera *I Capelleti e i Montecchi* is still performed with a female Romeo in man's dress. Shakespeare does not restore Romeo's feminine masquerade, but his version is sexually bold in other ways, offering perhaps the bawdiest language in Shakespeare, including the double-entendres often cut in the past in high school versions, the postcoital *aubade* and Mercutio's lewd wish that Romeo be a "pop'rin pear" and Juliet "an open etcetera" (or in some modern editions "open arse"). Luhrmann's Mercutio also draws on a more contemporary tradition, for Zeffirelli had opted in 1968 for what Renata Adler called a "softly homosexual" mood in the friendship between Romeo and Mercutio. Luhrmann of course knows the earlier film and alludes to it in a number of shots in which Romeo embraces and comforts the flaming, nearly hysterical Mercutio.

Drag is used here, coupled with fireworks and the psychedelic style that links both locales, to connect Mercutio's performance with that taking place at the Capulet mansion and to blur boundaries. Mercutio's entrance inserts countercultural "drag" style at the center of the ball, for he descends the grand staircase in his sequined costume, now enhanced by the addition of angel wings. The thin line between femininity as masquerade and as reality is underscored by the way in which this sequence exactly repeats Lady Capulet's earlier descent of the same staircase (to the andante movement of

Mozart's Symphony no. 25) in campy make-up, shower cap, and underwear, interrupting her own dressing up as Cleopatra to search for Juliet. The soundtrack commentary makes it plain that the visual echo was part of the design—in fact the boundary between male and female "drag" was considered so fragile that the designer, Catherine Martin, comments that the opening credits, in which each character is clearly identified in writing on screen, were added in part to identify Juliet's mother so she wouldn't be mistaken for a drag queen when she enters half dressed (Luhrmann 1996). While Olivier's triumphalist media allegory blends boy player and "real" actress at the end of Henry V, here femininity is doubly constructed, and drag with its own kind of "realness" takes precedence over its supposed original.

These sequences also link the film to recent Australian films such as *Priscilla, Queen of the Desert* (dir. Stephan Elliot, 1994). Like *Priscilla, Romeo and Juliet* makes numerous allusions (not always understood outside Australia) to the crucial role of the Sydney Gay and Lesbian Mardi Gras in Australia's cultural imaginary (Quinn 1994; Bziorak 1995; Jones 1997; Searle 1997; Perry 1998). The Mardi Gras, which began in 1972 as a gay-rights protest march at which many marchers were arrested, has become the largest outdoor festival in Australia, as well as the largest and most widely publicized gay and lesbian rally in the world. It is attended by more than 600,000 spectators and covered live on national television. The parade begins with an act of New Age refoundation, a display of fireworks, set off by scantily clad leather boys in harnesses, at the site of Arthur Phillips's settlement of Sydney in 1788 (Jones 1997).

Luhrmann's film and the culture/couture of the Sydney Mardi Gras are closely related in a number of ways. In the multimedia version of this chapter I presented evidence of several specific echoes of the 1995 parade in Luhrmann's 1996 film—including the performance of a marcher/performer who for years has appeared in a costume like that of the butterfly/angel-winged Mercutio in his grand entrance. Other elements, like the sacred heart imagery discussed earlier, also have analogues in the parade. In fact, the Mardi Gras is also a model for the film's repurposing of Catholic imagery. As in the film, the relationship between religious imagery as symptom of the meaningless proliferations of mass culture and religion as a locus of values that might—if repurposed or appropriated, "detourned"—constitute the basis for resistance to the regime of the spectacle, is a part of the parade. Floats feature "the Pope" as a spokesman for safe sex, handing out condoms from his mock Popemobile, and the Sisters of Perpetual Indulgence, an international collective that began in San Francisco, are marchers too—these are men, some mustached, habited as nuns and espousing a creed reminiscent of Rabelais's Abbey of Thélème, in the service of gay rights and support for AIDS research. But if some religious motifs are *détournés*, reversing their conventional meanings, the float devoted to the Blessed Mary McKillop, another perennial presence at the festival, creates its variation on mainstream significations in a different way, not through parody, burlesque or reversal, but simply by the inclusion of what might be a perfectly acceptable display such as might be seen in a Catholic street festival in many countries in the context of a gay event. The float consists of a performer dressed in a white dress with a large red pillow-like representation of the sacred heart sewn on the bosom. The Blessed Mother Mary McKillop, who worked for social justice and the education of the poor, died in 1909. She was a rebel within the hierarchy and was disciplined by the bishops, but eventually prevailed and founded her own order of the Sisters of Saint Joseph of the Sacred Heart. Her shrine has since become an international pilgrimage site (Hull 1995; Thorpe 1994). The appropriation of her image and that of the sacred heart in the parade is noteworthy for its respectful style, and in this context serves as a reminder that the devotion of the sacred heart itself began as a response to various strands of Protestant predestinarian theology. The meaning of the sacred heart, as used in the parade as in the multifarious images in the film and in the culture of Mexico where the film was shot and which the film tropes upon in multiple ways, all draw upon those aspects of the image that emphasize tolerance and universal charity. Central to the film's strategy is the idea that such an image participates in, but survives, its endless replication and its misuse as consumerist icon and firearms logo.

Read in this context, the Capulet ball as Luhrmann stages it can seem a momentary triumph of alternative cultures and styles; a benign form of the merger of illusion and reality, as if the Mardi Gras had moved permanently from the streets (or, in the film's terms, from the improvisational spaces at the margins of Verona) to the centers of wealth and power, gracing them with its liberationist energies. There are many indications, however, that the move from Sycamore Grove to the Capulet Mansion is a shift from creative exuberance to decadence: the hallucinogenic tab (marked with a heart) that Romeo consumes signals a queasy, seasick quality in the camerawork and especially in the vertiginous alternation of fast and slow motion and in and out of focus zooms. The Capulets' style of dress-up is eclectic, but Satanic (Tybalt), Ptolemaic (Lady Capulet), and decadent Imperial Roman (Capulet) costumes mark differences between Capulet drag and the Mardi Gras-influenced style of Mercutio. The psychedelic becomes threatening, as these snarling or confrontational figures loom suddenly in Romeo's field of vision, and lustful, as Capulet grabs repeatedly for the nearest scantily clad young woman or lifts up his garish toga to flash the camera.

Through a glass fishtank (but then face to face):
True Love and Optical Mediation

Like Mercutio, though in a very different way, Romeo brings with him to
the Capulet ball an alternative style and a mode of life that the film has established as closely associated with the "place of the stage" in Sycamore
Grove, with the ruined theater on the beach, and with the more easygoing
life of the city's past. And, as with Mercutio, Romeo's presence at the ball
(and his falling in love with Juliet there) raises the hope that the energies and
honesty of the youth cultures that subsist at the margins of Verona might
find a place closer to the center. The meeting of the lovers is set off from the
ball by a sequence that serves as a kind of ritual cleansing. Dizzy from the
effect of drugs and the vertiginous whirl of costumed figures, Romeo casts
his mask aside and soaks his head in a deep washstand to sober up just before he catches sight of her through the distorting and reflecting glass of a
tropical aquarium so large that it forms a kind of wall between them. They
move around it in a delicate dance, finding and losing eye contact before
coming face to face for a fleeting moment. We are encouraged to experience
this moment as "purer" in feeling than the ball, but it remains tinged by the
hyperreal. Intensely colored luminous ocean fish swim by, evoking the psychedelic imagery of the ball and the iconography of hallucinogenic vision.
The pair enjoy a moment of private contact here, but this is hardly an escape
to a "natural" or unmediated place of meeting. Their initial intimacy is made
possible, then enhanced, by the fact that it takes place as a shifting interplay
of mutual gaze, through glass, refracted by water, occluded by tropical fish—
their attempts to get a good look at one another are entrancing and at moments comically distorting. The spectral images we see in and through the
glass in this complex play of refraction and reflection allow us to see the relationship beginning while the couple themselves are still, as Prospero might
have put it, "surprised withal." Romeo sees Juliet through the glass (her refracted image is the object of his gaze). From another angle we see her image
through the glass and his image reflected on the surface of the glass. The two
images—one real, but seen through water, one a mirror image—form a couple in a way neither of them (each intent upon the other) can see.

The sequence is entrancing, but when Romeo takes Juliet's refracted
image for immediate presence, he bumps his nose on the glass, making the
same mistake, in a lighter key, as those literalist rubes of cinema legend who
mistook the maidens on the screen for living presences and tried to embrace
them. This optically mediated courtship dance is in some ways a visual
equivalent to the shared sonnet in the text, in the sense that even love at first
sight is made possible by a negotiation of formal boundaries, which the
lovers alternately transgress and respect. The glass, the water, the magic of

the couple that forms before us, like the constructive optical illusions in Lacanian illustrations of the workings of the gaze, all suggest the persistence, even the necessity of mediated communication even in this most intimate of the spaces the film has yet shown.

The first kiss takes place in the very temporary seclusion of an elevator between floors, and the balcony scene takes place in a swimming pool watched by a friendly security guard on an array of surveillance monitors. These scenes, too, develop the theme of the permeability of the Capulet space, its openness to the lovers' meetings and desires—and in this contrast sharply with Zeffirelli's more anxious construction of privacy and seclusion under surveillance. To this point, the film intimates a kind of coexistence of Debordian "spectacle" and alternative spaces, styles, and lifeways, as if the rhythms and the media of the past, the modes of romance, elegy, and meditation could blend and interpenetrate the world of the corporate and contemporary hyperreal; as if the ease with which the lovers find a place to meet and kiss augured a more permanent mode in which their love could continue.

Failures of Communication

The turn to tragedy, however, is marked by the failure of such mediations and accommodations. In the fight scene, the ruined theater, the locus of alternative and creative energy in the film, becomes a stage on which Mercutio delivers his last speech. In this sequence, the consequences of such a stage's inability to distinguish spectacle from reality become evident. The rear wall has been blown through as if by the large gun of a battleship, and if, in the early scenes this huge opening let in the light of dawn, here it frames an ominous confusion—both Capulets and Montagues watch Mercutio's death scene from the tattered seats on the audience side of the arch, which faces the city, while for his revelation to the screen audience of the extent of his wound he faces the beach side. His line "a plague on both your houses" is addressed to Capulets and Montagues, now seated as one house, but echoes more widely, perhaps implicating the cinematic audience as well. The sequence may be compared to the ways in which Olivier's *Henry V* makes transitions from stage to "real" space and from past to present— as if the voice of the great conqueror king, first heard in the film on the stage of the Globe, reaches out, through the medium of epic cinema, to later ages and to a whole nation. In *Romeo + Juliet* the bitterness of Mercutio's death speech is enhanced by its performance as an oration from a ruined stage, echoing in a void, the proscenium arch, itself framed by empty sky, sand, and ocean. What earlier seemed a creative elimination of barriers is now dangerous; there is no fourth wall, no "liminal" place to serve as sanctuary; the point is reinforced by shots of the stage from both sides as the storm (a serendipitously real, unplanned storm in Vera Cruz that occurred on the day of the shooting) darkens the sky.

Matching the failure of the "space" of alternative performance in Verona Beach, Romeo's exile (to the "Mantua Outback") is beyond the reach of urban communications media, but it is bleak and hopeless domain of seedy mobile homes in the desert, where even the express mail service (named "Post Haste Dispatch" in the film), cannot succeed in delivering the crucial message concerning Juliet's mock death. If community is defined by media coverage, as it is in the film, these are the media outlands or *eschatia,* not a refuge but a wasteland, a land of no return.

These sequences, in which alternative modes of communication such as improvised theater and slow "express" mail are seen to fail, and in which alternative spaces collapse into the center or are emptied of significance, prepare for and foreshadow *Romeo + Juliet's* powerful conclusion. In the final scenes, Romeo returns to "The Church of the Traffic Warden" at city center, and the most intimate medium of all—face to face speech at close range— trails off into inaudible whisper as the "society of the spectacle" triumphs and the pair of star-crossed lovers "take their life."

In the text, the death scene takes place in "Capels [sic] monument," an outdoor location outside Verona's center, perhaps in a churchyard. Romeo approaches it with "a mattock and a spade." Luhrmann shifts the location to the interior of a church at the center of town, a setting by now established as a part (perhaps the center and origin) of the culture of the spectacle. The interior of the Capulet chapel has been glimpsed as early as the credits, and then again, as a proleptic "flash forward" when Romeo senses "some consequence yet hanging in the stars" and we see him peering into a church interior we do not yet (quite) recognize as the space that will serve as Juliet's tomb. The chapel is the location in the film where the religious excess of the visual design reaches its point of greatest saturation, with thousands of votive candles of all sizes, and neon crosses by the dozens, Juliet laid upon a bier as upon an altar. Romeo, who has returned to Verona after hearing of Juliet's death, seeks refuge there from the glare and gunfire of police helicopters, but there is no sanctuary in the film; the lovers end their lives at the very center of the city, within the symbol of its fusion of religion, media and corporate power.

In what follows, Luhrmann alters the sequence of events in the text, having Juliet wake from her trance before Romeo dies so that the lovers are alive and conscious together briefly. But she is not conscious enough to restrain him from drinking the poison. Romeo, his hope extinguished, does not believe sufficiently in his senses (she is still warm, there is color in her face) to watch her long enough to see her move. He looks away (upward, reproaching God or the gods) makes a speech, and drinks. In Shakespeare, of course,

Romeo is dead when Juliet wakes from her trance, but in the context of the longer history of the story, from Da Porto in 1531 to recent stage productions of Shakespeare's play, the death scene has varied widely in the degree to which the lovers share a final scene. In Da Porto, Bandello, in Otway's *Caius Marius* of 1660, and in Garrick's adaptation the lovers converse, sometimes at length, before they die.

In a review of recent stage productions for *Shakespeare Survey*, Stanley Wells notes several in which Juliet shows signs of life before Romeo dies (Wells 1996; Holding 1992). Looked at in the context of the whole tradition, the Luhrmann version is notable for how early Juliet wakes and for its refusal of mutually shared last moments (there are pages of good-byes in Bandello). The pair are brought together, but not reunited; they are taken off screen on gurneys in separate body bags, but even before that the distance between Verona and Mantua has been, in a sense, internalized. In despair, Romeo cannot attend to Juliet enough to see her move and wake. There are wide-eyed close-ups of recognition in the sequence, referencing Zeffirelli's wonderful close-ups of Juliet's eyes—but here the recognition is ironic, registering consciousness of imminent death. Romeo is almost instantly paralyzed; he whispers "thus, with a kiss, I die" nearly inaudibly, but cannot manage a kiss or even a smile. The moment is visually poignant, but it also registers the lapse into silence of Shakespearean language in the film. Against the silence of the lovers, there is the grim contrast of the loud gunshot to the temple that ends Juliet's story.

As if to reinforce the bleakness of this close, there is almost immediate "coverage" of the events as we see news footage of the bodies loaded into separate ambulances just after the deaths, and the final sequences function as a conclusion not only to the tragedy but to the allegory of life under the regime of fetishized media spectacle which Luhrmann has constructed. In the final sequence, the setup of the Prologue is repeated in reverse, with the Epilogue spoken by the anchorwoman we saw in the beginning of the film, on the same television set, which slowly recedes and diminishes toward the back of the film image, and then disappears. There is something especially bleak about such an ending—Shakespeare's words fading a second time to silence as a television set shrinks to the vanishing point of the cinema screen. Here the historical sequence of media that includes Shakespeare's "original" play, its adaptation for the screen, its reduction to news story within that film—ends in oblivion, as if the world(s) we had glimpsed in and through the television screen vanish with it. This movement contrasts strongly with the triumphal *translatio mediorum*, the rehearsal of transition from "real" space to stage at the end of Olivier's *Henry V*, where Renaissance and modern media join, transitioning smoothly, "leaping o'er time and distance" just at the point at which Henry's double victory, success in battle and as wooer of Katherine, are sealed and celebrated. The Luhrmann ending joins media at their vanishing points, not in their plenitude and power, and in doing so echoes the final sequences of another recent Shakespeare media allegory, *Prospero's Books,* in which Prospero's acknowledgment of the loss of his magic powers is interpreted as a reduction of his image, seen now on a screen within a screen that then recedes into the darkness and vanishes (Donaldson 1997, 175; 1998).

The Double Ending:
From Citational Shakespeare to Techno-Baroque

In a sense the story of Romeo and Juliet has always had two endings, one tending to sentimental melodrama and the other toward the bleak acknowledgments of the tragic mode. David Garrick was said to have performed a "happy" ending in which the lovers survive, alternating this version on successive nights with Shakespeare's bleaker conclusion. Even in Shakespeare, where the lovers die in both the First Quarto and in the Second Quarto/Folio version, which is the basis of the modern edition, there are differences. In neither are the lovers conscious at the same moment, but Q1 suggest, far more strongly than Q2/F, that there will be a meeting after death. In the received text, Juliet's final lines are "Unhappy dagger/This is thy sheath; there rust and let me die," while the First Quarto suggests a reunion like that of Antony and Cleopatra: "this shall end my fear/ Rest in my bosom, thus I come to thee."

Luhrmann's version embodies the doubleness of the tradition. His media allegory concludes as a cruel triumph of the spectacle, with an astonishingly deliberate and poignant gunshot, all too familiar-looking footage of urban news coverage of the event, with the ubiquitous television screen having the last word. But within that framing, the death scene *also* honors the promptings of the text and the tradition toward a more redeeming and transcending conclusion, and I believe does so in a way that affects what the film has to say about the relation of contemporary media to the arts and media of the past.

First—the "Church of the Traffic Warden" is not only the most icon-saturated space in the film. It is also a space that we quickly come to see as a dignified, beautiful, ennobling setting for tragedy; perhaps, in the process, adjusting prejudices against visual excess the film itself has endorsed and deployed in its use of "Latin" religiosity as critique of commodified religion. At the beginning of the sequence, the saturation of the thousand and more candles, interspersed with large neon crosses threatens to overwhelm the human meaning of anything that might happen in it—there is no sanctuary, no space apart, no place not filled with the "brand names" of "Dark Ages." Yet as the sequence proceeds the harmony of this aesthetic may be distinguished from the jarring juxtapositions of mass-produced Christian images and breezy violence we have seen earlier, and this "techno-Baroque" interior joins with other elements in the staging and soundtrack to move, very firmly, toward the sacred and away from wit, satire, or critique. As Romeo first peers into the church, then enters it, walks down its aisle to the place of the altar where Juliet's body lies, we recognize this as the place where Romeo and Juliet were married; as shots proceed from wide shots to close-ups of Romeo, the myriad candles shift function, from markers of excess to resonance with his grief, and then, as we draw nearer still, to light sources, tender, appropriate, and, as life and death alternate as presences within the sequence, as images of a poignant transience.

If one image of the "end" of *William Shakespeare's Romeo + Juliet* is of body bags on gurneys moving into separate ambulances, another is the striking illusion that follows Juliet's death, created by filming the lovers with moving cameras hoisted on ropes and pulleys, in which Romeo and Juliet, embracing on the bier on which they die, seem to float above us in apotheosis, like the figures in a *trompe l'oeil* ceiling, while the *liebestod* from *Tristan and Isolde* plays on the soundtrack. This ending is closer to the hints of transcendental closure suggested by the First Quarto's "rest in my bosom / Thus I come to thee" and effects a final and powerful recuperation of the religious motifs in the film. Barbara Hodgdon (1999) has recently argued that the "double ending" mirrors both the realities of modern urban life that young people face as well as the continued vitality (and necessity) of romance traditions in contemporary youth culture.

In doing so, the sequence also continues and concludes the film's association of the alternative world the lovers hoped to create with the arts and media of the past. Traces and reminders of that world have been present in the film all along—in Mercutio's performances, in the dominating image of the ruined theater, and pervasively in the many ways in which the film's citations and surrogations make us aware that the film is not classical or authorized Shakespeare even as they reiterate and refresh the traditional construction of Shakespeare's *Romeo and Juliet* as a paradigm of romantic love. Now, in the final sequences shot in the cathedral, allusions to the past predominate, reaching beyond Shakespeare to include Medieval romance, Wagnerian opera, and Baroque illusionist painting, all invoked to reinforce the association of traditional art forms and legacy media with romantic love. Most important, such "citations" are no longer comic or ironic, but now blend seamlessly with the contemporary, slow-paced romantic style associated with the lovers and first seen in the film when Romeo is introduced writing Petrarchan poetry.

The convergence of Luhrmann's romantic style with an unironic use of Richard Wagner and Tiepolo may blunt the film's edge as media critique and call in question aspects of my argument, which has invited the reader to notice ways in which the film carries on radical traditions of ideological demystification, from Feuerbach and Marx through Guy Debord, punk, Gothic, and gay activist subcultures and styles. If Luhrmann's film is convergent with the aesthetic strategies and resignifications of the Syndney Gay and Lesbian Mardi Gras, it is also open to the valid criticism, urged even by the founders and original participants in the Mardi Gras, that the event has been co-opted, transformed by its success into a celebration of mainstream culture (Searle 1998; Jones 1997). But, understood differently, Luhrmann's double ending may deepen its value as critique. Following the rich ambivalences and oscillations of Shakespeare's ending, Luhrmann's *Romeo + Juliet* attempts to give its allegory of life in the age of media spectacle the stature of tragedy.

Works Cited

Anon. 1997. "Interview with Baz Luhrmann." *Mogul* [on-line magazine, http://mogulco.nz/stories/romeo/romeo/html], consulted May 26, 1997.

Baudrillard, Jean. [1981]1983. *Simulations.* Trans. by Paul Foss, Paul Patton, and Philip Beitchman. New York: Semiotext[e].

———. 1993. "Hyperreal America." Trans. by David Macey. *Economy and Society.* (May) 22(2):243–252.

Benjamin, Walter. [1936]1969. "The Work of Art in the Age of Mechanical Reproduction." In *Illuminations.* Ed. by Hanna Arendt. Trans. by Harry Zohn. New York: Schocken, 217–52.

Brook, Peter, Sir Peter Hall, Richard Loncraine, et al. 1998. "Shakespeare in the Cinema: A Film Directors' Symposium." *Cineaste.* 24 (1), 48–55.

Bziorak, Andy. 1995. *Priscilla and the Pink Dollar.* Australian Professional Marketing. February.

Crary, Jonathan. 1989. "Spectacle, Attention, Counter-Memory." *October.* 50, 97–107.

Da Porto, Luigi. [1530]1831. *Giuletta e Romeo [Istoria dei due nobilissimi amanti].* Pisa: Fratelli.

Debord, Guy. [1967]1994. *The Society of the Spectacle.* Trans. by Donald Nicholson-Smith. New York: Zone Books.

Debord, Guy and Asger Jorn. 1959. *Mémoires.* Paris, Internationnale situationniste.

Donaldson, Peter S. 1997. "Shakespeare in the Age of Post-Mechanical Reproduction: Sexual and Electronic Magic in *Prospero's Books.*" In *Shakespeare, the Movie: Popularizing the Plays on Film, T. V., and Video.* Ed. by Lynda Boose and Richard Burt. London, Routledge, 169–185.

———. 1998. "Digital Archives and Sibylline Sentences: *The Tempest* and the 'End of Books.'" *Postmodern Culture* 8.2 [on-line journal at http://muse.jhu.edu/journals/postmodern_culture/].

————. 1999. "'All which it inherit': Shakespeare, Globes, and Global Media." *Shakespeare Survey* 52: 183–200.

Hebdige, Dick 1979. *Subculture: The Meaning of Style*. London, Methuen.

Hodgdon, Barbara. 1999. "*Wiliam Shakespeare's Romeo + Juliet:* Everything's Nice in America?" *Shakespeare Survey* 52: 88–98.

Holding, Peter. 1992. *Romeo and Juliet: Text and Performance*. London: McMillan.

Hull, Geoffrey. 1995. *Building the Kingdom: Mary McKillop and Social Justice*. North Blackburn, Australia: Dove/Harper Collins.

Internationanal situationniste. 1963. *Internationale Situationniste* 8. Paris, Internationale situationniste.

Jones, Glynis, Judith O'Callaghan, and Robert Sweica. 1997. *Absolutely Mardi Gras: Costume and Design of the Sydney Gay & Lesbian Mardi Gras*. Haymarket, Australia: Powerhouse Publishing.

Marcus, Greil. 1989. *Lipstick Traces: A Secret History of the Twentieth Century.* Cambridge, MA: Harvard Univ. Press.

Modenessi, Alfredo Michel. 1998. "(Un)-Doing the Book 'by the book': Notes From the Receiving End of Baz Luhrmann's *William Shakespeare's Romeo + Juliet.*" *Poligrafía: Revista de Literatura Comparada* 2 (Mexico, D.F.), 191–227.

Mullancy, Steven. 1988. *The Place of the Stage: License, Play and Power in Renaissance England.* Chicago: Univ. of Chicago Press.

Murray, Timothy. 1997. *Drama Trauma: Specters of Race and Sexuality in Performance, Video and Art.* London: Routledge.

Perry, Nick. 1998. *Hyperreality and Global Culture.* London: Routledge.

Quinn, Karl. 1994. "Drag, Drags, and the Suburban Surreal." *Metro*. [Melbourne], Summer.

Sadler, Simon. 1998. *The Situationist City.* Cambridge, MA: MIT Press.

Searle, Samantha. 1997. "Queer-ing the Screen: Sexuality and Australian Film and Television. Australian Teachers of Media [ATOM], St. Kilda, Australia. Published as No. 5 of The Moving Image series.

Shakespeare, William. 1597. *Romeo and Juliet* [First Quarto]. London.

Shakespeare, William. 1599. *Romeo and Juliet* [Second Quarto]. London.

Shakespeare, William. 1623. *Comedies, Histories, Tragedies* [First Folio]. London: Jaggard.

Thorpe, Osmunde. 1994. *Mary McKillop*. 3d ed. North Sydney, Australia, Sisters of Saint Joseph of the Sacred Heart.

Wells, Stanley. 1996. "The Challenges of *Romeo and Juliet*." *Shakespeare Survey* 49: 1–14.

Worthen, W. B. 1998. "Drama, Performativity and Performance." *PMLA* 113: 1093–1108.

Films Cited

Almereyda, Michael, dir. 1999. *Hamlet.* Miramax. Sound, col. 113 mins.

Elliot. Stephan, dir. 1994. *The Adventures of Priscilla, Queen of the Desert.* United States/Australia. MGM. Sound, col., 104 mins.

Godard, Jean-Luc, dir. 1987. *King Lear.* USA. Cannon. Sound, col., 104 mins.

Greenaway, Peter, dir. 1994. *Prospero's Books.* Twentieth Century Fox. Netherlands/ France/Italy. Sound, col. 126 mins.

Loncraine, Richard, dir. 1996. *Richard III.* USA. MGM/UA. Sound, col. 104 mins.

Luhrmann, Baz, dir. 1996. *William Shakespeare's Romeo + Juliet.* Bazmark Productions. USA. Twentieth Century Fox. Sound, col., 120 mins. Video laserdisc.

Olivier, Laurence, dir. 1944. *Henry V.* U.K. Sound, col., 134 mins.

CHAPTER 3

"WE ARE THE MAKERS OF MANNERS"

The Branagh Phenomenon

MARK THORNTON BURNETT

This essay concerns itself with the development of Kenneth Branagh as a Shakespearean film director, producer, performer, and interpreter. It addresses all of Branagh's Shakespeare films to date, arguing that they can only be properly understood when discussed as a corpus and in relation to the cinematic work of his predecessors and contemporaries. Like Henry V, his alterego, Branagh is distinctive for having made (or created) the manners (or fashions) that have revitalized "Shakespeare" for a postmodern clientele. At the same time, however, Branagh has become the victim of these manners; although he has exorcized himself of the ghosts of previous luminaries of the establishment, he has now to compete with a host of related Shakespearean filmic interpretations, treatments that he himself has been instrumental in popularizing. In the same way that Frankenstein, another role reinvented by the *auteur,* is plagued by his creature, so has Branagh come to be haunted by his own screen progeny. As a result, Branagh's cinematic renditions of the Bard for the twentieth and twenty-first centuries reveal a movement from an entrenched, establishment-bound veneration for the dramatist to a much freer, more playful engagement with the "Schlockspearean." Through Branagh's career in miniature, then, we can glimpse the contours of a development that has marked Shakespearean studies in general, a critical position that begins with serious adaptation and ends with appropriation, kitsch, and even pastiche. More generally, the desire to bring Shakespeare to as broad a community as possible has involved Branagh in the production of "schlock" outside the strictly demarcated classical forum, the release of *Mary Shelley's "Frankenstein"* (1994), with its deployment of horror and slasher movie motifs, being but one example. Both the

Shakespearean and the Schlockspearean interpenetrate in Branagh's cinematic conceptions in ways that simultaneously undergird the reputation of England's most famous dramatist and dismantle it for mass consumption.

In *Henry V* (1989), his first major Shakespearean filmic outing, Branagh attempts to break free of the shackles imposed upon him by an earlier theatrical and cinematic tradition. Obviously, Laurence Olivier's *Henry V* (1944) was a seminal production with which to wrestle, and the film's influence can be detected in Branagh's frequently self-conscious references: in both versions, for example, the St. Crispin's Day speech is delivered from a cart, and hails of arrows descend on the French forces from the English archers. But Branagh equally endeavors to make his *Henry V* accessible to a modern audience, drawing upon the slow motion effects and tragic camaraderie characteristic of more recent Vietnam films, such as *Platoon* (dir. Oliver Stone, 1986), *Full Metal Jacket* (dir. Stanley Kubrick, 1987), and *Born on the Fourth of July* (dir. 1989) (Fitter 1996, 270; Guntner 1998, 58). The result, as contemporary tabloid reviews were quick to point out, was a seemingly anti-war film, a brutal, mud-soaked, and unflinching evocation of the horrors of the martial encounter. In pursuit of this perspective, newspapers noticed, Branagh was keen to include the speech before Harfleur and the execution of Bardolph, elements that the more heroically and nationally minded Olivier had chosen to excise.

From its earliest moments, Branagh's *Henry V* communicates a powerful sense of pervading gloom, a stony-faced attitude to the imminent conflict. Henry's entrance is made with a dark theatrical flourish, as the young king processes, Darth Vadar-like, into his court. An edgy undertone is elaborated in the ensuing discussion, with worried glances, gurgling cellos, and stealthy camera work all contributing to a conspiratorial air. As the film progresses, a restructured sequence of events offers an even more starkly dispassionate commentary on the war effort. For instance, having been introduced to the ailing and older world of the tavern, the audience is assaulted by the chorus's invitation to follow "These culled and choice-drawn cavaliers to France" (3, Chorus, 24): the juxtaposition points to the worrying gap between an idealization of war and its material underside. Similarly, the scene between Katherine and Alice, enlivened by its reliance upon silks, sunshine, and fluttering doves, is interrupted by the passing through the corridor of a grim-visaged royal party: as the princess (Emma Thompson) exchanges looks with her father (Paul Scofield), an impression of French fragility before the approaching martial machine of Henry is underscored.

But Branagh mainly communicates his theme, I would suggest, not through tonal engineering or scenic juggling but via a personalizing of the film's players. Inevitably, the central roles are granted cinematic prominence, yet Branagh also manages to endow even relatively minor performers with importance. Flashbacks initially announce this concern with the personal, as the announcement of the death of Falstaff is intercut with convivial snippets from *Henry IV, Part Two:* the implied visual similarity between Falstaff (Robbie Coltrane) and Exeter (Brian Blessed) moreover implies that the new monarch may still be in need of paternal protection. A comparable instance of the strategy occurs when Henry, after Harfleur has capitulated, collapses with relief into Exeter's arms: Branagh here personalizes his part in the suggestion that the threat to sack the town was merely a performance. A more self-assertive Henry emerges, however, during the execution of Bardolph. Although the tear on Henry's face and the flashback in which he indulges point to the personal struggle behind the execution order, the inclusion of his punitive speech at 3.6.104–10 illuminates a rejection of princely attachments and an embracing of the sovereign's authority.

Arguably it is with the film's combat scenes that the personal dimension comes to the fore. Time after time the camera's eye focuses on personalities whose actions reflect back upon Henry's soldierly efforts. Lack of textual support notwithstanding, Branagh elects to give Gower (Daniel Webb) a momentary prominence as captain of the king's archers. Both Henry and Fluellen (Ian Holm) embrace in a scene reminiscent of the "buddy movie," while on the battlefield itself the Constable (Richard Easton) is glimpsed dying in the arms of his compatriots. Forces antithetical to Henry are thus neatly banished, as is succinctly demonstrated in the stabbing of Nym (Geoffrey Hutchings), another nicely judged nontextual detail. What Branagh takes over here is a *mise-en-scène* more akin to Kubrick than Olivier. For in repeatedly concentrating on a host of impassioned faces—those of, for instance, Bedford (James Larkin), Gloucester (Simon Shepherd), and York (James Simmons)—Branagh adapts one of Kubrick's strategies for "personalizing" the legitimacy of the rebellion of Spartacus in the 1960 film of the same name. A greater emotional identification with Spartacus (Kirk Douglas) is encouraged when he tours the huddled masses who make up his army. Nowhere is Branagh's adoption of the method better exemplified, perhaps, than in his understanding of Burgundy's reflection upon the desperate state of the French nation (5.2.23–67). As Harold Innocent intones the words, a retrospective camera splices in images of many of the film's leading participants: the effect is, once again, to lend familiarity to otherwise anonymous representatives of the English imperative, to begin the celebration of Henry's achievement through a visual roll call of his supporters.

The issue, of course, is how far this mode of filmmaking manages to break with convention to deliver a radically new articulation. One might also ask if an interrogative realization of war is sustained into the film's final stages. For many critics, answers to such questions could be framed only in the negative. Upon the release of *Henry V,* one section of the academic profession was quick to label Branagh an unashamed Thatcherite, a venerating reader of the Bard who courted Prince Charles and deployed seasoned figures from the Royal Shakespeare Company to authenticate his entry into a sacrosanct arena. The film, according to Curtis Breight, glorifies a "divinely endorsed bloodletting" (Breight 1991, 107); defers, states Graham Holderness, to "monarchical power," reinventing patriotism through the "individualism of the new entrepreneur" (Holderness 1991, 84, 87); and "studiously," argues Donald K. Hedrick, "maintains . . . a conservative rather than a critical ambivalence" (Hedrick 1997, 49). To be sure, such assessments of Branagh are useful. Viewed from a later vantage point, the film might best be understood both as a felicitous remaking and reinterpretation that glosses over some of the play's more unpalatable ingredients. Narrative rejiggings and cameo-like biographical interventions make for a fast-paced, animated, and abundantly provocative cinematic statement. At the same time, the personalizing procedure can assume a sentimental cast and paradoxically a flattening of distinction: national accents are invariably Anglicized in the interests of easy identification, a move that plays down the social and political altercations highlighted in Shakespeare's play. Arguably, too, a perspective that reduces difference extends to the film's sexual politics. Although intriguing moments of homoeroticism pepper the scene involving the conspirators (Branagh, picking up on the reference to the King's "bedfellow" [2.2.8], introduces embraces and physical contact), no further elaboration of the hint is offered. And, finally, the film's music has a tendency to obscure the textual fabric. When Henry is bargaining with God to support his cause (4.1.282–98), for instance, a romantic refrain swells to drown out the unappealing fact of a monarch attempting to manipulate a deity. *Henry V* is an innovative reformulation of a national epic for postwar spectators. It is at the same moment an ideologically cautious telling of Shakespeare's history, a ultimately safe production that reflects flatteringly on protagonist and filmmaker alike.

Making manners in *Henry V,* then, Branagh steers an even course between a number of opposed positions. By contrast, Branagh's next Shakespearean film, *Much Ado About Nothing* (1993), a response to the Shakespearean filmic procedures popularized by Franco Zeffirelli (Jackson 1997, 118), might appear at first sight to come down only on the side of sexual conservatism. The stubborn recalcitrance of Claudio is eliminated (Moses 1996, 38); homoerotic implication is undercut by credits, music, and clothes (Deleyto 1997, 98); and the whole represents, in H. R. Coursen's words, no "subversive challenge to manifest content" (Coursen 1996, 115). But *Much Ado About Nothing,* I would suggest, is no tipsy Tuscan *Pietro's Friends,* a bourgeois *al fresco* frolic set in unthreatening Chiantishire. Rather, the film represents a more ambitious engagement with the Shakespearean, a ruthlessly selective reading that consistently privileges a particular interpretative paradigm and does not shirk from the play's notoriously problematic status. In this sense, *Much Ado About Nothing* makes manners with a greater economy and audacity than *Henry V,* its cinematic forerunner.

Much Ado About Nothing is primarily an intertextual undertaking. The opening alerts an audience to the play's "Sigh no more" refrain by bringing the words up on screen to the voice-over of Emma Thompson (who plays Beatrice). The initial effect is to blur the lines of demarcation between a song and a spoken delivery, a film and a drama, and a character and an actress. But the scene then shifts to a painting of a rural Italian landscape, which, in turn, is superseded by a shot of the "real thing" and a pan to Beatrice, sitting in a tree and reciting the same song to the amusement of her onlookers. Once again, the film's consumer is inaugurated into its particular frame of reference through multivalent levels, stages of intertextuality that purposefully confuse the representation and its material equivalent, the static text and its active enactment, and the camera's view and the specular experience of the filmic participants. As Douglas Lanier pithily puts it, Branagh here confronts "the perennial struggle of Shakespearean cinema to free itself from the constraints of bookishness" (Lanier 1996, 191).

As part of that urge to redress the "burden of the book" (Lanier 1996, 191), Branagh brings to his *Much Ado About Nothing* a peculiarly inventive understanding of both individual lines and eye-assaulting details. The film's language continually impresses with the freshness and insight of its delivery. In one of her early verbal tussles with Benedick, Beatrice is left to muse alone with the barbed reflection, "You always end with a jade's trick; I know you of old" (1.1.136–7). The statement is converted in Branagh's cinematography from a public declaration to a private rumination, thereby intimating an edge of vulnerability to Beatrice's typically grand-scale announcements. No less suggestive is Branagh's rendition of Benedick's characterization of Claudio as "Monsieur Love" (2.3.34). In Branagh's reading, "Love" becomes "Lurve": the stress upon an American-style pronunciation both enhances the gauche characterization of Claudio and allows Shakespeare briefly to make contact with Motown. If the film delights in pushing the text on the page into unexpected areas, it simultaneously invests in a gallery of imaginative visual accoutrements. Disguise is used with a thematically specific pertinence, a grinning mask emphasizing Benedick's mockery and a cherubic one highlighting Claudio's innocence. At a deeper level, props are enlisted as charged accompaniments to the film's visual business, whether they take the form of Benedick's collapsing deckchair, a *Leit-Motif* for his ineptitude, or Beatrice's knife, the concealment of which signals the onset of her romantic attachment. Such a richly communicative application of filmic machinery goes hand-in-hand with a comparably expressive deployment of location. The connotations of the chapel are put to fine use, for instance, in Beatrice's request that Benedick "Kill Claudio" (4.1.285). Because the demand unfolds in a sacred site, a glaringly sacrilegious note is struck. Beatrice's pleading further reinforces the tonal incongruity, since her appeal positions her as a supplicant and Benedick as a type of deity. Culminatively, remakings such as these have singularly successful outcomes, prompting an audience simultaneously to acknowledge Shakespearean textuality and the potential of the screen to transform the play into a more interpretively capacious utterance.

By lacing *Much Ado About Nothing* with such textual intricacies and scenic messages, Branagh is able to maintain his audience in a critically active state. Quickly indoctrinated into the film's cinematic mode, and used to similar experiences in the multiplexes, spectators become sensitized to shifts in tone, changes in perspective, narrative twists and turns, and the recurrence of similar scenarios. This is particularly apparent in the ways in which the film encourages the audience to spot the connections linking its various episodes. Much has been made of the opening of *Much Ado About Nothing,* with its cavalcade of galloping horsemen cribbed from John Sturges's *The Magnificent Seven* (1960). But it is also important to note the film's built-in parody of its own inauguration: the fictional horses ridden by Dogberry (Michael Keaton) and Verges (Ben Elton). Through such parallels, Branagh not only presents for amusement the class aspirations of a bumbling constabulary; he also critiques his own sources and borrowings. The film's capacity to comment upon and make connections with itself can be traced, I suggest, to the scenic condensations and realignments engineered by Branagh himself. Examined at leisure, the film reveals numerous structural splittings, indexes of the director's ability to create a more restless narrative than the play alone provides. For instance, 3.3, the scene introducing us to the watch, is cut across by 2.2, the hatching of the conspiracy between Don John and Borachio, which then, in turn, is shaped to flow into 3.2, the exchange between Claudio, Don Pedro and his brother. Immediately afterwards, viewers are wrenched back to the watchmen in 3.3 and taken forwards to Dogberry's muddling misapprehensions in 3.5. In these ways, the film plays fast and loose with the drama's traditional arrangements, insisting upon a breakneck pace, a relentless plot movement and a design that flashes back and forth between central players and dominant Shakespearean preoccupations. Remaking the play to suit the demands of the quick-thinking postmodern spectator, Branagh also manages to place a greater weight on the Don John subplot. Indeed, the film returns obsessively to the threat of Don John, habitually adding in images of Keanu Reeves tearing off his mask, striding through dank cellars and laughing with his henchmen. The effect is, once again, to unmoor the securities of the narrative, to make of the film a more nervous experience and constantly to show up the instabilities of romantic fantasy.

As a by-product of the concentration on the subplot, *Much Ado About Nothing* brings sexuality into prominence. The violence indulged in by Claudio (Robert Sean Leonard) at the aborted wedding ceremony finds its equivalent in the punishments meted out by the watch to the manacled Conrade (Richard Clifford) and Borachio (Gerard Horan), suggesting that sexual outrage is only one step away from physical abuse. Because of Branagh's pruning, moreover, Claudio can appear, at the close, to be an unconvincing convert. Upon learning of his mistake, Claudio suddenly begins to harp on "Sweet Hero" (5.1.238), the rapidity with which he abandons his earlier misogyny only half persuading an audience that he is transformed for the better. Given these difficulties, the final spectacle of the entire cast dancing about the Villa Vignamaggio to the fall of confetti arguably strikes a discordant note. Because of the manner in which the film concludes, however, residual discrepancies are seamlessly incorporated. The crane-shot rising above the trees to display, once again, the Tuscan panorama alerts an audience to the presence of the director stamping the play with his individual mark, while the return of the "Sigh no more" refrain, here sung as a choral symphony, reminds us of the intertextual suggestions with which the film began, of the fact that the Shakespearean script is endlessly open to manipulation and reformulation. In *Much Ado About Nothing*, Branagh wonderfully animates his core material even as he also comments upon his status as a Shakespearean practitioner and the processes of his own art.

As Branagh's Shakespeare films have progressed, they have developed in scope and crept steadily into the present. That is, they have taken on board increasingly imaginative conceptual templates in the same moment as they have embraced more contemporaneous time frames. With *Henry V,* the period evoked was roughly proximate to an Elizabethan juncture. But *Much Ado About Nothing*, as Branagh himself pointed out, unfolds in an "imaginary world" dating from "1700" onwards (Branagh 1993, xiv): the play is pushed closer to modernity. And, in his film version of *Hamlet* (1997), Branagh situates the play at the end of the nineteenth century, an indication of his predilection for exploiting images familiar to newer audiences and his willingness to locate Shakespeare in our own times. In *Hamlet,* indeed, it might be suggested that Branagh finally becomes an *auteur* in his own right: no longer tied solely to British funding agencies or stables of performers, and safely installed in corporate machinery, Branagh is able to advertise the film as "Kenneth Branagh's *Hamlet.* "

In other ways, too, *Hamlet* announced a coming of age for Branagh, particularly in terms of its aims, ambitions, and scope. Olivier is finally banished, surviving only in the bleached top-crop of Branagh as Hamlet and in the warning note sounded by the commemorative program: "If you think Hamlet by necessity means gloomy castles, dour costumes and pudding-bowl hairstyles, think again" (*Commemorative Programme* 4). While Olivier's somber, black-and-white filmic *Hamlet* (1948) is put firmly in its place by Branagh's color-saturated, spectacular take on the tragedy, so, too, is the notion that Shakespeare partakes only of a fusty theatrical tradition and *ennui*. To cite Branagh on the film, "We want this Hamlet to be a big, big treat. . . . The Ghost is going to be a lot scarier than some faintly benign old sort walking on stage in a white shirt. It ain't gonna be three-and-a-half hours of talking heads" (Arnold 1996, 36–7). As Branagh's language suggests, *Hamlet* is conceived of as a vehicle for mass entertainment, a production that, despite its Shakespearean origins, answers to the numerous generic requirements expected of the cinema-going public. Such is Branagh's confidence in the popular virtues of *Hamlet,* moreover, that he is even able to use the film to pose a challenge to another filmmaker, namely, David Lean. His *Doctor Zhivago* (1965), with its sumptuous appearance and sprawling snows, is frequently invoked and overtaken in the winter-clad landscape of Branagh's Elsinore. From a number of points of view, therefore, *Hamlet* represents an unprecedented undertaking, an approach to Shakespeare made possible by the cinematic reputation Branagh had accumulated. With his third Shakespearean film, a head-on confrontation with one of the most canonical texts of the western literary tradition, Branagh could lay claim to being his century's foremost Bardic interpreter.

Perhaps the most arresting element of the film is Branagh's performance as Hamlet, played in such a way as to bring out the multiple dimensions of a tortured psyche. Thus, from a grieving son lurking in the shadows at the start, Branagh moves to an explosive "man of action" in the later scenes, a knowing impersonator of madness and a theatrically dynamic presence. While Branagh clearly points up a personality-based and romantic reading of Shakespeare's play, the film is arguably more dominated by its political resonances. For this *Hamlet* constructs Denmark as a militaristic state. Already in the opening scenes there are glimpses of preparations for war; Hamlet marches past an arsenal on his way to encounter the ghost; and displays of fencing practice punctuate the narrative, foreshadowing the catastrophic conclusion. It is to Branagh's credit that he has restored to *Hamlet* its military subtexts, and the film does not hesitate to demonstrate the extent to which Denmark's power is dependent on the cooperation of a gallery of soldierly underlings—Rosencrantz (Timothy Spall) and Guildenstern (Reece Dinsdale) wear regimental sashes; guards invade Ophelia's chamber; and the gravedigger (Billy Crystal) arranges skulls side-by-side with all the precision of a campaigning general. Nor is this merely an extraneous interpretation. The play abounds in martial rhetoric, as when Claudius enjoins the "kettle to the trumpet speak, / The trumpet to the cannoneer without, / The cannons to the heavens" (5.2.272–74). Branagh takes his cue from the specific orientation of Shakespeare's text in a persuasive reconsideration of the material bases on which Elsinore's preeminence is founded.

It is part of the flexibility of the film's representational scheme that Branagh also develops the Fortinbras subplot, which is so often omitted from modern productions. Frequent use is made of parallel montage whereby the scene cuts between unfolding wrangles at Elsinore and the relentless advance of Fortinbras's army. At one point, newspaper headlines are deployed to highlight the threat of the Norwegian commander, played with an icy implacability by Rufus Sewell. As the film progresses, it would seem as if there is every justification for the nervousness of the sentry who patrols the castle's gates.

The innovativeness of such representational devices can be apprehended no less forcibly in set design and staging procedures. Joel Fineman's work on fratricide and cuckoldry has established the importance of *Hamlet's* "doubling" structures and mirrored arrangements (Fineman 180, 70–109). Branagh's *Hamlet* fits well with this assessment, since its interior scenes take place in a hall lined with windows and mirrored doors. In such a setting, Hamlet is forced to confront reflections of himself, such as Claudius (Derek Jacobi), who, with his blonde hair and clipped beard bears an uncanny resemblance to Branagh's Dane. The points of contact between the characters are also incestuously underlined when Hamlet pushes Ophelia (Kate Winslet) against one of the hall's mirrors, not realizing that Claudius and Polonius are hidden behind it. Branagh himself has observed that the set was intended to suggest "a vain world . . . looking in on itself . . . that seems confident and open but conceals corruption" (LoMonico 1996, 6). It is a bold and critically current view, and one for which there is considerable textual support. Once again, Branagh is keen to place a visual slant upon the concerns of the text, and this imperative is ably demonstrated in the presentation of court, which, as it contemplates its own self-image, faces only an inevitable decline.

To the broad brush stokes of the design can be added the nuanced local effects with which the film abounds. As the versatility of the film is exhibited in its overall montage, so is it discovered in a spectrum of more specialized scenic details and correspondences. First, several fresh areas of meaning come into play in images of domestic intimacy. After an assignation with a prostitute, Polonius (Richard Briers) dresses himself to tutor Reynaldo (Gerard Depardieu) in the arts of surveillance, which makes an intriguing link with the following scene where Ophelia describes Hamlet's appearance before her "with his doublet all unbrac'd" (2.1.78). As she recovers upon her father's bed, it is implied that Ophelia has been abused by Hamlet and will be prostituted by her brothel-frequenting father. Second, the density of scenic business reinforces the narrative continuum and creates surprising poetic points of contact. Claudius and Laertes (Michael Maloney) quaff brandy together as they plot Hamlet's downfall. Their conspiratorial drinking is immediately enhanced by the description of Ophelia's drowning and, subsequently, by the gravedigger's observation that a tanner's hide "is so tanned with his trade that a will keep out water a great while, and your water is a sore decayer of your whoreson dead body" (5.1.164–66). Through such networks of "liquid" allusion, visual stimuli in the film enrich the play's textual constitution, exposing reductive, consuming systems in which a woman's innocence is at the mercy of paternalistic hypocrisy.

By concentrating key scenes of the play in particular spaces, the film pushes to their furthest extent the areas of overlap between visual messages and verbal utterances. Notably the chapel, a dimly lit but ornate interior serves as a suggestive forum for the prompting of confessional revelations. Toward the beginning of the film, Polonius thrusts Ophelia into a confession box to quiz her about the "very ecstasy" of Hamlet's "love" (2.1.102). A more unsettling use of the box occurs when Claudius creeps into it to lament his "rank" (3.3.36) offence. Lighting upon Claudius, Hamlet forces his knife through the grill, becoming an unpunctual but unconsoling father confessor. As well as bolstering the impression of a world suffering from the effects of withholding secrets, these situational moments complicate the implications of the play's rhetoric. When Hamlet urges Gertrude (Julie Christie) to "confess [herself] to heaven" and "Repent what's past" (3.4.151–2), for instance, one is reminded of a developing intrigue that finds its expression in parodic gestures toward absolution. As confessional textual details are taken up in the film's confessional sequences, a lively sense of escalating frustrations is elaborated.

The partnership shared between the visual and the verbal is demonstrated most eloquently in the scenes involving the ghost. Played by Brian Blessed and shot from a high-angle perspective, the ghost is realized as a militant specter of colossal proportions. As the ghost confesses its secrets, bursts of flame break through the forest floor and smoke billows about the trees, apt metaphors for the opening of the sepulchre's "ponderous and marble jaws" (1.4.50) and for the "blasts from hell" (1.4.41) with which the supernatural visitation is associated. Similarly, when the ghost appears in Gertrude's chamber, an eerie music sounds, reintroducing the possibility that the apparition may be of infernal origin. True to the demonic implications of Shakespeare's text, the film images the ghost as a force of doubtful moral authenticity.

Characteristic of both the general representational strategies and the local coloring is the productively roving camera work. Often, repeated camera movements illuminate psychological connections. In the opening scene, the camera zooms outward to show the disappearing ghost, a trajectory followed again for Hamlet's "How all occasions do inform against me" (4.4.32) speech: the comparable tracking shot hints at a revitalized paternal and filial alliance. More striking, it might be suggested, are the ways in which the camera prowls around groups of characters, often exploiting 360-degree pans. When Claudius and Polonius agree to spy on the prince, they are circled by the camera, as is Hamlet on confronting his mother in her closet. In this scene, in fact, the voyeuristic impression created is reinforced by the chamber's Tiepolo-like wall paintings of eavesdroppers leaning over balustrades to watch an event of clearly spellbinding significance. This resonant deployment of the camera has several implications. At once, it adds to the sense of a court dominated by tawdry secrets and political espionage. In the same moment, it sharpens an awareness of the ever increasing danger of Fortinbras's army, a force that will eventually encircle the castle itself. The closer Fortinbras draws, the more exactly does he seem to represent the eye that subjects all of Elsinore to an uncompromising, comprehensive scrutiny.

It is perhaps after the intermission, when the break-up of Elsinore is an urgent prospect, that the film displays to their best advantage its innumerable merits. Clearly apparent in *Hamlet*'s latter stages is the shrunken character of the court: only a handful of attendants are present at Ophelia's funeral, a stark contrast with the swelling numbers flocking to enjoy the play-within-the-play and a register of Claudius's waning control. Even before Fortinbras makes his spectacular final appearance, monarchical authority is wavering, as Gertrude's increasingly sour expressions indicate. When the climax arrives, Fortinbras's troops crash through the state hall's windows and mirrored doors, a timely lesson for a court that has been incapable of recognizing its own fragile illusions. Hamlet is given a soldier's funeral, a move that identifies him with Fortinbras, the commander whose superior military prowess allows him to declare himself the state's inheritor.

But Branagh's *Hamlet* goes beyond a simple dichotomy between military technology and political supremacy. In many respects, it probes levels of meaning that lie beyond the merely filmic and textual relationship. Above all, this *Hamlet* builds upon the precedent of *Much Ado About Nothing* intertextually to contemplate its connections to a host of other texts and histories. Faithful to the 1623 First Folio version of the play, the film is suitably bookish, and a favorite retreat for Hamlet is his book-lined study: it is here, not accidentally, that he consults a treatise on demonology before setting out to confront the ghost. Branagh, it seems, is concerned to authenticate himself as a leading Shakespearean by stressing the decision to realize the entire play, an endeavor unparalleled in the theatrical record. To this end, he is aided by many of the seasoned veterans of the Shakespearean scene. There is more than a passing intertextuality involved in casting Derek Jacobi as

Claudius, for the actor played Hamlet in 1979 at the Old Vic, took the part in a BBC version of the play in 1980, and directed Branagh in the title role for the 1988 Renaissance Theatre Company production (Branagh 1996, vi-vii; 175). If Jacobi is Branagh's filmic father, then Branagh is Jacobi's theatrical son, the descendant of a metaphorical parent who both throws into relief and justifies the younger actor's colonization of hallowed terrain. A legitimating imperative would also appear to lie behind the casting of John Gielgud (Priam) and Judi Dench (Hecuba) in nonspeaking appearances, and an intertextual dimension is certainly detectable in Charlton Heston's cameo role as the Player King. By drawing upon the pooled resources of Stratford-upon-Avon dignitaries, and of Hollywood "epic" legends, Branagh, with typical audacity, sets himself up as another epic filmmaker, as a bardic interpreter with impeccable credentials and as a performer who, in the words of Courtney Lehmann and Lisa S. Starks, "plays out an Oedipal rivalry" to execute a "fantasy of theatrical succession" (Lehmann and Starks 2000, 6; 9). What is additionally distinctive about *Hamlet* is the fact that this process is thematized on the surface of its narrative. Just before the play-within-the-play, Hamlet, in a moment stylishly snitched from Adrian Noble's 1996 film version of *A Midsummer Night's Dream*, peers inside a toy theater in which there stands a cardboard model of a king. The cutout is then flicked over by Hamlet, a move that both summarizes and breaks the personal and professional filaments binding the actor and the director, the director and the playwright, the *auteur* and the cast, and Branagh and his past.

Nor does the film's intertextuality end with casting implications. Part of the grandeur of the film depends upon the numerous exterior views of Blenheim Palace (masquerading as Elsinore), which is shot in a wide-screen 70mm format. From this landscape of epic architectural magnificence a number of intertextual resonances can be inferred. Following the defeat of the French at the battle of Blenheim, Germany in 1704, the palace was constructed for the Duke of Marlborough as thanks for a landmark victory. Sir Winston Churchill was born at Blenheim Palace in 1874, and members of the family still live at the palace. With these contexts in mind, it might be argued that Branagh's *Hamlet* finally operates as synecdoche for historical conflicts between England and France, between England and Germany, and even between the English royal family and a more powerful political entity. The film is too multivalent to be straitjacketed within a simple allegory, however, and is equally interested in provoking contrary readings that go against its more obvious contextual correspondences. At the close, the imposing statue of Hamlet Senior is toppled to the ground, and any spectator attuned to the collapse of the communist countries in the 1990s will not miss the parallel. Branagh's *Hamlet* is an eloquent disquisition on the perils of theatrical, aristocratic, and royal authority; it is also a covert celebration of the plebeian forces that contest the ownership of power and privilege.

Using his film to entertain such considerations did not come to Branagh without a struggle. For in the activities surrounding the film's production is inscribed a nervousness about the play's status as an enshrined monument of English-speaking culture. Just before *Hamlet*, Branagh had written, produced, and directed *In the Bleak Midwinter* (1995), a black-and-white comedy about a group of actors rehearsing and finally performing *Hamlet* in the abandoned church of an English country town. Via its fantasy scenario (the production is a spectacular success and heals the emotional rifts dividing the cast), Branagh addresses anxieties about the relevance and availability of *Hamlet* in the postmodern era. No less importantly, *In the Bleak Midwinter* offered Branagh an opportunity autobiographically to negotiate, at his own expense, the implications of his grand plan to stage *Hamlet* as a big-budget cinematic extravaganza. Certainly, in related projects prior to *Hamlet*, the vexed position of the drama as a millennium masterwork seems to have been an issue. Even before it was released, Branagh published an annotated screenplay and diary of the film's making. What is striking about the accompanying notes is the alternating between a number of seemingly incompatible positions. References to Goethe (Branagh 1996, viii) sit happily alongside a commentary that, in its demotic discontinuity, suggests a desire to schlock: Claudius is described as being in "Norman Schwarzkopf mode" (Branagh 1996, 12), the players put on a "good gig" (Branagh 1996, 67), the gravedigger is likened to both "Judge [Lance] Ito" (Branagh 1996, 142) and "Einstein" (Branagh 1996, 143), and Hamlet and Laertes are resemble "two graduates of the Robocop academy" (Branagh 1996, 163). On the screenplay's release, a number of reviewers took exception to this populist perspective. A *Times Literary Supplement* notice objected to Branagh's "low interjections," the "boorish" participation, it stated, of "a rather louche character, someone from *Eastenders*" (S. D. 1996, 16). But such criticism ignores, I think, the necessarily shifting markers that both cut across and characterize Branagh as a Shakespearean interpreter. As an end-of-the-century artist, Branagh is constituted by straddling "high art" and "popular culture" at one and the same time, precisely because, as the thrust of this volume demonstrates, these distinctions no longer hold as indicators of traditional social arrangements. Partly thanks to Branagh, Shakespeare has been reclaimed as a figure whose work reaches beyond a narrowly selective constituency, and film is an essential element in that process. The more recent Bard is an amalgam of a host of interpenetrating cinematic, televisual, and musical vernacular influences, and out of that melting pot is born Branagh's multivoiced mind-set. As Branagh has made Shakespeare in the image of his own manners, so has Branagh been fashioned by the emergence of Shakespeare as a mass media icon.

By the same token, and accompanying the changing "Shakespeares" that animate the postmodern moment, Branagh has developed (or has had developed for him) a distinctive sense of himself as a media personality. In the earlier part of his career, encapsulated most forcefully in his autobiography, *Beginning* (1989), Branagh appeared as a fresh-faced "Belfast boy," distinguished by a combination of youth, self-deprecation, and chirpiness. More recently, however, largely through press constructions, Branagh has come to be associated with a blokish image. Clearly, this new guise shows once again the coming to maturity of the *auteur:* no longer does Branagh fit the part of Olivier's inheritor. But Branagh as bloke is also Branagh as celebrity, as testified to by the current vogue for using blokishness as part of a celebrity appeal. Blokishness, then, marks the new breed of public performer. It enables Branagh to play the part of a soccer *aficionado* who quotes Bill Shankly, the football manager (Branagh 1996, viii), to wear "jackets and trousers that look slept in" (Morgan 1999, 7) and to present himself as, in the words of one journalist, a "chain-smoking, foul-mouthed bag of nerves" (Smith 2000, 34). At the same time, blokishness functions as a sign of Branagh's ability to continue to mediate Shakespeare, enduring symbol of high cultural capital, for the cinema-frequenting punters of the twenty-first century. Simultaneously the subject of a major retrospective at the National Film Theatre in 1999, the recipient of the Gielgud Award in 2000 and the self-elected communicator of Shakespeare to the populace via the big screen, Branagh remains a figure of multiple and sometimes contrary identifications.

Branagh is able continually to revise Shakespeare to match the demands of modern taste because of his investment in the film industry as a whole. In recent years, the actor/director has been participating with a growing vigor in non-Shakespearean cinema. *The Theory of Flight* (dir. Paul Greengrass, 1998), *Wild, Wild West* (dir. Barry Sonnefeld, 1999), *The Road to El Dorado* (dir. Bibo Bergeron and Will Finn, 2000), and *Alien Love Triangle* (dir. Danny Boyle, 2000) are but four of Branagh's newer filmic excursions. In all of these productions, but particularly in *The Proposition* (dir. Lesli Linka Glatter, 1998), a dramatic meditation on Virginia Woolf's invention of "Shakespeare's sister," and *Celebrity* (dir. Woody Allen, 1998), in which he plays a down-at-heel screenwriter, Branagh retains a Shakespearean aspect. Indeed, it might be suggested that Branagh keeps returning to Shakespeare because he has not found a clearly demarcated role outside it. Whatever part the actor performs, he discloses his theatrical antecedents. One type of film feeds off and depends upon a host of others; as twenty-first century Hollywood strives to better itself, so must Branagh's Shakespeare move imperceptibly away from the context, conception and content of the Bardic original.

Such a hypothesis is abundantly illustrated in Branagh's film version of *Love's Labour's Lost* (2000). Having established himself as an *auteur,* Branagh was empowered to move to the text with impunity. And because he had earlier defined his credentials by garnering success both as an epic director and a star player in Shakespearean productions not of his own making (his performance as Iago in Oliver Parker's *Othello* [1995] is an apposite instance), Branagh found himself authorized to interpret Shakespeare's comedy through a musical lens. By placing the action in the period between the wars, *Love's Labour's Lost* endeavors to make manifest the currency of its Shakespearean material. In this sense, Branagh's evolving sense of Shakespeare shows itself to be acutely responsive to recent televisual and filmic trends. *Love's Labour's Lost* adapts for cinema the nostalgia more commonly associated with television series: Dennis Potter's *Pennies from Heaven* (1978), which broke the TV mold by weaving a romantic narrative in and out of songs from the 1930s and '40s, is the most obvious analogue. Furthermore, by availing itself of the appeal of celebrities (Alicia Silverstone suggests Batgirl more quickly than she does the French Princess in the social imaginary), *Love's Labour's Lost* takes a leaf from more recent Shakespearean cinematic offerings, films that Branagh himself has helped to generate. One has only to think here of the casting of Calista Flockhart and Anna Friel in Michael Hoffman's *A Midsummer Night's Dream* (1999), the late Victorian romp in which Ally McBeal meets Beth Jordache in a mud-wrestling match. Finally, because *Love's Labour's Lost* is staged as a singular combination of play and musical, it can be suggested that Branagh is now not so much persisting in Shakespearean adaptation as moving toward Bardic appropriation.

In a recent interview, Branagh chose to query this theorization of his *oeuvre* (Wray and Burnett 2000, 174). However, he is also on record as recognizing that "We have broken away from the various earlier periods of Shakespeare movie-making that were linked more closely to theatre. . . . Now these stories are free for exploration in a way they weren't before. The canvas is blank again" (Gristwood 2000, 13). Certainly, *Love's Labour's Lost* represents Branagh's boldest attempt yet to make Shakespeare speak to the present generation: lines and scenes are dispensed with, tried and trusted cinematic ploys are exploited, and an energetic score keeps the action perpetually on the boil. In this connection, it is not unreasonable to maintain that *Love's Labour's Lost* is intricately enmeshed in both appropriation (as it revealed itself, for instance, in the comedy, *Ten Things I Hate about You* [dir. Gil Junger, 1999], a reworking of *The Taming of the Shrew*) and more strident "Shakespearean" modernizings (such as Baz Luhrmann's pop-soaked *William Shakespeare's Romeo + Juliet* [1996]). Like Branagh's *Love's Labour's Lost,* it might be argued, these films were distinctive for directing themselves to reanimations of the "teen flick" and the potential conversion of a younger respondent (see Burt 2001).

Despite its seeming distance from the source, *Love's Labour's Lost* still manages to dress in fresh colors familiar moments in the Shakespearean text. Consciously modeled to connote the mood of the late 1930s, Branagh's production deploys its Oxbridge-style setting to evoke a halcyon interlude, a period of innocence and calm before the explosion of hostilities. But reminders of larger realities are not forgotten, for, as in *Hamlet,* newspaper reports, flashed onto the screen, hint at military developments unfolding beyond the film-world's perimeters. In such an environment, the repeated requests of the King of Navarre (Alessandro Nivola) to "subscribe" (1.1.23) begin to sound like a demand for national allegiance. Similarly, when the King dwells upon monies never "received" (2.1.134) and rights in Aquitaine, one is reminded of Neville Chamberlain's famous announcement that, because no promise from Hitler to withdraw from Poland had been received, war would be declared. Such contemporary glosses on the comedy are consistently provocative, working to infuse particular passages with political valency and to remind an audience that romance is very often the vehicle for subversive critique. If the filmic ambience permits a reconceptualization of Shakespearean language, the accompanying music translates the play's situations into more meaningful idioms. Thus the dominating question—"What is the end of study, let me know?" (1.1.55)—and the onerous obligations of academe are newly phrased, in Branagh's revision, in the George Gershwin and Desmond Carter song, "I'd Rather Charleston," whose references to "mind" and "intellect" precisely concatenate the dramatic implications of renouncing 'the world's delights" (1.1.29). In many respects, such musical interruptions represent the means with which the wit and invention of the Shakespearean original are given a more familiar, but no less expressive, verbal guise.

Felicitous reformulations extend no less importantly to the play's gender politics. Of course, *Love's Labour's Lost* is one of Shakespeare's most generically anomalous comedies, since stylistic badinage is invariably seen as female and the rituals of courtship fail to materialize in expected marital outcomes. Although Branagh rectifies this omission in the reunions of his interpolated epilogue, he makes available a rich vocabulary for a resistant femininity through his musical decisions. Thus the women's testy rejection of their suitors' "commendations" (2.1.116) finds an eloquent home in the rendition of Jerome Kern's song, "I Won't Dance," while the stance of willful singleness occupied by the Princess and her entourage in 4.1 is aptly encapsulated in the performance of Irving Berlin's "No Strings," with its "I'm Fancy Free" refrain. When the courtship takes on a reciprocal character, even more exact musical equivalents are elaborated. The decision to "woo these girls of France" (4.3.347) becomes a prelude to Irving Berlin's song, "Let's Face the Music and Dance," which is acted out so as to suggest the lords' new romantic resolve. Particularly resonant are the points of contact linking the play's generic inconsistencies—as Berowne states, "Jack hath not Jill" (5.2.864)—and comparably bitter-sweet musical correlatives. George and Ira Gershwin's "They Can't Take That Away from Me" sounds as the central players being their protracted separations, and its repeated line, "Our romance won't end on a sorrowful note," draws a heightened attention to a momentary rejection of accepted modes of resolution and closure. In the same way that the play breaks its mold, so, too, are the songs made to play fast and loose with their own codes and conventions.

Music is similarly invaluable in placing a contemporary cast on the comedy's immersion in intertextuality. Perhaps the most linguistically showy and stylistically aware work in the canon, Love's Labour's Lost is rife with a density of Elizabethan allusion to script, writing, playing, and mental production. Branagh's take on the play loses none of Shakespeare's self-consciousness. "Let me hear a staff, a stanza, a verse" (4.2.103), the request of Holofernia (Geraldine McEwan), is answered by an ensemble execution of Jerome Kern's "The Way You Look Tonight": the verbal fencing of 4.2 is here nicely glossed, with the song becoming a demonstration of poetic facility. No less suggestive is the filmic dovetailing between Berowne's realization that "love . . . hath taught me to rhyme" (4.3.12–13) and the prompt delivery of the George and Ira Gershwin song, "I've Got a Crush on You," the rhyming plenitude of which recalls a dramatic concern with the processes of versification. Such sequences of musical intertextuality form a platform from which the film is able to contemplate, with an intensity unmatched in the Branagh *oeuvre,* its status as a cinematic artifact. A small globe in *Love's Labour's Lost* Radcliffe Camera-style interior recalls another acting space, the Globe Theatre, while the ascension of the lords to the heavens of the library during the singing of Irving Berlin's "Cheek to Cheek" constitutes a signal reminder of an Elizabethan theatre's heavens. Because astrology and philosophy are represented on the domed ceiling from which, magically suspended, Berowne and his companions perform their musical "harmony" (4.3.321) of the gods, it would seem as if Branagh is making two playful references—the first to the early modern concept of the musical concord of the spheres, the second to the potential of his filmmaking to feature as one of the traditional arts.

In this sense, Branagh is able to introduce through *Love's Labour's Lost* an autobiographical element. Many of Branagh's Shakespearean films, sometimes because they have received their *premières* in Belfast, communicate a powerful sense of the actor/producer/director's personal preoccupations. The *première* of *Hamlet* at Belfast's Waterfront Hall, for instance, bristled with homecoming motifs: Julie Christie introduced the film by presenting Branagh (who was born in Belfast but brought up in England) to the audience as "your boy." At the same time, the occasion was witness to an attempt to internationalize the local context, since the screening was supported by First Run Belfast, a charity dedicated to sponsoring thespians to pursue theatrical ventures or study drama outside Northern Ireland. *Hamlet,* one might suggest, therefore, represents Branagh's attempt to negotiate a tricky movement (and a narrative of exile and return) between London, Stratford-upon-Avon, Hollywood, and Belfast.

But in *Love's Labour's Lost* Branagh thematizes the implications of his chosen craft with a greater autobiographical brio. In particular, the film becomes, in Branagh's hands, a paean to a filmic world no longer available to him as postmodern artist. At its release, much was made in the popular press of the choreographical and musical amateurishness of the film's performers, with Lindsay Duguid striking a particularly critical note: "Possibly Branagh means to recreate a cheery amateurishness of technique as well as atmosphere. . . . It is hard to know for whom all this expensive foolery is intended" (Duguid 2000, 34). The nonprofessional enthusiasm of his cast, however, is precisely the point: Branagh is highlighting the consummate skills and expertise of the Hollywood musical by imitating them in a twenty-first century cinematic medium. In so doing, Branagh is empowered to pass further comment on his filmmaking phenomenon. Particularly through the rendering of Irving Berlin's song, "There's No Business Like Show Business," the film's most spectacular number, Branagh addresses his career as a Shakespearean interpreter and rehearses the mechanisms he has perfected in seeking to make the Bard "our contemporary." Crucially, the social trajectory traced by the song—it moves from the plebeian frustration of the "butcher, the baker, the grocer, the clerk" to the emancipatory glitter of popular entertainment—chimes with Branagh's own, while the accompanying musical reflection on "steal[ing] that extra bow" points up the measures that the *auteur* is obliged to institute to reanimate Shakespeare for a mass consumership. And, on any director's list of vital cinematic ingredients, the kinds of appropriations and parodies flirted with in *Love's Labour's Lost* would surely occupy pride of place. Branagh's spectral presence in his production is nowhere more obvious than in his reading of the line, "You that way; we this way" (5.2.920). In the play, of course, Armado's words self-consciously separate cast from audience: spectators are enjoined to "leave the theater" in the same moment that the performers are instructed to depart by the wings. By contrast, Branagh has this final injunction appear as skywriting, which brings together in a marvelous choreographic arrangement all the film's major motifs—writing, script, the heavens, intertextuality, the implications of periodicity, the claims of the *auteur.* Of course, at the level of the film, "You that way; we this way" functions as a felicitous accompaniment to the *Casablanca*-inspired leave-taking scene which, faithfully remade, increases the Bogart-Bergman-Henreid triad into an octet of parting lords and ladies.

Yet at the level of Branagh's personal vision the aerially inscribed line executes a two-way movement: it looks back to the heyday of Hollywood, dissolving its conjured ghosts, and it looks forward to new Shakespearean possibilities, to the future forms of the Bard on screen.

An absorption in the cultural applications of film, a will to make Shakespeare transparently communicative and a penchant for personally meaningful intertextual borrowings—all of these components of the Branagh phenomenon are at work in his two ongoing Shakespearean projects. "The ultimate goal is to make this completely contemporary in feel," Branagh has said of *Macbeth,* his next Shakespearean production, adding, "maybe with this one I will get to the present day" ("Branagh" 9). The shift into the present day is significant, a sign of the director's abandonment of the Elizabethan and of his entry into the Shakespearean postmodern. Current *Macbeth* certainly appears to be. The Intermedia press package for the project (which shows an outreached hand looming in front of a skyscrapered background) describes the film being set at "the beginning of a new millennium. An utterly modern setting in which Shakespeare's warfare takes place amid the corridors of power in financial centres around the world. The bloody battle for leadership centres on the control of a global media empire" (*Kenneth Branagh's "The Shakespeare Film Company,"* n.p.). Clearly, the idea here is for *Macbeth* to follow in the footsteps of another recent dystopian representation of corporate capitalism, Oliver Stone's *Wall Street* (1987), recreating Shakespeare for the new century by seeing the play through the lens of a communications network mogul rather than a medieval Scottish tyrant. It is equally possible to suggest, however, that the film constitutes Branagh's attempt to counter not only Ian McKellen's version of another Shakespearean empirebuilder in Richard Loncraine's *Richard III* (1995) but also the spirit of Michael Almereyda's *Hamlet* (2000), with its Manhattan setting, big business accoutrements (the Denmark Corporation has its headquarters in a skyscraper), and liberal use of Generation X slacker iconography.

These, of course, are films whose genesis can be taken back to the revolutionizing movie-making of Branagh himself. As the twenty-first century gets underway, therefore, Branagh is faced with the challenge of rivaling as well as outdoing this plethora of wares engulfing the Shakespearean cinematic market. Comparable speculation can be brought to bear on Branagh's *As You Like It,* his second Shakespeare-in-production project. The play will be taken, publicity informs us, to Japan's Kyoto and "all the excitement and pageantry of Samurai tradition. European influences clashing dramatically with the ancient order" (*Kenneth Branagh's "The Shakespeare Film Company,"* n.p.). One can only guess at the film's final form, but it may be that, with this production, Branagh will build upon the example of another director, Quentin Tarantino, utilizing cultural *bricolage,* purposefully discordant elements and productively conflicting registers to translate Shakespeare's problematic pastoral. In this sense, Branagh, cast in the guise of a blokish director, may yet inherit something of the Tarantino charisma.

This, at least, is one possible prognosis. The other is that advertised in a gossip column from the British tabloids. Current rumors maintain that Branagh's "grand £30 million scheme to make a trio of new-look Shakespearean films has hit the buffers" ("Ken's Labour" 2001, 39). Apparently because *Love's Labour's Lost* (which cost £8 million to make) realized only £350,000 in the U.K., Branagh has put on possibly permanent hold the plan to eclipse his Shakespearean superstardom via a triumvirate of generously budgeted movies. Branagh's unexpected departure from Shakespeare raises some timely issues. On the one hand, it supports the notion that Shakespeare has moved so far in the direction of adaptation and citation that even appropriation is not enough to guarantee commercial profit. The state of play at the present juncture shows Shakespeare having evolved into a *mélange* of content and capital, iconicity and desacralization, revered quotation and spin-off association. Caught in the cross fire of this historical impasse, Branagh is perhaps acknowledging that, even though the unadulterated Shakespeare has had his day, the appropriation also needs to touch the pulse of the times with a particular finesse. On the other hand, to take on board Richard Burt's theory of "hyperunproductivity," the productive dimensions of Branagh's non-Shakespearean interlude need to be emphasized. Due, in large part, to Branagh's example, modernity is witness to a proliferation of Shakespeares unparalleled in recent memory. If this takes us away from Shakespeare, it also takes us back and, in particular, alerts us to the variety of technological instruments through which the Bard now communicates. Although *Love's Labour's Lost* had a limited run in the cinema, for instance, it has been granted a much longer life via an arsenal of print and digital mediums: a soundtrack CD, an edition of the play, a video, a DVD, and a website. Shakespeare after mass media, then, may appear ripe for extinction even as he is also multiplying, diversifying, and expanding, constructively reaching the attention of a newly polymorphous consciousness.

Over the course of an extraordinarily dynamic and culturally transformative career, Branagh has turned Shakespeare on film into an industry, an achievement that has made the "popular" respectable and given an energetic boost to academia (including this volume). Making filmic manners, Branagh has created an *oeuvre* that has been profitably responsive to increasingly various cinematic requirements. With Olivier's doublet and hose put firmly into the wardrobe, Branagh has gravitated to the filmic examples of his own moment and, in the process, has self-consciously granted his audience a version of his own narrative. He has simultaneously transcended, as least as he is represented in mass media, a royal label (a *Spitting Image* sketch featured

"Ken and Em" as the new King and Queen) to embrace a more populist, transatlantic persona. Branagh, then, has progressed and grown alongside the currents of Hollywood, but he has also matured with one eye cocked toward the academy, recognizing that the range of "Shakespeares" that mark the present condition are just as fascinating as objects of study as the playwright's imagery or dramaturgy. At the beginning of the twenty-first century, as films such as John Madden Jr.'s *Shakespeare in Love* (1998) demonstrate, Shakespeare is no longer a holy representative of iconic status; rather, judged from the standpoint of the "cultural logic of late Shakespeareanism" (to adopt Donald K. Hedrick's essay title), his name has fractured outwards to signify a broader ideological trajectory, to the extent that the dramatist is now inseparable from debates about, for instance, the post-colonial mindset, the subaltern experience, education and cyberspace. The Branagh phenomenon suggests ultimately that Shakespeare can, in the space of one filmic incarnation, shed the vestiges of his visual history and embrace a postmodern Bard, one characterized by fluidity, hybridity, and even a Schlockspearean anti-bardolatry.

Works Cited

Arnold, Gary. 1996. "Branagh Breathes New Life into Classics." *Insight on the News*, January 15: 36–7.

"Branagh Brings the Scottish Play up to Date." 1999. *Belfast News*, May 13: 9.

Branagh, Kenneth. 1996. *"Hamlet" by William Shakespeare: Screenplay, Introduction and Film Diary*. London: Chatto and Windus.

Branagh, Kenneth. 1993. *"Much Ado About Nothing" by William Shakespeare: Screenplay, Introduction, and Notes on the Making of the Movie*. New York and London: W. W. Norton.

Bright, Curtis. 1991. "Branagh and the Prince, or a 'royal fellowship of death.'" *Critical Quarterly*, 33, 95–111.

Burt, Richard. 2001. "T(e)en Things I Hate about Girlene Shakesploitation Flicks in the Late 1990s, or, Not So Fast Times at Shakespeare High." In *Screening the Bard: Shakespearean Spectacle, Critical Theory, Film Practice*. Ed. by Lisa Starks and Courtney Lehmann. Madison, NJ: American Univ. Presses, 205–232.

Commemorative Programme: William Shakespeare's "Hamlet," Directed by Kenneth Branagh. 1997. Belfast: Graham & Heslip.

Coursen, H. R. 1996. *Shakespeare in Production: Whose History?*. Athens: Ohio Univ. Press.

Deleyto, Celestino. 1997. "Men in Leather: Kenneth Branagh's *Much Ado About Nothing* and Romantic Comedy." *Cinema Journal*, 36(3): 91–105.

Duguid, Lindsay. 2000. "No Kicks in a Plane." *Times Literary Supplement*, April 7: 34.

Fineman, Joel. 1980. "Fratricide and Cuckoldry: Shakespeare's Doubles." In *Representing Shakespeare: New Essays*. Ed. by Murray M. Schwartz and Coppélia Kahn. Baltimore and London: Johns Hopkins Univ. Press, 70–109.

Fitter, Chris. 1991. "A Tale of Two Branaghs: *Henry V,* Ideology, and the Mekong Agincourt." In *Shakespeare, Left and Right.* Ed. by Ivo Kamps. New York and London: Routledge, 259–75.

Gristwood, Sarah. 2000. "What Is this Thing Called *Love's Labour's Lost?.*" *The Guardian: Arts.* March 27: 12–13.

Guntner, Lawrence. 1995. "Recycled Film Codes and 'The Great Tradition of Shakespeare on Film.'" In *Negotiations with Hal: Multi-Media Perceptions of (Shakespeare's) "Henry the Fifth."* Ed. by Peter Drexler and Lawrence Guntner. Braunschweig: Univ. Braunschweig, 51–61.

Hedrick, Donald K. 1997. "War Is Mud: Branagh's Dirty Harry V and the Types of Political Ambiguity." In *Shakespeare, the Movie: Popularizing the Plays on Film, TV, and Video.* Ed. by Lynda E. Boose and Richard Burt. New York and London: Routledge, 45–66.

Holderness, Graham. 1991. "'What ish my nation?': Shakespeare and National Identities." *Textual Practice,* 5: 74–93.

Jackson, Russell. 1997. "Shakespeare's Comedies on Film." In *Shakespeare and the Moving Image: The Plays on Film and Television.* Ed. by Anthony Davies and Stanley Wells. Cambridge: Cambridge Univ. Press, 99–120.

"Ken's Labour Lost on the Bard." 2001. *The Daily Express.* January 30: 39.

Kenneth Branagh's "The Shakespeare Film Company." 2000. London: Intermedia.

Lanier, Douglas. 1996. "Drowning the Book: *Prospero's Books* and the Textual Shakespeare." In *Shakespeare, Theory, and Performance.* Ed. by James C. Bulman. New York and London: Routledge, 187–209.

Lehmann, Courtney, and Lisa S. Starks. 2000. "Making Mother Matter: Repression, Revision, and the Stakes of 'Reading Psychoanalysis' into Kenneth Branagh's *Hamlet.*" *Early Modern Literary Studies.* 6(1): 1–18.

LoMonico, Michael. 1996. "Branagh's *Hamlet*—Power and Opulence." *Shakespeare* 1(1): 6–7.

Morgan, Hilary. 1999. "Made in Belfast." *The Sunday Mirror,* August 1: 7.

Moses, Carol. 1996. "Kenneth Branagh's *Much Ado About Nothing:* Shakespearean Comedy as Shakespearean Romance." *Shakespeare Bulletin* 14(1): 38–40.

S., D. 1996. "N. B." *Times Literary Supplement,* November 22: 16.

Shakespeare, William. 1987. *Hamlet.* Ed. by Harold Jenkins. New York and London: Methuen.

Shakespeare, William. 1975. *Henry V.* Ed. by A. R. Humphreys. Harmondsworth: Penguin.

Shakespeare, William. 1982. *Love's Labour's Lost.* Ed. by John Kerrigan. Harmondsworth: Penguin.

Shakespeare, William. 1983. *Much Ado About Nothing.* Ed. by R. A. Foakes. Harmondsworth: Penguin.

Smith, David James. 2000. "In the Company of Ken." *The Sunday Times Magazine,* February 20: 34–40.

Wray, Ramona and Mark Thornton Burnett. 2000. "From the Horse's Mouth: Branagh on the Bard." In *Shakespeare, Film, Fin de Siècle.* Ed. by Mark Thornton Burnett and Ramona Wray. Basingstoke: Macmillan, 165–78.

Films Cited

Allen, Woody, dir. 1998. *Celebrity.* USA Sound, b/w, 113 mins.

Almereyda, Michael, dir. 2000. *Hamlet.* USA Miramax. Sound, col., 106 mins.

Bergeron, Eric, dir. 2000. *The Road to El Dorado.* USA Disney. Sound, col., 89 mins.

Branagh, Kenneth, dir. 1989. *Henry V.* U.K. Renaissance Films. Sound, col., 132 mins.

————, dir. 1997. *Hamlet.* USA Castle Rock. Sound, col., 232 mins.

————, dir. 1995. *In the Bleak Midwinter.* U.K. Castle Rock. Sound, col., 95 mins.

————, dir. 2000. *Love's Labour's Lost.* USA Intermedia. Sound, col., 90 mins.

————, dir. 1994. *Mary Shelley's Frankenstein.* USA Tristar Pictures. Sound, col., 118 mins.

————, dir. 1993. *Much Ado About Nothing.* U.K. Samuel Goldwyn and Renaissance Films. Sound, col., 104 mins.

————, dir. 1992. *Peter's Friends.* U.K. Samuel Goldwyn and Renaissance Films. Sound, col., 98 mins.

Glatter, Lesli Linka, dir. 1998. *The Proposition.* USA PolyGram. Sound, col., 107 mins.

Greengrass, Paul, dir. 1998. *The Theory of Flight.* U.K./USA Sound, col., 101 mins.

Hoffman, Michael, dir. 1999. *A Midsummer Night's Dream.* USA Twentieth Century Fox. Sound, col., 116 mins.

Junger, Gil, dir. 1999. *Ten Things I Hate about You.* USA Touchstone Pictures. Sound, col., 93 mins.

Kubrick, Stanley, dir. 1987. *Full Metal Jacket.* USA Warner Brothers. Sound, col., 111 mins.

Kubrick, Stanley, dir. 1960. *Spartacus.* USA Universal. Sound, col., 186 minutes.

Lean, David, dir. 1965. *Dr. Zhivago.* USA Warner Brothers. Sound, col., 192 mins.

Loncraine, Richard, dir. 1996. *Richard III.* U.K./USA United Artists. Sound, col., 150 mins.

Luhrmann, Baz, dir. 1996. *William Shakespeare's Romeo + Juliet.* USA Twentieth Century Fox. Sound, col., 115 mins.

Madden, John, dir. 1998. *Shakespeare in Love.* USA Universal. Sound, col., 119 mins.

Noble, Adrian, dir. 1996. *A Midsummer Night's Dream.* U.K. Capitol Films/Channel Four. Sound, col., 100 mins.

Olivier, Laurence, dir. 1948. *Hamlet.* U.K. Two Cities Films. Sound, b/w, 155 mins.

————, dir. 1944. *Henry V.* U.K. Two Cities Films. Sound, col., 131 mins.

Parker, Oliver, dir. 1995. *Othello.* USA Castle Rock, Sound, col., 119 mins.

Sonnenfeld, Barry, dir. 1999. *Wild, Wild West.* USA Warner Brothers. Sound, col., 105 mins.

Stone, Oliver, dir. 1989. *Born on the Fourth of July.* USA Universal. Sound, col., 138 mins.

————, dir. 1986. *Platoon.* USA MGM. Sound, col., 114 mins.

————, dir. 1987. *Wall Street.* USA Twentieth Century Fox. Sound, col., 120 mins.

Sturges, John, dir. 1960. *The Magnificent Seven.* MGM. USA Sound, col., 127 mins.

CHAPTER 4

SHAKESPEARE
The Theme Park

DIANA E. HENDERSON

From whence "Schlockspeare," and where is it going? Is it the creation of twentieth-century mass media, or has mass culture merely changed the technological particulars of how "Shakespeare" is represented outside canonical, licensed artistic venues? While many accounts of the decontextualized commercial appropriation of Shakespeare (what Richard Burt has dubbed Schlockspeare) presume it to be a modern phenomenon and bastard kin to a "legitimate" tradition in text and performance, one might just as well argue that their origin is unitary: Schlockspeare was there "in the beginning," in the texts performed and pirated in seventeenth-century London. When Hamlet addresses the players, attempting to constrain and counter current professional practices; when courtiers mock amateurs for including Moonshine and bungling classical allusions; when Antigonus is caught between a bear and a Bohemian seacoast and Hecate dances through Scotland, Schlockspeare is the specter and Shakespeare the author who polices or indulges him. In other words, it was ever thus, with purists and crowd-pleasers as Siamese twins, the strange stage-fellows unable to survive alone. That which was deemed out of bounds, unworthy of interpretation, incoherent, or wrong predates mass media, and is therefore not so much "post-hermeneutic" (again, Burt's term) as non- or antihermeneutic.

The phenomenon of Schlockspeare, then, would be intrinsic to the perpetuation and study of Shakespeare itself, rather than a degrading sideline. And yet, though this ultimately seems historically more accurate as well as a useful counterpoint to the cultural jeremiads accompanying each generation's nostalgia for a putatively less fragmented past, to simply celebrate Schlocks-peare can also likewise serve as a form of scholarly evasion, a refusal to address the difficult question of value in a world where the sheer quantity of Shake-schlock as well as Bardolatry could fill (or waste) a lifetime. It is here that the "post" in posthermeneutic takes on significance. Quick acceptance of the schlock with the Shake may displace careful analysis of the particularity of different forms of indulgence at different moments, that is, attention to the ways that technological changes allow or disallow our seeing and hearing various elements of the multimedia events that have always accompanied the name of Shakespeare. Thus a short trek to explore a few of the schlockier habitats of the Bard may not be amiss at this historical juncture, at least as a means to diagnose more accurately the reasons for "Shakespeare's" ubiquity and the queasiness rather than enjoyment it often induces. At the risk of indulging myself by not policing the boundaries of the professional essay form and thereby approaching Schlockspeare as muse, I here recall some memories, revealing some of my own origins and location, in order to address the questions with which I began.

*ళ· *ళ· *ళ· *ళ· *ళ·

When I was eighteen, I worked in a parking lot called Scotland. Wearing a tartan miniskirt and wool tam in the Virginia heat, I drove a double-decker bus full of tourists from their cars to the main gates of "Busch Gardens: The Old Country." This amusement park thematized American ancestry and links to the past through areas linked with certain Western European countries, primarily England, France, and Germany. There was a side area, "Hastings," between the larger ones we called as shorthand England ("Banbury Cross") and France ("Aquitaine"). In recalling the battle of 1066 that brought the French to power in England, someone involved in the park's planning may have had a wry sense of humor about its nationalist design. French-Canadian clog dancing in "New France" also pushed the envelope slightly, acknowledging some intermediate stages between old and new, not to mention an older America outside the United States. And then there was Scotland, on the margins, a bit of forest inside and the parking crew outside the main gates. As if to add insult to injury in the days before Tony Blair's Labour policy of "devolution" (which allows limited self-government to the old "Celtic fringe" areas of Great Britain heretofore ruled by Parliament in London), we Scots carted visitors in buses imported from London itself. Thus the only "authentic" objects in the enterprise, with old-fashioned double-pump clutches and diesel engines, were English.

At the main entrance, Handel's *Water Music,* composed for English royalty by a German-born naturalized British subject, played unceasingly. One then passed through turnstiles to find England itself, which meant—along with the ubiquitous tacky gift shops and eateries—a village clock tower we called "Big Ben," and the Globe Theater. (See figure 4.1.)

And with the appearance of the Globe, one's frame of reference for reading the "Old Country" must shift a bit. Big Ben and black-and-white frame houses might prompt yearnings to be back in England, if one ignored their ersatz qualities; "German dancers" in the reconstructed Munich beer hall likewise tried to create a folksy feeling for a willing audience. Transmuting Germany into "Oktoberfest" during the lifetime of those who fought in World War II or had relatives exterminated might seem an act of breathtaking bad faith (all history lost its edge here), but it was a different kind of oddity than was involved in reconstructing the Globe. For nobody could "think back" to her or his own idealized image, or even his or her family's distant memories, of the Globe Theatre in England: the old ones had burned down centuries before, and the new one on the South Bank of the Thames now sold as "Shakespeare's Globe" hadn't been built yet. So where *were* we, and who was the "Old Country" designed for?

If we were to take the countries deemed worthy of representation as a guide, a small fragment of historically privileged white America. Not only were Asia and Africa off the map, but this brave new world's historical gaze excluded even those "later" waves of immigrants who came to the United States in the mid- to late nineteenth century from Eastern and Southern Europe, as well as from Ireland and Scandinavia. But it seems this theme park "old country" is nobody's authentic home anymore, only a phrase to be invoked. It is a composite of the most familiar national stereotypes and images derived from mass media, as distilled in brochures for the "grand tour" in seven days. And as a tourist fantasy, the plastic buildings worked better if one hadn't seen them in stone and in scale. The target audience may still have included people whose ancestors lived in England, France, and Germany—but it was really targeting, or at least was most successful with, those who could not afford or did not care to travel to Europe and see the "real thing." As a fantasy substitute for a European holiday (with plenty of rides to keep the kids amused), this old country addressed a wider audience than one might have at first presumed, predominantly middle and lower-middle class families and teens from the South and mid-Atlantic region.

But again the presence of the Globe made this place different: it not only added an overtly historical dimension but outdid "reality" by presenting what has come to epitomize both the glory days of merry olde England and "culture"—but can't be visited on the package tour. Like the "Hastings" area, this building testifies to a memory of English history and mythology as formative, as the originary "old country" for the United States—at least until about the time Busch Gardens was built. The linguistic tie obviously is fundamental to this originary myth, so who better to personify that connection than Shakespeare, what better building than "his" theater? Naming that theater still has caché and drawing power, at least in millennial London; but the local meanings and uses of the Globe vary widely in the age of multimedia. And while some still hold on to visions of the Bard as an aesthetic icon rising above the crassness of mass marketing, in many quarters, the boundaries between "Shakespeare" and other forms of theme park entertainment have become virtually indistinguishable. Nor, as noted in my introductory remarks, is this a new phenomenon. However, in the wake of high-tech mass media's increasing centrality in culture, theme park Schlockspeare may be drowning out alternative versions, eclipsing historically or theatrically grounded ideas of Shakespeare.

When I worked in Scotland, Shakespeare still had a role at Busch Garden's Globe Theater. But what did it mean then, in the theme park world, to present "Shakespeare"? Certainly not to put on whole plays with texts attributed to Shakespeare: nobody coming for a day at the theme park wanted to spend so long a time in one place, away from the rides, nor would management want customers detained from spending more money at the food and gift concessions. A thirty- to forty-five-minute performance could still have presented a sequence of "greatest hits" scenes by Shakespeare, or a truncated play; the Westinghouse and the Hallmark Hall of Fame television shows of the 1950s, and numerous children's versions and spin-offs, provided precedents. But a handful of famous characters and lines from Shakespeare was as close as this Globe show got, interspersed with other elements to make sure the audience remained amused. Nor was this a reconstructed outdoor theater: we were firmly ensconced indoors, in a darkened theater with our seats in what would have been the pit. The actors came onto a raised stage making sweeping gestures as they lip-synched to a tape (as a result not earning Equity scale for speaking roles, keeping the wages low). Falstaff bounced in—as did Queen Elizabeth I. She has so often been viewed as a kind of benign companion to Shakespeare that the audacity of the move no longer registers. What did provoke comment, and was certainly unusual, was the addition of technological special effects to spice up the proceedings. The witches from *Macbeth* not evoking the sort of fear they once would, the producers supplemented the stage event. In the upper levels of the theater, where once the high-paying customers would have sat, were lines of statuary—vaguely classical busts that seemed mere adornment. At the crucial moment, in thunder, lightning, and in rain, they came to "life": through superimposed projections and mechanical manipulation, their mouths appeared to move and the faces gained expression. This, then, was the highlight at the Globe Theater: Shakespeare as a trip to the haunted house. Schlockspeare with spooks.

In playing with Shakespeare, the Busch Gardens show was of course doing nothing new. Even before recent scholarship emphasized the shifting, collaborative nature of Shakespeare's playtexts, those acquainted with performance history knew that there has never been a stable, unchallenged, and unaltered version of his plays. From William Davenant's Restoration spectacles through Nahum Tate's and Colley Cibber's textual alterations to the nineteenth century's continued cuts, tableaux, and myriad burlesques, Shakespeare has always been theatrical *material*. At least from the time of David Garrick's Jubilee at Stratford-upon-Avon in 1769, Shakespeare has also been an idea and an institution—though the content of what he/it signified has been as changeable as performance itself. We cannot rightly attribute to the era of mass media, then, the tendency to muck about with (or even "butcher") Shakespeare's plays.

Nor, more arguably, should we attribute to the class profile of the audience the responsibility for choices to cut and alter text so radically that we are left wondering what "Shakespeare" means. The implicit assumption here would be that the producers are forced to dumb down the material because it won't be comprehensible or enjoyable for an audience of, say, teenage boys and working-class adults. They are supposed to be the ones who can't handle the language and need extra spectacle. This is an old argument, and kindred to assumptions about the role of the "groundlings" in Shakespeare's own day. Almost inevitably, my undergraduates assert unselfconsciously that the "low-life" material in Shakespeare's plays was there to please the crude sensibility of the groundlings; so I infer that many high school teachers are still working from a highbrow/lowbrow model that equates expensive seats with cultivated taste and wit, while only bawdry and dogs please the standing workers. John Dover Wilson may have exaggerated the protodemocratic qualities of an Elizabethan playhouse, and Ann Jennalie Cook may have overcompensated by making privileged a category so capacious as to describe most everybody attending, but none of this debate seems to have forced major rethinking of assumptions about class and taste derived from the nineteenth century, at least not outside small cadres of academics and performers. Were apprentices, who clearly did enjoy allusions to themselves onstage, unable to enjoy a great speech as well? Are teenagers who watch Leonardo DiCaprio in Baz Luhrmann's *William Shakespeare's Romeo + Juliet* (over and over) unable to enjoy anything except his visual image and the spectacle? Like the fictional Cher in *Clueless* who knows her Mel Gibson (and thus can correctly attribute a line from Zeffirelli's *Hamlet*), one need not be a scholar or a highbrow to have an ear and a brain.

Likewise, if one knows a smattering of performance history, the assumptions behind these widespread class-based comments appear groundless. As regards spectacle, Samuel Pepys enjoyed the balletic sequences added to

Restoration Shakespeare; William Macready, Charles Kean, and Charles Calvert added huge tableaux to their nineteenth-century productions thinking them historically apt and edifying; and the twentieth century has produced its share of high-toned spectacles and gallimaufries to amuse. The idea that "highbrows" can enjoy evenings of static recitation is not entirely without foundation, but they certainly seem to have enjoyed a bit of lively stage business as well. Conversely, as Lawrence Levine has documented in his admirable study of Shakespeare's place in nineteenth-century America, small town and popular entertainments played with audience familiarity with Shakespeare, to great effect and success.

Nevertheless, simplified and often inaccurate class-based interpretations have segued into assumptions about mass versus elite audience expectations in the twentieth century. And here, it seems to me that even Levine succumbs, perhaps because of his interest in proving that the cultural bifurcation between *Highbrow/Lowbrow* had occurred by the start of this century. Thus, when mentioning an early twentieth-century extravaganza, *Caliban by the Yellow Sands* (1916), he follows Charles Shattuck's analysis in attributing its success, despite the words not being Shakespeare's (it was scripted by the poet Percy MacKaye), to the fact that Shakespeare was now "archaic and inaccessible" to the people.

What "Shakespeare" means here, however, is the language and story in its "pure" form (or some approximation of that unrealizable idea), which is quite a different standard for audience appreciation than was applied to earlier instances of burlesques and popular entertainments. The 1916 event, moreover, clearly belonged to a different genre than Shakespeare play production: it included a cast of over 1,500 performers singing and dancing as well as acting (in New York City, where bigger means better), and had Caliban bowing down at Shakespeare's feet. It thereby honored the occasion, which was the 300th anniversary of Shakespeare's death. Nor was it more absurd than, for example, the theatrical tribute at Sir Walter Scott's death in 1832, which imagined a bard thousands of years hence venerating the dead poet alongside Shakespeare. In other words, "free play" with language and character befits the tribute genre in a way that links the early nineteenth and early twentieth centuries, rather than in itself signaling a radical change or great divide between high and low, as Levine would have it.

I would argue that the Busch Gardens show likewise extends this tribute genre, the difference being not the looseness (and to a Shakespeare devotee or purist, absurdity), but the nonoccasional nature of the performance. Here is where the true effect of mass culture enters. The 1916 show ran for ten days and its total Lewisohn Stadium audience is reported to have numbered 135,000. Its timing was determined by the venerated author, in that it took place around the anniversary of his death. By contrast, the Busch Gardens show was performed six to eight times a day, six days a week all summer long, and on weekends in late spring and early autumn—that is, theme park business hours. Each Globe show's audience numbered in the hundreds rather than thousands, but those hundreds added up, over time, to many more attendees than were at the 1916 extravaganza. What has been lost is the aura created by a special time, a commemorative ritual, a shared holiday of sorts; now, both the business of Busch and the audience member's own vacation timing determine the conditions, and Shakespeare "fits in" to both their schedules. The Globe show was also one of many entertainments to choose among, others including a puppet show and live dancers—that is, an array of alternatives not unlike those competing with the first Globe Theatre in 1599. Shakespeare had returned from the mausoleum to be back in business at the Busch Gardens Globe. In addition, one might claim that the theme park show authentically attempts to include even those who do not have a prior involvement and commitment to Shakespeare—that is, it could be said to be more democratic, inclusive, and welcoming than earlier self-selecting tributes organized around "Shakespeare" rather than a day's holiday.

❧ ❧ ❧ ❧ ❧

Two decades later, I returned to the theme park. Times have changed: in the "real world," Scotland has its own (bickering) parliament again after centuries of control by London. At Busch Gardens, Scotland ("Heatherdowns") is now a petting zoo. In each case an ironic enactment of progress—though the baby goats have a charm that might even lure a Touchstone back to nature. No longer do teenagers drive tourists to the gates by London transport. Electric trolley carts have replaced pump-clutch buses, and many of the drivers are older Americans. In the late 1970s, most Busch workers were college students. Nowadays, college students don't do as much manual labor in the summer because, with high-tech training and internships, they don't have to. The new arrangement cuts the staff in half and is environmentally friendlier, though it erases the last trace of authentic "old country" materiality from the park.

Greece and Italy now merit inclusion, if primarily for the sake of more roller-coasters and a water ride. There is even one gesture that the naive might expect to signal the recognition of culture beyond Europe: mention of Marco Polo's journey to Asia in the "Festa Italia" area. This recognition, however, turns out to consist of a teacups ride (made into Turkish Delight by having them painted as coffee cups), a carousel, and similar fairground amusements. It might as well have been Mr. Toad's Wild Ride as Mr. Polo's. Beginning in the summer of 2001, Busch also adds Ireland to its empire; they seek actors who are "proficient at Irish dialects and who have the 'gift of the gab'" (Auditions Brochure, Autumn 2000). But with the expansion comes a loss: this theme park no longer claims to represent the "Old Country," but merely "Busch Gardens, Williamsburg." The new name is geographically accurate but also a neat evasion of a loss of focus, and signals a shifting awareness of and within national identity. Being perceived as old has even less commercial caché than it used to. Still, the Busch Gardens website admits to the European focus and advertises "an old-world adventure full of modern-day fun"; it even claims to possess "the charm and flair of 17th century Europe" tied up neatly in a package deal so that it can be visited "all in one day."

Historic Williamsburg itself—that is, Colonial Williamsburg, the corporation that runs the reconstructed pre-Revolutionary "downtown"—has also changed. It has been forced to reexamine its assumptions about the nation, and has itself been accused of being a theme park. Ada Louise Huxtable, in *The Unreal America: Architecture and Illusion,* regards Colonial Williamsburg as the ancestor of Disneyland and theme parks in general. She claims its falsity of representation paved the way for these simulacra, and her claims have merit: both in "cleaning up" history and in mixing Rockefeller-financed replicas with eighteenth-century buildings, "CW" forfeits any claim to historical purism and has participated, at least until very recently, in the whitewashing of U.S. history. Those attacks have historical validity and yet seem odd, rather like targeting the indie movie for violence while another Stallone or Schwartzenegger blockbuster rakes in millions. At the top of Duke of Gloucester Street, William & Mary remains, after all, a state school. For many of us Virginians, it allowed access, at a comparatively affordable price, to what seemed a less mechanized and anonymous time, a nobler, Jeffersonian past. Of course we were wrong. But of course we never really believed in CW literally, given that our classmates were among those with the dashing loose-sleeved white shirts and the hoop skirts, serving in taverns and strumming "What shall we do with a drunken sailor?" We knew it was a re-creation when a friend played Cornwallis at Yorktown, but we also knew it was a more interesting and historically thoughtful re-creation than was involved in being a Globe performer. It was better theater. The past, for all its deformation, was at least allowed to speak.

The whitewash of history is beginning to be addressed, though the theme park aspects of CW are also more overt: there are slave quarters and stories of the ill used, and there are also special night tours focusing on witches and things ghoulish. In its efforts to keep the crowds coming, CW hasn't changed dramatically, but it seems less "elevated," costs more, and is less distinct both from the commercial enterprises and leisure sites that surround it (Williamsburg having become a mecca for retirees) and from the theme park world of Busch Gardens.

4.1. Globe Theater, Busch Gardens (Photo: Diana Henderson)

Or so it struck me until I returned to the "real" theme park. What was the Globe Theater showing in the summer of 2000? Despite skepticism borne of experience, I was taken aback. There was the building, same as ever, right past the ticket takers, shaping one's impressions and grabbing the audience before they got to the more seductive rides. But now the banner screamed *Pirates!* (See figure 4.2).

Obviously, they were no longer pretending to market Shakespeare at the Globe. And yet, on the walls of the fake timber-frame houses all around, there were still attempts to recreate an Elizabethan mood. Granted, the

4.2. Pirates! (Photo: Diana Henderson)

"parchments" tacked on the walls were made of metal, but they were quite good, historicist reproductions of a London map and a sixteenth-century title page. Meanwhile, the Globe was showing *Pirates!*, a "4-D" experience.

Customers filed into the lobby and were given plastic viewing glasses. Inside the Globe, we took our seats in front of a massive screen: no longer was the stage to be used at all, nor the upper galleries (even for ghostly grimaces). Other than two gunship structures framing the screen, lit with a waterwheel effect, the walls were draped in black. We had come to the Globe to watch a movie. As the brochure announced, this "high-tech comedy adventure whisks you to a Caribbean island, where you become immersed in the hilarious misadventure of a hapless pirate crew and its wacky captain." The premise is more *Treasure Island* than *The Tempest:* our hero is preteen-age, once cabin boy to the corrupt Captain played by Leslie Nielsen, who on an earlier visit to the island killed his crew and stole all the treasure. He failed to kill our hero, however, who has rigged the island to get his revenge, booby-trapping and creatively torturing the crewmen in the process. The mayhem allows a good deal of cheap humor (with "Frenchie" Eric Idle leading the way) and use of "4-D"—sensations, sounds, and visuals that seem to break out of the screen's perspectival illusion. Bats flew out of the picture and rustled past our ears, causing a windy chill (that is, air was blown out of our seats at ear-level); bees hovered around our faces, leading even cynical adults to swat at the air. The glasses worked. Finally the corrupt but unsinkable Captain onscreen spit water from the ocean, and we got wet (this time, the seatback in front was the engine that shot streams of water while we gazed ahead through our glasses). This, plus spyglasses extending out of the visual frame, titles floating in midair, and the general silliness, did in fact make a far better show than in olden days.

Where was Shakespeare? A mini-send-up of *Hamlet* was the film's trace tribute, as the dastardly Captain Lucky contemplates whether he will allow Pierre "To be, or not to be?" In another glimmer of memory that words can also delight, the Captain makes an improvisatory joke out of his overheard intention to kill the crew, explaining that "kill" was a "metaphor" for "reward." But these are moments so slight as merely to reinforce the change of emphasis and interest. Film has trumped theater and virtual reality has become the only means to collective engagement. Holography, computers, and machinery in the audience rather than onstage allow effects that forcibly isolate each viewer within her own plastic eyeglass world, even as she shrieks alongside her neighbors. Next to this, *Caliban by the Yellow Sands* seems positively pure Shakespeare.

Is this what the market is demanding? Could "Shakespeare" (in any manifestation) no longer hold a mass audience? Again it is tempting to leap to such conclusions. But this was a management choice, not an inevitable sign of mass culture's direction. As it happened, a college friend of mine had been involved in trying to "pitch" a more literary spectacle to the Globe during the waning years of its Schlockspeare show. He and his cocreator developed a musical show in which a book came to life and magically led audiences through the centuries, with big, splashy production numbers (Radio City was set to coproduce) and *at the same time* plenty of literary allusions and exposure to reading for the kids. For reasons of expense or territoriality, Busch rejected the show and put on another "in-house" production for about a half million dollars less—which flopped and was removed after a year. *Pirates!* was the salvage operation that followed.

Certainly it is of a piece with the rest of the new Busch Gardens, where the Oktoberfest entertainers now intersperse polkas with a conga line sing-along to "Hot, hot, hot!" Theme park global culture may not be up-to-date (in the movie, a character was raised on "the island of Ceylon") but it provides an excuse, if Americans still need one, to forget about the specifics of history entirely. Yet in a way, this, rather than a nostalgic trip into national pasts, is to represent the world as it is: you can get french fries in every "country" inside the park, but that is increasingly true outside the park as well.

◆◆ ◆◆ ◆◆ ◆◆ ◆◆

Another Globe Theater opened during the last decade of the twentieth century, to much more acclaim than the Busch Gardens Globe. It joined a number of other Globes (in San Diego, Stratford Ontario, etc.) in being a "real" theater that puts on some Shakespeare plays. It also meshes with the larger phenomenon of summer Shakespeare festivals, especially popular in North America, whose seasonal business schedule resembles that of the theme park. The difference in this case being location, location, location. Or almost: "Shakespeare's Globe" on the South Bank of the Thames isn't precisely what it professes to be, even if precision and authenticity are its supposed claims to fame and distinction. As many have observed, the space had to be modified from the already speculative designs of architects and scholars who have culled what we can exhume from early modern documents and dirt. Building codes, audience sensibilities, and the demands of unhappy actors led to a variation on the theme of an accurate reconstruction. Moreover, the spot isn't exactly right, since that would have displaced business buildings rather than a street-sweepers' station: Shakespeare may be valuable to business, but not that valuable. Or not valuable in a way that involves historical accuracy rather than commodity trading as its first priority. And so, we have "Shakespeare's Globe" as a tourist attraction that, like Colonial Williamsburg, traffics quite successfully in a prettified, slightly ersatz version of the past. Likening this Globe to a theme park, as Huxtable does in the case of "CW," seems both right and wrong, a case of overkill given so many more egregious places to look for signs of corporate bad faith and consumerist self-delusion. But perhaps because of the competing forces within the Globe project, and despite much that has already been written about it, a few words remain in order.[1]

Unlike most critics of Shakespeare's Globe, I will not address the quality of the productions by the company headed by Mark Rylance. My interest lies in the type of cultural tourism and consumerism that this place promotes, and in this regard I follow in the path of Dennis Kennedy and Kathleen McLuskie.[2] McLuskie has remarked that in our time, "Shakespeare is used to stand in for an ethical engagement with the modern world: the ethical and the aesthetic are elided but the economics of their production are invisible." But whereas she is discussing play productions, I want to stop next door to the theater, or rather, in the areas of the building complex adjacent to the stage itself: the "Shakespeare's Globe Exhibition" area. For it is here that one sees the clash of agendas in the world of Shakespeare after mass media most vividly, and it is here that the aesthetic, made to stand for the ethical, only partially veils the economic; it is here that Shakespeare the theme park mingles and collides with other images or attempts at understanding Shakespeare differently. Graham Holderness and Barbara Hodgdon have written of the cultural materialist and the material consumer in Stratford, birthplace of Shakespeare and of the modern Shakespeare industry.[3] Many of their observations can now be transplanted to the South Bank as well, to the neighborhood where Shakespeare was involved in the productions that, after all, still form the core of his appeal and justify any interest in his biography. But in a way that reiterates the changes over twenty years at Busch Gardens, this newer Shakespeare exhibit simultaneously tries to invoke history and nation, yet goes further than the Stratford sites in effacing historical distance and national distinction. If Stratford was Merry Olde England entrenching Tory royalist interests, the London Globe Exhibition is the transnational Shakespeare media conglomerate, the artbiz where every visitor can become a "sharer."

Whereas the critics of the Shakespeare industry contemptuously deconstruct (Holderness) or alternatively find fractured forms of postmodern delight (Hodgdon) in the myths and products generated by "the Bard," I am more interested in describing the results of what seem to me clearly conflicting perceptions as to what is possible or demanded of those who still try to present a version of Shakespeare to a mass audience. The assumptions of those producers end up shaping the audience perception, and their marketing mentality constrains them and changes the substance of what we consume. At the same time, some involved in the effort are trying to work with a different vision and a different set of priorities from those of the mass market—or at least, from those who presume to know about that market. The methods of those employed to do market research prompt no more confidence than do those scholarly methods informing assumptions about what the groundlings wanted. In any event, these forces have created a strange hybrid at the new shrine.

In the past, the Exhibition might have been called the Shakespeare Museum—and who better to place at home with the muses? But given the absence of artifacts connected to Shakespeare, or even inclusion of much from the time period, perhaps this title is more honest. The choice has been to emphasize the reconstructed Globe building and the process of theater, rather than to memorialize the past. Signs of a desire to understand the past do persist, however, struggling with the dominant "present-centered" experiential planning. Here at ground zero of Shakespeare's professional career, simple tourism or reconstruction is not felt to be adequate. And so attempts are made to educate as well as amuse the visitor.

My own visit exemplified the struggles involved in achieving this aim. One might expect a pressure to include digital and multimedia displays, since they have come to be signs of currency (in all senses), and that was true enough. But even before I got to the displays, I encountered the opposite problem, perhaps a manifestation of a defensive desire to hold on to theater's centrality when talking about Shakespeare. I had not realized, when reading in the 2000 season brochure about this Exhibition being "the biggest in the world dedicated to Shakespeare and his workplace" (perhaps size being a sign of substantial U.S. investment in this project), that the subsequent sentence's "will" was imperative: "A visit will include a guided tour of the Globe Theatre." The young man at the entrance desk would not sell me a simple ticket to the Exhibition, because that day a special offer was being touted, by which one could both visit the Exhibition and take a tour of the stage of the Globe for a reduced fee. But I had attended several plays at the theater, had worked in others, and had neither desire nor time that day to take the stage tour. I just wanted to visit the Exhibition. I was willing to pay the same amount as the combined visit, and yet my request still was unacceptable. Clearly, the mass machinery did not anticipate such a visitor, nor did it wish to make space for someone who might want the scholarship or the modern media without a sense of the theatrical space, and moreover without attention to the current troupe and their acting space. Only after a good deal of pleading did I manage to shuffle inside, by this time feeling guilty about imperiling the young man's job (he might get "caught" letting someone in to study rather than go onstage). Shakespeare meets Kafka.

Inside, attempts at learning were not entirely thwarted, but they were not unambiguously encouraged either. Barbara Hodgdon remarks that Stratford's "Empire of Shakespeare" "turns tourists into readers—and, moreover, readers of English." The new Exhibition, by contrast, is enough to make one nostalgic for what Hodgdon critiques. Though more subtly than at Busch Gardens, modern technological effects sometimes seemed to be displacing rather than displaying Shakespeare, and with him, even the partial versions of "history" that Stratford sells. Getting past the self-congratulatory corridor about the financing and building of the new Globe, featuring the transatlantic alliance of American Sam Wanamaker and British Mark Rylance, I finally reached the material about Shakespeare's world. Several glass cases, interspersed between interactive screens and video machines, did include textual information and a few objects from the time of Shakespeare. But the designers did not deem this to be of sufficient interest in itself, and so had arranged the lighting to dim and brighten periodically, spotlighting one area and then another. At first I thought this was meant to highlight certain ideas or associations, a train of thought and information, within the case, but I soon discovered otherwise. Just as I made it through about half of the text in one area, the light was gone, hopping to another section of the cabinet randomly, and not returning for several minutes. Unless one had speed-reading skills and exceptional patience, it was nearly impossible simply to take in the information displayed—much less consider its value and sequence. It took quite some time for me to decipher what a single case "said," by which time I had realized that the lighting was simply for effect and worked on the assumption nobody really wanted to stand and read text. The designers did not trust us to, indeed hardly allowed us to, become engaged with the historical material. It was there for show.

What the Exhibition lacked in dedication to history, it partially made up for in its interest in the theatrical workplace of Shakespeare, with areas for children to play with costume-making and makeup pigments. As in the older-fashioned Stratford heritage sites, the Globe Exhibition attempts to bridge the historical gap as well as acknowledge it, but here with a greater emphasis on what this organization regards as valuable now. If times have changed, by pretending and using "the same" methods and materials, historical distance supposedly disappears. Video programs allow one better to understand the processes by which gods descended on stage machinery, blood was spilt, or characters were hung. Small booths also allow one to listen to an impressive array of great actors performing short passages from Shakespeare's plays, nicely representing the audio of modern performance. One expects that the Exhibition, like the Globe itself, will become more ambitious and capacious in time, especially given its success as a tourist attraction. Currently it could only be called the "biggest" in terms of square feet, many of which are empty; what sort of material will come to fill it, and whether it will make the Exhibition another theme park version of Shakespeare, remains to be seen. If it continues as it is going, this will not be a faux-nostalgic royalist construction of the sort Hodgdon perceives at Stratford, but rather a faux-historical celebration of theater people as presently conceived (with an emphasis on emotions, process, and celebration, acknowledging the market but acting as if they themselves are neither tainted by it nor a mere product of it).

Indeed, the entire "Shakespeare's Globe" enterprise hovers, sometimes in schizoid fashion, between theme park entertainment and mystified Bardic tributes, on the one hand, and attempts at something closer to re-creation of early modern staging and dedication to repertory theater, on the other. The author figure here functions more to serve the troupe than vice versa. And yet, at the same time, rather bold attempts are being made to recover what earlier troupes played. Two of the main-stage productions each season are not familiar Shakespearean moneymakers, thus affording audiences a chance to see plays that no filmmaker or Broadway producer will ever finance: Richard Brome's "The Antipodes," for example. On Bank Holiday Monday in August, a summer revels show included not only the entertainments one might find on "ye olde Renaissance faire" circuit, but also a production of George Peele's *The Old Wives Tale*. And the Globe-to-Globe International Theater season allows a more vital form of international representation, certainly, than was ever seen at Busch Gardens. Meanwhile, down the street, the distinction between "real" history and theme park entertainment has been architecturally elided, as one can see the "original" Big Ben hazily pointing skyward through the spokes of the Millennium Wheel.

The oscillations evidenced by Shakespeare's Globe are ultimately comparable to those made by hundreds of repertory theaters and college professors, vying for attention in a busy mass media world while trying in some way to hold on to a process, a text, or a tradition that contains something they consider of value. What is interesting is how often this shared, conflicted position is overlooked or even denied by academics and theater people alike, with one group turning on the other. In my experience, this most often takes the form of theater practitioners mocking academics or incorrectly imagining professors taking positions that can serve in a straw man argument against some imagined pure, rigid adherence to an idolized Shakespeare and a letter-perfect representation of the past (cf. Al Pacino's *Looking for Richard* (1996), which also, oddly given his performative biases, finds him seeking cosmic vibrations at Shakespeare's house *and* at this new Globe simulacrum, as if they were equivalent). I have, within the preceding anecdotal accounts, in some places given fodder to those who would see me as such a professor. But in the process of recounting these experiences with Shakespeare after mass media I have also tried to complicate such views, in a sense exemplifying the same schizoid play between present celebration and adherence to historicism that can be discerned at "Shakespeare's" many, mass-marketed Globes. I would like to conclude by sketching some of the positions that I have noticed coming into conflict, less with the aim of erasing them than with the idea that articulation may make the falseness of some of the dichotomies (and the smugness and despair among some subcultures) less seductive.

Attitudes within the academia toward the representation of Shakespeare are one notable case of a general phenomenon that arises when one considers artworks from other times being adapted to contemporary media. Extreme positions do exist, though fairly occasionally, on each side—and are then turned into the whole opposition by those wishing to escape the schizoid realities of Shakespeare after mass media. One extreme position is that of the antiquarian purist, who thinks we can never do justice to the particularity and texture of the past, and our representations thus block and mar access to the "original" (be that Shakespeare's brain or his text or the political culture). The other extreme is that of the cultural narcissist (the term is intentionally polemical, and best describes a subset of those involved in new media studies and performance), who thinks that the past is completely inaccessible and hence there's no point in trying to be anything other than ourselves; moreover, that the delight of performance is its exploration of that "freedom" in one's own moment of creativity, prompting the audience to "relate to" it directly—in its worst manifestations, this basically being a form of idolatry of one's own image.

Idolatry was one of the charges against the Elizabethan stage too, and is a frequent charge against artistic representation when it represents anything of value; that is, the image or embodiment replaces or damages the thing being represented. The bizarre and interesting form of performance idolatry tries to collapse the distinction between past and present entirely, or between presentation and representation. It would seem quite different to put a mystical faith in Shakespeare's First Folio and to put a mystical faith in one's own body and its present-day freedom to enact that Folio text, yet these are conflated in the performance version of Shakespeare idolatry.[4] In the academic/historicist version, a similar collapse takes place: between devotion to Shakespeare's text(s) and to the cultural contexts in which they were generated. In each case, "Shakespeare" takes on much more importance than a mere theme park show, and becomes the shadowy occasion for indignation at those with a different temporal focus. The idolatry comes in the attitude toward Shakespeare as the immanent location of what matters then or now; rather than recognizing his texts as representations *and* his own figure as a representation for these phenomena, priorities, or valued experiences, he becomes the thing itself, the site of the authentic. To mess with Shakespeare, then, becomes an act of messing with those beliefs.

If, to rephrase in a simplified form that addresses the temporal distinction, the two extremes toward historical or artistic representation in modern media are the idolator of the past and the idolator of oneself, the more moderate positions from which the extremes derive make good sense: one is a sense of history, of the need to understand another time and culture and human being; the other is a sense of performativity, the delights of drama as involving an event in the moment, in living bodies and in the resources of theatricality and, in a more complicated way, new media.

As digitalization has again made the medium the message in a particularly urgent way, there is a perceived imperative to use new media whenever possible, a perceived imperative current not only among practitioners in new media and in marketing, but in traditional fields. Certainly any project with a mass market audience at present will feel pressure from many quarters to make it current and multimedia. In response to that pressure, some celebrate, just as they do with performativity, while others perceive constraint and historical erasure. This gets acted out in most cases not as a worry about history, however, but as a worry about the author figure. In thinking back to Shakespeare at the Busch Gardens Globe, or in *Caliban on Yellow Sands,* or at the Shakespeare's Globe Exhibition, one keeps discovering a double image: a mass media experience, and the figure of an originary author lurking behind. Only in *Pirates!* has Shakespeare almost completely disappeared. It is as a result an easier show simply to enjoy without vexation or concern: it has no loyalty to a past at all, being all about experience. Yet even there, the maps on the walls remain as traces, and some ghost of a desire to remember history remains, perverse and perverted as it may be. And in that sense, maybe the new Busch could help us in the work of untangling the threads that have become entwined in a less than useful ball with the result that some wish simply to break free rather than think back at all. If we can decenter the author without decentering either historicism or an interest in live performance processes, more common ground might be found between those currently on opposite ends of the academic/theater divide. Instead of being at one another's throats, we might turn to investigate the economics that make this distinction—outside certain professional fields—fairly trivial. And with that might come more innovative ways of collaborating in the production of "Shakespeare" entertainments that talk to, rather than kowtow or patronize, a mass audience.

Mass media in the form of advertising works to make us idolators not of the past but of the present—or rather, of the absent presence of our contemporaries who have what we are trained to desire. Mass media versions of Shakespeare the theme park necessarily include marketing divisions and modern mechanics, yet those machines and people can also work with performers and scholars, reanimating a past with different values or modes of thinking. Within the world of global capitalism, such an action can be something other than mere nostalgia or reactionary mystification, in that it fights against mass amnesia and tries to give consumers access to more than the present model in which they buy and are sold. The people who have tried to sell Shakespeare and literary history to Busch Gardens again, unsuccessfully, saw themselves not as old-fashioned upholders of the Bard, in fact, but as marketing a better show, which respected its mass audience's intelligence a bit more—because they were interested in "history" in a fanciful form. Those who continue to teach the poetry of Shakespeare do so not only because it is somehow elevating but because it is more fun when you "get it," and they do so on the presumption that anybody who takes some time can do so. To continue in these endeavors is to reject the merely "post-hermeneutic" status of much Schlockspeare, without retreating from the recognition that mass appropriations and media play are intrinsic to any vital study of "Shakespeare." Such study will not necessarily make us any purer or less embedded in economic structures that market Shakespeare the commodity. That would take a massive cultural and political change. But while we ponder that larger prospect, may the most imaginative actors and most careful scholars soon sign on and add their voices to whatever becomes the newest, best version of Shakespeare, the theme park.

Notes

1. See John Drakakis, 24–41, and Howard and Shershow. The Globe's initial offerings, problems, and potential were much discussed at the SCAENA conference (Shakespeare and His Contemporaries in Performance) at St. John's College, Cambridge University, U.K., August 13–15, 1997, in talks by Andrew Gurr, John Barton, and Dennis Kennedy, among others.
2. See also Bristol's more wide-ranging discussion of Shakespeare in modern America. I refer particularly to Kennedy's SCAENA keynote and his subsequent article in *Theatre Journal*, and McLuskie's talk at the Shakespeare Association of America meeting in Montreal, Canada, Spring 2000, revised as an essay on the consumerist bard for *Renaissance Drama*. My thanks to Professor McLuskie for sharing her working draft of that essay with me.
3. See Holderness's "Bardolatory" and Hodgdon's "Stratford's Empire of Shakespeare; Or, Fantasies of Origin, Authorship, and Authenticity: The Museum and the Souvenir" (*The Shakespeare Trade*, chapter 6).
4. See for example Kristin Linklater's method throughout *Freeing Shakespeare's Voice;* William B. Worthen has well documented these contradictory impulses among a wide range of performance scholars and artists.

Works Cited

Bristol, Michael. 1996. *Big-Time Shakespeare,* London, Routledge, 1996.

Drakakis, John. 1988. "Theatre, Ideology, and Institution: Shakespeare and the Roadsweepers." In Holderness, ed., 24–41.

Hodgdon, Barbara. 1998. *The Shakespeare Trade: Performances and Appropriations.* Philadelphia: Univ. of Pennsylvania Press.

Holderness, Graham. 1988. "Bardolatory: or, The Cultural Materialist's Guide to Stratford-upon-Avon." In Holderness, ed. 2–15.

———. ed. 1988. *The Shakespeare Myth.* Manchester: Manchester Univ. Press.

Howard, Jean and Scott Cutler Shershow. 2001. *Marxist Shakespeares.* London and New York: Routledge.

Huxtable, Ada Louise. 1997. *The Unreal America: Architecture and Illusion.* New York: The New Press.

Kennedy, Dennis. 1998. "Shakespeare and Cultural Tourism." *Theatre Journal* 50.2: 175–188.

Levine, Lawrence W. 1988. *Highbrow/Lowbrow: The Emergence of Cultural Hierarchy in America.* Cambridge, MA: Harvard Univ. Press.

Linklater, Kristin. 1992. *Freeing Shakespeare's Voice: The Actor's Guide to Talking the Text.* NY: Theatre Communications Group.

McLuskie, Kathleen. "The Commercial Bard." Forthcoming in *Renaissance Drama.*

Worthen, William B. 1997. *Shakespeare and the Authority of Performance.* Cambridge: Cambridge Univ. Press.

CHAPTER 5

HARLEQUIN PRESENTS

That '70s Shakespeare and Beyond

LAURIE E. OSBORNE

Throughout the late twentieth century and in to the millennium, we have grown accustomed to Shakespearean allusions in several forms of mass culture. Not only does a talking Jack Russell terrier play Prince Hal, Romeo, and Ariel on assorted episodes of the PBS show *Wishbone*, but the novelizations of those episodes rewrite Shakespeare for the terrier's audience. From a *Romeo and Juliet* Pokémon episode (with warring Pokémon masters owning a pair of Pokémon lovers named Maria and Tony) to *Shakespeare: The Animated Tales* and comic book versions, children's mass culture may seem a traditional locus for Shakespearean plots; however, adolescents are watching *10 Things I Hate about You* (dir. Gil Junger, 1998) and playing computer games like *The Curse of Monkey Island* (1997), wherein they can see Slappy Cromwell rehearse bits of *Speare*, his forty-five minute compilation of Shakespeare plays, and *Safecracker* (2000), in which they read a parody called MacBreath, by William Shapesphere. Although they may have trouble finding it, they can even play *Hamlet: A Murder Mystery* (1997), which uses extensive footage from Kenneth Branagh's 1996 film but allows the gamer as Hamlet to retrieve his ten wits, survive, and be crowned king of Denmark by punishing the guilty and sparing the innocent. They read novels like Carol Matas's *Cloning Miranda* (1999) and Welwyn Wilton Katz's *Come like Shadows* (1993). Young fans of Bruce Colville's *Alien* series probably also read his novel *The Skull of Truth* (1997), starring Yorick's skull from *Hamlet*.

Shakespeare also appears throughout adult popular fiction. Susan Baker has argued that Shakespeare and the Shakespearean artifacts that populate murder mysteries help to justify the literary status of classic detective fiction. Her essays on the detective story's use of Shakespearean relics and allusions predate *Shakespearean Whodunnits* (1997), wherein 1990s mystery writers take their own crack at solving and sometimes creating Shakespearean mysteries. However, the recent Shakespeare craze has not been limited to the near-high art of mysteries or books ratified by *New York Times* bestseller list like John Updike's *Claudius and Gertrude* (2000) or Robert Nye's *The Late Mr. Shakespeare* (2000). In a culture that has produced an astonishing three films of *Hamlet* in eleven years, it is not surprising that the problems facing the Danish prince also make an unexpected but pointed appearance during a discussion about the duty to revenge fathers in Lois McMaster Bujold's *A Civil Campaign* (1999), the latest in the Hugo Award-winning science fiction series featuring Miles Vorkorsigan. Even more extensively, John Varley follows a transgalactic Shakespearean actor from his performances of Romeo to King Lear in *The Golden Globe* (1998). Even self-help books are not immune; witness *Will Power: Using Shakespeare's Insights to Transform Your Life* (1996).

The much maligned genre of romance fiction has produced an enormous array of Shakespearean references. Christina Dodd's 1994 novel (reprinted in 1999), *The Greatest Lover in All England,* includes both Shakespeare and "Rosencrantz," the boy-actress who is really the actress-heroine who first plays Ophelia. Among recent historical romances, Julie Beard's *Romance of the Rose* (1998) features Shakespeare, and its heroine, Rosalind, is the ghostwriter of *The Taming of the Shrew;* and, more dramatically still, in Malia Martin's *Much Ado About Love* (2000) Shakespeare *is* the heroine, whose real name is Olivia and who turns out also to be Queen Elizabeth's illegitimate daughter.

All these allusions fit admirably in "Schlockspeare," as Richard Burt has defined it in the introduction to this book. Even substantive appearances by Shakespeare or his plays in genre fiction especially partake of the designedly ephemeral quality of disposable entertainment. The sheer range of these allusions leave us to wonder what purpose Shakespeare serves in cultural productions that eschew "high art" aspirations and often celebrate their own specialized, even topical appeal to small transitory audiences.

Nowhere is the planned obsolescence of genre fiction more pronounced than in serial romance fiction. Harlequin initially sold series romances as explicitly mass media commodities, even marketing sample books in boxes of Kotex and distributing them with Avon cosmetics (Glescoe 1996, 86–69). Published monthly in defined categories rather than as individual, freestanding novels, series romances acquired their name not because their narratives are linked and ongoing (as in soap operas), but because their "brand name" is issued in a series and even numbered. The appeal is not the hook on going narrative (or even of author recognition until recently) but of the repeated and regular appearance of recognizable generic forms. In this mass production of books, Shakespeare has developed a surprisingly large presence. Among recent Silhouette Romance offerings, Helen Myers draws on *Shrew* for *Kiss Me, Kate* (1990), Kasey Michaels offers *Romeo in the Rain* (1990), and Natalie Bishop foregrounds her Shakespearean theme with *A Love Like Romeo and Juliet* (1993) (although the novel only briefly alludes to the play). Harlequin publishes Judith Arnold's *Just Like Romeo and Juliet* (1993), in which the heroine touches Juliet's statue in Verona for luck and receives the ghostly aid of Juliet herself. Even more striking, Regency series romances abound in Shakespeare. During the nine months from October 1999 to June 2000, Shakespeare figures in thirteen of twenty-seven Signet Regencies released.

This recent inundation of Shakespeare tends to obscure the fact that Shakespeare has appeared throughout the history of series romances. The Bard sightings/citings in series romance occur within a complex history and reflect the contention for readers between romance lines from different publishing houses and especially between subgenres. Using both Harlequin's own account and Paul Glescoe's aptly titled *The Merchants of Venus*, which recounts Harlequin's remarkable success since its inception, I track the ebb and flow of Shakespearean references in the context of the development of series romances through the 1970s, '80s, and '90s. Harlequin's complex publishing history provides the context for surprisingly various elaborations on Shakespeare's plays and characters. I argue that the significance of Shakespearean references within series romance is crucially tied to its generic development, particularly to the emergence of subgenres.

Moreover, series romance serves as the test case for my larger contention that looking only at the current flood of Shakespearean allusions is not sufficient to analyze Shakespeare's position in mass culture, in part because mass culture, imposed and formulaically constructed, is not monolithic, never entirely just "mass" rather than "popular" media. (See Richard Burt's introduction for a discussion of the two.) Burgeoning Shakespearean references in the late 1990s responded in part to challenges facing emergent or endangered subgenres in the marketplace of mass fiction. Moreover, the variations in Shakespearean citation during the development of particular genres of popular fiction are crucial for understanding the appropriation of Shakespeare into these different formats. As Shakespearean allusion becomes one component in the struggle for difference in the outwardly homogeneous racks of monthly series romances, Schlockspeare evolves as the forms themselves carve out audiences, status, and, as a result, their relative claims to escape the disposable conditions of their own production. Shakespeare's connotations of permanence and status are apparently dismissed in the inevitable loss and critical dismissal of genre fiction; however, invoking his name or works at the same time stakes the claim that Shakespeare can enable a change in status as specialized productions in mass culture constitute themselves as popular culture. To put it another way, there is trash Shakespeare and there is trash Shakespeare that attempts to distinguish itself from trash Shakespeare.

Early Harlequin Shakespeare

At first Shakespeare appeared erratically in series fiction, in part because the original Harlequins, the first to explore marketing books in North American supermarkets, drugstores, and mail-order, appeared in the 1940s and '50s and played out fantasies linked to early adventure fiction rather than romance. For the first two decades or so, there were male writers as well as a healthy proportion of female novelists. Marketed out of Canada, Harlequin soon recognized that the occasional doctor/nurse romances were selling well and contracted for the North American rights to publish the British Mills and Boon romances in paperback. Harlequin's enormous success in marketing their slender romances soon came to be matched by huge numbers of these books produced and purchased monthly. Although Harlequin achieved enough success by the late 1970s to become the "name brand" of romance, by the early '80s their strategies and a misguided move in canceling their distribution contract with Simon & Schuster soon created rivals as other publishing houses created their own series.

The relative paucity of Shakespearean allusions in the original Harlequin series through 1979 (only nine novels bear Shakespearean titles in over two thousand published between 1949 and 1979, and a smattering more contain references) is not an accurate index of later series or of the significance of the allusions. (See *Thirty Years of Harlequin: 1949–1979*). Some early Harlequins offer a surprisingly sophisticated level of engagement with Shakespeare, interactions that differ notably from their successors in the 1990s. Overt multiple references to Shakespeare in recent romance novels do not arise in a void but within genres and subgenres as they emerge and compete for audiences.

Admittedly, some early Harlequins include only slight references like Flora Kidd's *Love Alters Not* (1968), which offers just a Shakespearean title, epigram, and single allusion to Sonnet 116.[1] However, even the slightest references can carry more weight than you might expect. For example, Janet Dailey, the first U.S. novelist to publish with Mills and Boon and thus break into writing Harlequins, incorporates Shakespeare briefly into an early novel. Dailey's U.S. settings and especially her heroines were different, as Paul Glescoe notes: "Dailey . . . did write a heroine with a certain American-style spunk. . . . Typical was *Valley of the Vapours* [1976] . . . the setting is the Ozark hills of Arkansas, and the 19-year-old heroine, Tisha (or Red, as the hero prefers), drives a Mustang, pursues a career in art, knows her Shakespeare, and says things such as 'Sometimes I wish I had been born a man'" (120–21). However, Tisha's "spunk" disappears when a happy ending overtakes her, and Glescoe's comment draws on a single exchange between Tisha and Roarke, where she recognizes his allusion to *Taming of the Shrew* and counters with her own. Nonetheless, for Glescoe, a single allusion becomes the mark of acceptability for both the American author and the American character breaking into the solidly British publishing base of early Harlequin romance.

Other 1970s Harlequins incorporate Shakespeare more thoroughly. Among three early novels by Elizabeth Ashton that invoke Shakespeare, both *Sigh No More* (1973) and *My Lady Disdain* (1976) announce their connections to *Much Ado About Nothing* in their very titles. In *Sigh No More*, the opening two lines of Balthazar's song become the heroine's talisman against future heartache. Given as the epigram, "Sigh no more, ladies, sigh no more / Men were deceivers ever" surfaces first when Imogene encounters a Shakespearean TV production after the faithlessness of her longtime swain, Raymond, and the disturbing volatility in her latest interest, Christian: "This was a Shakespeare production, *Much Ado About Nothing*, and the song in it seemed to have a personal message for her. . . . [song] Men were deceivers all, and she would sigh after none of them, neither Christian nor Raymond, but let them go. Shakespeare knew what he was writing about" (56–57). The deceit of men becomes her refrain whenever she uncovers bad male behavior, even though the novel's point is that Christian will ultimately assure that she "sighs no more." The Shakespearean reference here is little more than a displaced romantic mantra, offering the principle that Shakespeare knows what he is writing about.

The more elaborate treatments often include explicit critiques of the very Shakespearean situations that the novels invoke. As a result, Shakespeare may "know what he was writing about," but his knowledge is rejected, sometimes violently. Like Imogen, Jacqueline in Ashton's *My Lady Disdain* receives her Shakespearean tag rather than seeking it out. When she finally asks why Gino calls her "my lady disdain," he directs her to read her Shakespeare:

> She searched through the family bookshelves, and did find a battered Shakespeare. She proceeded to wade through *Much Ado About Nothing*, but could not make much of Beatrice's archaic wit, which seemed close akin to rudeness. . . . Regarding the play, she got the message. The couple sparred whenever they met, yet eventually, with the help of some engineering on the part of their friends, they fell in love. She closed the book with a bang. Possibly it made good comedy from a theatrical point of view, but it was too unrealistic to be true to life, and nothing could be more improbable than a romance between her and Gino Rossellini. (Ashton 1976, 26)

Nonetheless, Beatrice's fate proves impossible to avoid; at the end of the novel, Gino says, "I'll stop your mouth" and kisses her. She acknowledges the reference in telling fashion: "dimly she recalled the words he had used came from the play that he had once told her to read. Beatrice's and Benedick's 'merry warfare' had ended in marriage, and so had hers" (Ashton 1973,189). Although the heroine may indeed seem dim in accepting the Shakespearean ending she has once rejected, she also remembers the line, read and discarded months ago. Her knowledge here is both functional and romantic. Her awareness of the line's origin signals her current alliance with Gino as well as her status as his mate; Shakespeare's happy ending under-scores hers—and her silencing.

The Taming of the Shrew serves the same function even more explicitly at the end of Valerie Thian's Oh, Kiss Me Kate (1971). Though most of the novel has little Shakespearean content beyond the constant quarrelling of the main characters, Kate, like Jacqueline, has been ordered to read Shakespeare and confesses finally that she followed the advice:

> One night, after you'd made me so mad, calling me [shrew], I fired my Shakespeare right across the room in a tantrum. But in the morning I read the Shrew right through. . . . And I remember the bit at the end when Kate swears her obedience:
> > "I am ashamed that women are so simple
> > To offer war where they should kneel for peace,
> > Or seek for rule, supremacy and sway
> > When they are bound to serve, love, and obey."
> > It made me cross at the time. . . . But now, darling, it's so ex-
> > actly right. You've tamed your shrew. (Thian 1971, 186)

Kate in this scenario expresses her anger by physically throwing Shakespeare away, but she ultimately submits by quoting Kate's most troublesome speech and accepting it as her own. The twist is that her lover then rejects her new docility, asking "are you really tamed, my love? Tamed by your Petruchio? Not completely, I hope—I always felt that Katharina was rather too subservient in the end. Stay a little on the wold side, just for me. It's such fun, darling!" (Thian 1971, 187). The novel overtly embraces the logic in Shrew that feminist critics like Lynda Boose have critiqued so vigorously, and the minimal space it leaves for affirmation of aggressive female speech allows that speech as "such fun" for men.

As these two novels illustrate, Shakespeare's plays, and specifically their models of comic union, can serve as focal points of the female anger that Tania Modleski has identified within the romance novel (1982, 24–37). As the lightning rod drawing the heroine's anger, Shakespeare becomes available to a notable level of early feminist critique. The Harlequins of the 1970s that engage his plays most thoroughly often expose the patriarchal dangers to women within them rather than simply acknowledging that Shakespeare "knew what he was writing about."

For example, in Ashton's *The Player King* (1975), our actress-heroine, Jocelyn, falls for the actor-hero while playing a member of the fairy chorus to his Oberon in *A Midsummer Night's Dream*. However, the fairy king that so fascinates her is not a benign figure: "according to robust Elizabethan humour, the trick Oberon plays upon his wife would be considered a great joke and it is necessary to the plot, but it was no joke in Dorian's hands. He brought to his interpretation of his role a vindictiveness that was spine-chilling" (Ashton 1975,13). Long before current readings of Oberon's vindictiveness and abuse, Ashton identifies the troubling aspects of Oberon's character and uses them throughout Jocelyn's romance which develops around Dorian's own "changeling boy."

More extensively, Jane Donnelly's *Dear Caliban* (1977) uses Shakespeare's *Tempest* and self-conscious, critical revisions of its social dynamics in order to explore and partially debunk the conventionally passive Harlequin heroine identified so critically by Ann Bar Snitnow (1983, 248–50). In this novel the passive heroine is Abigail, the pampered princess daughter of famous actor, Leo Lansing. He and his wife Helen met while playing Shakespeare's star-crossed Romeo and Juliet and produce a daughter who becomes a Miranda figure. Leo is identified as an egocentric, manipulative Prospero-father throughout the novel. Although Abbie first invokes *The Tempest*, her hero, Max Routledge, recognizes the coercion of Prospero and consequently of Miranda's father:

> She said, "It's magical by moonlight, your island. Like the island in Shakespeare's *Tempest*. . . . Perhaps we're Prospero and Miranda?"
>
> "As one Miranda was a princess and another a mermaid you could well be Miranda," he said.
>
> "And as you have a magical island you should be Prospero." Tall and strong and powerful, but old, so that wasn't Max. He laughed and asked,
>
> "How many fathers do you want?"
>
> The last thing she wanted was to be a daughter to Max . . .
>
> "I think I've got the wrong cast list."
>
> "I could always be Caliban."
>
> "The Monster." She acted shocked. "The demi-devil?"
>
> "I've always felt that Caliban had a bad deal. Turned into a one-man chain gang for making a pass at Miranda. . . . Strictly speaking, the island was Caliban's. He should have been nobody's slave."
>
> "So it was. . . . Caliban was there first, wasn't he?"
>
> (Donnelly 1977, 105)

Recasting Caliban's attempted rape of Miranda as "making a pass" is just the sort of exculpatory account of male violence that feminist critics of romance deplore, but Max is equally involved in reframing Prospero's account of his own benevolence and of Miranda's character. Initially, Abbie may concede that she and Caliban are misrepresented, but it takes her longer to recognize the accuracy of Max's reading of Prospero's character—and her father's—if the suitor is not a demi-devil.

If Leo Lansing plays Prospero as the nasty, obstructive parent of a Harlequin romance, Miranda/Abbie proves to be far stronger and less passive than her enforced, public role as princess to his king seems. She does all the cooking, cleaning, and hard housework to maintain their "castle" in order to protect the arthritic family housekeeper whom her father would dismiss without a second thought for her disability. In addition to domestic competence—here portrayed as a tough and unacknowledged job—Abbie also swims through perilous waters and actively pursues the hero, provoked by his open dislike of her on sight. Although she accepts her Miranda-role, Max's palpable scorn for it echoes her own discontent and shocks her out of her normal mode.

When she stows away on his boat and they end up working together to restore his island house, she proves her toughness and capability, winning his love. He recognizes her father as his principal rival long before she does, especially when she propositions him:

"What do you think would have happened if Miranda had made the pass at Caliban, on their magic island, instead of the other way around?"

"Not a thing," said Max promptly. "Prospero would have seen to that."

Miranda's father, the magician. . . . "My father played Prospero in the other Stratford-on-Avon, the one in Ontario, a couple of seasons ago."

"That figures," said Max. (Donnelly 1977, 138–39)

Abbie's comments use the Shakespearean play to reveal the force separating the lovers, although she herself does not fully realize it. Despite numerous difficulties created by her father, who attempts to bribe Max, blackens her character (she is frail, needy, and totally dependent on wealth), and ultimately feigns illness to separate them, Abbie persists in her love for "Caliban" over "Prospero," firmly established as the alternate identities for lover and father. However, Prospero/Leo is not fully cast as the villain, since his ultimate capitulation and exploitation of what he cannot change will mean that he will "play the proud father of the bride" (186–87), much as Prospero himself does.

If Donnelly's sympathetic reading of Caliban as the owner of the island and winner of the girl, rather than rapist, offers an unexpectedly contemporary

take on the play, Kay Thorpe's *Curtain Call* (1971) foreshadows and complicates Linda Charnes's argument that criticism of *Antony and Cleopatra* has
been waylaid by "the love story . . . one of the most pervasive and effective—
yet least deconstructed—of all ideological apparatuses" (1992, 1). Although
Charnes notes that "this isn't to say that Shakespeare has written a Harlequin
romance or even anticipated it" (3), Thorpe has certainly anticipated Charnes's
question: "how is reading Shakespeare's play like reading a Harlequin romance?" (4). However, Thorpe offers her answer from within a romance. In
Curtain Call, the naive heroine is Kerry West, an actress trying out for the part
of Charmian in *Antony and Cleopatra*. The hero, Ryan Maxwell, is inevitably
the lead actor who plays Antony. Though approving his portrayal, Kerry criticizes the lead actress's interpretation: "There was something in her interpretation of Cleopatra, even now emerging, which Kerry herself did not care for.
Unless she was very much mistaken, the lovely and temperamental actress saw
her role as that of twin protagonist. And that, temptation though it undoubtedly was, was entirely wrong because Shakespeare himself had intended only
one—Antony" (37–38). Kerry's complete faith that the play belongs to
Antony jars with her frequent assertions that the play offers "a vision of perfect love between two people who have experienced almost all that life has to
offer" (20), and with Harlequin's own generic requirement that the *heroine* be
the primary protagonist.

Maxwell's analysis, in turn, deflates her "vision," pointing out that both
characters are "totally unscrupulous in their ambitions" (20). Despite his
presence in a Harlequin novel, Maxwell espouses the more opportunistic
view that Charnes opposes to the Harlequin-style ideology of romantic love:

> "I mean for what she is and never ceases to be: wanton, possessive, and totally
> ruthless."
>
> "Oh, no, that's not true!" Kerry's voice was impassioned, the identity of
> her advisor forgotten for the moment. "At first, yes, she is all those things. But
> not after Antony dies. She kills herself for love!"
>
> "She kills herself," returned Ryan evenly, "because her pride and vanity can-
> not accept the degradation planned for her by Caesar. Certainly she's toyed
> with the idea before, but it isn't until Dolabella confirms what her instincts
> have told her that her resolve finally hardens. . . . Shakespeare conceived her as
> a woman of shallow nature, and that's how she should be played. It wouldn't
> be a popular interpretation but it would be a true one." (Thorpe 1971, 70–71)

When his niece then worries whether he can play opposite an interpretation that he does not believe, Maxwell acknowledges that "Cleopatra has been
idealized for so long in the theatre, it would take a very brave actress indeed
to try putting her across in any other manner but the accepted one" (71).
Maxwell makes precisely Charnes's point that the ideology of sacrifice for love

obscures the actual decisions made in the play. Of course, he does so within the very genre that Charnes identifies as promoting that "pernicious" ideology. Although Ryan, like Max in *Dear Caliban,* offers a masculine-voiced Shakespearean critique, Thorpe and Donnelly are using those male voices, as well as Shakespeare's plots and characters, to explore and challenge some crucial conventional features of the popular genre in which they write—the Mills and Boon/Harlequin romance. The love story, perhaps especially when it alludes to Shakespeare, interrogates its own conventions.

For example, in *Curtain Call* Thorpe explores the theatrical problems of interpreting Cleopatra in terms of female rivalries as typically presented in Harlequin romance during its most dominant period. Paula Vincent, the beautiful, experienced actress playing Cleopatra and trying to play Ryan, does well in the first two acts but cannot achieve the necessary transformation into great love required in the third section of the play (as staged by this director). Her reviews praise the first part of her performance but not the last. Just as important, when she tries to scuttle the performance by conveniently claiming a migraine and refusing to go on, Kerry must play Cleopatra. Paula in effect commits professional "suicide," risking her theatrical career in her Cleopatra-like desire for center stage. Kerry, on the other hand, although initially terrified of the task and hesitant in her performance, "grows" into the role as play progresses (with Ryan's support, of course). Her final act is spectacular because she has decided to play her love for him. Thus the novel solves the problem expressed in the conflicting readings of Cleopatra's nature by splitting her role between the two actresses.

Although the book ultimately espouses the "romantic" reading of Cleopatra that Maxwell asserts is inescapable, Thorpe also encodes the opposing reading within the classic Harlequin plot and characters. The doubled possibilities for interpreting Shakespeare's Cleopatra expose and test the established Harlequin female character types—the naïve yet triumphant heroine and the sexually experienced, opportunistic woman who loses at love. The novel in effect achieves the split characterization of Cleopatra in ways that criticism supposedly cannot, and, in the process, pushes the naive heroine into acting the *entire* role of Cleopatra.

The Harlequins of the 1970s inadvertently betray the complacency of an emergent yet dominant new genre, albeit one basically ignored by traditional publishers and literary critics. The marked ascendancy of Harlequin in romance publishing until the early '80s translated into the stricter generic formulas dictated by the need for many manuscripts to satisfy established reader tastes. Unchallenged by external competition and committed to a winning formula, Harlequin achieved a success that ultimately enabled some of its authors to meditate on the genre's features and conventions, as Donnelly's and Thorpe's novels demonstrate. These popular Harlequin writers used Shakespeare to ratify their generic model—impossibly naive heroines, rapacious female losers, manipulative, powerful fathers and father figures, and transcendent true love are features that Shakespeare apparently shares with Harlequin romance novels. However, neither Harlequin conventions nor Shakespeare's plots and characters emerge in these novels without critique.

Romance Wars

The 1980s featured extensive upheavals both in Harlequin and in more traditional publishing houses that began to launch their own romance lines in response to Harlequin's unexpected success and emerging distribution problems. In addition to their American Romances, Harlequin began to develop an array of specialized lines: "Harlequin Temptations, 'sensually charged contemporary romantic fantasies,' . . . Romantic Intrigues 'set against the backdrop of suspense and adventure,' Gothic romances 'with [an] element of foreboding or hidden evil,' and Regency Romances 'set in England between 1811 and 1820'" (Glescoe 1996, 189). At the same time, other publishing houses were releasing their own romance lines, following the lead of Simon & Schuster which produced its Silhouette Romances, written by American authors.

The upshot of the "romance wars," as they were called, was a proliferation of the number and kind of romances being published: "In 1981, there were 30 romance titles being published each month; two years later there were a 100 more, 22 of them published by Harlequin, whose market share had shrunk by half" (Glescoe 1996, 168). Sheer competition for readers produced different marketing approaches (like Loveswept's author-based series), different degrees of sensuality (Second-Chance-at-Love by Berkeley, Harlequin Temptations, etc.), and different locales and historical contexts (Harlequin American Romances and Regency romance series by Coventry, Dell, Jove, Signet, Avon, and later Zebra Books). Mass market romances also began to appear—lengthy historical romance novels not published explicitly under a series "brand name." Such competitive self-definition produced a greater Shakespearean presence in series romance. In 1982 alone, at least twelve novels in six different series allude to the plays or quote lines. That increase might seem a predictable result of increased publication, but all twelve examples I have found so far from 1982 appear in Regency or Georgian series. The allusions range from minor ones like the heroine's visit to the theater to see Kean play Richard III in Joyce Lee's *Perchance to Dream* (Dell Candlelight Regency 1982) to extensive, even exhausting Shakespearean allusions in Joan Smith's *Lover's Vows* (Coventry Romances 1982). Regencies also include dramatically different modes of Shakespearean allusion. Joan Wolf typically uses Shakespearean chapter epigrams in *An American Duchess* (Signet Regency 1982) and her noble heroine in *His Lordship's Mistress*

(Signet Regency 1982) acts Shakespeare on the public stage to gain a wealthy "patron" and enough funds to save her family. Amateur Shakespearean theatricals are the backdrop for both Smith's *Lover's Vows* (Coventry 1982) and Elizabeth Kidd's *My Lord Guardian* (Avon 1982). In *The Tenacious Miss Tamerlane* (Avon 1982), Kasey Michaels creates Aunt Lucinda, whose habit of speaking only in quotations enrages a beloved friend whenever she dares to quote Shakespeare, and a distant Shakespearean scholar-father names his daughters Calpurnia, Olivia, and Rosalind in Charlotte Hines's *The Earl's Fancy* (Second-Chance-at-Love Regency 1982). In Elizabeth Mansfield's *Frost Fair* (Berkeley Regency 1982), the amnesiac heroine begins to regain her memory when she completes a Shakespearean sonnet the hero is reading aloud. Among the emerging subgenres of a burgeoning romance market, Shakespeare proves a frequent resource for series romances specializing in seventeenth and eighteenth century England.

Kasey Michaels's books underscore the distinction between the Shakespeare-rich Regencies (and the closely related Georgians) and the other contemporary romance series that appear during the early 1980s. Her Aunt Lucinda continues to quote Shakespeare in *The Playful Miss Penelope* (1988) and even as a ghost in *The Haunted Miss Hampshire* (1992). In contrast to the persistent Shakespearean content of her Regencies, her contemporary series romances during this period may allude to Shakespeare, but *Romeo in the Rain* (1990) has minimal Shakespearean content, despite its title. Although I have not researched extensively in *all* the subgenres and series (Connie Beck's romance database, BYRON, lists almost twenty-two thousand series romances), notable examples from contemporary series and the disproportionately large number of allusions in Regencies support my contention that, as content and generic features have changed in the competition for romance readers, so Shakespeare has served such distinctions.

Two of the more thoroughly Shakespearean series contemporaries of this period underscore these variations. Carole Buck's *Love Play* (1985) and later Judith Arnold's *Just Like Romeo and Juliet* (1993) both appear in series predicated on more experienced heroines and overt sexuality before marriage, Second-Chance-at-Love and Harlequin American Romances respectively. In both romances Shakespeare's plays are a pervasive reference point for erotically charged principal relationships. However, despite the extensive allusions, both novels are principally involved in using Shakespeare to further their investigations of lust and love rather than the kind of mutually inflected critique offered in the early Harlequins or the varied Shakespearean functions in the Regencies, to which I will return.

Published in the fourth year of the Second-Chance-at-Love series, *Love Play* opens with an epigram from *As You Like It*, "No sooner met but they looked, no sooner looked but they loved, no sooner loved but they sighed; no sooner sighed but they asked one another the reason, no sooner knew the reason but they sought the remedy" (title page). The novel then completely belies the immediate courtship and marriage of Oliver and Celia through 180 pages of the couple's struggle with career issues and independence and more than twenty-eight direct allusions to Shakespeare's plays. Our heroine, Dr. Torie Clavel, is a Shakespearean professor working on a biography of Edmund Kean, while her hero, Nick Forsythe, is a British Shakespearean director currently staging *A Midsummer Night's Dream*. They have been exchanging virulent letters across the Atlantic, expressing "literate but escalating hostility over their very divergent interpretations of Shakespeare's attitudes towards women" (Buck 1985, 4). Of course, they no sooner meet than they look, etc. As they love, sigh, and seek remedy, they quote *Taming, Romeo and Juliet, Othello, Henry VI* and most of all *Hamlet* at each other. They eat beef bourguignonne "à la Macbeth" (74) and make love on "a bank where the wild thyme blows" (133) in the middle of his *Dream* set.

This romance is saturated with Shakespearean quotations, repeatedly alluding to Ophelia's line about rosemary in *Hamlet*. After their first "burning, branding kiss," he sends roses and a note: "The florist shop was out of rosemary. It will have to be roses for remembrance" (21). Pursuing the same Shakespearean reference, Forsythe acknowledges the misquotation at their next meeting and later sends her dried rosemary as a goodbye present when she flees both his proposal and his country in order to preserve her independence. She in turn discovers that she is strong enough to marry him, accepts a writing position in London, and cables him: "Dried rosemary isn't enough. Stop. Fresh memories needed. Stop. Yours, Torie" (164). In their reunion, her lover flings a full-grown rosemary bush into the middle of her lecture: "'Here's rosemary,' quoted a vibrant male voice that would have filled the Globe Theater of Shakespeare's day to the back row, 'for remembrance!'"(168). The line is Shakespearean, but the context and significance have been completely reworked to fit Torie's successful romance rather than Ophelia's madness and suicide. Aside from his quotation from Oberon about Titania's bower that potentially alludes to Torie's fears of being overwhelmed by him, for the most part Shakespeare is sent up, revised, and played with here with everything from deliberate misquotations to playful reworkings. By the end of *Love Play,* "rosemary for remembrance" belongs to the novel more than to Hamlet.

In sheer abundance of references, Buck's novel substantially out-Shakespeares even Thorpe's *Curtain Call.* Functioning as the flag of intellectual status and compatibility, Shakespeare also underscores the writer's literary knowledge. Buck overtly notifies the readers when Shakespearean allusions appear and, though the protagonists have reportedly argued about Shakespeare's women before they meet, that promising contention almost completely disappears during their courtship. Shakespearean quotations become the background noise to their amorous adventures and their difficulties with two-career conflicts.

Judith Arnold's *Just Like Romeo and Juliet* (1993) ranges less widely in its allusions since almost all come from one play. However, it appropriates Shakespeare more directly to serve its romantic argument. As the novel opens, the ghosts of Romeo and Juliet overlook the statue of Juliet in a Verona Square. As Juliet yearns for one true love story, Romeo reveals that she has helped countless lovers who have touched her statue for good luck. Arnold is drawing on the literal situation in Verona, where lovers not only touch Juliet's statue, but even write letters to her, care of the Verona post office, effectively blurring fiction, fact, and even life and death.[2] Arnold's heroine, the similarly named Gillian Chappell, doesn't buy the romantic good-luck charm and, like earlier Harlequin heroines, rejects Shakespeare, though her traveling companion urges her to touch the statue. Needless to say, Juliet, the ghost of a dead fictional character, enables the romance of the star-crossed lovers, Gillian and Owen. Romeo and Juliet, as ghosts, offer commentary throughout the novel—as prologue and epilogue as well as the italicized openings for five other chapters, thus structurally recapitulating the play. As the contemporary couple move through their own star-crossed, compulsive love affair, Shakespeare's lovers blatantly discuss parallels to their own sad history (à la Shakespeare) and question whether the couple experience love or lust for each other. Juliet does, at last, get her happy ending, however, when Gillian's and Owen's letters to each other, thrown into Juliet's tomb, enable them to reunite after each thinks the other has been unable to forgive.

In *Just Like Romeo and Juliet,* Arnold carefully identifies all the parallels between Shakespeare's lovers and hers, as Shakespeare's play become the "real" history of "real" ghosts who intervene in the lovers' difficulties. Although Romeo and Juliet discover that violence is still unavoidable and comment extensively on their own love story, calling Shakespeare into question is less an issue than validating the romance form. Carefully established parallels to the canonical romance figures outweigh even the interrogation into the distinctions between love and lust that potentially critique both Shakespeare's lovers and Arnold's.

The competition that spawns differently focused series within Harlequin and elsewhere in the 1980s and early '90s turns Shakespearean allusions, when they appear in series contemporaries, into unchallenged guarantees of the heroine's intellect, authorial literacy, and the validity of genre. Historically based series romances use Shakespeare more subtly and more provocatively.

Shakespeare at the Turn of the Centuries

Throughout the 1980s, extensive Shakespearean allusions appear in Regencies from all the publishers who embarked on the series: Coventry, Dell, Harlequin, Jove, Avon, Fawcett Crest, Zebra and Signet. In 1986 Susan Car-

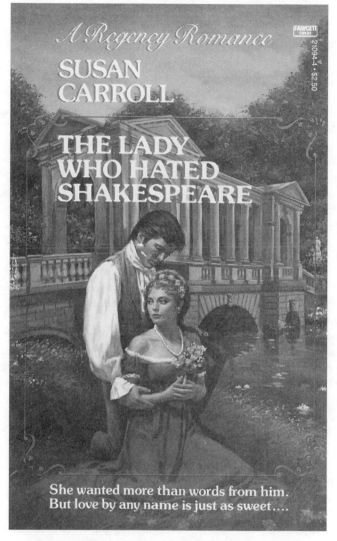

5.1. Susan Carroll's *The Lady who Hated Shakespeare,* makes the investment in the Bard explicit. (Courtesy Fawcett Crest, Ballantine Books).

roll's *The Lady Who Hated Shakespeare* from Avon takes on the culture of Stratford tourism and amateur productions of Shakespeare in the Regency. Among the Harlequin Regencies, Brenda Hiatt's *The Ugly Duckling* (1989) offers Touchstone's "Truly, I would the gods had made thee poetical" from

As You Like It on the cover and uses Shakespeare to signal the unacceptable intellect of its bluestocking heroine. By the early 1990s, *Miss Grimsley's Oxford Career* (Signet Regency 1992) employs Shakespeare to explore class and female education, and Margaret Porter Evans's *Toast of the Town* (Signet Regency 1993) follows Flora Campion from Drury Lane Shakespearean actress to noble marriage. Michelle Martin's *The Hampshire Hoyden* (1993) from Fawcett Crest reworks *Much Ado About Nothing*, and at Zebra Books, Jean Ross Ewing's Charles de Dagonet in *Scandal's Reward* (1994) quotes Shakespeare, among others, to keep the heroine and his own murky past at bay. Throughout the publishing history of series Regencies Shakespearean allusion is frequent and varied as I have noted in my essays "Romancing the Bard" and "Sweet, savage Shakespeare."

However, by the late 1990s Regencies became an endangered species. Four of the remaining publishers of the subgenre, Harlequin, Jove, Avon, and Fawcett Crest, dropped their Regency lines, and several authors I mentioned above stopped writing in the subgenre. In fact, the prominent romance fan magazine, *Romantic Times*, devoted a significant part of their October 1998 issue to supporting and saving the Regency. Describing what Regencies are, beyond being short romances set in England between 1811 and 1820, Gail Eastwood focuses on the peculiarly strong role played by Regency society— its rules, its preoccupations, and its language: "society plays such an active role in the stories, it is almost another character" (14). Shakespeare's plays onstage, his language quoted by characters, and his dramatic situations all contribute to this character, society. As Jean Ross Ewing puts it, "one reason Regency characters freely quote Shakespeare is because this is what Regency people actually DID!!! At least, that's what they did in their letters, diaries, etc." (Regency@egroups.com). RITA Award-winning Regency author Nancy Butler points out further purposes for Shakespearean citation, "The reason I include references to his work in my books, is that he furnishes a wonderful timeline from the Elizabethan period through the Regency into our own century. Readers can relate to his name more than if I used a playwright specifically from the Regency who is no longer in vogue. And of course, his words are always apt, deft and true, a writer's dream source" (e-mail correspondence). Regency writers take their Shakespeare seriously and employ his work as part of their historical bridge to the early nineteenth century.

If anything, Shakespearean allusions in the last couple of years of "Regency crisis" have become even more pervasive. Almost half the Signet Regencies in the last nine months allude to Shakespeare. Some employ slight references to theatrical performances or characters, but others use Shakespeare more extensively and in various modes. Not only does Lynn Kerstan's *Lord Dragoner's Wife* offer Shakespearean epigrams for every chapter, but Dragoner speaks and even THINKS in Shakespearean quotations (in italics). He uses the Bard as a verbal self-defense, turning every situation into a sardonic Shakespearean allusion. His wife of convenience, abandoned for six years and now seeking to start her marriage, proves her spousal worthiness by recognizing and completing his quotations ("My lady disdain" of course). She is well aware of his Shakespearean strategy for fending off unwanted intimacy and even responds testily to one quotation, "O, for pity's sake, sir. Don't start *that* again!" (1999, 204). The author's Shakespearean epigrams suggest a pervasive appropriation of Shakespeare's language, but Dragoner's quotations use that language as the barrier that romance must breach.

Dragoner himself recognizes both his tendency to quote and its limitations: "*What's gone and what's past help should be past grief.* Should be. And wasn't. Shakespeare didn't always get it right" (118). More important, when he finally asks her to be his wife in truth, he promises to stop quoting Shakespeare:

"And to prove my good intentions, I shall even stop quoting bits of Shakespeare at you."

"Oh, but I wouldn't dream of asking so great a sacrifice. . . . In fact, Charles, I mean to go through all the plays and underline every passage where a man extravagantly praises his lady. You may then memorize the lines I've marked and give them back to me."

Chuckling softly, he wrapped his arm around her . . ."I doubt even Shakespeare has written enough praise for you, lady mine." (Kerstand 1999, 214–15)

Shakespeare ultimately turns out not to be enough and not always right. The hero must abandon or adapt his Shakespeare to prove the authenticity of his feelings, yet Shakespearean language nonetheless pervades the text, often verifying his growing affection for his bride.

Although Kerstan wrote Fawcett Regencies previously, none of her earlier Regencies contains such extensive Shakespeare. In fact, the high percentage of Shakespearean references in the 1999–2000 Signet Regencies cannot merely derive from the publisher's absorption of authors from other now-defunct Regency lines, since many authors most prone to quoting and using Shakespeare have now begun to write series contemporaries or the more lucrative historical novels. Increasing numbers of Shakespearean allusions coincide with an array of strategies that broaden the genre's appeal. The strict setting and "realistic" historical detail have been augmented by time travel plots, supernatural elements (ghosts, vampires, Cupid, and, in Butler's forthcoming story, Puck himself), and alternative settings like Regency Scotland and Ireland, rather than just London or country house settings. Shakespearean citation functions quite differently in this stage of the subgenre's development since they also secure the position of the series Regency as "the 'intelligentsia' of the romance novel" (Michaels 2000, introduction i).

Although Kasey Michaels suggests that it has regrettably deterred new readers from trying Regencies, that intellectual reputation also secures diehard Regency fans who insist on accuracy in historical details and slang while embracing an eroticism of suggestion and restraint. Shakespearean allusions ratify the status that Regencies assume among romance subgenres, even as the strategic use of Shakespeare has shifted. For example, theatrical Regencies, in which a lower-class actress matches the noble hero's Shakespearean knowledge, have dropped out of the current series while matching or completing each other's quotations still often signals the future success of the couple.[3] Shakespeare as the mediator of class— a frequent mode in the early 1990s—yields to Shakespeare as a consolidator of audiences, drawing established Regency fans who understand his significance in the period and new readers who recognize his name and recent alliance with romance.

I am not arguing that Regency novelists consciously draw on Shakespeare to "rescue" their endangered genre. Increased use of Shakespeare emerges within a complex blend of factors: the pressures of fewer publishers producing Regencies; readers' perceptions/expectations of their intellectual content; the sudden alliance of Shakespearean wit and romance in the highly popular film *Shakespeare in Love* (1998); and the Regencies' long-standing engagement with Shakespearean themes and language as embraced in early nineteenth-century Britain. Shakespeare appeals to established Regency fans and potential new readers; his current popularity across genres thus also serves the particular needs of Regency authors.

Conclusions

When we explore the appearance of Shakespearean plots, language, or artifacts in mass culture, we risk letting our investment in Shakespeare supercede the very concerns of context, production, and reception on which we would insist if we were analyzing a particular Shakespearean production or edition. In fact, since Shakespearean allusions are undoubtedly of secondary concern to the creators of these commodities, we must examine carefully generic development as well as the pressures of production and consumption in assessing such allusions. As this chapter demonstrates, even analyzing Shakespearean allusion in a narrowly defined section of mass media, the series romance, reveals that competitive challenges and generic changes, like the emergence and decline of subgenres, influence Shakespeare's function. There are clearly dramatic differences between the relative subtleties of 1970s Harlequin Shakespeare and the superficial blatancies of Shakespearean reference during and after the '80s romance wars. The emergence, endangerment, and now resurgence of Regency series prove an even more significant context, given the fact that the Regencies outdo all other series romances in both extent and method of Shakespearean allusion.

Although the apparent disposability of much mass-produced fiction may imply a less rich and therefore concomitantly less significant history of production than, for example, scholarly editions of Shakespeare, the very volatility of popular mass cultural forms (of which Shakespeare's quartos were once part) exacerbates the importance of generic contexts, including several that I have not touched on directly, including contemporaneous political and social movements, authorial biographies and publishing histories, and so forth. Pervasive Shakespearean allusion in a specific text always exists within the interaction of genres, authors, publishers, and readers.

The validity of this argument could be tested by applying it to other emerging and established genres of mass culture. For example, we could examine the relatively recent emergence of young adult fiction. Two books aimed at early and mid-adolescents, Bruce Colville's *The Skull of Truth* (1997) and Welwyn Wilton Katz's *Come Like Shadows* (1993), use props from Shakespeare's plays as magical talismans that ultimately challenge both the authenticity of their respective plays and the truths surrounding their young hero and heroine.

Colville's skull turns out to be Yorick's skull from *Hamlet* with an uncanny ability to enforce speaking the truth in those who possess it. Charlie Eggleston not only learns some relatively unpalatable truths about his family but also unwillingly tells the truth about his feelings for a female classmate. He even learns the truth of Yorick's history and demise—rewriting and reinterpreting *Hamlet* in the process since Yorick was, in this version, cursed by an old woman to tell nothing but the truth and lost both freedom and life for telling the truth about Gertrude.

A comparable combination of talisman and Shakespearean revision appears in Katz's book because of the magic mirror in *Macbeth*, which, as it turns out, allows the witches to live forever by taking on new bodies of female victims. Because the historical Macbeth intervenes in their ritual, he gets caught in the mirror despite his resistance to their influence throughout his reign. As the witches chase through time to retrieve their key to eternal life they rewrite Macbeth's "real" heroic history by influencing Shakespeare when he briefly gains possession of the mirror. The heroine of Katz's book, influenced by the witches, picks up the mirror from an antique store as the prop mirror for a doomed production of *Macbeth* at the Stratford Ontario Shakespeare festival where she is an apprentice.

The common reliance on Shakespearean props as magical talismans is notable, and given the similar ways these books use those items, it is tempting to suggest that Shakespeare becomes a touchstone for truth within adolescent confusion over truth, origins, and destinations. The fact that these talismans predate and even generate the Shakespearean plays they invoke adds another layer to the quest. The "truth" is anchored magically in a prop that is itself authenticated by its presence in a Shakespearean play. The circularity here, which resembles the circular reinforcement invoked in Arnold's *Just Like Romeo and Juliet* and Kerstan's *Lord Dragoner's Wife*, ultimately depends on Shakespeare to insure truth, mostly by the sheer endurance of his plays.

What this thumbnail reading omits is significant contexts that differentiate the talismanic quality of Shakespeare in the two novels. Colville's novel has not only the background of his Shakespearean adaptations for much younger readers but also the context of his genre fiction—the *Alien* and supernatural novels that bookstores tend to stock with Christopher Pike's youth horror books. The topical specialization of young adult fiction into "minigenres" that mirror adult popular fiction (romance, sci-fi, fantasy, horror, etc) is another relevant context for *The Skull of Truth*.

Katz's *Come the Shadows* is even more intriguing. Her novel echoes an early youth-oriented romance novel, *The Shakespeare Girl*, by Mollie Hardwick, which follows sixteen-year-old Miranda's career through a comparable, though less magical, British Stratford apprenticeship. Also Katz, who is Canadian, offers an account of a *Macbeth* production reworked to vilify Quebec's greatest hero, General Montcalm, a "misuse" of Shakespeare's play that seriously bothers the heroine. By means of this updated production, questions of authenticity and history are inflected through specifically Canadian history and conflicts. Macbeth, and thus General Montcalm, become simultaneously reinstated as heroes in the novel. Where Colville's *Skull* offers a personal journey to family truth, Katz's novel invokes contemporary political conflict in Canada. And both participate in the establishment of "magical" genre fiction for young adults that ultimately derives from British children's books by C. S. Lewis and Edward Eager.

This brief consideration of young adult fiction underscores my larger point. Mass culture, whether grouped under the title of series romance or young adult fiction, is embedded in complex publishing histories that interact with equally complicated histories of generic development. We omit these histories at our peril. If we consider Shakespearean allusions in isolation or in only the context of the current abundance, we risk missing how very differently Shakespeare can function even in mass cultural forms that seem highly conventional and similar.

As much of the publishing industry faces proliferating forms of textual reproduction, Shakespeare comes to represent a fascination with the potential durability of popular fiction, read most often as topical, transient, and eminently disposable. Consequently, the proliferating Shakespearean allusions in the late 1990s often engage concerns about truth and authenticity, not just in series romance but also across different generic boundaries. Such Schlockspeare, apparently as ephemeral and disposable as the genres that incorporate it, becomes part of a growing (pop) cultural mediation on what authenticity might be in the late twentieth century, but that mediation is only available if we acknowledge the publishing history from which it emerges.

Notes

1. Titles appear initially with their publication dates to underscore their place in the history of series romance.
2. Elvis Costello has produced a record with the Guarneri Quintet, entitled *Juliet's Letters* and based in the premise of lyrics found in the mail to Juliet which arrives daily in Verona.
3. The most recent actress novel is Eileen Putman's 1997 *A Passionate Performance,* which predates the *RT* plea to save the regency.

Works Cited

Baker, Susan. 1994. "Comic Material: 'Shakespeare' in the Classic Detective Story." In *Acting Funny.* Ed. by Fran Teague. Cranbury, NJ: Associated Univ. Presses, Inc.
———. 1995. "Shakespearean Authority in the Classic Detective Story." *Shakespeare Quarterly* 46: 424–48.
Boose, Lynda. 1991. "Scolding Brides and Bridling Scolds: Taming the Woman's Unruly Member." *Shakespeare Quarterly* 42: 178–213.
Charnes, Linda. 1992. "'What's love got to do with it?' Reading the Liberal Humanist Romance in Shakespeare's *Antony and Cleopatra.*" *Textual Practice* 6: 1–16.
Coddington, L. 1997. "Wavering Between Worlds: Feminist Influences in the Romance Genre." *Paradoxa* 3(1–2): 58–77.
Eastwood, G. (October) 1998. "Saving the Regency: A Sub-Genre at the Crossroads." *Romantic Times* 175: 12–14.
Glescoe, P. *The Merchants of Venus.* 1996. Vancouver: Raincoast Books.
Heyer, Georgette. 2000. With introduction by Kasey Michaels. *The Corinthian.* Toronto: Harlequin Books.
Krentz, J. A. ed. [1992]1996. *Dangerous Men and Adventurous Women: Romance Writers on the Appeal of the Romance.* New York: Harper Collins.
Modleski, Tania. 1982. *Loving with a Vengeance: Mass Produced Fantasies for Women.* Hampton, CT: Archon Books.
Osborne, Laurie E. 1999. "Romancing the Bard." In *Shakespeare and Appropriation.* Ed. by Christie Desmet and Robert Sawyer. New York: Routledge.
———. 2000. "Sweet Savage Shakespeare." In *Shakespeare Without Class: Misappropriations of Cultural Capital.* Ed. by Donald Hedrick and Bryan Reynolds. New York: Palgrave.
Rabine, L. W. 1985. *Reading the Romantic Heroine: Text, History and Ideology.* Ann Arbor: Univ. of Michigan Press.
Radway, Janice. [1984]1991. *Reading the Romance.* Chapel Hill: Univ. of North Carolina Press, 1984.

Snitnow, Ann. B. 1983. "Mass Market Romance: Pornography for Women Is Different." In *Powers of Desire: The Politics of Sexuality: New Feminist Library.* Ed. by A. B. Snitnow, C. Stansell, and S. Thompson. New York: Monthly Review Press.
Thirty Years of Harlequin: 1949–1979. 1979. Toronto: Harlequin Books.

Genre Fiction and Popular Culture

Arnold, J. 1993. *Just Like Romeo and Juliet.* Toronto: Harlequin Books.
Ashley, M. Ed. 1997. *Shakespearean Whodunnits.* New York: Carroll & Graf.
Ashton, E. 1976. *My Lady Disdain.* Toronto: Harlequin Books.
———. 1975. *The Player King.* Toronto: Harlequin Books.
———. 1973. *Sigh No More.* Toronto: Harlequin Books.
Beard, J. 1998. *Romance of the Rose.* New York: Berkeley.
Buck, C. 1985. *Love Play.* New York: Jove/Second-Chance-at-Love.
Bujold, L. M. 1999. *A Civil Campaign.* New York: Baen Books.
Butler, N. 2000. E-mail correspondence. May 24.
Carroll, Susan. 1986. *The Lady Who Hated Shakespeare.* New York: Fawcett Crest Regency.
Colville, B. 1997. *The Skull of Truth.* New York: Harcourt, Brace and Company.
Curse of Monkey Island. 1997. LucasArts Entertainment.
Dodd, C. [1994]1999. *The Greatest Lover in All England.* New York: HarperPaperbacks.
Donnelly, J. 1977. *Dear Caliban.* Toronto: Harlequin Books.
Ewing, J. R. E-mail correspondence. <regencylist@egroups.com>.
———. 1994. *Scandal's Reward.* New York: Zebra Books.
Hamlet: A Murder Mystery. 1997. CastleRock/EMME.
Junger, Gil, dir. 1999. *10 Things I Hate About You.* USA. Touchstone Video. Sound, col., 93 mins.
Kelly, C. 1992. *Miss Grimsley's Oxford Career.* New York: Signet Regency.
Kerstan, L. 1999. *Lord Dragoner's Wife.* New York: Signet Regency.
Katz, W. W. 1999. *Come Like Shadows.* Toronto: Penguin Books Canada.
Kidd, E. 1982. *My Lord Guardian.* New York: Avon Books.
Kidd, F. 1967. *Love Alters Not.* Winnipeg, Canada: Harlequin Books.
Lee, J. 1982. *Perchance to Dream.* New York: Dell Candlelight Regency Special.
Malcolm, M. 1974. *A Bright Particular Star.* Toronto: Harlequin Books.
Martin, Malia. 2000. *Much Ado About Love.* New York: Avon Books.
Martin, Michelle. 1993. *The Hampshire Hoyden.* New York: Fawcett Crest Regency.
Matas, Carol. 1999. *Cloning Miranda.*
Michaels, K. 1992. *The Haunted Miss Hampshire.* New York: Avon Books, 1992.
———. 1988. *The Playful Lady Penelope.* New York: Avon Books Regency.
———. 1990. *Romeo in the Rain.* New York: Silhouette Books.
———. 1982. *The Tenacious Miss Tamerlane.* New York: Avon Books Regency.
Myers, H.R. 1990. *Kiss Me Kate.* New York: Silhouette Books.
Nye, R. 2000. *The Late Mr. Shakespeare.* New York: Penguin.
Porter, M. E. 1993 *Toast of the Town.* New York: Signet Regency.
Safecracker. 2000. Dreamcatcher Interactive.

Searle, S. 1965. *Green Girl*. Winnipeg, Canada: Harlequin Books.

Smith, J. 1982. *Lovers' Vows*. New York: Coventry Romances.

Summerville, M. 1982. *Lord Wicked Wolf*. New York: Dell Candlelight Regency Special.

Thian, V. 1971. *O Kiss Me, Kate*. Toronto: Harlequin Books.

Thorpe, K. 1971. *Curtain Call*. Toronto: Harlequin Books.

———. 1968 *Devon Interlude*. Winnipeg, Canada: Harlequin Books.

Updike, J. 2000. *Claudius and Gertrude*. New York: Knopf.

Weinberg, D. H. and Rowe, D. 1996. *Will Power! Using Shakespeare's Insights to Transform Your life*. New York: St. Martin's Press.

Wolf, J. 1982. *His Lordship's Mistress*. New York: Signet Regency.

———. 1982. *An American Duchess*. New York: Signet Regency.

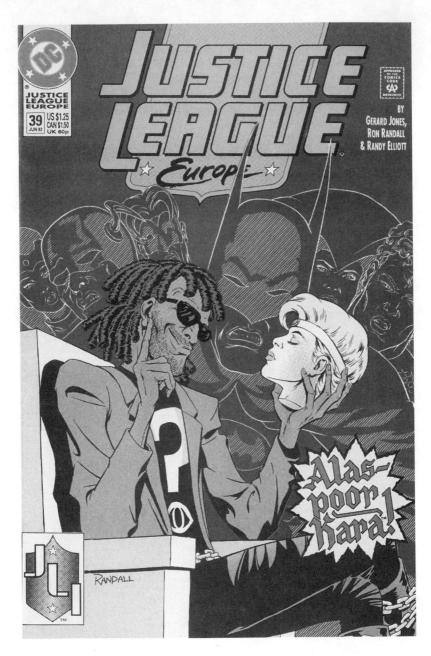

6.1. Alas, poor Hamlet?

CHAPTER 6

SUGGESTED FOR MATURE READERS?
Deconstructing Shakespearean Value in Comic Books

JOSH HEUMAN
AND RICHARD BURT

"Alas, poor Kara," mourns supervillain Deconstructo on the cover of DC Comics' *Justice League Europe* 39 (June 1992), as the Hamlet-like villain holds aloft the detached head of superheroine Kara Starr.

A quick reading of this comic, the third and final issue in a series of three focusing on the villain Deconstructo, who gains his superpowers from a magic wand left behind by aliens, might lead one to conclude that there's just not very much Shakespeare to interpret here. "Alas, poor Kara" acknowledges the notoriety of *Hamlet's* graveyard scene, for example, but seemingly without any commitment to substantial engagement with the play itself. One should never judge a comic book by its cover, however. The three-part series suggests more than passing engagement with Shakespeare. As issue 37 opens, the Justice League Europe, composed almost exclusively of American superheroes, finds itself leaderless and in disarray, frustrated by a crisis of authority only tentatively resolved by the appearance of Green Lantern in the last panel of the concluding episode in issue 39. Secretly a disgruntled, dreadlock-sporting London artist named Archie Tipple, Deconstructo makes his entrance in issue 37 by mounting a verbal attack outside an art gallery where a fundraiser for the JLE is being held. In one of his typical sidewalk jeremiads, Tipple/Deconstructo rants:

> Cultureless Americans calling themselves "Justice League Europe." Imposing their naive lie on countries that know better but are too weak to fight back.

The Lie of Hero. It's the same imperialism as the art patrons. The superheroes of wealth who sponsor the art that erects the lie of meaning. There is no meaning. In art, in life, in history, in heroes . . . meaning is dead!

An art critic named Mr. Ruskin explains to Bruce Wayne that the guy shouting outside their reception is "just a local deconstructionist artist. Rather bitter about being ejected from our exhibit, I'm afraid." Wayne responds, as no doubt do many of the comic's readers: "I'm afraid I'm fuzzy on deconstructionism, Mister Ruskin." Ruskin replies in a compressed way that makes it extremely difficult to tell how seriously his account is meant to be taken and even if the primary audience is assumed to be adult:

> Quite the academic fad in France and America, it has become passe now, I understand. It holds that all thought is dictated by the structures of the mind and language. Therefore no human creation can reveal anything except about itself. All efforts to create meaning and values are pointless. This chap's submission was a sieve with super heroes half-melted through it. That seemed inappropriate with the justice league helping with our fundraiser.

And in issue 39, Batman, a quick study, later gives an account some readers might find equally serious or hilarious depending on their interpretation of the comic. Batman explains to the assembled JLE:

> Archie Tipple, once a politically conscious artist who became disillusioned by the lies of the world. He used intellect to rebel against the cultural establishment and his own violent family. Until he came to believe that the mind controls reality. He became obsessed with the Dutch philosopher Paul de Man, whose guilt over the Nazi propaganda he wrote in his youth, caused him to question the self-deceiving power of language.

In this bizarre, possibly ironic and amusing mixture of familiar, sometimes head-scratching, befuddled "superheroes-save-the-world-from-mad-villain" formula, literary theory, and references to "epistemological debate" and "ze existentialism . . . ze nihilism" made by these same superheroes, Shakespeare is, perhaps unsurprisingly, deconstructed. He is cited by both Deconstructo and by Mrs. Dibny, the coordinator of the JLE and the wife of one of its members, Elongated Man. In a full-page panel, Deconstructo recycles in punk-rock fashion lines from John of Gaunt's deathbed speech in Richard II: "Ah, the glory that was Britain! This sceptered isle, this shoppered aisle, this kippered eel, this England!" And Ms. Dibny similarly parodies Richard III's famous line delivered as he is about to lose the Battle of Bosworth Field, "A Leader! My Kingdom for a Leader!" Shakespeare is on the side of the cultural establishment and the disenchanted avant-garde, on the side of the heroes and the villains, both of whom misquote him. And this latter opposition is in turn deconstructed: The villain Deconstructo is linked to the tragic hero, Hamlet, while the heroine Mrs. Dibny is linked to the villain, Richard III. If "Alas, poor Kara" were insufficient indication, this JLE series wants to make clear that something's rotten in the state of comic books.

Tipple deconstructs artistic value to speak forcefully against what he calls American artistic "imperialism" even as he reinscribes British cultural imperialism, at one point becoming a giant version of Admiral Nelson's statue atop the column in London's Trafalgar Square. The value of Shakespeare citations in these highly self-conscious comics is difficult to assess, or one might even say "undecidable": Should they be elevated to the ranks of serious academic criticism (or parody thereof) or should they be dismissed as incidental and meaningless in a medium properly relegated to a trash bin? The very existence of a character named Deconstructo who cites Shakespeare and Milton immediately raises questions about who this comic book is addressed to, younger readers or adult graduate students and academics, or both? How is Deconstructo meant to be taken? Is he a tragic hero along the lines of Milton's Satan, whom Deconstructo also deliberately misquotes, and Shakespeare's Hamlet?[1] Or is he merely a joke, a magic wand-waving parody of deconstruction? Are the literary references, mostly clichéd lines well known even to a public who has never read a play by Shakespeare, meant to be taken seriously, as evidence of how high-minded comics can be, or just another register of how Shakespeare gets reduced to familiar tag lines when he enters a medium like the comic book? Is Batman's account of Paul de Man meant to endorse right-wing attacks on him and his writings, or is the enunciation of that attack in a medium such conservatives dismiss meant to deconstruct that attack, show it up as a cartoonish parody of real literary criticism and intellectual debate? Rather than answer these questions, the JLE Deconstructo story implicitly deconstructs the cutthroat ways in which comic books are valued by our culture in terms of their place on one side of a series of binary oppositions: between art and trash, literature and comics, and adult and juvenile readers, among others. And more broadly, the JLE story suggests the cutthroat character of comic book production in general: recognition of any sort of artistic legitimacy in some comic books presumes distinction from others, which remain merely trashy comic books.

The relative complexity of the JLE Deconstructo story may be thrown into relief by comparing it briefly to two other uses of Shakespeare in DC Comics: the *Flash* no. 197 May 1970 entitled "Into a Four-Star Hero" and *The Adventures of Superman* no. 579 June 2000 entitled "Pranked." In the *Flash* story, Barry Allen's secret identity is about to be exposed, so he sets up a performance of *Hamlet* and literally seems to be in two places at once. But rather than deconstruct the difference between superhero identity and secret alter ego identity (it seems perfectly clear given that Allen is the Flash, given that the Flash plays Hamlet with his face unmasked), the story gives its readers an incoherent display of the Flash's virtuosity, his ability to play all the roles of the play. Shakespeare is here unambiguously on the side of the hero. In *The Adventures of Superman*, Shakespeare is, by contrast, unambiguously on the side of the villain. Superman's nemesis the Prankster cites Hamlet's speech about Yorick and a line from *Romeo and Juliet*. In contrast to the honorific attitude the Flash takes toward Shakespeare, the Prankster takes a mocking attitude. Although Hamlet's speech about Yorick in the gravedigger scene is cited in its entirety, it is interrupted and disrupted by plenty of asides, and fragmented across a series of panels. Moreover, for comic effect the Prankster mixes citations from Shakespeare with references to filmic adaptations by Kenneth Branagh, and he plays off Shakespeare's high cultural status against the lower cultural film *The Wedding Singer* and the cartoon character Porky Pig. Unlike the Deconstructo *Justice League Europe* series, Shakespeare occupies one side of a stable binary opposition between hero and villain in the *Flash* and *Adventures of Superman* episodes.

In examining some of the many citations of Shakespeare's comic books, it is not our intention to appreciate their artistic value or condemn them for their lack thereof, but to interrogate how the medium of comic books in general comes to have cultural value by invoking (for may different effects) Shakespeare's cultural authority. Not surprisingly for a medium commonly dismissed as juvenile, claims to artistic distinction made by comic book authors and their readers tend to come couched in the language of maturity with such consistency that it becomes difficult to think about comic book value outside of that language. As a measure of comic book value, maturity refers descriptively to the reader's age, often with warning labels like "suggested for mature readers," or "sophisticated suspense" on DC's *Swamp Thing*—e.g., *Swamp Thing's* sophistication is inappropriate for an eight-year-old. In this sense, maturity obviously marks an important distinction between adult and child comic book audiences. At the same time, the evaluation of comic books that proceeds only from this sense of maturity involves complications. Very often it's simply difficult to distinguish between comics for children and comics for adults. The ambiguous diversity of the comic book audience seldom conveniently breaks down into adults reading adult comics, and children reading children's comics. As our reading of the Deconstructo storyline suggests, sometimes adults read apparently juvenile comics in (relatively) mature ways—indeed as adult comics and even, perhaps, as philosophy.

The persistent devaluation of comic books within the broader culture coincides with the cultural image of their immature audience. Because of this coincidence, the real or imagined reader plays a pivotal role in the formation (and transformation) of comic book value—within and especially *beyond* the comic book medium. Through his association with scholarly literary value and valorized styles of critical reading, Shakespeare lends the comic book reader a certain ethical maturity, we argue, which in turn imparts legitimacy to the comic book itself, making it into an art form in its own right. In the first section of this chapter, we consider various series of adaptations published under the Classics Illustrated imprint. While they differ sharply across the different series, these comics raise a series of questions: How does Shakespeare's work play in the comics? How does the language of readerly maturity translate into the seemingly incommensurable language of pictures and words? The second section examines DC's *Sandman,* a series that appropriates the work of Shakespeare within a remarkably effective enterprise of upward cultural mobility, one that arrogates the prestige both of the new comic book deconstruction and of its hypercompetent mature reader. A short final section looks to Viz Comics' *Ranma 1/2* for an alternative, more benignly deconstructive way of negotiating cultural value to those practiced by *Sandman* and the CI adaptations, whose every step forward toward artistic legitimacy depends on another comic's further step back toward illegitimacy. While certainly *Ranma 1/2* offers no simple escape from the binary oppositions on which a winner takes all economy of cultural value (and perhaps any economy) is founded, the Japanese series might offer a kinder and gentler version of readerly maturity as measure of distinction.[2]

Classics Illustrated:
(Mal)Adaptations of Shakespearean Value

Though popular nostalgia favors only the original with its memory, the Classics Illustrated imprint has graced three series of adaptations, published by successive property holders Gilberton, First, and Acclaim. While the three series represent distinct modes of adaptation, and imply distinct kinds of readers, they all participate in the common—though shifting—problem of the comic book's formal specificity. Certainly the problem of form and value haunts any adaptation across hierarchized cultural forms; as Graham Holderness comments, "[t]heatrical, film, and television productions have always been accorded a place and a potential value within the broad conspectus of a literary education: the question is what place, and what value?" ([1985]1994, 207). More than film and television productions, however, comic book adaptations of Shakespeare bridge a seemingly boundless gap of cultural value between their highbrow sources and their lowbrow form. No wonder, then, that the CI adaptations should so forcefully raise the pressing question of *mal*adaptation: Does the comic book form allow democratization of the "true" Shakespeare, or only massification of a debased, "dumbed down" version? Or closer to the reader than the text: Does comic book adaptation conserve the civilizing influence of literary education, or only foster juvenile indiscipline underneath a patina of maturity? Whether figured as elevation or fall, this encounter between high and low tells only half the story. The other half takes place within the low comic book field itself, where mediated through the figure of the reader, Shakespearean value offers a means of distinction for the CI adaptations.

In the great-man narratives of popular and fan historiography, the history of Classics Illustrated is the story of Albert Kanter.[3] Within CI lore, Kanter ventured into adaptations after seeing his children reading comic books rather than the classic literature he cherished. Though his adaptations were aimed at children, already we can see how they aimed to bring a certain maturity to the juvenile audience. Only in lore, however, does he fit the role of the romantic author: partners financed the venture, and managed its outsourced creative production; other publishers engaged in similar projects to market edifying comics for children. Kanter and company released their first "Classic Comic," *Three Musketeers,* in 1941 (the name would change to "Classics Illustrated" in 1947); after 167 installments, all but a few put out by Gilberton, American publication of new adaptations ended with 1962's *Faust* (reprints and overseas production continued afterward). Books ranged from forty-eight to sixty-four pages, across titles and even printings (variation owed to production costs rather than aesthetic consideration). Adaptations concentrated and accelerated their source stories, remaining broadly faithful to major plotlines, if sometimes not much else. It smacks of anachronism to discuss CI "art"; the books' "pictures" followed conventional styles of illustrated children's fiction. Selections for adaptation derived overwhelmingly from the genre of boy's adventure fiction (Dumas, Poe, Stevenson), with occasional exceptions like *Faust, Alice in Wonderland,* and of course the Shakespeares: *Julius Caesar* (1950), *Midsummer Night's Dream* (1951), *Hamlet* (1952), *Macbeth* (1955), and *Romeo and Juliet* (1956).

Like other Classics Illustrated adaptations, the Shakespeares favored the broad trajectory of the reproducible tale over the finer points of its authentic telling. Indeed, in their commitment and fidelity to major monologues, they sometimes resemble a collection of Shakespeare's Greatest Hits (as word balloons expand to fill the page). But while theatrical performance moves in real time, the adaptations often race along in summary. If their supplementary narration translates theatrical stage directions for print narrative, for example, it also hastens along the action, condensing what's most salient and suturing over deletions of what's not. Such Procrustean tendencies do not suggest unambivalent betrayal, however. Fortinbras disappears, leaving Hamlet thinner without one of his foils. The ambiguity of Hamlet's madness withers nearly expunged, largely reduced to a single line of narration:

"As days pass, a strange madness, part real and part feigned, comes over Hamlet." His advice to the players is cut, along with his discussion of the play with Ophelia, and much of Polonius's rhetorical richness. Like the other Shakespeares, this adaptation preserves the tale, while frustrating close reading of its telling.

Perhaps even more than other titles in the series, the Shakespeares must be read against the backdrop of their social context. Postwar America witnessed a rekindled mass-culture debate, one that derived special anxiety from the problematic relationship between mass-media effect and democratic citizenship. This anxiety drifts readily toward the figure of the vulnerable child; notions of ill-effected citizenship played an important part in constructing the figure of the 1950s juvenile delinquent. Delinquency panic attached firmly to comic books, especially but not only to EC Comics' lurid horror stories.[4] Estes Kefauver's Senate subcommittee on juvenile delinquency reported "substantial . . . agreement among the experts that there may be detrimental and delinquency-producing effects" of reading comics (Kefauver 1955, 33). A New York legislative committee arrived at a stronger conclusion, calling to declare comics "a basic factor in impairing the ethical development of minors and a menace to the health, safety, and morals of the people of the state" (Carlino 1952, 19–20). Or as librarian Jean Gray Harker put it, "If we were to set out to deliberately undermine the future of our country, to rob our future generations of the ability to think, to talk, to read, to act with intelligence, we could have no more effective weapon than the comic book" (1948, 1705). It's tempting to write this episode off as a medley of folly: the mutual justification of performed politics and "expert" social science; Dr Fredric Wertham's masterful entrepreneurial turn as psychiatric Comstock in his panic-peddling *Seduction of the Innocent* (1954); the formation of the Comics Magazine Association code in 1954, with its nakedly *de facto* censorship of EC. Despite their hyperbolic alarmism, however, the 1950s moral reformers continued a long-standing association between (im)proper reading styles and cultural (in)civility—the same noted by Hunter at work within popular literary education.

As a reform project, Classics Illustrated tendered a version of cultural uplift drawn from the same imagination as this crusade against mass culture. The accessible adaptations would operate as gateways, spoonfuls of sugar to lead reluctant juvenile palates toward mature literature. "Now that you have read the Classics Illustrated Edition," closed most books, "don't miss the added enjoyment of reading the original, obtainable at your local school or library." More than mere enjoyment, uplift suggests that cultured maturity carries a payoff in cultural capital. One suggestive promotional campaign enlisted banks to give away CIs to children who opened accounts. A recent letter to the *New York Times* pushes the metaphor of capitalization further:

When I was born in 1947, my father began making two biweekly purchases without fail: a United States Savings Bond and a Classics Illustrated comic book. . . . By 1964, he could send me (without financial aid) to a university where I eventually read the entire canons of Austen, Conrad and James, among others, and earned a Ph.D. in English. (Levy-Reiner 1996)

This letter understands with unusual clarity the promise of cultural uplift. Nicola Beisel locates nineteenth-century Comstockery in a crisis of family status reproduction (1997); nebulous 1950s anxieties toward mass culture disclose similar concern for the fate of the vulnerable child. Against the questionable march of "civilization," CI presented parents and librarians with the preservation of a specific form of culture—one that mobilized Shakespeare as privileged element, not only within an aesthetics of elite culture, but also a bankable ethics of cultured civility.

Of course, uplift only assumes so unlikely a form as the comic book with discomfort. In a variety of industrial maneuvers, Gilberton aimed to distance Classics Illustrated from the salacious taint of "immature" comics. Even before Classic Comics became CI, it accepted neither advertisements nor vendor returns; though subscriptions were available, and mailed as second-class periodicals, on the racks CIs were discrete and nonperishable books, rather than ephemeral serials. Since he was not a comic book publisher, Gilberton refused to join the Comics Magazine Association, and held a stiff upper lip against what it saw as accordingly misguided legislative attention. Release of the Shakespeares seems conveniently timed to mark more distance from comic book immaturity—especially given the difficulty of supporting sharp distinction with a backlist of barely literary and paraliterary genre fiction. CI earned appreciative coverage for *Julius Caesar;* a *New York Times* piece reads like a press release in its message of fidelity, legitimacy, and authenticity:

Heeding the pleas of educators and parents, the Gilberton Company is offering this version of Shakespeare in the hope of loosening the hold of video and Superman on countless youthful minds, Mr. Kanter explained yesterday. After months of research conducted with the cooperation of authorities at New York University, the picture version of "Julius Caesar" will start selling next week. . . . "In 'Julius Caesar', as in all other literary works we have presented as comic books," Mr. Kanter said, "we have adhered rigorously to the author's language and plot." ("Shakespeare Bows to 'Comics' Public" 1950, 24)

There are comics and then there are comics, goes this party line; a properly executed adaptation can conserve the literariness of its source, and by extension the democratic promise of uplift, with no lapse toward immature delinquency.

This *Times* write-up notwithstanding, party lines play better within parties than outside of them; and in the shadow of mass-culture debates, the promise of democratization carries the peril of massification. In the last year of Classics Illustrated adaptation, Habermas asked whether the democratic promise of the market held true or false:

> whether it created an initial access to cultural goods for a public and then, in keeping with the cheapening of the cost of the products, *economically eased* the access for an ever larger public; or whether it adapted the content of the cultural goods to its own needs in such a way that it also *facilitated* access for broad strata *psychologically.* ([1962]1989, 166)

In Habermas's tale of decline and fall, "psychological facilitation" undermines rational-critical literacy, portending the withering of citizenship—thus again the association of civility with a normative literacy, inflected more positively by Habermas than by Hunter. Alongside how Habermas conveniently captures the spirit of the mass-culture debates, it's worth noting how his ideal of mature citizenship derives from the same Kantian notion of maturity as undergirds the rationality of popular literary education. Unlike typical CI fare, Shakespeare's work holds privileged place within the readerly ethics of literary education; and the bigger they are, the better targets they make. Their detractors could find ample evidence that adaptations remained mired in the immature facility of the comic book form, that their gateway led down rather than up. As texts they stripped their sources of the very complexity prerequisite for cultivation of the critical attitude. As regards authorship, despite Gilberton's moves to distance itself from the comic book culture industry, its own creative staff worked for hire within a similarly Fordist organization of production—for almost literal disintegration of the authored coherency of their sources. At the scene of reading, Wertham found customary formulae for delinquency in occasional horror sequences (unsurprising given the concentration of titles in juvenile genres). Along with many librarians and teachers, he saw their promise of upward literary mobility straightforwardly controverted by what Harker called "their primitive dependence upon pictures" (1948, 1705); even Shakespeare can't repair the essential immaturity of the comic book form. The closing exhortation to read the original work smacks of disingenuousness; with selections for adaptation aligned with school curricula, students could read the adaptation in order *not* to read the original.

Whether figured as tragedy or triumph, this is the reversal of reform, the deflection of popular literary education. Certainly reversal, deflection, and outright failure haunt any project of cultural reform; but in 1950s America, preoccupied with policing lines between democratization and massification, the potential for failure would have appeared especially perilous in the comic book Shakespeares. Again, the central question is that of the relationship between official culture and the apparently degraded and degrading forms of mass culture. No definitive authority emerged to resolve that question then, and it remains unresolved and open to debate today.

With the imprint's resurrection by Berkley/First Publishing in 1990, however, the terms of the question shift with a revaluation of the comic book form as art. Unlike the Gilbertons, whose bid for cultural legitimacy derived exclusively from the authority of their literary sources, the First adaptations aspired to an artistry proper to the comic book form—an aspiration decidedly more attainable, and more intelligible, in 1990 than in 1940. Comparison between Firsts and Gilbertons registers a half-century of change within the comic book field, change that goes far beyond any simple narrative of aesthetic progress. If Gilberton "illustration" looks simplistic next to First "artwork," for example, apparent technical advancement in representation depends on technological advancement in reproduction. Similarly, the prestige of First's "name" artists presumes institutions of criticism, (para)literary public spheres like the critical fan press, in which names are *made*. Likewise the limited scale of direct-market distribution distinguishes First from the mass market, a distinction only partially and fitfully achieved by Gilberton. And perhaps most importantly, children composed an overwhelming proportion of Gilberton's market from the 1940s through the '60s. The recent contraction of the comic book market favors an older audience, and more broadly a maturation of the medium itself—the aestheticization of popular art forms demands a measure of distance from the everyday. More than ever, comics aren't just for kids; the '80s and '90s saw the comic book community mounting soapboxes to proclaim that point. That First's "aesthetic progress" follows the comic book's upward mobility so closely should sound a note of caution against derision of last-year's models within developmental narratives—as in First "name" Gahan Wilson's characterization of the Gilbertons as primitive hackwork (see Kelman 1990).

Nevertheless, the effect of artistic maturity in the First adaptations suffers little for its historical contingency. They indeed seem more modern than primitive, not only with more attention to the style of their literary sources, but also with more stylistically practiced artwork. Pictures no longer play poor relations to maladapted words; rather pictures and words together participate in a relatively credible bid for artistic legitimacy. *Hamlet* (1990, the short-lived series' only Shakespeare) repeats many of the questionable Gilberton elisions; but it also includes more of Shakespeare's words (including the role of Fortinbras), with fewer cuts and synopses, and more thoughtful visual representation of dialogue—a relatively mature sense of narrative and form. The painted art reflects a cinematic turn in comic book storytelling: the panel as flexible film frame, composed and sequenced for stylistic effect. In "frame analysis," one might contrast First artist Tom Mandrake's active style of shot variation across a free panel space, as against Alex Blum's seemingly a stylistic reliance on a few favored "utilitarian" shots across more static and rectilinear panel space in Gilberton's *Hamlet*.

But the cinematic metaphor does more than offer a way to appreciate the comic book equivalent of film style; it allows the comic book reader to bask in the reflected maturity of film criticism. This readerly maturity works as an important support for a wider revaluation of comic books—not only within the comic book field, increasingly autonomous relative to official institutions of artistic evaluation, but also beyond, through various and variously effective projects of entrepreneurship. Once again, straightforward comparison of adaptations risks losing this forest for the trees. That the Firsts met warmer reception than the Gilbertons (though importantly and not coincidentally, much *smaller* reception) indicates not simple differences in artistic value between the two kinds of adaptation, but the fact that the First comics could be valued as art—if not on par with Shakespeare, at least on the same order of cultural value. The character of negative reaction to the new adaptations tells much toward this point. From a multiculturalist perspective, Professor Barbara Burnaby worried over the *preservation* of the canon, rather than its degradation (in Kelman 1999). In Phi Beta Kappa's *American Scholar*, J. C. Furnas called the paper "slick" and the artwork "pretentious" (1992, 251), a very different kind of complaint than the labels of juvenile immaturity applied to the Gilbertons. Still more provocative is an earlier encounter between the *Comics Journal*, *de facto* journal of record for artistically legitimate comicdom, and Brazilian artist Von's *Macbeth* (1983), from another series of adaptations published by Oval Projects. In his *CJ* review (1983), Dale Luciano pillories Von not so much for simple betrayal of Shakespeare, but seemingly more pointedly for betraying the proper artistry of the comic book form. It's not Luciano's disciplined reading alone that shepherds the comic book form across some threshold of aesthetic maturity; but some threshold has been crossed.[5]

When First folded in 1991 after thirty-odd adaptations, the property lay dormant until acquired by Acclaim Books in 1997. In its own short Classics Illustrated publication history, Acclaim reprinted about a third of the Gilberton titles (including all five Shakespeares), recolored and repackaged with new sections of commentary as CI "Study Guides."[6] Most often written by graduate students, junior faculty, and ex-academics, commentaries acknowledged the limitations of the adaptations, noting lines and subplots dropped from source texts, indicating approaches toward critical analysis (poetics, thematics, narrative structure), and more generally attending to context (politics, culture, source material, performance). Thus if the Acclaim guides returned to the Gilberton project in announcing themselves as "doorway[s] to the classics," they presented a more properly scholarly kind of doorway. "Over the centuries since *Hamlet* was written," Debra Doyle writes, "students of the play have been attracted to the play because it's so rich in 'problems,' points which can be argued and analyzed and approached from many different directions" (1997). In that formulation and in the list of problems that follow, Doyle issues a clarion call to ethical criticism. If the ethics of criticism's the thing, she effects an apparently winning redemption of Shakespeare in comics.

Needless to say, this apparent "reschooling" of comic book adaptation is shot through with ambivalence, most notably in its questionable relationships with both literary education and the comic book field. Acclaim marketed its titles as study guides rather than comic books; and so if it shepherds Gilberton's comic book Shakespeare closer to the scholarly scene of critical reading, it's only for a closer shot at subversion of that scene. The Gilberton series appropriated Shakespearean value through the promise of uplift packaged along with the pleasure of reading, even if the pleasures of the comic book form reversed the uplift of properly literary value. The First and Oval Projects series founded claims of artistic legitimacy upon transformations within the comic book medium, including the new emergence of a proper comic book criticism, the purest form of a newly appropriate critical attitude toward comic books. Their implicit parity with the literary value of their sources certified their claims, even if revaluation remained importantly local and limited. With no such grand aspirations, the Acclaim series might seem the degenerate member of the Classics Illustrated family. But in the end, it illustrates utterly without pretense (if not without perversion) the connection between Shakespearean value in comic books and the scholarly ethics of critical reading.

Sandman: the Value of Mythology, Mythologies of Value

Sandman is a comic strip for intellectuals, and I say it's about time.

—*Norman Mailer*

Sandman mobilizes the figure of Shakespeare within an expansively effective enterprise of cultural value; with an audience imagined as not only mature, but intellectual, the series achieved not only broad recognition of legitimacy, but of literariness. As in the Gilberton series, Shakespeare plays a relatively small role, but one of disproportionate consequence. And as in the First series, engagement with Shakespeare works to certify revaluation of comic books in relation to an acknowledged measure of cultural value. Not bound by the constraints of adaptation, however, *Sandman* incorporates the work of Shakespeare much more freely, as pliable elements of mythology within a narrative of many, rather than as discrete and inflexible texts for translation. If the adaptations borrow the legitimacy of Shakespearean maturity, *Sandman* practices a much stronger appropriation, with its own proper inflection of Shakespeare. This storytelling strength participates in another kind of mythology: the insistent and ubiquitous tale of exceptionalism that constructs *Sandman* as the paradigmatically literary comic book, a beacon of maturity in a sea of immaturity. Given the currency of this second mythology, Mailer's pull-quote begs a more interesting question than it answers: How does a comic book become one for intellectuals? In brief, occasional traffic with Shakespeare, a (meta)mythology congruent with the mature critical attitude.

In DC's official version, the story of *Sandman* begins in late 1987, when "Neil Gaiman suggests a radical new take on the old DC Sandman character to British liaison editor Karen Berger and company president Jenette Kahn" (1995). Already this narrative advances the creep of exceptionalism. *Sandman*'s emergence in late 1988 rides the tide of the much broader British invasion of American comics discussed above; Berger fashioned DC as beachhead, editing Alan Moore's *Swamp Thing* (1984), Jamie Delano's *Hellblazer* (1988), Grant Morrison's *Animal Man* (1988) and *Doom Patrol* (1989), and Peter Milligan's *Shade* (1990). Leaving aside for now why Mailer never favored *Hellblazer* with his evaluative authority, *Sandman* ended in 1996 with Gaiman's finale in issue 75, survived by various spin-off projects by other writers. In bird's-eye view, *Sandman*'s broad narrative trajectory follows Morpheus, the lord of Dream; from issue to issue, a succession of more or less self-contained storylines assume prominence as they wind around that thread. Thus in an elegant (if not unique) reconciliation of seriality and variety, Gaiman decenters his protagonist, reconstructing his narrative role as something like a player and host of anthology drama—one with more suspense and horror in the earliest issues, more melodrama and fantasy later on. But Morpheus not only sets and takes the stage for the various *Sandman* stories; he *is* the stage, the very personification of the plurality of mythology. Perhaps more than any other element, the resulting aura of hyperliteracy has come to define the series: "*The Sandman* plays with myth and fantasy and storytelling," comments DC publicity manager Martha Thomases. "You should know your Shakespeare, you should know your mythology, and you should know your history. The writer assumes you've read a lot" (quoted in Wilson 1995). By this point, of course, it shouldn't surprise that Thomases explains the series' hypersophistication with reference to the hypercompetence of its implied reader.

Within *Sandman*'s play of collaged stories, Shakespearean mythology holds a position of privilege. William Shakespeare makes a first cameo appearance in issue 13, "Men of Good Fortune," as Will Shaxberd, hack playwright envious of the talent of friendly rival Kit Marlowe. Morpheus approaches him with a bargain: In return for storytelling skill, Shakespeare will pen two commissioned plays. In this meeting of mythologies, Shakespeare stands subordinate to Morpheus, a favored pet within the dreamlord's menagerie of stories. Certainly Morpheus's power to enclose Shakespeare within *Sandman*'s narrative won't suffice to set Gaiman and Shakespeare on equal footing outside of it; but one of the earliest lessons from the series' reception history is that a little metanarrative can go a long way. . . . And so of course Shakespeare accepts the bargain, fulfilling his first commission in issue 19, "A Midsummer Night's Dream." With Burbage and company, Shakespeare journeys to the green countryside to perform the play, as a gift from Morpheus to the departed Faeries. As lesser Faeries play unruly groundlings, fascinated by their own representations, the lord of Dream watches with Titania and Auberon. Afterward, he explains the performance to King and Queen, with a remarkable flourish:

> MORPHEUS: They shall not forget you. That was important to me: that King Auberon and Queen Titania will be remembered by mortals, until this age is gone.
> AUBERON: We thank you, Shaper. But this diversion, although pleasant, is not *true*. Things never happened thus.
> MORPHEUS: Oh, but it *is* true. Things need not have happened to be true. Tales and dreams are the shadow-truths that will endure when mere facts are dust and ashes, and forgot. (21)

Affirmation, that's what dreams are made of. This story about stories that affirm the value of stories (Shakespearean and otherwise alike) flatters our investment in stories, affective and critical; and it became the first and last comic book to win a World Fantasy Award. WFA's subsequent exclusion of comics reinforced the mythology of *Sandman*'s exceptional literary value.

Shakespeare completes his bargain with Morpheus in the final issue of the series, "The Tempest." Where "Midsummer Night's Dream" told of performance, "Tempest" tells of composition; it tells a story of storytellers rather than stories. The tale finds Shakespeare and Morpheus in momentous and pregnant weariness: the playwright at the end of his career, charged with a final creation; the lord of dreams granted a final appearance in a story set before his death and wake (in the two previous storylines). Once again, the patron explains his play: "I wanted a tale of graceful ends. I wanted a play about a King who drowns his books, and breaks his staff, and leaves his kingdom. About a magician who becomes a man. About a man who turns his back on magic" (35). Like nested dolls, the figures of Shakespeare, Morpheus, and Gaiman collapse here across concatenated levels of narrative. And not only here: Story endings disproportionately determine story meanings, and *Sand-*

man's ending draws the meaning of the series' entire run toward this chain of authorial equivalence. Thus in the end, *Sandman* cashes in the cultural value of the Shakespearean mythology accrued within its own (meta)mythology.

Since Habermas mourned the fall from active cultural debate to passive cultural consumption (as corollary of culture's own fall from medium of democratization to instrument of massification), more recent work has acknowledged the persistence of an active audience. *Sandman* has occasioned a vibrant fan community, with dozens of often elaborate websites devoted to the series and its writer. But the mature quality of fan attention tells more than its quantity. A detailed critical annotation of the series circulates on the web, for example, glossing each issue almost panel by panel. More than an outpost of popular literary education, however, *Sandman* comes home to roost in the academy. The number of on-line term papers, masters' theses, and even dissertations on the series only hints at the volume of critical academic attention it receives, including consistent, emphatic, and authoritative entrepreneurial support from UC-Santa Barbara's Frank McConnell: "If *Sandman* is a 'comic,' than *The Magic Flute* is a 'musical' and *A Midsummer Night's Dream* is a 'skit.'" (1995). As implied in Habermas's narrative, the cultural value of texts correlates with the cultural value of their associated reading practices; most fundamentally, reading *Sandman* critically for its literary value enacts its literariness.

Reading for literariness depends on the series' insertion within a frame of reference to distinguish it from comic book paraliterature. Typically genre and form work together to set styles of reading. But *Sandman* practices a fascinating legerdemain: through affiliation with genre fiction, it transcends its form; and by disavowing its genre, it becomes literature.[7] This alchemy proceeds first through repudiation of mainstream comic book superheroics. In the mythology of exceptionalism, *Sandman* heroically deconstructs unsophisticated heroism—never mind the neglect of other comic books that practice a similar deconstruction, nor the presumption of dismissing the undeconstructed as unsophisticated. *Sandman* excepted (sometimes along with a few others), the field of comic books collapses into a ghetto of juvenile paraliterature. Most notably and notoriously with its World Fantasy Award, the series escapes that ghetto wearing the colors of genre fiction: file it under fantasy, goth, metaphysics, subculture, but not under comics. "Midsummer Night's Dream" captures this capacity for crossover well: the charmed coupling of Shakespeare and metamythology plays well at the science fiction/fantasy bookstore. Of course, genre fiction carries pejorative connotations; in its ascension to literariness, *Sandman* simply sheds the mark of genre. Journalists follow Gaiman and his readers to dismiss spandexed superheroes, for example, but suppress the markedly generic quality of Morpheus's resemblance to characters from science fiction/fantasy illustration.

Another kind of frame constitutes the text more directly. Among the most limiting aspects of the comic book form is its association with seriality; the critical attitude prefers to favor discrete texts. DC collects the complete run of *Sandman* in a set of numbered trade paperbacks, shifting distribution from newsstands or specialty stores to more legitimate bookstores, with a more distinguished clientele. And of course the series' very completeness leads away from lowbrow seriality: "For a story to have a meaning, it has to end," Gaiman contends; "It's the difference between a play and *Days of Our Lives*" (quoted in Henrickson 1996). This is a very revealing comment. Most generally, this juxtaposition might imply the contingency and labor-intensiveness of *Sandman*'s upward cultural mobility, in light of similar, though often much more politically and sociologically self-conscious, projects to revaluate soap opera (see Brunsdon 2000). Gaiman nips that implication in the bud with fairly callous dismissal of soap opera. Second, his intimate association of meaning and ending goes to confirm the structural privilege of "The Tempest" (and Shakespearean mythology) within the narrative as a whole. Finally, he understands *Sandman*'s termination through an implicit distinction between artistic and industrial culture—one that bleeds into a distinction between artistic and industrial authorship.

As the comic book text suffers the taint of industrialized seriality, the comic book writer endures the disrepute of industrial production: collaboration and incorporation spell the end of romantic-individualist authorship. Gaiman has straightforwardly diminished the importance of pencils and inks in *Sandman:* "*Sandman* is a writer's book. It doesn't matter who's on it" (interviewed in O'Donnell 1991). Penciller, inker, and writer alike, however, earn their paychecks from DC's parent company, Warner Brothers, perhaps the very emblem of corporatized culture. Once again the series' ending carries important weight: first for its mythologization of authorship in which Gaiman is a kind of Shakespeare; and then also for its place within mythologies of creative control, Gaiman being a romantic opponent of cultural industrialization. Yet of course sometimes mythologies of creative control serve the interests of the cultural industries, and the DC party line participates in the mythology of exceptionalism. "It's not often you get an author as identifiable as Neil," says editor Stuart Moore, personalizing institutional transformations in relations of intellectual property; "We felt the book was so much Neil that it wouldn't have been productive to continue" (quoted in Hakim 1995). Nevertheless DC continued to release spin-offs from *Sandman,* as well as T-shirts, figurines, and plush dolls.

Moore's strategic omission represents something other than mere falsification; it *spins* the romance of Gaiman's authorship for the benefit of the mainstream press, the springboard of cultural entrepreneurship. Along with other elements of the mythology of *Sandman*'s literary value, it makes for good copy; various elements recur in the popular press with striking consistency, reproduced with the fond reverence accorded favorite stories of high-school glory. *Sandman*'s mythology of value translates serendipitously within the conventions of journalism. Gaiman is cast in the role of great man (an assignment he accepts without reluctance), as the romantic personification of an emergent comic book authorship—a trope that conveniently truncates the untowardly long, complicated, and sometimes decidedly *un*romantic history of that emergence. The construction of *Sandman* as the exception to the comic book rule similarly streamlines the journalistic narrative, violently flattening the field of mainstream comic books, letting the exceptional standout exemplify, and very often thus exclude the precursors that allow for its possibility. And for journalistic narratives, *Sandman* mythology offers compelling ornamentation: academic dissertations on comic books, comic book usurpation of prose-fiction awards, and of course comic book stories about stories from Shakespeare.

With or without its hyperbolization in journalistic circulation, this broader mythology of value should not be mistaken for a simple lie, any more than it should be mistaken for simple truth. It's a mythology, more profitably considered for its effects than for its truth or falsity. *Sandman*'s mythology of value derives from the value of mythologies, especially of the Shakespearean kind, within certain bankable configurations of readership, textuality, and authorship. *Sandman* mythology appropriates Shakespeare for its own artistic legitimation, and unlike the adaptations it does so within its own proper terms. A resistant appropriation? In some ways "yes"; but at the same time, revaluation of *Sandman* reproduces certain rules of value with uncomfortable force. The effectiveness of its implied reader's much vaunted intellectualism, for example, trades upon opportunistic and insistent reference to the juvenile immaturity of the implied audiences of other comic books. This is not to endorse some putatively radical rejection of value and evaluation, as if we should (or could) try never to distinguish between good and bad. Yet in the relentless disparagement of "undeconstructed" comic books (not to mention occasional defamation of soap opera), *Sandman* mythology might prove more complicit than resistant.

"Ranma and Juliet": A Carnival of Value?

By way of conclusion, a brief consideration of Viz Comics' *Ranma 1/2* might indicate an alternative to the cutthroat negotiations of value in Classics Illustrated and *Sandman*, in which enterprises of upward cultural mobility look up toward Shakespearean maturity, and inevitably downward upon unredeemed comic book immaturity. Viz graphic novels translate and repackage

Rumiko Takahashi's Japanese "gag manga" (lighthearted comic) *Ranma 1/2*, serialized in the magazine *Shonen Sunday* between 1987 and 1996. *Ranma 1/2* tells the story of Ranma Saotone, schoolboy martial artist who becomes a school*girl* when touched by cold water. In the "Ranma and Juliet" storyline, Ranma's school produces an idiosyncratic *Romeo and Juliet*, frustrated at every iconic turn by the misadventures of its young cast. Reflected across cultures and then back again, Shakespeare appears in a dizzy carnival of funhouse mirrors. Within contemporary criticism, the storyline's gender-bent queerness might represent the most faithful aspect of its Shakespeareanism; or it might read as allegory for the disruption of scholarly literary education. Despite such temptation to recuperate the story within familiar terms, what's more salient in *Ranma 1/2* is precisely its unfamiliarity, its distance from the conventions of intelligibility common to Classics Illustrated and *Sandman*. Across this cultural distance, Japanese manga holds a position of distinction with respect to American comics. But crucially as against the kind of distinction aimed for by CI and *Sandman*, appreciation of manga implies no deprecation of comics. On the contrary, manga carries connotations of legitimacy for all comics, beyond the zero-sum economy of value—as in the ritualized observation that comics in Japan aren't just kids' stuff, but an entertainment form esteemed by all. Clearly the language of maturity as measure of distinction loses some if its teeth. At the same time, however, the marginality of western manga fandom fosters a different economy of value, structured most notably around the reader's critical connoisseurship of a relatively obscure cultural other. In *Ranma 1/2* Shakespeare participates in a reflected play of cultural difference and similarity, within an economy of value indeed much less competitive than that of Classics Illustrated and *Sandman*. Yet while *Ranma 1/2* marks a partial break from their harshly competitive negotiations of value, the break is only ever partial, and the cultured reader's distinction remains. Perhaps Deconstructo's self-defeating struggle to undo binary oppositions he ends up reinscribing is a more accurate account of comic value after all.

Notes

1. Deconstructo says to Kara in issue 38, "What do you know about Hell? Hell is a word and a word is a world. As Milton didn't say, 'A word is its own place and can make a Hell of Heaven.'"

2. We choose these examples for their prominence and for the sake of argument, but there are of course other comic book Shakespeares worth noting. In Dik (and now Chris) Browne's syndicated strip *Hägar the Horrible*, Norse conquerors Hägar and Helga name their melancholy son "Hamlet." In the world of Marvel Comics' X-Men, one supporting player borrows his name

and feral nature from Shakespeare's Caliban. Long before the JLE met Deconstructo, DC's Superman, Batman and Robin, Flash, and Teen Titans all played at Shakespeare in one fashion or another. In these more developed allusions, a range of narrative devices join faraway fictional worlds: performance, rehearsal, or recitation of plays-within-the-comic book; looser adaptation of play storylines; even collaboration between Shakespeare and a time-travelling Superman on *Macbeth*. Kyle Baker's *Cowboy Wally Show* features a jailhouse production of Hamlet; against the illegitimacy of trash-entertainment producer Cowboy Wally, the story interestingly aligns author and reader together on the side of Shakespearean legitimacy. Though not without ambivalence, Baker displaces abjection of comic books upon "trash culture," pleading innocence by association with high culture. Eddie Campbell inverts this formula of association in his "Shakespeare" strips, projecting the cartoonist's abjection onto the playwright, shown writing a series of collection letters. Instead of genuflection to the Bard sacralized within aesthetic ideology, the strips present Shakespeare as accounts-receivable clerk, mired along with the cartoonist in everyday necessity. See also *Fightin' Army* 4 "The Lonely War of Captain Schulz" (American Comics Group) and *Batman Gotham Adventres* 39 (August 2001, DC Comics), "Bringing Down the House," for references to *Macbeth*. And see Justice League *A Midsummer's Nightmare* 1–3, DC Comics 1996. The daily *Terry and The Pirates* comic strips in the 1930s and 40s also has a series of quotations from Shakespeare. See 5/6/39 and 4/20/38, among others. *Macbeth* is cited in *Dick Tracy Monthly*, no. 17, (El Cajon: Blackthorne Publishing Company, September, 1987.) Our thanks to Mike Jensen for bringing *Terry* and *Dick Tracy* to our attention.

3. For sometimes fascinatingly partial correction of academic historiography's neglect of CI, see Overstreet 1970/2000, Sawyer 1987, Malan 1991/1996, Richardson 1993.

4. On mass-culture debates, see for example Rosenberg and White 1957; on media effect, see Hardt 1992; on delinquency, see Gilbert 1986; and on horror comics, see Nyberg 1998 and Barker 1984/1992 on the British case.

5. In a peculiar epilogue to this chapter of Shakespearean adaptation in comic books, the cover of Sinfield's *Faultlines* (1992) displays nine partial panels from Von's *Macbeth*, and Holderness's *Shakespeare Myth* (1988) reprints a page from Oscar Zarate's *Othello*. Quoted without discussion or explanation (save attribution), the comic book clippings occupy an ambiguous position with respect to the academic analysis around them. Do Sinfield and Holderness enlist Von and Zarate as equal partners in crime (against Shakespearean traditionalism)? Or do they appropriate them as souvenirs from the popcult slum? Given the academic's very low credibility as criminal, and attendant propensity to derive credibility from vampirism, one might incline toward the latter. Furthermore, Sinfield and Holderness might not only cite but also reproduce Von and Zarate's artistic marginality and illegitimacy. Both artists draw in a "primitivist" style; but when removed from most favorable context

(critical attention to positive style), primitivism looks merely primitive. Blocked at the threshold of aestheticization, the adaptations play their assigned roles of romantically marginal prey for academic vampirism. Of course, this is only one reading of Sinfield and Holderness; and it's only a provocative turn that this blockage should occur in such unexpected places as left-revisionist academic sociologies of Shakespeare. But the broader point is that blockage occurs at all. If transformations within the comic book field lend a certain authority to reading comic book Shakespeares toward artistic legitimacy, that authority encounters limits—here, perhaps, in readings invested in the illegitimacy of comic books.

6. In a similar though much more limited redeployment, in 1981 Regents Publishing released expanded versions of some Gilbertons for classroom use.

7. Properly speaking, of course, *Sandman* practices not very much at all; here and elsewhere, I use this kind of rhetoric that attributes agency to comic books in the name of convenience rather than analytic rigor. More strictly speaking, it's *Sandman*'s readers who associate the series with genre fiction, and so on.

Works Cited

Barker, Martin. 1984/1992. *A Haunt of Fears: The Strange History of the British Horror Comics Campaign.* Jackson, MS: Univ. of Mississippi Press.

Beisel, Nicola. 1997. *Imperiled Innocents: Anthony Comstock and Family Reproduction in Victorian America.* Princeton, NJ: Princeton Univ. Press.

Bruggerman, Lora. 1997. "'Zap! Whoosh! Kerplow!'" *School Library Journal.* January, 22–27.

Brunsdon, Charlotte. 2000. *The Feminist, the Housewife, and the Soap Opera.* NY: Oxford Univ. Press.

Carlino, Joseph. 1952. *Report of the New York State Joint Legislative Committee to Study the Publication of Comics.* Albany: Williams Press, New York Legislative Documents. 175th Session. Volume Eight, Document 64.

Dollimore, Jonathan and Alan Sinfield. 1985/1994. *Political Shakespeare: Essays in Cultural Materialism.* 2nd ed. Ithaca, NY: Cornell Univ. Press.

Furnas, J C. 1992. "Why Johnny Needn't Read." *American Scholar* (61) 247–253.

Gilbert, James. 1986. *A Cycle of Outrage: America's Reaction to the Juvenile Delinquent in the 1950s.* NY: Oxford Univ. Press.

Habermas, Jürgen. [1962]1989. *The Structural Transformation of the Public Sphere: An Inquiry into a Category of Bourgeois Society.* Trans. by Thomas Burger with Frederick Lawrence. Cambridge, MA: MIT Press.

Hakim, Danny. 1995. "Good Night, Dark Prince; Neil Gaiman Puts His Sandman Comic to Sleep." *Washington Post.* November 1 (Style) B1.

Hardt, Hanno. 1992. *Critical Communication Studies: Communication, History, and Theory in America.* NY: Routledge.

Harker, Jean Gray. 1948. "Youth's Librarians Can Defeat Comics." *Library Journal.* December 1, 1705–1707: 1720.

Henrickson, Eric. 1996. "The Sandman Cometh: Mainstream Wakes Up to Cult Comic Book Creator; New Adventures Lie Ahead." *Detroit News* March 2 (Accent).

Holderness, Graham. 1985/1994. "Radical Potentiality and Institutional Closure: Shakespeare in Film and Television." In Dollimore and Sinfield, eds., 206–225.

————. ed. 1988. *The Shakespeare Myth*. Manchester: Manchester Univ. Press.

Jones, Gerard. 1992. Justice League Europe 37–39. NY: DC Comics.

Kefauver, Estes. 1955. *Comic Books and Juvenile Delinquency: Interim Report of the Committee on the Judiciary.*

Kelman, Suanne. 1990. "A New Comic Version of the Classics." *Toronto Star.* February 1 (Magazine) M3.

Levine, Lawrence. 1988. *Highbrow/Lowbrow: The Emergence of Cultural Hierarchy in America.* Cambridge, MA: Harvard Univ. Press.

Levy-Reiner, Sherry. 1996. "The Trickle-Down Theory." *New York Times.* October 20. Magazine Desk Section 6, 28.

Luciano, Dale. 1983. "Parody, Poetry, Perversion, and a Bludgeoned Bard." *Comics Journal.* (81) May: 44–45.

Malan, Dan. 1991/1996. *The Complete Guide to Classics Illustrated (Volume One: The U.S. Series of Classics Illustrated and Related Collectibles.* Revised ed. 1996). St. Louis, MO: Malan Classical Enterprises.

McConnell, Frank. 1995. "Epic Comics." *Commonweal.* 20 October, 21.

Morrow, Greg, and David Goldfarb, ed. *Sandman Annotations.* Available online at http://theory.lcs.mit.edu/~wald/sandman-index.html.

Nyberg, Amy Kiste. 1998. *Seal of Approval: The History of the Comics Code.* Jackson, MS: Univ. of Mississippi Press.

O'Donnell, Whitley. 1991. "Neil Gaiman." *Comics Interview.* 103, 4–13.

Overstreet, Robert. 1970/2000. *The Overstreet Comic Book Price Guide.* NY: Harper Collins.

Richardson, Donna. 1993. "Classics Illustrated." *American Heritage.* May/June 78–85.

Rosenberg, Bernard, and David Manning White, eds. 1957. *Mass Culture: the Popular Arts in America.* NY: Macmillan/Free Press.

Sawyer, Michael. 1987. "Albert Lewis Kanter and the Classics: The Man Behind the Gilberton Company." *Journal of Popular Culture.* 20: 4 (Spring), 1–18.

Sinfield, Alan. 1985/1994. "Give an Account of Shakespeare and Education, Showing Why You Think They are Effective and What You Have Appreciated About Them. Support Your Comments with Precise References." In Dollimore and Sinfield, eds. 1985/1994, 158–181

————. 1992. *Faultlines: Cultural Materialism and the Politics of Dissident Reading.* Berkeley, CA: Univ. of California Press.

Takahashi, Rumiko. 1997. *Ranma 1/2* (Volume 7). NY: Viz Comics.

Wertham, Fredric. 1954. *Seduction of the Innocent: The Influence of Comics on Today's Youth.* NY: Rinehart.

Wilson, Terry. 1995. "The Big Sleep: Popular 'Sandman' Comic Reaches the End of the Line. *Chicago Tribune.* (Tempo) November, 1. 7.

CHAPTER 7

THE SHATNERIFICATION OF SHAKESPEARE
Star Trek and the Commonplace Tradition

CRAIG DIONNE

Nothing is more distinctive, more distinguished, than the capacity to confer aesthetic status on objects that are banal or even "common" (because the "common" people make them their own, especially for aesthetic purposes), or the ability to apply the principles of a "pure" aesthetic to the most everyday choices of everyday life. . . . In fact . . . the different ways of relating to realities and fictions, of believing in fictions and the realties they simulate, with more or less distance and detachment, are very closely linked to the different possible positions in social space and, consequently, bound up with the systems of dispositions (habitus) characteristic of the different classes and class fractions.

—Pierre Bourdieu, *Distinction*

"Hath not a Q eyes? Hath not a Q hands, organs, dimensions, senses, affections, passions? Fed with the same food, hurt with the same weapons, subject to the same diseases, healed by the same means, warmed and cooled by the same winter and summer as the Captain is?"

—*Star Trek: The Next Generation*

It could be argued that science fiction has one distinctive narrative feature, defined by the genre's ability to depict the future as a direct outcome of the present. Specifically, its representation of the future implies a temporal causality that civilization progresses through history as a result of material conditions of the past. The world we live in now, these stories suggest, places limits and constraints on the unfolding history of our future. In some examples of the genre—where society in the future is rendered as chaos and catastrophe, the dim horizon of a postnuclear winter or the victim of technology in an overly industrialized world (here for examples we might think of Ursula Le Guin's *Lathe of Heaven* or Philip K. Dick's *Do Android's Dream of Electric Sheep*, or the films *Metropolis*, or *Robocop, Terminator*)—the narrative mode has the potential to demystify one of the fundamental ideals of modern Western capitalism: the myth of progress, the idea that history naturally progresses toward a more prosperous and democratic civilization.

As Fredric Jameson has suggested, the cultural importance of this variety of science fiction is its ability to destablize this all-powerful myth: "its deepest vocation is to bring home, in local and determinate ways, and with a fullness of concrete detail, our constitutional inability to imagine utopia itself" (1984, 247). Ideologically, science fiction does not merely give us images of the future, then, but works specifically on our awareness of reality in a way "to defamiliarize and restructure our experience of our own present" by "accustoming" us to "rapid innovation, of preparing our consciousness and our habits for the otherwise demoralizing impact of change itself.[1] [These narratives] train our organism, " Jameson continues, "to expect the unexpected and thereby insulate us . . . [with] an elaborate shock-absorbing mechanism for the otherwise bewildered visitor to the new world of the great . . . industrial city" (1984, 244).

I wonder, however, if there is not a dimension to science fiction that runs counter to this dialectical impulse to teach each of its readers about the rapid changes associated with modernity. Science fiction's use of allegory to make its political messages explicit can sometimes place limits on just how "shocking" and "unexpected" the future world is rendered. When science fiction uses a tableau of loosely analogous characters and plots to provide topical commentary, it functions, as does most allegory, to organize the otherness of the Real into a recognizable object world for the reader. Consider, for example, the way the *Star Trek* television series modishly represents its future hippies in the famous "Way to Eden" episode as an allegory of the 1960s youth movement. There is nothing shocking or unexpected here: America's resistant youth are meant to look like a misdirected cult, as indeed the establishment chose to see them at the time. An easy formula might suggest that the more overtly allegorical the story means to be, the more it must depend on stock visual representations and habitual cultural patterns to make its message clear, as if the more Captain Kirk goes looking for new life and new civilizations the more he finds himself everywhere. The use of allegory can be thus interpreted as the narrative device that constrains the more progressive impulses of the genre to help its audience visualize difference.

Though I am not suggesting that allegory functions in science fiction as it did in the traditional liturgical or courtly literature, there is a degree to which the conventions of narrative form place limits on science fiction's claim to interact and transform the reality it depicts, so that rather than interpolating a subject into a providentially ordained cosmos, allegory in science fiction writes the crisis (or alternatively the utopia) of an impending future-present in a way that confirms for the reader on a deeper level that their beliefs and attitudes will survive all social change. "Ahhh, the hippies of planet Tiburon are weird and impetuous too." On a more insidious level, though, this form of ideological closure works to reproduce stridently reactionary representations of racial difference. The representation of different species in the future worlds of science fiction can be read as allegories of racial difference, and as such they work to essentialize seemingly genetic differences between the humanoids of the cosmos.[2] All the different species seem to have predominating character traits common to their people, as the show promotes associations between the humanoids of tomorrow and their present-day equivalents: "See? the Vulcans are genetically predisposed to excel in math, just like Asians." Or, even more insidiously, "See these Ferengi? Money-grubbing and materialistic, just like Jews." The more allegory is used to render our potential historical future recognizable, the more it tends to realign and reconstitute that future in the idiom of cultural hegemony.

This clash between the liberating and conservative impulses of science fiction—to decenter the myth of progress while confirming difference and the social hierarchy—can be identified as the central animating dialectic of science fiction generally, a definition that brings us closer to talking about *Star Trek's* varied narrative gestures in using Shakespeare to speak to its audience about the future. From its inception as the brainchild of Gene Rodenberry's popular television series to the latest elaborations in the wagon train theme, *Star Trek: Voyager,* the references and allusions to Shakespeare appear at key moments when the future is meant to speak to us like the twenty-third-century Elizabethan world it seems to be, oddly familiar as telos and origin to a Western culture that sees itself everywhere in the cold alien remoteness of an (as yet) uncolonized space.

On the surface, references to Shakespeare in *Star Trek* are playful responses to the question, what will literary tradition look like in the future? Or, more specifically, what will literacy look like in the future? A question that is more heartfelt today in the dot.com age when new modes of digitalized communication call into question old-world ideas of book and print; these lingering doubts about reading literature in turn underscore on a larger scale a new and zealous fixation on older printed texts that is now beginning to write various modes of commodity culture. (Think of the company Levenger's "Tools for Serious Readers"—with its gold-tipped wooden styluses, leather-wrapped reader's tables, and ivory bookmarks, all accentuating an "antiquated" form of reading for private pleasure—as the fullest expression of this fetishism, and perhaps the new literalism, "history of the book" project, with its particularity of bibliographic minutiae as an academic counterpart). Allusions to Shakespeare on *Star Trek* in this context mark moments where deeply felt anxieties about the effect technology will have on our relation with canonical literature are treated ostensibly as misguided fears, since the message we receive in these quirky moments when the Bard is quoted on the holodeck of the *Enterprise* or the bridge of a Klingon Bird of Prey, or when Captain Kirk receives a pair of eyeglasses and a leather-bound book as a quaint joke about his old age, is that Shakespeare not only survives in the future but remains in untouched form as an icon of poetic truth and authority for *all* cultures.

As a popular cultural text that represents the problems of a post-colonial politics read through the new frontier narrative of "exploring new worlds," *Star Trek* frames the anxiety about the loss of literary tradition within the context a larger global history. Specifically, these references to Shakespeare speak to deeper apprehensions over the role Western art or literature will have in defining a new and truly global cultural pluralism. All uncertainties about the Bard's defining position in the future are dispelled, however, when we see the intergalactic company of actors, the Karidian Company of Players, perform *Hamlet* for the crew of the original *Enterprise* ("Conscience of a King"), or the android Data receive acting lessons on how to portray Prospero ("Emergence"), or Captain Picard refer to his leather-bound copy of Shakespeare's works in his ready room. Such scenes confirm for viewers that Shakespeare's writing will persevere through the tempests of any or all postmodernities. Moreover, these scenes demonstrate the commingling of viewer interests, as they address a consumer equally at home with learning the vibrant fictional detail of fully realized alien cultures—Vulcan mating practices, Klingon kin structures, Cardassian feuds, the precise techno-babble of a psuedo-scientific discourse of phasers, forced plasma beams and neutrino inverters—next to allusions and references to *Julius Caesar, The Tempest,* and *Henry V.* What is reproduced through *Star Trek's* Shakespeare is a middlebrow audience attempting to distance itself even further from the popular lowbrow that defines mass culture generally, as a vaguely high-brow Shakespeare promises to help the series push its orbit even further from the aesthetic options located only a channel or film screen away.

But such distancing is overdetermined by the complex mediations of consumer culture. Bourdieu's theory of *habitus* accounts for the conferring of aesthetic status on the objects that litter the everyday consumer world, and may help define the move a popular culture text makes to hail an audience hungry to envision themselves as distinct, "above the masses," as a moment that is traversed with the performative politics of class and status. When *Star Trek* was originally produced in the 60's, it was semiotically situated against a backdrop of camp sci-fi shows like *Flash Gordon* and *Lost in Space*. The allegorical structure and moral tone of its first episodes ("The Cage," "Where No Man Has Gone Before," "The Corbomite Maneuver") were immediately recognized as attempts to elevate the genre's mediocre place of pulp television and to resituate it on par with other aesthetically equivalent alternate-reality and sci-fi shows like *Twilight Zone* and *Outer Limits,* though clearly within the hugely popular western motif. Rodenberry pitched the series to executives as "*Wagon Train* to the Stars" (the other show that mixed these generic features more patently was *Wild Wild West*).

The *Star Trek* pilot was described by one television executive as "too cerebral" for television. But Rodenberry was not deterred, as he set his goals to construct, in his own words, "a devoted fan-following of topflight scientists, engineers, and educators who recognized the ingenuity and foresight behind the fictional façade" (Tulloch and Jenkins 1995, 6). Such history speaks to the way in which *Star Trek,* from its inception, was inscribed as a middle brow narrative meant to cordon a meritocracy consumer with intellectual tastes. Such history also speaks to how *Star Trek* became the perfect medium for the transformative gestures Bourdieu speaks of, since this audience (Rodenberry's list seems more like an ego ideal than a realistic approximation of who actually grew to watch the show—a mainly youth culture keenly attuned to the show's liberalism) would also identify with any attempt to confer distinction to the aesthetic textures of the series.

But Bourdieu's theory of retooling the object world of consumerism begs many questions about some of the terms he uses to define the relative degrees of status implied in such terms as "vulgar," "banal," and "common," suggesting that his theory of social process might itself be one that applies to a history of consumerism when such categories had a meaningful relation to the modes of cultural production current at the time. *Star Trek*'s early history testifies to the fact that these ideas of distinction were relevant to its production as a highbrow form; the references and allusions to Shakespeare have been a mainstay since the Karidian players performed *Hamlet* on the *Enterprise* in the 1967 "Conscience of the King."

As Richard Burt suggests in *Unspeakable ShaXXXspeares,* however, much more complicated permutations in capitalist production in the last twenty years of a more broadly "mass" culture have forced us to reconsider the extent to which such ideas of aesthetic taste and distinction are not themselves outmoded by an intensified consumerism that calls into doubt the high-low boundaries implied in the idea of a "popular" (as opposed to an "elite") culture. This anxiety of a boundaryless, post-MTV "kiddie culture," as Burt calls it, is registered in those moments in film and television when Shakespeare is meant to signify one horizon or position in a cultural or regional domain buts ends up taking on a rather fuzzy zoneless quality of the commodity relation itself. As Burt argues, the recent interest in Shakespeare in all of the various markets of the media industry function as "unconscious efforts at reterritorializing Shakespeare" at a time when "relations between world powers are reconfigured in the post–Cold War globe" ([1998]1999, xiv). As such, Shakespeare gets to become, for corporations that cannot be defined by national boundaries and regional interests, a commodity "exported" from an idealized "native" Anglo-American culture. The truth of the matter is that this cultural locus gets lost in the hyperreal logic of this new phase of multinational capitalism, and Shakespeare becomes hard to define in the mixed forms of a principally tourist-driven industry.

The commodity logic of this industry defines the conflicting ideological motives behind Star Trek's latest assimilations of Shakespeare, since in its attempt to align the genre's aesthetic interests with textual appreciation of a high art form—"Shakespeare" as an icon of perjuring artistic value—it nonetheless ends up assimilating Shakespeare, like the Borg do to all worlds, as another recognizable form of cult paraphernalia. The best example of this would be *The Klingon Hamlet by William Shakespeare*, composed by the Klingon Language Institute, which purports to be the original ur-*Hamlet*, marketed as a "must have" item for the fan who owns *The Klingon Dictionary: English/Klingon Klingon/English*. Shakespeare is represented as the plagiarist of an original Klingon fable. At best, *The Klingon Hamlet* is a playful work that parodies what a postmodern revisionist scholarship looks like—a satire to those bibliographic attempts to uncover the lost and unread ur-text (a clever screenwriter is probably now devising a narrative where Klingons transport to Elizabethan England and leave their legendary tale for Kyd to stumble upon); at its worst it is a perfect expression of the commodity logic at the heart of the assimilating gesture, to use Shakespeare to clear more shelf space in the trekbook section of Barns n' Borders.[3]

The most important aspect of *Star Trek*'s Shakespeare in the manner in which it contextualizes his writing in seemingly incoherent ways; quotations and references seem to have little connection to the ongoing storyline. A brief tour of the website "William Shakespeare's STAR TREK" will demonstrate this. The site is an amusing compellation of passages that parrot different lines from different plays. "Is Picard a plagiarizer?" we're asked next to Patrick Stewart's photograph. "There is nothing either good or bad, but thinking makes it so," and then: "Sisko, Sisko, wherefore art thou Capt. Sisko. / Deny thy Starfleet and refuse thy commission. / Or if thou not, be sworn my love, / and I'll no longer be a Cardassian." The site serves to remind viewers just how immersed in Shakespeare *Star Trek* really is. But there is no real attempt to explain how these lines—or the context in which they appear in the plays—have anything at all to do with the *Star Trek* narratives. It merely suggests that, in case they haven't noticed, viewers have been exposed to Shakespeare in their favorite *Next Generation* episodes, whose local history lurks behind the website's glib references to the Bard.

As an entertainment industry defined its markets to include a broader consumer base in the late 1980s, an anxiety over the loss of a normalized hegemonic white-bread "center" was registered in mass media's attempt to account for the space women and minority consumers would have in this once-sanctioned white haven of middle-class mass-consumerism. It could be argued that *Star Trek*'s Shakespeare became more intense, more frenetic during this period, as it introduced in the *Next Generation* the Shakespearean Captain Picard to provide a halo of Anglocentric security to a crew whose diversity was meant to signify a rainbow society of collective, team-centered management. It could be argued that the Rodenberry franchise expanded during a time when an incipient mass culture threatened to reorient its hallmark gestures of allegory and social critique as an unwanted elitism akin to the History channel or PBS's educational programming. In response, *Star Trek: The Next Generation* seemed to retreat from overtly political themes by choosing loosely humanist narratives whose moral themes of difference and acceptance would not get in the way of its exciting special effects made possible by new technology and increased production budgets. *Star Trek*'s use of Shakespeare must be situated in this larger history when territories between consumer groups and boundaries between aesthetic practices were shifting to account for a more complex set of social relations in the public sphere. Readers cannot help but notice how the visual images on the website underscore the allusions to Shakespeare with references to the malshaped faces of the many species that populate the future world of the *Next Generation*'s culturally diverse universe, as if to say Shakespeare now gives expression to an even *more* universal culture.

But what of the website's form? This site exposes how closely Shakespeare is parsed and digested as a collection of saws and maxims whose messages have little or nothing to do with the underlying theme of the episode in question, as if the dizzying amount of allusions are meant to reassure viewers of the value of the narrative experience offered by the show. The Shakespeare of science fiction's future appears at times as if he has been reduced to a series of sound bite passages, bits and pieces of him meant to represent unspoken wholes, his work emptied of anything that might look like a theme and condensed to an icon that signifies the brute value of cultural capital itself. When considering the actual mode of editing involved on the website, one notices that this restless cutting and pasting is reminiscent of the commonplacing practices of Renaissance learning.[4] But the tradition has closer ties to the nineteenth-century famous quotations manuals and the high school oratorical "readers."

What I want to suggest in the following is that there is a long and—to the eyes of literary critics, at least—subterranean tradition of this kind of Shakespeare in American popular culture, one that defines a particular mode reading and appreciating his work that belongs to the extratextual, or more broadly defined sociological uses of Shakespeare in mass culture that this anthology is dedicated to examining. The practice of quoting Shakespeare, I would argue, does not have to be conceived as merely a top-down history in the sense of conceptualizing Shakespeare's influence as one where stage productions, critical readings, or scholarly editions are used to stand for society's sense of his importance. This is to assign a privileged status only to those relatively elite institutions like theater, universities (and even film companies), defining them as constitutive forces in the dissemination of his writing while overestimating the role of the professional or intellectual in determining how Shakespeare's writing is assimilated into culture generally. Most importantly, it leaves out of the picture a large section of other mediating influences like educational texts and quotations manuals which compose a different sector of the publishing industry and have a nearly autonomous relation to these other sites of cultural production.[5]

The history of Shakespeare's influence—even in those studies that putatively examine "Shakespeare's America" and vice versa—tend to neglect altogether that aspect of life implied in Bourdieu's theory of social practices that constitute everyday modes of communication and social interaction determined by these other "productions" of his writing. In the present essay, I make the case for a different interpretive strategy when looking at the curious history that Shakespeare has played in the different *Star Trek* stories, a strategy that may appear counterintuitive, but one that will address how his writing has played a role in the cultural shifts I have briefly outlined above. When looking at the curious allusions and references to his work that appear in different episodes, we may find ourselves at times at a loss to explain the contradictory or uneven parallels that seem to elusively suggest themselves. (Is Data's performance of Prospero at the beginning of "Emergence," say, meant to contextualize the cool rationality and emotional distance of Shakespeare's brave new world read through the androids of tomorrow?)

I do not doubt that the writers of the episode meant to communicate these things. But if we rely on our scholarly instincts as hermeneutic critics trained to find hidden themes suggested in all of these parallels, we are missing an important sociological piece of the puzzle. This is because we are trying to find theme where theme as such may not exist. These textual moments must be situated in the long-standing American tradition of reading and using Shakespeare in that other middle-brow practice of literary appreciation: the famous-quotation conduct manual. When confronted by many parallels in theme suggested in references to Shakespeare, it is perhaps best to begin by understanding the larger cultural meanings of using allusions and famous quotations in speeches and public forms of address, a stylized mode of self-display that is situated in a different history of literacy than the one suggested by the hermeneutic tradition of theme-making and interpretation—less the realm of self-consciousness through textual interrogation and more the realm of self-invention and self-promotion through textual adaptation, less in the mode of Coleridge and more in the mode of Shatner.

Akin to the commonplace tradition of the Renaissance, where allusions and "all saws and maxims" were used by the student as free-floating passages meant to help him signify his wit and learning in what Keith Thomas has termed the "Imitative Society," the ability to quote random passages of Shakespeare has always meant—at least in the American context of nineteenth- and twentieth-century oratorical pedagogy and the ensuing industry of middle-class conduct manuals—to signify one's erudition, one's middle-class status as "educated," "refined," and one's affinity with the larger mission of liberal culture to shape a narrowly defined consensus through formal diction.[6] The "Shakespeare's STAR TREK" website does not look too far out of place when situated next to other examples of this tradition.

Take for example E. D. Hirsch's *Cultural Literacy*, which makes its case about the declining literacy rates in the United States by telling a story about how his father was able to communicate succinctly and richly in a business memo by using phrases like "there is a tide" to explain the urgency of a transaction. Hirsch expresses the degree to which Shakespeare's writing had formed the cultural idiom of the American middle class. But one wonders if Hirsch's father was taught the entire *Julius Caesar*, to invoke the pathos behind this passage? As a holdover of the nineteenth-century oratorical textbook, the famous-quotations manual reproduced an ideology of moral conduct by thematizing key scenes and passages in Shakespeare's plays around solidly genteel ethics of ambition and virtue. In so doing they created a commonsense paradigm that has imparted a general interpretive approach to Shakespeare's plays, so much so that it would have only been natural for Hirsch's father to quote *Julius Caesar* on issues concerning expediency and trust, or *Macbeth* on ambition, loyalty, and turpitude. This tradition is so pervasive, so much taken for granted, that it defines how Shakespeare is to be used in practically every discourse outside of the narrowly defined academic confines of literary and dramatic appreciation. Consider how lawyers and judges repeatedly use Shakespeare in summations, briefs, and opinions to ground legal rulings in the firm soil of unquestioned aesthetic truth, free from anything that might look like a thematic understanding of the plays, using a reference to *King Lear* to support a ruling that it is legally sound to teach the idea of obeying fathers, and *Othello* to support the idea that the word "Indians" can be used to describe different native people of the Americas.[7]

What I am arguing here is that *Star Trek*'s seemingly reductive use of Shakespeare is not reductive at all in the way it mirrors a long and largely unexamined aspect of Shakespeare's "common place" in American culture. A more thorough understanding of how Shakespeare's writing has functioned in this commonplace tradition might help us understand the divide between the different arguments in today's culture wars, especially if we see how two ideological camps are working within distinct traditions of reading. When the left-leaning critic Stephen Greenblatt makes a case for the importance of teaching *The Tempest* in understanding the moral implications of colonialism, it seems to fall on the deaf ears of right-leaning William Bennet—whose famous *Book of Virtues* uses a quotation from *Macbeth* to teach children the value of ambition (!?), in part, because both political camps belong to different interpretive traditions. One framework means to understand the play as a whole text, applying a hermeneutic method to fathom its deeper thematic meanings; the other means to parse the play, to "commonplace" it as a storehouse of quotable quotes to impart wisdom and aesthetic delight.

One mode of reading belongs to the tradition of Coleridge and postromantic criticism, seeing the text in its entirety as a coherent and autonomous art object. The other approaches Shakespeare's writing much like the Renaissance commonplace book, a storehouse of oratorical exercises and moral maxims. Bennet's call for a return to Western culture speaks from within this commonplace tradition, which has its own implied pragmatic mode of defining the literary text as a malleable compendium of moral exemplars, quotations that reflect fixed and unchanging truths. This is the tradition that defines the use of Shakespeare in *Star Trek*, borrowing as it does from the middle-brow reader's editorial practice of arranging passages of his writing in epigrammatic, textual "chunks" to be transcribed in encyclopedias of common wisdom—Shakespeare's *Quotable Quotes*, Shakespeare's *Witty Comebacks*, but also think of Bartlett's *Familiar Quotations*. This is an incredibly influential mode of reading Shakespeare that is generally ignored by literary historians because it falls outside the standard categories of aesthetic response and theater history defined by literary scholarship (with the notable exception of Helen M. Whall's study included in this anthology). Nonetheless, it is a mode of appreciating (and interacting) with Shakespeare that shapes an entire industry of publishing and consuming his writing. In the case of *Star Trek*, the allusions and references to Shakespeare tend to do the similar cultural work of enhancing the gravity and aesthetic texture of its allegorical messages. The best example of this kind of textual allusion is to be found in *Star Trek VI: The Undiscovered Country*, which figures as a paradigmatic expression of this type of commonplacing and the way it is used to reconcile the social contradictions attendant to the collapse of a distinctly Eurocentric aesthetic tradition.

The narrative of *Undiscovered Country* works as a thinly veiled allegory that comments on several important political occurrences in postwar history. The three-part structure of Hollywood works well in providing a "grammar" to this story: in the beginning of the movie we find the newly recognized Captain Sulu cruising the cosmos on a routine mission when his vessel is hit by the powerful effects of a mysterious explosion from beyond the neutral zone behind the Klingon border. It turns out the blast originates from the Klingon moon, Praxis, where the planet's energy facility is located. This is the situation that draws the audience into the narrative's major conflict: the Klingon empire now only has fifty years of life left and cannot maintain its military budget. Hence, it is forced to recognize the economic benefits of making peace with the Federation. In the first scene with our familiar heroes, we learn that Captain Kirk has been selected to lead the first peace mission. The main tension of the narrative is centralized around Kirk's individual prejudice against Klingons: can he learn to set aside his anger over the loss of his son (is this a revenge narrative?), can he make peace with the alien world of the Klingons, who are now doomed to become dependent economically and politically, on the Federation? The history of an entire planet's people now depends on one individual's ability to change. In this scene, Kirk discovers that Spock volunteered the *Enterprise* to work as envoy of peace and make first contact with the hated Klingons:

KIRK: We volunteered? . . .
SPOCK: My father requested that I open negotiations . . .
KIRK: (interrupting) I know your father is the Vulcan ambassador, for heaven's sake. But you know how I feel about this. They're animals!
SPOCK: Jim, there's an historic opportunity here.
KIRK: Don't believe them! Don't trust them!
SPOCK: They're dying.
KIRK: Let them die!

The unfolding resolution of this conflict follows succinctly the Hollywood style. The recognizable fragments of Cold-War politics speak through the allegory. Here, the catastrophe on Praxiz appears vaguely like the lesson of Chernobyl and the economic crisis of the Klingons as the erosion of the Soviet infrastructure by Reagan's war of attrition. But both of these broader conflicts are collapsed into a moral choice to be made by a single person. What is important about this scene is that Kirk does not want to be the one to lead the mission. Kirk—the one who disobeys prime directives, disobeys Federation mandate, something of an intergalactic loose cannon himself— is the one chosen to represent the Federation's interests. And the audience is asked to delight in this irony. "Only Nixon could go to China." The Federation needs him, and the audience is placed in a position to read this scene as a kind of western. Dodge City needs its marshal, though the role is not one of protecting society from lawless criminals, but of providing a model for cultural tolerance. Kirk reflects in a monologue, the "Captain's Log":

> Captain's log. Stardate 9522.6. I never trusted Klingons, and I never will. I could never forgive them for the death of my boy. It seems to me our mission to escort the Klingon High Chancellor to the Peace summit is problematic at best. Spock says this could be an historic occasion. I'd like to believe him. How on earth can history get past people like me?

The ideology behind this narrative structure is one that, as Robert Ray has argued in his influential *A Certain Tendency of the Hollywood Cinema*, reconstitutes the ethos of individualism by subtly demonstrating that society is a world of laws and rules that constrain the natural freedoms and liberties of the real (outlaw) heroes of the world. Kirk's freedom to feel hatred and spite toward Klingons (read: the freedom to hate communists, but also freedom to differentiate ethnic difference) must be overcome if the conflict of this movie is to find a resolution. Thus, the allegory suggests a more complicated kind of individualism is required to reconcile the contradictions of a post - Cold War world. Kirk's individual choice will symbolize in the movie a new age of liberal pluralism in this latest stage of history where one united Federation—and one economic system—will define the different and competing cultures and ethnicities of all remaining life forms.

When coming to face the enemy, however, Kirk and the crew of the *Enterprise* are surprised to discover that Klingons are not the uncultured Slavic rogues they imagined. The whole Klingon race is reimagined here as romanticized warrior heroes of a bygone age, mixed in a cultural mingle-mangle as Third Reich aristocracy and Japanese Shogun. More importantly, the Klingon's "cultured" warriors can quote Shakespeare. Put simply, we might read the following scene, where Klingons quaff Romulan ale and quote Shakespeare at ease with their hosts, as a burlesque of an elite stateroom dinner at the Pentagon, a window into the bankrupt paradigm of liberal culture itself, where the mission of conservative pundits to return to the cultural literacy of an imagined past is played out in all of its contradictions when quotations of Shakespeare appear as rather gratuitous attempts at self-fashioning a genteel character more than thematic commentary on plot. The following scene also foregrounds the way Shakespeare will be meant to fit into the postwar world, since the ensuing discussion of the future and the western notions of rights seems to occasion momentously a return to Shakespeare, quoted by Chancellor Gorkon (the Klingon version of Gorbachev) in a toast at the first peaceful meeting between Starfleet and Klingons: "'The undiscovered country!' (pause) The future!" Spock immediately responds: "Act 3, Scene 1."

KLINGON GENERAL CHANG: You have not experienced Shakespeare until you have read him in the original Klingon.

KLINGON: Tak Pah, Tak Beh

ALL: [laughter]

UHURA: (to Klingon who is eating live thing): Are you fond of Shakespeare, General. . . . (repulsed)

CHEKHOV: We . . . believe that all planets have a sovereign claim to inalienable human rights . . .

KLINGON AZETBUR (daughter of Gorkon): Indeed. If you could only hear yourselves. "Human rights." The very name is racist. The Federation is no more than a homo sapiens-only club.

CHANG: (to Spock) Present company accepted, of course.

KLINGON: In any case, we know where this is headed. The annihilation of our culture.

NIMOY: That's not true!

KLINGON: No?

SPOCK: No!

CHANG: To be, or not to be. That's the question which preoccupies our people, Captain Kirk. We need breathing room.

KIRK: Earth. Hitler. 1938. (Spock surprised)

CHANG: I beg your pardon.

GORKON: Well . . . I see we have a long way to go.

General Chang is a stock evil character reminiscent of the cultured Nazi who plays Mozart while marching his victims to their death. Kirk's line helps viewers place him as such. The conflict between the two old warring groups is interspersed with random quotations from the Bard. One might ask, what does the "undiscovered country," as it appears in *Hamlet* (Spock reminds us of the line) as a reference to death, or immortality, have to do with the plot of the movie? Why would Gorkon toast to this? And does Chang's reference to Hamlet's lines, "to be or not to be," suggest that his people are considering mass suicide? Such questions force these lines to do what they are not meant to do, since commonplacing Shakespeare means that speakers can re-order and transfigure the signification of these lines to fit any topical context. Here, Shakespeare is merely used to sanctify the occasion of defining a new moment in history free from older animosities and Cold War strife. No other "country matters" are suggested here.

But another allegory might be suggested in this scene, particularly if we consider the cultural politics of commonplacing as it is depicted through the movie. I would argue that the scene serves as a parody of how the William Bennets and Dinesh D'Souzas of the world, who admit that Shakespeare wrote in "their" language and spoke their themes, make Shakespeare a kind of commonplace book of worldy wisdom to aid in the construction of the middle-brow idiom of "polish" and "deference" that contemporary conservative pundits see so lacking in public political discourse. In this context, the idea of the cultured post–cold warrior takes on the energy of expressing the ethical contradictions at heart in the project of liberal culture itself, where the promised ethics of Literature's ennobling affects—capital L—seem unable to explain much of the atrocities committed in twentieth-century history by the cultured heroes of Western societies, a contradiction that is embodied in the image of a Chang wiping blood from his lips as he quotes *Hamlet*. The unfolding plot—the imprisonment of Kirk and McCoy as fall guys for an attempted coup from within the Federation, which was meant to resurrect Cold War antipathies), their escape from the work camp, and their "saving" of the peace mission—never quite resumes the same energy or power of this one scene.[8] Shakespeare is used to heighten the aesthetic "pitch" of the movie's allegorical message, an argument for a new kind of individualism meant to transcend or, at least, distance itself from the liberal idealism of age-old, Eurocentric literacy. Kirk's growing awareness of his own prejudices is meant to foreground the overall theme that a new global community will have to be keen to cultural difference and open to ethnic diversity. In a crucial scene in the prison camp, where Kirk and Nimoy serve their life sentences as patsies to Gorkon's assassination, Kirk realizes that he must transcend his racism in order to construct a new future for the Federation:

> KIRK: Some people are afraid of what might happen. I was terrified.
> BONES: What terrified you, specifically?
> KIRK: No more neutral zone. I was used to hating Klingons. It never occurred to me to take Gorkon at his word. Spock was right.
> BONES: Try not to be hard on yourself. We all felt exactly the same.
> KIRK: No, somebody felt a lot worse. I'm beginning to understand why . . .
> BONES: Well, if you've got any bright ideas, now's the time.
> KIRK: Time's the problem. You and I are nothing. . . . Whoever killed Gorkon is bound to attempt another assassination unless we can get out of here . . .

Yet the lesson misfires. As much as Kirk becomes a revolutionized subject— "you and I are nothing," as if to say, bourgeois individualism may not be the template for subjectivity in this new world—he never fully realizes this transformation. After this scene the beautiful prisoner, Martia (played by the international model Iman), comes to Kirk and promises that she will deliver him safe outside the walls of the prison. Later, however, Kirk and Bones are betrayed by the shape-shifting Martia, whose beauty as well as her gender are as malleable as her allegiance to the captives. Martia can be read as the object of Kirk's newfound empathy, a general sign of the film's idea of cultural pluralism writ large as it envisions her racial difference in a patently orientalist manner. A tall, green-eyed, cigar-smoking femme fatale, Martia's the forgotten "other" of Kirk's Federation, doomed to work out her days in a slave camp on a remote asteroid. When Kirk later realizes that she has given them up to his Klingon conspirators, his openness to the global spirit of glasnost is revealed for the flimsy, romantic idealism it always was.

What we really need, this film suggests, is a hero who will protect himself inwardly from the transgressions of those who will take advantage of liberal society's open generosity. In moments like this, the film articulates the contradiction at the heart of New World Order ethos, as it conceives of cultural difference outside the supposed old-world prejudices that shaped Kirk and his "homo sapiens-only club." *Undiscovered Country's* representation of otherness reproduces the ideology upon which colonial notions of identity are founded. When Martia shape-shifts into Kirk in a comic scene before his rescue from the work colony, we see Shatner fulfill his fantasies to "play himself." (The film foregrounds this when it tells us Kirk always fantasized about kissing himself). Viewers get to delight in the doubling of Kirk's identity; as he struggles with Martia he is fighting to find himself after the ideological sea change that has occurred in his prejudiced self.

Shakespeare is brought back into the film at the end to help viewers visualize how a commonplacing practice will not sufficiently provide a substantive cultural model for the new global community. Chang may know Shakespeare, the movie suggests, but he's no Kirk. In Chang, we are made to witness the excesses of a commonplace tradition, as he chants over the comlink to Kirk while bombarding the defenseless *Enterprise:*

Now be honest, warrior to warrior. You do prefer it this way, as it is meant to be. No peace in our time. Once more unto the breech, dear friends. Tak Pah, Tak Beh? Tickle us, do we not laugh? Prick us, do we not bleed? Wrong us, shall we not revenge? . . . Ah, the game's afoot, huh? Our revels now are ended, Kirk. Cry "havoc!" and let slip the dogs of war. I am constant as the northern star.

Like a broken record. As Richard Burt suggests, the excessive citations of Shakespeare in the film lead to a filmic aporia: the number of citations such as these "deconstructs the distinction between the original and the (parodic) sequel but also undermines the capacity of the original or sequel to open up a controlling distance form the film's narrative and genre" ([1998]1999, 144). A parody is indeed suggested when considering how the film editors set up the viewer's reactions immediately after these line by cutting to Spock, who utters: "Gas." (He has finally found a way to trace the cloaked vessel). Such blatant and heavy-handed citations do stink of a kind of flatulence. But when considered in the tradition of commonplacing, the question of aesthetic distance is moot, since all citations are by their definition "excessive" in the sense that they are not expected to frame the narrative at all, nor to grant it authority as a "revision" of an original; rather, in keeping with the tradition, the references are used merely to enrich the gravity of the character's oratory, to enshrine his words with golden passages from an unspoken book of virtues.

As Chang continues to scream over the intercom, "I'm as constant as the northern star . . . ," McCoy speaks for the audience by responding: "I'd give good money to make him shut up." When the newly rigged cruise missile finally vaporizes Chang's ship, it signifies the utopian moment in the movie where what is really destroyed is not so much the old warrior mentality but the limitations of an outmoded and ideologically suspect literacy that was used in the twentieth century to put the lie to brutality and colonial exploitation. We hear quotations from Shakespeare as the Bird of Prey explodes and disappears in space, and we are exhilarated that such bad uses of Shakespeare may finally be put to rest. The scene works to displace the anxieties of the new Federation as it redirects the focus of its own dodgy and vaguely colonialist policies of "noninterference" and theories of "progress" and "evolution" of alien civilizations onto the cultured enemies like Chang. When Kirk, our revitalized hero of the new millennium, saves the Chancellor from being assassinated, he is asked, "What is the meaning of this?" His last lines indicate that Shakespeare is the true romantic hero of the film, since his endless return is signaled in Kirk's reiteration of the movie's central focus:

"It's about the future, madam Chancellor. Some people think the future means the end of history. Well, we haven't run out of history quite yet. Your father called the future "the undiscovered country." People can be very frightened of change."

People can indeed be very frightened of change. The film offers to console us about the role Shakespeare will play in the future. At least in the present-future of *Star Trek*'s grand vision of the destiny of Western liberal culture as it is configured through the commonplacing of moral truths and exemplars of virtue from the pages of the Bard. Perhaps the text doth protest too much. As this flat and rather disappointing scene proposes, there is nothing quite unexpected nor undiscovered in our unfolding future. "We haven't run out of history quite yet." Nor have we run out of ways to commonplace Shakespeare, apparently. At the very least such a prolonged and unremitting articulation of Shakespeare's power in *Star Trek* to shape the lives of those in the future might inspire some of us to ask, why so anxious?

Notes

1. This defamiliarization effect has been identified by other critics like Carl Freedmen in *Critical Theory and Science Fiction* as the dominant feature of the genre. 21–23. See also Seed.

2. See Katrina G. Boyd's "Cyborgs in Utopia: The Problem of Radical Difference in Star Trek: The Next Generation," and Leah R. Vande Berg's "Liminality: Worf as Metonymic Signifier of Racial, Cultural, and National Differences." Michael C. Pounds' definitive *Race in Space: The Representation of Ethnicity in Star Trek and Star Trek: The Next Generation* investigates the idea of race in the *Star Trek* episodes in the context of the underlying tensions in the television and film production unions, as well as the shows reflection on civil rights issues. Camille Bacon-Smith's *Science Fiction Culture* details the relationship between fans and producers of the television series, suggesting another complex model of science fiction's view of difference, particularly the role women, gays, and lesbians play in this culture.

3. Maisano examines the way the *Klingon Hamlet* reinvents an Enlightenment humanism in his "Shakespeare's Alien Abduction: *The Klingon 'Hamlet'* as the Last, Best Hope for Humanism." Forthcoming.

4. See Moss's *Printed Common-Place Books and the Structuring of Renaissance Thought.*

5. Helen M. Whall's "Bartlett's Evolving Shakespeare," also in this anthology, one of the only notable exceptions to my claim, attests to a more immediate relation between the post - World War II publication of Bartlett's *Familiar Quotations* and those "experts" in academia that are asked to report which passages form the canon of "famous" and "familiar." Her study of Bartlett's evolving use of Shakespeare does not account for how the famous quotation manual emerges next to and in concert with that other nineteenth-century oratorical model the high school "reader," from which it borrows the eclectic encyclopedic form, and as such belongs to a more complicated history commonplacing practices that I want to make a case for.

6. See Thomas's "The Meaning of Literacy in Early Modern England."

7. Respectively: *Mitchell v. Helms*, 530 U.S. 793A cites as follows: "A teacher could, for example, easily use Shakespeare's *King Lear,* even though set in pagan times, to illustrate the Fourth Commandment. See Exodus 20:12 ('Honor your father and your mother'). Thus, it is a non-sequitur for the dissent to contend that the textbooks in Allen were 'not readily divertible to religious teaching purposes' because they 'had a known and fixed secular content.' Post, at 28." The 1998 U.S. Supreme Court brief 818 uses the following note to consider that "The Founders Knew that the "Indian" Peoples Were Politically and Ethnically Diverse." "By 1600, Shakespeare's audience readily understood Othello's sad likening of himself to "the base indian" who "threw a pearl away richer than all his tribe." (V.ii.348–49).

8. John Pendergast, in "A Nation of Hamlets: Shakespeare and Cultural Politics," has also noted that this one scene marks a particularly "American style" of using Shakespeare. "Most of the Shakespearean references in Star Trek VI," he notes, "can be found in Hirsch's list." As provocative as Pendergast's description of Shakespeare's role in this film is, his identification of this style of quotation as a form of "propaganda" implies an aesthetic bias toward theatrical productions that remain (aesthetically) true to a "real" Shakespeare.

My own reading intends to invert this hierarchy of real, aesthetic over false, propaganda so that the appropriation of Shakespeare in quotation manuals and other commonplace books speak to the actual "lived" modes of identity making—marshalling of cultural capital, incorporating the great phrase—so that this conservative style has a broader historical habitation and a name in our understanding of Shakespeare's place in middle-brow American culture.

Works Cited

Bacon-Smith, Camille. 2000. *Science Fiction Culture.* Philadelphia: Univ. of Pennsylvania Press.

Bennet, William J. 1993. *The Book of Virtues: A Treasury of Great Moral Stories.* New York: Touchstone.

Bourdieu, Pierre. 1984 *Distinctions: A Social Critique of the Judgement of Taste.* London: Routledge.

Boyd, Katrina G. 1996."Cyborgs in Utopia": The Problem of Racial Difference in Star Trek: The Next Generation." In Harrison et al., eds.,

Burt, Richard. [1998]1999. *Unspeakable ShaXXXspeares: Queer Theory and American Kiddie Culture.* 2nd ed. New York: St. Martin's Press.

Freedman, Carl. 2000. *Critical Theory and Science Fiction.* Hanover: Wesleyan Univ. Press.

Hirsch, E. D. 1988. *Cultural Literacy.* New York: Random House.

Jameson, Fredric. 1984. "Progress Versus Utopia: Or, Can We Imagine the Future?" *Art After Modernism: Rethinking Representation.* Ed. by Brian Wallis. New York: New Museum of Contemporary Art, 239–52.

Pendergast, John S. 1995. "A Nation of Hamlets: Shakespeare and Cultural Politics." *Extrapolation: A Journal of Science Fiction and Fantasy* 36, (1): 10–17.

The Klingon Dictionary : English/Klingon Klingon/English (Star Trek). 1992. Marc Okrand and the Klingon Language Institute. New York: Pocket Books.

The Klingon Hamlet by William Shakespeare. 2000. New York: Pocket Books.

Maisano, Scott C. Forthcoming. "Shakespeare's Alien Abduction: *The Klingon 'Hamlet'* as the Last, Best Hope for Humanism."

Moss, Ann. 1996. *Printed Common-place Books and the Structuring of Renaissance Thought.* Oxford: Clarendon Press.

Pounds, Michael. 1999. *Race in Space: The Representation of Ethnicity in Star Trek and Star Trek: The Next Generation.* London: Scarecrow Press.

Ray, Robert B. 1985. *A Certain Tendency of the Hollywood Cinema, 1930–1980.* Princeton, NJ: Princeton Univ. Press.

Seed, David. 1999. *American Science Fiction and the Cold War.* Chicago: Fitzroy Dearborn Publishers.

Thomas, Keith. 1986. "The Meaning of Literacy in Early Modern England." In *The Written Word : Literacy in Transition.* Ed. by Gerd Baumann. Oxford: Oxford Univ. Press, 97–132.

Tulloch, John and Henry Jenkins. 1995. *Science Fiction Audiences: Watching Doctor Who and Star Trek.* New York: Routledge.

Vade Berg, Leah R. "Liminality: Worf as Metonymic Signifier of Racial, Cultural, and National Differences." In Harrison et al., eds., 1996.
William Shakespeare's STAR TREK. http://homepage.interaccess.com/~fast5lgt/Shakespeare_Trek/quotes.html.

Films Cited

Meyer, Nicolas, dir. 1991. *Star Trek VI: The Undiscovered Country.* USA. Paramount Pictures. Sound, col., 110 mins.

PART TWO

HISTORIES OF SHAKESPEARE'S APPROPRIATION

Case Studies

CHAPTER 8

WSHX
Shakespeare and American Radio

DOUGLAS LANIER

Film is evil, radio is good.

—Harold Foreman

Famously, *Henry V* opens with a lament about the limitations of Shakespeare's chosen medium. The Globe Theatre, the Prologue declares, is a rickety sign of its own inadequacies, "a wooden O," unable to present the epic breadth of the story's action, the mighty presence of "the warlike Harry," or the exhilarating clash of mighty armies. All it can offer is the shoddy mechanics of Renaissance staging, "flat unraised spirits" on an "unworthy scaffold" (I Cho 9–10). Yet what at first seems an insurmountable deficiency turns out to be an advantage. The very inadequacy of the medium—with some help from the Prologue's repeated exhortations—prompts the audience to "piece out our imperfections with your thoughts" (I Cho 23). Through their imaginations playgoers can negotiate transitions between settings or time schemes impossible to stage convincingly and can supply the pageantry and multitudes that "four or five most vile and ragged foils / Right ill-disposed in brawl ridiculous" (IV Cho, 50–51) cannot portray. Claiming "'tis your thoughts that now must deck our kings" (I Cho 28), the Prologue prompts the viewer to become an imaginative participant (or coconspirator) in Henry's exercise in military and royal self-fashioning. We, along with the king's peers and enemies, learn how to imagine Henry as an epic hero-king rather than as a manipulator of appearances and rhetoric, that is, an actor.

In a curious way, the Prologue's discussion of the fortunate failure of the theatrical medium anticipates recent criticism (what little there has been) of radio drama. Nearly all discussions begin by emphasizing what distinguishes radio from stage performance, its lack of a visual dimension. And nearly all argue that this seeming "defect"—its reliance on the aural—is in fact radio drama's strength, an absence that prompts the listener to supply the missing visual elements with the imagination. Commentators and practitioners agree that radio drama is, in the words of *CBS Radio Workshop*, "the theater of the mind." It requires its audience to envision a fictional world—characters, blocking, settings, props, time frames, and the like— from aural cues, from dialogue, sound effects, music, and the actors' intonation and delivery. Indeed, radio drama arguably improves upon the situation articulated by Shakespeare's Prologue. Unlike theatergoers, who must to some extent disregard the visual information before their eyes, radio listeners are freer to imagine scenes on their own terms. And because these scenes exist only in the listener's mind, radio drama is immensely flexible, allowing for intimate or epic scopes and for lightning changes in setting, time frame, and point of view, all with great economy of means. If Shakespeare's Prologue articulates an ideal for the experience of theater, radio, it is tempting to think, is that "muse of fire" that Shakespeare claims he longs for, a means capable of conveying his vision without the practical encumbrances of stageplay.

It is not surprising, then, that radio has been regarded as a promising performance medium for Shakespeare's plays. What might challenge suspended disbelief on the stage or in film, particularly where cost is prohibitive or material limitations can't be overcome, can be performed with relative ease on the radio. Because they were ephemeral (at least before the advent of tape and LP), radio performances of Shakespeare retained the frisson of live stage performance. This live effect was, at least in American radio, often enhanced by introductions that invite listeners to attend a stage performance, complete with sounds of an on-air audience. The fiction was that radio merely extended the audience for the theater, rather than transforming it into something phenomenologically different. Moreover, the lack of the visual apparatus of performance—involving the hands of scene designers, costumers, and directors—placed emphasis back on the actors and the text, on vocal characterization and the verbal music of Shakespeare's poetic language. This may suggest why for American radio, with its distinctively modern, colloquial idiom, the problem of Shakespearean language—its poetic density, its formality and archaic diction— loomed especially large.

The emphasis upon language is only one way in which radio performance transforms Shakespeare. Because the listener imagines Shakespeare's characters and settings into being, on radio his plays become somewhat abstracted rather than being clearly located by details of place, period, or design concept. Characters tend to become archetypical rather than specific, the emphasis falling on their inner emotional and psychological states rather than on external reality, which tends in radio drama to be relatively unspecific and fluid, having substance only insofar as it is continually aurally confirmed. Of course, those abstractions differ from listener to listener, since each is constructing his or her own individual imaginative experience. Radio listening, Martin Esslin argues, tends to produce a kind of dream state in which "the mind is turned inwards to a field of internal vision" (1985, 7). The conditions of reception often nudge Shakespeare's plays, particularly the tragedies, in the direction of psychological dramas centered on the interior world of the protagonist, with other characters and events a function of that psychology (rather than having a firmly established exterior reality). The dream-like intimacy of radio drama, where the external and internal realities are often blurred, is thus particularly amenable to the Shakespearean soliloquy, which has affinities to such radio conventions as the interior monologue and the voiceover.[1] This predisposition toward narrative interiorization can be a metathematic resource. In radio performance *Macbeth* tends to play as a Gothic nightmare (rather than as, say, a political drama) because Macbeth's creation of ghostly realities out of his guilty imagination so parallels the radio listener's situation and thus invites identification. Yet this formal resource can also pose a barrier to Shakespearean adaptation. A passage like Gloucester and Edgar's encounter on the Dover Heath in *King Lear* 4.6, a scene that depends for its meaning on the utter disjunction between what we see and Edgar's false description of it, poses a nearly intractable challenge for radio adaptation, since without additions to the script the listener has nothing but Edgar's description to work from. Such challenges are not confined to the tragedies, as illustrated by the scenes in the Columbia Shakespearean cycle's *Much Ado* where Benedick and Beatrice overhear gossip about each other (2.3 and 3.1). Since in radio what is not heard does not exist, in performance the first of these scenes are strange and confusing, for as Claudio, Leonato, and Don Pedro speak, we tend to forget that the silent Benedick is listening and we cannot benefit from his reactions to their conversation. More than merely broadcasting the lines over public airwaves, radio Shakespeare requires that Shakespearean theater be accommodated to a phenomenology specific to radio.

Orson Welles was one of the first adapters to understand radio's distinctiveness as a medium, and his 1938 production of *Julius Caesar* for *The Mercury Theatre of the Air* demonstrates that process of formal accommodation in practice. Welles was not the first to adapt Shakespeare to American radio, but he was among the first to control all aspects of production, from scripting and casting to direction and sound design to hosting and acting (Fink 1981, 220). That is, Welles brought auteurship to radio. His *Julius Caesar* blends Marc Blitzstein's score, sound effects of crowds, and Shakespearean oratory into a well-orchestrated commentary on rising fascism, the aural equivalent of his 1937 Federal Theater stage production. Welles's mastery of sound design is particularly apparent in Marc Antony's oration, where he juxtaposes Antony's speech against a crescendo of whispers and shouts from the mob. And he underlined the relevance to contemporary events by providing narration from Plutarch delivered by CBS news reporter H. V. Kaltenborn, who was at the same time reporting on German forays into Eastern Europe (Anderegg 1999, 50). This last touch was telling, since it framed Shakespeare's play within a form—the news broadcast—and a voice already familiar to listeners. Welles's technique was to manipulate codes of reception rather than update the language in order to harmonize Shakespeare with the radio medium. As Nachman observes (1997, 439), his experiments with radio Shakespeare in the late 1930s lent American radio drama an air of theatrical prestige at a crucial moment in its history, though, it should be added, that prestige was to prove relatively short-lived. Perhaps more important, Welles's productions established him as a Shakespearean auteur in the public's mind, paving the way for his subsequent Shakespeare films and his lifelong association with artistic quality. It is revealing that Welles verbally signed his broadcasts, "your obedient servant, Orson Welles."[2]

However, to frame the challenge of adapting Shakespeare to radio as a question of form is to tell less than half the story. To stress the distinctiveness (and thus aesthetic authenticity) of radio drama as a form, as so much academic criticism has done, is to obscure the extent to which radio drama has developed under particular institutional conditions. Radio is not merely a medium but a culture industry, shaped by its modes of finance, production, and distribution, its systems of programming and scheduling, its matrix of genres, its rivalries and affiliations with cultural alternatives like theater, film, popular fiction, and TV, and its star system and fan culture. And insofar as Shakespearean theater appears on the radio, it must accommodate, or at the very least address, those institutional protocols. Chief among them was American radio's early self-definition as a popular rather than high cultural medium. American radio drama addressed the individual listener at home in a largely informal, intimate tone somewhat distinct from more public, spectacular media like theater and film. Radio took great pains to establish its credentials as a "popular" medium and consequently was, at least in its American incarnation, characteristically inhospitable to cultural elitism. This "popularism" posed a serious challenge for "proper" Shakespeare, associated as it was with classical theater and high culture.

This issue of register has been masked by the fact that academic studies of radio Shakespeare have concerned themselves almost exclusively with British examples. It is certainly true that British radio has had a long, robust history of broadcast Shakespeare, extending back to the first broadcast in Great Britain in 1923 of scenes from Shakespeare. Yet that tradition has been profoundly shaped by the fact that the BBC is a state-sponsored public corporation, with the explicit charge of preserving and promoting its national culture, regardless of commercial considerations. When the broadcast of American-style radio drama to British audiences during World War II raised concerns about declining standards of quality, the BBC responded by dividing its radio broadcasts into three distinct, class-coded programs, the Home Service, the Light Programme, and the Third Programme. The last of these, later to become Radio 3, was devoted to high cultural and intellectual fare and thus became (and continues to be) the primary home of Shakespeare on the British airwaves. In the case of British radio, then, Shakespeare has largely been protected from the demand that it be "commercial" or accommodate itself to "popular" tastes or genres. For that reason commentators have addressed Shakespeare on radio primarily as a formal or technological issue rather than one of commerce and cultural class. The example of American radio, my focus here, offers a rather different perspective. The institutional history of radio in America has been anomalous among developed countries, for its development has been driven by the vagaries of corporate capitalism rather than by state charter and cultural custodianship (Esslin, 1985, 109). Nevertheless, Shakespeare's place in American radio is instructive because it suggests the extent to which institutional pressures, particularly the relationship between commercialism and cultural register, frame the problem of adapting Shakespeare to a mass medium and, more generally, frame the public's perceptions of Shakespeare. From the 1930s to the '50s, the so-called "golden age" of American radio, the overriding issue for Shakespeare on the radio, I will argue, was the mismatch between lowbrow medium and highbrow Bard. The challenge was *how* to convert Shakespeare's indisputable cultural capital to the medium's own register.

Early on, American radio did develop a very rough equivalent to the BBC's Third Programme in the form of what were called sustaining programs. Most dramatic programming on American radio developed under the sponsorship of advertisers, whose interests were commercial and whose influence extended even to the writing and producing of shows. Networks distributed the shows nationally through individual stations.[3] The early airwaves were dominated by three major networks, the National Broadcasting Corporation (NBC, divided into two programming units, the Red and Blue networks), the Columbia Broadcasting System (CBS), and the Mutual Network. The networks, along with a handful of individual stations, also financed and produced their own programming, the bulk of which was educational or "quality" programming, shows that had limited commercial potential but that lent the networks and radio medium a veneer of artistic prestige. Such "sustaining programs"—examples include *Radio Guild, The Mercury Theater of the Air* (later sponsored by Campbell Soup), *Great Plays,* and *The Columbia Workshop*—were typically (though not exclusively) relegated to non-prime-time hours where listenership (and therefore potential profit) was low. It is through sustaining programs that most early full-scale Shakespeare productions on American radio were broadcast. *Radio Guild,* for example, pioneered in bringing classical and contemporary theater to the airwaves, and its very first production, on November 6, 1929, was an hour-long *Romeo and Juliet.* From 1929 to 1940 on the Blue Network, it made forty Shakespeare broadcasts (some in two parts), including a complete cycle of the histories from November 1935 to February 1936 and productions of lesser known plays like *Coriolanus* and *Cymbeline* (with Shaw's rewritten fifth act). *Radio Guild* also broadcast a fictional biography of Shakespeare ("Will Shakespeare"), a biography of Garrick which featured dollops of Shakespeare, and a "greatest hits" show entitled "Shakespeare-ana." *Great Plays,* also produced by the Blue Network, extended the formula established by *Radio Guild* to Sunday afternoons. From 1938 to 1942, principally in November, it broadcast eleven Shakespeare adaptations, using its rotating core of directors, writers, and actors. Though these broadcasts have been largely forgotten, in part because few have survived, they—not the more prestigious productions of Orson Welles's *Mercury Theater* and the *Columbia Workshop*—established the basic terms for adapting Shakespeare "proper" to American radio. It was precisely because sustaining shows were relegated to fallow periods in the programming schedule that they were given the freedom to produce Shakespeare on a regular basis, since there they were exempt from pressure to be commercial.

This is not to say, however, that Shakespearean production on sustaining shows existed in a cultural realm unto itself. It is striking, for example, that there was so much Shakespearean activity on American radio in the latter half of the 1930s, particularly in 1937 and 1938. Though this Shakespearean boomlet might be traced to several causes, four events stand out: the formation of the Mercury Theater in the summer of 1937, and the immediate notoriety of its first production, an antifascist *Julius Caesar,* in November; the Federal Theater Radio Division's productions of classical drama; the appearance of two Shakespeare movies, Warner's *A Midsummer Night's Dream* (1935) and MGM's *Romeo and Juliet* (1936); and Congressional hearings, much rumored in the summer of 1937, into radio's monopolistic practices and undue influence on the FCC. The first of these events has gotten the more attention because it led in the summer of 1938, to Welles's creation of *First Person Singular,* the innovative radio series that became, with the broadcast of *Julius Caesar, The Mercury Theater on the Air.* However, for all his reputation as a radio Shakespearean, Welles produced only three radio Shakespeare programs during the 1930s, *Julius Caesar* for *The Mercury Theater on the Air* and *Hamlet* and *Macbeth* for *The Columbia Workshop.*[4] Arguably of more impact were the productions of the Federal Theater Radio Division and Hollywood's attempts to produce Shakespeare films in the mid-1930s. The Federal Theater Project, active from September 1935 to June 1939, produced government-subsidized classical and contemporary theater throughout America, and its Radio Division, the Federal Theater of the Air, extended that mission to broadcasting by using airtime donated by the networks. The success of its 16-week Shakespearean cycle in the mid-1930s spurred network production of "quality" programming between 1937 to 1939; essentially, commercial radio quickly sought to co-opt a potential market. Film too was an important catalyst. Though Hollywood was initially wary of radio, by the '30s the two media had worked out a complementary relationship: film studios supplied radio with star power and some of its best plot material, and radio provided Hollywood with an extension of its publicity machine into millions of homes. Even so, there was no cultural or institutional consensus as to which of these media might lay claim to the prestigious legacy of the theater, symbolized by Shakespeare. Indeed, radio drama of the 1930s, still produced largely in New York and with ties, albeit tenuous ones, to Broadway, could be said to have the more direct lineage to the stage, as words like "playhouse," "theater" and "plays" in the titles of radio series suggest. In part a bid by Warner and MGM for artistic prestige and in part a response to early '30s concerns about cinematic sex and violence, the major film productions of Shakespeare seemed to ignite the cultural fantasy of a (re)popularized Shakespeare. In effect, film was establishing itself as the primary means for bringing Shakespeare to the public, positioning itself as a medium with artistic potential while radio remained (or became by default) merely a purveyor of lowbrow entertainment. The proliferation of radio Shakespeare from 1936 to 1938, then, suggests radio's response: it attempted to capitalize upon the technique of using film stars in Shakespearean roles (with far lower production costs than film), while it sought to establish its own credentials as an heir to the theater and a culturally uplifting influence.

This response would result in one of the most instructive chapters in the history of Shakespeare on American radio, the 1937 so-called "Battle of the Bard." In keeping with the practice of producing Shakespeare as sustained programming, William Paley masterminded what CBS billed as an unprecedented summer Shakespeare series for radio, designed to bolster the upstart network's reputation for quality programming. The "Columbia

Shakespeare Cycle" featured eight one-hour productions—of *Hamlet, Much Ado, Julius Caesar, Lear, Shrew, As You Like It, Henry IV,* and *Twelfth Night*— directed and adapted by Brewster Morgan (Gilbert Seldes adapted *Shrew* and Archibald MacLeish *Lear*). Scheduled for prime-time broadcast on Monday nights, the series received elaborate promotion, including a lavish brochure trumpeting "the first major radio production of William Shakespeare's plays." That assertion incensed John Royal, vice president for programming at NBC, who hurriedly cobbled together his own summer Shakespeare series to air in an overlapping time slot on NBC's Blue Network. It would star John Barrymore, then well into a downward spiral as a film star but with a still viable reputation as a Shakespearean, revived by his appearance as Mercutio in the 1936 *Romeo and Juliet.* "Streamlined Shakespeare" featured six forty-five minute adaptations by Forrest Barnes of *Hamlet, Richard III, Macbeth, The Tempest, Twelfth Night,* and *Shrew.* In an effort to upstage CBS's series, Barrymore's series began broadcasting on June 21, three weeks before CBS's *Hamlet* was scheduled to air on July 12. Once "Streamlined Shakespeare" had run its course, NBC continued its counteroffensive by programming a four-episode cycle of O'Neill plays in the same time slot. With remarkable candor, Royal was to confess, "We didn't put it on because we were great enthusiasts for Shakespeare . . . we put it on for Exhibit A, to show educators . . . that we were adding something to culture" (Smith 1990, 144).

This was more than a battle between radio networks for prestige; it was a contest between two ways of accommodating radio Shakespeare to Hollywood star-power. The Columbia cycle assigned film stars to the key roles: Burgess Meredith as Hamlet; Leslie Howard as Benedick and Rosalind Russell as Beatrice; Reginald Denny as Julius Caesar, Claude Rains as Cassius, and Raymond Massey as Antony (replaced at the last minute by Morris Ankrum); Edward G. Robinson as Petruchio; Walter Huston as Henry IV and Humphrey Bogart as Hotspur; and Cedric Hardwicke as Malvolio, Tallulah Bankhead as Viola and Orson Welles as Orsino. Even so, the adaptations emphasized plot rather than characterization, ensemble rather than individual stars. By contrast, "Streamlined Shakespeare" trained the spotlight squarely on the bravura performances of Barrymore and his wife Elaine Barrie, supported by a minimal cast. Barrymore even doubled parts in three of his productions, playing both Hamlet and the Ghost in *Hamlet,* Sir Toby Belch and Malvolio in *Twelfth Night,* and Prospero and Caliban in *Tempest* (Elaine Barrie played both Ariel and Miranda). The opening line of each program gave a revealingly co-equal billing: "the words of William Shakespeare, the voice of John Barrymore." Predictably, the adaptations tended toward a "greatest hits" approach, stringing together big speeches and climactic scenes with just enough narration to make them comprehensible to the average listener.[5] And consonant with his grandiloquent style, Barrymore's florid introductions stress the flamboyance of his protagonists: Richard III offers, for example, "a veritable Roman Holiday of dramatics," and Macbeth is "a strong, violent, splendid figure of his times, a potential flaming sword."

The press promoted the competing shows as a theatrical war of the networks, in the words of *Newsweek*, "a phalanx of high-priced [CBS] voices against the lone knight of NBC" (quoted in Dunning 1998, 644), and it is true that the publicity briefly encouraged the production of other "quality" radio drama. But the ratings only tended to confirm assumptions about Shakespeare's lack of popular appeal.[6] Though reviews were generally favorable for both series, by splitting what was no doubt already a limited audience, both were beaten out week after week by the enormously popular *Fibber McGee and Molly*, which aired at the same time on NBC's flagship Red Network. This episode points up the central challenge posed by Shakespeare for American radio. Beyond being an instantly recognizable trademark of quality, Shakespeare was a reservoir of familiar plot lines, characters, scenes, and lines, a valuable resource for an industry that needed to produce vast amounts of drama to fill its daily schedule. But Shakespeare "proper," in Shakespearean language, was marked with the stigma of learned, antiquated high culture that was regarded—not without reason—irremediably uncommercial. For that reason, as they incorporated Shakespeare into commercial programming writers and producers pursued a variety of strategies for addressing Shakespeare's association with high cultural tastes and institutions. By and large these radio shows did not challenge Shakespeare's highbrow reputation. Quite the contrary: in many cases that reputation was actively promoted and even exaggerated in order to establish by contrast radio's status as a *mass* medium. To put this another way, radio tended to circulate the image of highbrow Shakespeare *sous rature*, on the one hand preserving Shakespeare as a sign of artistic quality, while on the other using the theatricality and antiquated language of stage Shakespeare as a foil for expressing vaguely class-coded resentments about high culture, in the process identifying radio with popular taste. Certainly sustaining programs continued to broadcast Shakespeare throughout the 1940s and '50s; one of the few sponsored cultural programs, *The Theater Guild on the Air* (underwritten by U.S. Steel), offered five Shakespeare broadcasts during its run. But by far most American listeners encountered Shakespeare on the radio not in the form of sustaining programs but as free variations on and allusions to Shakespeare scattered through the soaps, mysteries, westerns, situation comedies, and variety shows that made up the bulk of the broadcast schedule. Five tragedies provided the major points of reference: *Romeo and Juliet, Hamlet, Macbeth, Julius Caesar,* and *Antony and Cleopatra.*

Given the ways in which sustaining programs used stardom as a promotional device, it is no surprise that the Shakespearean star becomes an identifiable type on variety and drama programs. After his Shakespeare radio series, John Barrymore became a regular on *The Rudy Vallee Sealtest Show* and was instrumental in the show's shift from crooning to comedy (and to its recovery in the ratings). Barrymore played a caricature of himself as a pompous, sodden Shakespearean has-been, but he used the opportunity to deliver the occasional serious Shakespearean performance. Orson Welles was also a frequent guest Shakespearean on radio, notably *The Fred Allen Show, Duffy's Tavern, The Edgar Bergen/Charlie McCarthy Show,* and *Command Performance,* and he was paired with Barrymore more than once on *The Rudy Vallee Sealtest Show.* Their December 19, 1940 broadcast, ostensibly a biography of Barrymore, was structured as a comic contest between Barrymore and Welles for the title of greatest Shakespearean, with Barrymore as a stage ham and Welles the boy wonder of radio (his work as the voice of the Shadow is pointedly referenced). The program closes with a moving performance of *Julius Caesar* 4.3, the meeting of Brutus and Cassius before the battle of Phillipi. Given the way in which the show casts Barrymore the Shakespearean as the representative of an outmoded medium, the classical stage, the scene takes on added significance when as Cassius Barrymore impotently declares that he is "older in practice, abler than yourself / To make conditions" and laments that he is "aweary of the world: . . . braved by his brother, / Checked like a bondman, all his faults observed / Set in a notebook, learned, and conned by rote, / To cast into my teeth." The "conflict" and "reconciliation" between competing Shakespeareans Welles and Barrymore, in other words, transforms Shakespeare's scene into an allegory of the relationship between stage and broadcast Shakespeare.

Other Shakespeareans also appeared on variety shows. To name but two, Charles Laughton appeared on *The Kraft Music Hall* to coach Al Jolson in the balcony scene from *Romeo and Juliet,* an episode that made much of the gap between Laughton's British and Jolson's minstrel accents, and Maurice Evans, an important American Shakespearean at midcentury, was featured performing *Hamlet* on *The Fred Allen Show.* In these appearances emphasis fell upon the divide between highbrow Shakespeare and lowbrow comedy, the contradiction typically manifesting itself in the program's form, a lampoon focused either on Shakespeare's high-falutin' language or the actor's snobbery, followed by a reverent Shakespearean set piece. In Evans' case, his performance of the ghost scene from *Hamlet* is sandwiched between a comedy routine in which Fred Allen demands a refund for *Hamlet* and a sketch starring Evans as Shakespeare. The sketch's topic could hardly be more telling: "what would happen if Shakespeare tried to get a job in radio today?" Shakespeare interviews with the Rubicam Advertising Agency as a serial writer, and as he describes his *Hamlet,* the ad exec insists that each detail be changed to match the conventions of radio drama: the scene must be not Denmark, but Centerville, USA; Claudius must be renamed Papa Mayor, Hamlet Sam, and Polonius Lorenzo Fink; the show must be retitled *Ophelia Faces Life;* and the murders must be cut because "no one is ever murdered on the radio in the morning." Although the sketch spoofs the conventions of sponsored radio programming, it also reinforces the sense that being "commercial" is a fundamental obligation from which no performer should be exempt. What prompts the sketch is Allen's accusation that Evans is engaging in a Shakespearean "racket" because he doesn't have to pay his writer royalties. In the end, commercialism triumphs over "culcha": Shakespeare commits suicide, and when he intones "to be or not to be" as his dying words, the ad exec decides to do a quiz program.

Shakespearean parodies were to become a staple of variety programs, in part because Shakespeare was a widely recognizable point of reference and a safely symbolic target against which to express resistance to authority. It is tempting to set such lampoons in the context of the working-class legacy of variety shows, stretching back to vaudeville, music hall, and minstrel shows. This legacy is made explicit by the 1936 minstrel show *Romeo and Juliet* aired by *The Jack Benny Show* (it previewed on October 25 and aired a week later), a show clearly intended to capitalize upon MGM's *Romeo and Juliet.* Susan Douglas has argued that the linguistic slapstick of 1930s radio should be seen the aural counterpart of the physical slapstick of vaudeville and silent film, both of which were often directed against class-oriented codes of decorum through which established social order was maintained (1999, 100–106). Focusing on the balcony scene, Benny used both linguistic and physical slapstick (the latter achieved through sound effects) to skewer not so much any specific performance in MGM's film version as its relentlessly high-minded tone. In the preview, the familiar conflict between "something high-class" and commerce dominates. When his sponsor calls to object that *Romeo and Juliet* is not sufficiently familiar to his audience, Benny tells him off, then considers the consequences and presents as his own the sponsor's idea that they do a minstrel show instead. In the minstrel show itself, much of the undeniably racist comedy springs from the gap between Shakespeare's elevated idiom and black dialect rather than a parody of any specific passage. Romeo's ascent to Juliet's balcony, with its connotations of romantic transcendence, is reduced to a competitive scramble up a ladder: Benny's Romeo is repeatedly shunted aside by other Shakespearean suitors, Antony, Macbeth, and Othello (renamed Othello Jell-O, in acknowledgment of Benny's sponsor). The parody works on several levels at once: as a skewering of Benny's persona, with pretensions to "class" and sex appeal; as a send-up of Norma Shearer's prim, overidealized Juliet; and, perhaps most interestingly, as a metonymic discussion of "the popular" in relation to Shakespeare. Shakespeare's Juliet refuses to be tied to the marriage market (just as Shakespeare is exempt from the demand to be commercial), yet this modernized Juliet gleely embraces and embodies the principle of wide appeal. Even when Benny's Romeo tries to thwart other suitors (and restore a "properly Shakespearean" Juliet!) by destroying the ladder, yet another suitor—this time Tarzan—passes him by. To Benny's objection that she is unfaithful, she replies, "I ain't unfaithful, I'm jus' popular."

More often than not, Shakespearean parodies highlighted the mismatch between Shakespeare's works and the conventions of genre dramas. It became something of a standard routine to reimagine Hamlet as a private eye (as in "Hamlet Revisited," *The Henry Morgan Show*), and in a tour-de-force Danny Kaye produced three versions of *Romeo and Juliet*—as a soap opera, Western, and quiz show, all in goofy accents—in a single show. The point of such parodies was typically not to suggest parallels between Shakespeare and popular culture, but to reinforce the perception that conventions of commercial programming, not high culture, had become a cultural norm. By the 1950s, this norm extended even to sustaining programs, if one judges by "Another Point of View, or *Hamlet* Revisited," produced for *CBS Radio Workshop*. Its predecessor, *The Columbia Workshop*, had regularly offered full-scale Shakespeare productions, but *CBS Radio Workshop* offered only occasional anthologies of Shakespeare performances ("Lovers, Villains, and Fools" and "Colloquy #2: Dissertation on Love") and a show devoted to the Shakespearean authorship question ("Colloquy #1: An Interview with William Shakespeare," hosted by Dr. Frank Baxter, a well-known Shakespeare popularizer). "Another Point of View" suggests why: the show features a performance of *Hamlet* intercut with wry commentary by William Conrad. In effect, Shakespeare's drama is read through the conventions of 1950s middle-class family drama rather than Elizabethan revenge tragedy, with the result that Hamlet emerges as the play's villain, not its hero. The show was presented as a tongue-in-cheek exercise in "analytical misrepresentation," but it nonetheless acknowledges that by this time a certain interpretive paradigm, established by popular genres, held sway. This gap was exploited to rather different effect in "More Than Kin," an episode of *The Six Shooter*, a Western starring Jimmy Stewart as Britt Ponset. The episode concerns an old friend of Britt's, Archie Plunkett, once a dry goods dealer and now a Shakespearean actor, and his wife Maggie. Faced with unruly audiences in Virtue City, they are about to slip out of town when they meet P. T. Barnum, who announces he wants to attend their *Hamlet*. Recognizing that this, their big break, will be disrupted by the same unappreciative hooligans, they talk Britt, a famed gunfighter, into joining the show and intimidating the hecklers. Much of the episode's gentle comedy springs from the mismatch between florid Shakespearean language and Britt's stammering delivery and Texas drawl (contrasted with Archie's fake British accent), and from the irony that the popular audience's "appreciation" of Shakespeare springs not from what Barnum mistakes for "stage presence" but from Britt's reputation with a six-gun. In the quintessentially American context of the West, Shakespeare as "high culture" turns out to be a sham.

If comedy sought to exploit the difference between Shakespeare and popular radio drama, dramatic programming sought to assimilate Shakespeare in a variety of ways, with mixed success. Faced with deadlines, radio writers could in a pinch turn to Shakespearean motifs. True Boardman, writer for "Silver Theatre," claimed to "have written *Hamlet* twice, *King Lear* once, *Julius Caesar* four times, and *Romeo and Juliet* oftener [sic] that I should confess . . . The same people in the same basic situation with clothes of a different age and dialogue to suit. It's almost always a sure way out" (quoted in Maltin 1997, 38–9). "Best Laid Plans,"[7] an episode of *The Lone Ranger,* provides an apt example. This tale of a forbidden romance between rancher Chick Thompson and homesteader Mary Seton unmistakably adapts motifs from *Romeo and Juliet,* but it never directly signals its Shakespearean source and like many such adaptations might be said to resist it. Whereas Shakespeare's play moves inexorably toward the lovers' deaths, in "Chalmers" that tragic trajectory—and the feud between ranchers and homesteaders that underlies it—is avoided through the Lone Ranger and Tonto's heroics. This revision points to a deep structural gap between Shakespearean tragedy, often concerned with the ironies and contradictions of "heroic" action in a complex universe, and adventure drama of the period, largely preoccupied with providing models of can-do individualism that triumphs over all foes and circumstances. Yet when the Shakespearean source is openly acknowledged, such rewriting often generates unease. "Romiette and Julio," an episode of the college comedy *The Halls of Ivy,* makes updating Shakespeare its main topic. Clarence Wellman, trustee of Ivy College and member of its Atheneum Drama Club, objects to a modernized student production of *Romeo and Juliet,* a production that, anticipating *West Side Story* by six years, features a lower-class Romiette and Julio in an urban slum. Much of the episode focuses on the absurdity of reverence to dramatic tradition, exemplified by the irrational and thoroughly unpleasant Wellman. Although in the end his objection is silenced (literally, when Wellman reads the script so loudly that he becomes hoarse), the attitude of the episode and its protagonist, Dr. Hall, the college president, toward updating Shakespeare seems ambivalent. For one thing, the verse in the student production is dreadful, hardly a promising model. From the balcony scene:

> 'Tis Julio, with ready smile and lips all ready
> For a jest or kiss, needing a woman who

Can tell the two apart. For when a man jests
With his kiss, a kiss is just a jest, and true love
Puts his foot in door until the joke doth end.
For sentiment and wit are cousins much too near,
And cannot wed. . . .

For another, Hall himself seems less to endorse modernization than to object to Wellman's high-handed, elitist attempt at censorship. He asks the author of *Romiette and Julio*, "For one who has tampered with the immortal works of Shakespeare, you appear quite unabashed. Have you ever considered pepping up the New Testament in your spare time?" Pointedly absent is what we might expect for the episode's ending, a triumphal performance of the adaptation. For all its critique of Shakespearean traditionalism, the episode seems to leave open the question of whether Shakespeare can be successfully translated into another, more modern idiom.

More interesting are those shows in which the Shakespearean influence is acknowledged and Shakespeare thus becomes an explicit topic for commentary. It is striking how many of these concern Shakespeare on stage, and how often Shakespearean theater serves as the scene or instrument of crime (as in *Suspense's* "Fire Burn and Cauldron Bubble"). In radio drama's waning years in the late 1940s and '50s, it is as if the prestige of radio's high-cultural rival, the theater, takes increasingly pathological form, and for that reason Shakespearean allusions—particularly from *Macbeth* and *Othello*—begin to drift in the direction of mystery shows. (The connection was sufficient that Elliott Lewis, veteran radio writer, mounted a two-part production of *Othello* for *Suspense*.) "Banquo's Chair," a popular episode of *Suspense*, demonstrates this link. In a clever amalgam of *Hamlet's* "Mousetrap" and the banquet scene from *Macbeth*, master sleuth William Brent arranges for unrepentant murderer John Bedford to attend a banquet where he has contracted a Shakespearean actress to play the victim's ghost. Because the other guests pretend not to see the ghost, the frightened Bedford, like Macbeth, guiltily confesses. Only afterward do the host and guests learn that the actress never arrived and that they had been visited by a *real* ghost. The effect of the episode is to invest Shakespeare with uncanny power while detaching that power from the art of theater, here associated with fakery.

Of parallel interest is the figure of the Shakespearean stage star, often portrayed as a comic, pitiful, hypocritical, or villainous figure, out of step with mainstream society.[8] In an episode of *Gunsmoke* entitled "The Tragedian," for instance, the title refers to Edward van der Man, a Barrymore-like figure who once played Shakespeare in Europe but now is reduced to drink and card-sharking. Though Marshall Matt Dillon tries valiantly to reform him, refusing to jail him and even getting him a job, van der Man cannot be assimilated into middle-class society and soon falls back into his old ways, redeeming himself only when he accidentally takes a bullet for the lawman and dies. The conviction that the Shakespearean is always suspect is so strong that in "The Actor," an episode of *The Clock,* a young woman need only hear of her new beau's predilection for Shakespeare and classical theater to become convinced (wrongly, it turns out) that he is a serial killer. "I Always Marry Juliet," a superb episode of *Quiet Please,* exemplifies the trend. It is a first-person portrait of a second-rate Shakespearean, Rambeau Bainbridge, who has fallen on such hard times that he has become a sometime radio pitchman for phonograph needles. We learn that he has thrice married his costars in *Romeo and Juliet* only to become disenchanted with them, murdering them one by one. As in Robert Browning's "My Last Duchess" on which it is modeled, the episode's grimly ironic effect springs from the way in which the actor nonchalantly reveals his crimes. The episode ends with a second surprise: the actor's interlocutor is, it turns out, Shakespeare, who identifies himself as Juliet's first murderer—"Juliet had to die to make the play"—and the two, we discover, are doomed endlessly to replay the balcony scene with their victims as punishment. As the original source of the violence in which Bainbridge engages, this Shakespeare is in stark contrast to the kindly but largely impotent author we meet in *Favorite Story*'s "Mister Shakespeare." Portrayed by Vincent Price, Shakespeare is resurrected in modern Hollywood to find that his poetic talents are regarded as useless. When a studio executive rejects his sonnet-writing as uncommercial and forces him to script a vapid film, *The Capulets,* Shakespeare muses, tacitly endorsing radio's reliance on language, "after three centuries, I thought maybe people would learn to appreciate beautiful words by themselves without having them strung on stale plots. I was wrong." Though his poetry finds a diminished audience with a romancing couple (Shakespeare crows, "the old stuff still works!"), at episode's end he can do little but fade away.

This set of issues—the disparaged figure of the Shakespearean, the tension between Shakespearean theater and commercial media, the shifting cultural status of radio drama—come together in *The Magnificent Montague,* an NBC series broadcast from November 1950 to November 1951, only a few months after NBC reaired Barrymore's "Streamlined Shakespeare" series in abbreviated form (in August 1950). Edwin Montague, played by Monty Woolley as a variation on the Barrymore persona, is the last scion of a dying theatrical dynasty, a Shakespearean whose faded grandeur has soured into acid-tongued condescension. His closest friends are his aging peers at the Proscenium Club, devoted to "keeping alive the last flickering flame of theatrical culture." Unappreciated and unemployed, he consents secretly to play Uncle Goodheart "who lives on the sunny side of the lane," hero of an afternoon radio serial. The comedy turns on Montague's efforts to keep his role secret and return to the Shakespearean stage, and to maintain his dignity in the face of what he sees as the effrontery of American philistinism.

The series was remarkable not just for focusing on the institutional situation of Shakespeare in an age of mass media, but also for the ambivalence with which it treated its premise. As the representative Shakespearean, Montague is far more concerned with defending his dwindling cultural authority than actually performing the plays. One oft-repeated routine has him mangle line after line of Shakespearean dialogue as his actress wife, Lili, supplies corrections; those lines he does cite correctly mostly bemoan his fallen status. Montague's aristocratic self-absorption, exclusive club, and taste for imported kippers and star treatment only reinforce the stereotypical association of highbrow Shakespeare with blue-blood privilege. On the other hand, with the exception of his feisty maid, Agnes, Montague was the only character with any style. The film studio executives and drama coaches he meets in Hollywood when he screentests for *Macbeth* (a storyline that stretched over four episodes from January 12 to February 2, 1951) are dim-witted lotus-eaters who want to turn *Macbeth* into a musical and "polish up the dialogue." Though he marvels that a single broadcast can reach ten million listeners at once, Montague loathes radio as "the electronic monster that's killed theater," and what radio we do hear—excerpts from the *Uncle Goodheart Show*—is sentimental tripe, particularly when measured against Montague's razor-sharp wit. In its portrayal of film and radio, the series purveys what Ien Ang has termed "the ideology of mass culture"(1985, 15ff.), the conviction that mass culture, as the creation of corporate capitalism, is merely a series of degraded commodities fashioned for consumption by a gullible public. Despite the show's skewering of Shakespearean theater as outmoded and pompous, Shakespeare nevertheless emerges as the unequivocal standard of quality against which commercial media always come up short. Even so, the show also purveys a parallel ideology, what one might call "the ideology of high culture," the conviction that high culture is little more than a means through which a certain social class lays claim to privilege. The series is built upon the premise that Montague the Shakespearean's rantings about the vulgarity of American pop culture are secretly and hypocritically underwritten by his participation in that culture.

The episode "Shakespeare on the Radio" epitomizes the double-edged nature of the series' satire. Montague learns that his radio producer and writer will produce a fifteen-minute adaptation of *Romeo and Juliet* for Shakespeare's birthday. He finagles his way into the part of Romeo, but fearful that his wife Lili's performance as Juliet will overshadow him, he insists that another actress be found for the role. Meanwhile, Lili's falsetto-voiced brother Teddy, with unlikely dreams of broadcast stardom, comes to live with the couple. Much of the episode juxtaposes Edwin Montague's practicing of Shakespeare and Teddy's obsessive recitation of radio tag-phrases, both comically overwrought. Predictably Montague learns that the play has been vulgarly modernized, with a show-tune score, modern traffic noises for street scenes, and suicides removed (because "people don't die on radio"), but the *coup de grâce* is that his Juliet is none other than Teddy, the castrated, mindless voice of popular radio. Their juxtaposition casts a plague on both lowbrow and highbrow houses, leaving the middle-brow listener capable of appreciating both registers of allusions yet safe from implication in either critique.

The Magnificent Montague marks the last major attempt to couple Shakespeare with commercial radio in America. By the end of the 1950s, dramatic programming had definitively migrated to television, which came to occupy the place in American culture once held by radio, and radio responded by turning to pop music for programming. Periodically there were attempts to revive radio drama, and in those, perhaps in acknowledgment of its uncommercial reputation, Shakespeare played no more than a minor symbolic role. One of the most ambitious was the *CBS Radio Mystery Theater*, produced from 1974 to 1982, an hour-long series broadcast daily by many involved in radio's golden era. For the week of Shakespeare's birthday in 1976, the show broadcast a series of seven Shakespeare performances, each an hour-long adaptation advertised (tellingly) under new titles (*Hamlet*, for example, became "Long Live the King is Dead," *Antony and Cleopatra* "The Serpent of the Nile"). Though strictly not a radio broadcast, one last production suggests the persistent impulse to wed Shakespeare with radio-style drama, long after the passing of the medium's "golden age." In the late '60s, the Firesign Theatre, a radio foursome who had honed their craft on Los Angeles' Radio Free Oz (on KPFK-FM), produced several recordings blending inventive sound design, stream-of-consciousness parody, and complex wordplay into what were, in effect, postmodern radio plays for LP. Rife with highbrow and pop allusion, these works paid homage to American broadcast history and to experimental writers like Joyce and Borges. Among Firesign's productions is *Anythynge You Want To*, an extraordinary Shakespearean parody first recorded in 1972 as *Not Insane* and expanded a decade later as *Shakespeare's Lost Comedie*. Touching on scenes from *Lear*, *Hamlet*, *Macbeth*, and *The Tempest*, as well as more general Shakespearean motifs, *Anythynge* relates a preposterous battle for the Phlegmish throne between the foundling Edmund and his bastard twin Edmund Edmund. Lampooning Shakespeare's conventional gestures toward social order, the play ends with the rightful heir Edmund and his father accidentally dying when, knives in hand, they rush to embrace. Most striking about Firesign's production is not the story, however, but its pseudo-Elizabethan wordplay. Edmund's meeting with the ghost gives the flavor:

EDMUND: A ghost! What? Ghost? Methought you spoke of goats upon the battlements! . . . Well, be he ghost, or goat, or ghost of goat, or both, I'll spirits need to goad my spirits on! (He drinks) (Firesign 1997, 8)

Throughout radio's golden age Shakespeare's language, the conspicuous mark of his incompatibility with the dominant broadcast idiom, was typically an object of ridicule or suspicion. By contrast, *Anythynge* celebrates Shakespeare's wordplay as the mark of his countercultural status, treating Shakespeare as a fountainhead of the kind of linguistic anarchism and aural psychedelia that was Firesign's forte.

This brief overview suggests the characteristic ambivalence with which Shakespeare was assimilated by American radio, establishing how Shakespeare would be accommodated to its successor, television. It also reveals the extent to which discussions of the relationship between Shakespeare and popular culture have focused almost exclusively on the example of the moving image, in part because film has an established theoretical apparatus—notably auteurism—for conceptualizing the process of adaptation and, just as important, because Shakespeare films have become readily available on videotape for scrutiny. More ephemeral media for which there is no developed analytic vocabulary— radio is a cardinal example—have tended to attract less critical attention, with the result that accounts of Shakespeare and popular culture have often been skewed in directions we have been slow to recognize. Most important, the example of American radio reveals how unexamined principles of canonization have hovered over our choice of study materials. Though "proper" productions for sustaining programs were responsible for introducing many listeners to live Shakespeare and resulted in memorable, even occasionally groundbreaking, performances, the full range of Shakespeare's presence in commercial broadcasting offers a more varied and complex picture of Shakespeare's status in mid-century America. Such "Shakespeareana," I would argue, provide a necessary countercontext for understanding "proper" Shakespeare in performance. These works theorize, debate, and resituate the cultural significance of Shakespeare from outside those institutions that purvey "authentic" Shakespeare, and they insist that the meaning of Shakespeare's works cannot be divided from questions of cultural status. They remind us that the issue of Shakespeare and radio (or any mass medium) is more than merely a matter of transposing from one form to another. Rather, it is a matter of the interests of and commerce between the cultural institutions that mediate our experiences of Shakespeare.[9]

Notes

1. See Drakakis's superb discussion in "The Essence That's Not Seen" and "Introduction"; for a practitioner's perspective, see Evans.

2. All citations from radio programs are taken from tape transcriptions of the programs.

3. For a concise history of American broadcasting, see Fink 185–243. The standard history remains Barnouw's three-volume "History of Broadcasting in the United States," especially *A Tower in Babel* and *The Golden Web,* which should be supplemented by Douglas, chapters 1–6. For more critical accounts of the relationship between corporate commercialism and American radio, see Breitinger, and Streeter 59–110.

4. Welles did act in a few radio Shakespeare productions during this period, most notably as Orsino in the Columbia Shakespeare Cycle's presentation of *Twelfth Night* on August 30, 1937. In the late 1930s his attention was devoted not to radio Shakespeare but to recorded Shakespeare: in 1939 he produced a *Julius Caesar, Twelfth Night,* and *Merchant of Venice* for Mercury Text Records (released in conjunction with the reissue of his *Everybody's Shakespeare* series), and a *Macbeth* followed in 1940. For a cogent discussion of these recordings, see Anderegg 39–56. Welles was to return periodically to radio to produce Shakespeare as summer replacement programming. *The Cavalcade of Literature,* produced during the summer of 1941, yielded multipart presentations of *Julius Caesar, Twelfth Night,* and *The Merchant of Venice.* Welles revived the Mercury Theatre for the summer of 1946 as *The Mercury Summer Theater on the Air;* sponsored by Pabst Beer. The September 13 installment featured a half hour presentation of King Lear, starring, written, and directed by Welles.

5. For a sympathetic close reading of Barrymore's approach to Hamlet in this radio performance, see Kliman 286–89.

6. For evidence of those assumptions, see Dunlap; "News and Gossip"; and "Radio's Twelfth Night."

7. According to Al Hubin, this episode reworks with minor changes an earlier episode, "School for Ranchers," broadcast January 30, 1942.

8. Some examples from westerns include "The Actor Outlaw" (The Lone Ranger), "The Actress" (Frontier Gentleman), and "Shakespeare" (Gunsmoke).

9. I would like to thank members of the old-time radio fan community, particularly Tom Monroe, Walt Pattinson, Al Hubin, and Donna Halper, who supplied me materials and information.

Works Cited

Anderegg, Michael. 1999. *Orson Welles, Shakespeare and Popular Culture.* New York: Columbia Univ. Press.

Ang, Ien. 1985. *Watching Dallas: Soap Opera and the Melodramatic Imagination* London: Methuen.

Barnouw, Erik. 1966–1970. *A History of Broadcasting in the United States.* 3 vols., New York: Oxford Univ. Press. Vol. 1, *A Tower in Babel, to 1933.* Vol. 2, *The Golden Web, 1933 to 1953.*

Breitinger, Eckhard. 1978. "Towards the Golden Age of American Radio." In *Papers of the Radio Literature Conference 1977.* Ed. by Peter Lewis. Durham: Durham Univ. Publishing, 73–84.

"The Columbia Shakespearean Cycle." 1937. Adapted by Brewster Morgan, Gilbert Seldes, and Archibald MacLeish. Radio adaptations of *Hamlet, Much Ado About Nothing, Julius Caesar, The Taming of the Shrew, King Lear, As You Like It,* and *King Henry IV.* Unpublished typescripts.

Douglas, Susan J. 1999. *Listening In: Radio and the American Imagination.* New York: Time Books.

Drakakis, John. 1981. "The Essence That's Not Seen: Radio Adaptations of Stage Plays." In *Radio Drama.* Ed. by Peter Lewis. London: Longman, 111–133.

———. "Introduction." 1981. In *British Radio Drama.* Cambridge: Cambridge Univ. Press, 1–36.

"Drama: John Barrymore Will 'Air-Streamline' Shakespeare." 1937. *Newsweek* 9 (June 26): 22.

Dunlap, Orrin E., Jr. 1937. "Shakespeare is Radio's Midsummer Night's Dream." *New York Times,* July 11, sec. 10, p. 8.

Dunning, John. 1998. *On the Air: The Encyclopedia of Old-Time Radio.* New York: Oxford Univ. Press.

Esslin, Martin. 1985. "Drama and the Media in Britain." *Modern Drama* 28.1 (March): 99–109.

Evans, Stuart. 1987. "Shakespeare on Radio." *Shakespeare Survey* 39: 113–21.

Fink, Howard. 1981. "The Sponsor's vs. the Nation's Choice: North American Radio Drama." In *Radio Drama.* Ed. by Peter Lewis. London: Longman. 185–243.

The Firesign Theatre. 1977. "Anythynge You Want To or, Waiting on the Count of Monte Cristo or Someone Like Him." Unpublished typescript.

———. 1972. *Not Insane, or Anything You Want To.* Columbia KC 31585.

———. 1982. *Shakespeare's Lost Comedie.* Rhino RNLP 807.

Foreman, Harold. 1992. "Film Is Evil, Radio Is Good." In *Unbalancing Acts: Foundations for a Theater.* Ed. by Ken Jordan. New York: Theater Communications Group. 147–202.

Grams, Martin, Jr. 2000. *Radio Drama: American Programs, 1932–1962.* Jefferson, North Carolina: MacFarland & Company.

Kliman, Bernice W. 1988. Hamlet: *Film, Television, and Audio Performance.* Rutherford, NJ: Farleigh Dickinson Univ. Press.

[Landry, Robert J.]. 1937. Review of "Columbia Shakespearean Cycle" *Hamlet* and "Streamlined Shakespeare" *Hamlet. Variety,* July 14, p. 49.

Maltin, Leonard. 1997. *The Great American Broadcast: A Celebration of Radio's Golden Age.* New York: Dutton.

Nachman, Gerald. 1997. *Raised on Radio.* New York: Pantheon.

"News and Gossip of the Studios: Showmen Study Results of Shakespearean Broadcasts." 1937. *The New York Times,* August 30, sec. 10, p. 10.

Priessnitz, Horst P. 1978. "Problems and Characteristics of British Radio Drama." In *Papers of the Radio Literature Conference 1977.* Ed. by Peter Lewis. Durham: Durham Univ. Publishing. 45–72.

"Radio's 'Twelfth Night.'" 1937. *The New York Times,* September 5, sec. 10, p. 10.

Smith, Sally Bedell. 1990. *In All His Glory: The Life of William S. Paley.* New York: Simon & Schuster.

"Streamlined Shakespeare." 1937. Adapted by Forrest Barnes. Radio adaptations of *Hamlet, Richard III, Macbeth, The Tempest, Twelfth Night,* and *The Taming of the Shrew.* Unpublished typescripts.

Streeter, Thomas. 1996. *Selling the Air: A Critique of the Policy of Commercial Broadcasting in the United States.* Chicago: Univ. of Chicago Press.

Radiography

Anthology. Dir. John Malcolm Brennen. NBC Network.
> *Shakespearian Festival* (in four parts). June 11 and 27, July 18 and 25, 1954.
> *A Midsummer Night's Dream.* September 19, 1954.
> *The Three Witches of Macbeth.* October 31, 1954.
> *Shakespeare: Romeo and Juliet.* April 24, 1955.

The Cavalcade of Literature. Dir. Orson Welles. CBS Network.
> *Julius Caesar* (in three parts). July 12, 19, and 26, 1941.
> *Twelfth Night* (in two parts). August 2 and 9, 1941.
> *The Merchant of Venice* (in five parts). August 16, 23, and 30, and September 6 and 13, 1941.

CBS Radio Mystery Theater. Dir. Himan Brown. CBS Network.
> *That Hamlet Was a Good Boy.* June 25, 1975. Rebroadcast October 15, 1975, November 14, 1980 and November 19, 1998.
> *Murder Most Foul.* April 19, 1976. Rebroadcast May 9, 1977 and April 28, 1979.
> *The Assassination.* April 20, 1976. Rebroadcast May 10, 1977 and April 6, 1979.
> *The Love Song of Death.* April 21, 1976. Rebroadcast May 11, 1977 and September 30, 1979.
> *The Green-Eyed Monster.* April 22, 1979. Rebroadcast May 12, 1977 and April 7, 1979.
> *Long Live the King Is Dead.* April 23, 1976. Rebroadcast May 13, 1977 and April 21, 1979.
> *The Prince of Evil.* April 24, 1976. Rebroadcast May 14, 1977.
> *The Serpent of the Nile.* April 25, 1976. Rebroadcast on May 15, 1977 and August 4, 1979.
> *The Murder of Caesar.* September 24, 1980.
> *Lady Macbeth at the Zoo.* May 31, 1982.

CBS Radio Workshop. Various directors. CBS Network.
> *Colloquy #1: An Interview with William Shakespeare.* February 24, 1946. Rebroadcast on Voice of America, April 12, 1964.
> *Lovers, Villains, and Fools.* May 18, 1956.
> *Another Point of View, or Hamlet Revisited.* June 22, 1956.
> *Colloquy #2: Dissertation on Love.* August 17, 1956.

The Clock. Dir. William Spier. ABC Network.
> *The Actor.* November 10, 1946.

The Columbia Shakespearean Cycle. Dir. Brewster Morgan. Adaptations by Brewster Morgan, Archibald MacLeish, and Gilbert Seldes. CBS Network.

Hamlet. July 12, 1937.
Much Ado About Nothing. July 19, 1937.
Julius Caesar. July 26, 1937.
The Taming of the Shrew. August 2, 1937.
King Lear. August 9, 1937.
As You Like It. August 16, 1937.
King Henry IV. August 23, 1937.
Twelfth Night. August 30, 1937.
The Columbia Workshop. Various directors. CBS Network.
Hamlet (part I). September 19, 1936.
Hamlet (part II). November 14, 1936.
Public Domain: Characters of Fiction Freed from the Copyright Lane. January 2, 1937.
Macbeth. February 28, 1937.
As You Like It. December 7, 1939.
The Taming of the Shrew. March 21, 1940.
King Richard III. June 2, 1946.
The Danny Kaye Show (also Blue Ribbon Town). Dir. Dick Mack. CBS Network.
Modern Romeo and Juliet. March 10, 1945.
The Edgar Bergen/Charlie McCarthy Show. Dir. Earl Ebi. CBS Network.
Romeo and Juliet. December 11, 1955.
Family Theater. Various Directors. Mutual Network.
Julius Caesar. July 26, 1950.
Favorite Story. Ziv Syndication.
Mister Shakespeare. January 14, 1947 (West Coast) and April 10, 1948 (East Coast).
The Fred Allen Show. NBC Network.
Guest Star: Maurice Evans. January 13, 1946.
Frontier Gentleman. Dir. Antony Ellis. CBS Network.
The Actress. March 23, 1958.
Great Plays. Dir. Blevins Davis. NBC Blue Network.
A Midsummer Night's Dream. March 26, 1938.
A Midsummer Night's Dream. November 13, 1938.
Julius Caesar. November 20, 1938.
Othello. November 27, 1938.
Romeo and Juliet. November 12, 1939.
Much Ado About Nothing. November 19, 1939.
Macbeth. November 26, 1939.
Love's Labor's Lost. November 10, 1940.
The Merry Wives of Windsor. November 17, 1940.
The Tempest. November 24, 1940.
The Taming of the Shrew. December 28, 1941.
Gunsmoke. Dir. Norman Macdonnell. CBS Network.
Shakespeare. August 23, 1952.
The Tragedian. October 26, 1958.

The Halls of Ivy. Dir. Nat Wolff. NBC Network.
  Romiette and Julio. April 18, 1951.
The Henry Morgan Show. Dir. Charles Powers. NBC Network.
  Hamlet Revisited. April 23, 1950.
The Jack Benny Program (also The Chevrolet Program and The Jello-O Program).
  NBC Blue Network.
  Preview of Romeo and Juliet. October 25, 1936.
  Doc Benny's Minstrels–Romeo and Juliet. November 1, 1936.
Kaleidoscope. NBC Network.
  Twelfth Night. January 24, 1953.
  Richard II (in two parts). February 28 and March 7, 1953.
  Measure for Measure (in two parts). March 21 and 28, 1953.
  On Acting Shakespeare. April 18, 1953.
The Kraft Music Hall (also The Al Jolson Show). NBC Network.
  Guest Star: Charles Laughton. February 12, 1948.
The Lone Ranger. Dir. Charles Livingstone. NBC Blue Network.
  School for Ranchers. January 30, 1942.
  The Actor Outlaw. March 14, 1951.
  Best Laid Plans. February 20, 1952.
The Magic Key (of RCA). NBC Blue Network.
  Romeo and Juliet. October 18, 1936.
  Richard II–A Scene. April 25, 1937.
  Julius Caesar. January 2, 1938.
  All the Men and Women Are Merely Players. January 16, 1938.
  Balcony Scene. February 20,1938.
  Marc Antony and Cleopatra. June 4, 1939.
The Magnificent Montague. Dir. Nat Hiken. NBC Network.
  Starring Role in Radio. November 10, 1950.
  Aunt Agatha. November 17, 1950.
  To Play Romeo. November 24, 1950.
  To Shave or Not to Shave. December 1, 1950.
  Movie Offer. January 12, 1951.
  Lost in Hollywood. January 19, 1951.
  Screen Test. January 26, 1951.
  Sharing Bungalow. February 2, 1951.
  Road Show. April 13, 1951.
  Shakespeare on the Radio. April 20, 1951.
  School. June 2, 1951.
  Culture in Brooklyn. June 23, 1951.
The Mercury Summer Theater on the Air. Dir. Orson Welles. CBS Network.
  King Lear. September 13, 1946.
The Mercury Theater on the Air. Dir. Orson Welles. CBS Network.
  Julius Caesar. September 11, 1938.
The Philip Morris Playhouse. Dir. William Spier. CBS Network.
  Banquo's Chair. March 25, 1949.

Quiet, Please. Dir. Wyllis Cooper. Mutual Network.
I Always Marry Juliet. April 5, 1948.
Radio Guild. Dir. Vernon Radcliffe. NBC Blue Network.
Romeo and Juliet. November 6, 1929.
As You Like It. January 15, 1930.
Julius Caesar. November 21, 1930.
The Merchant of Venice. January 30, 1931.
Hamlet. March 20, 1931.
Macbeth. April 17, 1931.
Will Shakespeare. April 24, 1931.
A Midsummer Night's Dream. October 23, 1931.
Julius Caesar. October 30, 1931.
Hamlet (in two parts). November 6 and 13, 1931.
The Merchant of Venice. November 20 1931.
Coriolanus. October 24, 1931.
Romeo and Juliet. October 31, 1932.
King Henry V. November 7, 1932.
As You Like It. November 14, 1932.
King Richard III. November 21, 1932.
Julius Caesar. October 16, 1932.
Will Shakespeare. April 24, 1933.
The Tempest. April 23, 1934.
A Midsummer Night's Dream. August 13, 1934.
Othello. September 17, 1934.
David Garrick. September 24, 1934.
Macbeth. November 19, 1934.
Twelfth Night. December 31, 1934.
King Henry IV. March 4, 1935.
A Midsummer Night's Dream. July 29, 1935.
Much Ado About Nothing. October 17, 1935.
King John. November 7, 1935.
King Richard II. November 14, 1935.
King Henry IV, Part I (in two parts). November 21 and December 5, 1935.
King Henry IV, Part II (in two parts). December 12 and 19, 1935.
King Henry V (in two parts). December 26, 1935 and January 2, 1936.
King Henry VI, Parts I -III. January 9, 16, and 23, 1936.
King Richard II. January 30, 1936.
King Richard III. February 6, 1936.
King Henry VIII. February 13, 1936.
Twelfth Night. November 27, 1936.
The Merry Wives of Windsor. March 5, 1937.
Shakespeareana. April 23, 1937.
Antony and Cleopatra. November 12, 1937.
Julius Caesar. April 23, 1938.
Cymbeline, with George Bernard Shaw's rewritten fifth act. June 3, 1938.

The Rudy Vallee Sealtest Show. Dir. Dick Mack. NBC Network.
 Guest Stars: John Barrymore and Orson Welles. December 19, 1940.
The Six Shooter. Dir. Jack Johnstone. NBC Network.
 More than Kin. December 13, 1953.
Sleep No More. Dir. Nelson Almstead. NBC Network.
 Banquo's Chair. February 6, 1957.
Streamlined Shakespeare. Adaptations by Forrest Barnes and John Barrymore. NBC
 Blue Network.
  Hamlet. June 21, 1937.
  King Richard III. June 28, 1937.
  Macbeth. July 3, 1937.
  The Tempest. July 11, 1937.
  Twelfth Night. July 19, 1937.
  The Taming of the Shrew. July 26, 1937.
Suspense. Various directors. CBS Network.
  Fire Burn and Cauldron Bubble. April 6, 1943.
  Banquo's Chair. June 1, 1943. Rebroadcast in revised form on August 3, 1944
   and March 9, 1950.
  Othello (in two parts). May 4 and 11, 1953.
Theater Guild on the Air (also The United States Steel Hour). Dir. Homer Fickett.
 ABC and NBC Networks.
  Macbeth. April 11, 1947.
  Romeo and Juliet. February 8, 1948.
  The Taming of the Shrew. April 10, 1949.
  Hamlet. March 4, 1951.
  Julius Caesar. June 7, 1953.
Theater USA. Various directors. ABC Network.
  Hamlet. April 21, 1949.

CHAPTER 9

SHAKESPEARE, BEARD OF AVON

FRAN TEAGUE

"Brush up your Shakespeare," sings a gangster who's hanging around back-stage to collect an overdue gambling debt, "Start quoting him now . . ."

> Brush up your Shakespeare,
> And the women you will wow.
> Just declaim a few lines from Othella,
> And they'll think you're a hell of a fella.
> If your blonde don't respond when you flatter 'er,
> Tell her what Tony told Cleopatterer . . .

The number stops *Kiss Me, Kate* so completely that Cole Porter added encore verses because "we realized that . . . [it] was a 'boff' number—a show stop-per" (McBrien 1998, 313–14; 116). The number uses a comic tempo "to conjure up images of middle-class gentility and sentiment," and "outrageous rhyming and increasingly bawdy imagery that Porter derives from Shake-speare's titles" (Swain 1990, 134;136). Initially it simply alludes to Shake-speare's plays with cleverly forced rhymes to amuse the audience ("Othella / hell of a fella," with its piled up rhyme, for example, or "flatter 'er / Cleopat-terer," with a dialect gag). As the song progresses, Shakespeare's titles become double entendres, so that references to the eminently respectable Shakespeare permit the lyric to suggest the startlingly unrespectable:

> If she fights when her clothes you are mussing
> What are clothes? Much Ado about Nussing. . . .
> If she says your behavior is heinous
> Kick her right in the Coriolanus. . . .

When your baby is pleading for pleasure,
Let her sample your Measure for Measure.

The meaning is slippery, as Cole Porter ostensibly endorses the heterosexual, yet covertly engages the homosexual (McBrien 1998, 313). Shakespeare's presence is essential, heightening the incongruity to make us laugh, as high-culture titles and vulgar implications work together to permit the impermissible. The song's claim for Shakespeare's value, for high culture, for the legitimate stage, is placed in the mouths of two low-lives who acquired their culture during "eight years in the prison library in Atlanta" and who think him of value because invoking his name permits sexual success. In other words, the song relies upon the audience's perceiving a split in culture, a division between high and low. Yet even as it relies on that split, it unsplits culture: the gangsters have spent eight years in a library; the composer used a classical education and European musical training to produce a novelty song. Even the basis of that split—the perception that Shakespeare has worth and hence value—is simultaneously undermined and underscored by displacement of his worth from the respectable (marker of education) to the naughty (seduction). The song slides back and forth because its jokes make it function now as a marker of low, and now as a marker of high, culture: we get its jokes because we too are low and high. Even the song's place in the musical's plot works in this slippery way: the gangsters threaten to stop the show by injuring the male lead; they also take part in the production to stay near him; and they ultimately become the way that Fred Graham (Petruchio) maintains the production and retains his leading lady, Lilli Vanessi (Kate): they are enemies to, participants in, and saviors of the Shakespearean play. Finally they have the power to stop and save the show because, as their show-stopping number demonstrates, Shakespeare is and isn't Shakespeare: he's naughty, knotty, not-He.

The split upon which the song depends is not an essential part of American culture, according to Lawrence Levine, who thinks that it appears around the time of the Astor Place Riots in 1849.[1] In this chapter, I shall examine Shakespeare musicals on Broadway, so for my purposes what is important about Levine's argument is the way that the split into highbrow/lowbrow affects American musical theater. Initially theatrical practice was mixed, for as Levine remarks, "the play may have been the thing, but it was not the only thing. It was the centerpiece, the main attraction, but an entire evening generally consisted of a long play, an afterpiece (usually a farce), and a variety of between-act specialties." By midcentury, however, the separation had occurred and a play stood alone on the bill in the legit, while the comic sketches, singing and dancing, and animal acts that had once accompanied the play were performed in the variety theater (which in turn split into minstrel shows, vaudeville, and burlesque, and ultimately became musical comedies). Douglas Gilbert notes the opposition between variety and the legit:

Variety was a curious hit-or-miss activity, a theatrical shot in the dark. It was of the stage, yet distinct from the legitimate theater whose "Harolds and Arthurs" regarded variety performers as low persons of no moment. ([1940]1963, 24)

The oppositional nature of legit and variety is important to the way that Shakespeare is treated in musical comedy; another important feature is that two topics occurring regularly in Shakespearean musical comedies are central to variety: sex and ethnicity. As Gilbert notes, before 1880, "in beer halls and for-men-only dives, roughhouse turns and afterpieces were smuttily "blued" to amuse the tosspots, strumpets, dark-alley lads, and slummers who in those days made up variety audiences," and both Levine and Gilbert comment how variety performers depended on ethnic and racist jokes for laughs. Nadine George-Graves points to the problems that such a feature posed for African-American performers when she writes:

The ultimate irony was that the emergence of African American people in the theatrical workforce perpetuated degrading stereotypes of black people. . . . Although recognized as a grotesque genre and decried by black intellectuals at the time (especially philosopher Alain Locke and sociologist W. E. B. DuBois) for sustaining stereotypes, minstrelsy and the practice of blacking up must nevertheless be understood as the first professional performance opportunities for African Americans, and its participants should be regarded as pioneers. For many black performers, minstrelsy was a way out of hunger, out of the Jim Crow South, and into adventure and other opportunities" (2000, 35).

Because book musicals grew out of variety theater, operating in opposition to the legit, the place of Shakespearean musicals is tricky from the outset, because in them variety performers take over legit texts, then use the play to overtake legit's "Harolds and Arthurs" as performers. What starts out in vaudeville as performers mocking another theatrical style becomes direct competition when book musicals use Shakespeare. In the book musical, a show invokes Shakespeare, yet dismisses most aspects of the legit, including the text; moreover, a musical's descent from variety theater leads it to employ sex and race to sell the show, even when the performers using such topics might themselves be made uncomfortable by them.

Shows building Shakespearean elements into the book invoked him to provide greater freedom for a transgressive purpose (*Boys from Syracuse*, 1938; *Swingin' the Dream*, 1939; *Kiss Me Kate*, 1948; *West Side Story*, 1957). By the 1970s, however, this development had largely run its course. *Your*

Own Thing (1968) and *Two Gentlemen of Verona* (1971) enjoyed success, but nine more Shakespearean musicals flopped. Recent Shakespearean musicals that succeed may have substantial distance from Shakespeare (*The Lion King*, 1997), invoke race directly (*Play On!*, 1997), or use race and sex indirectly (*The Bombitty of Errors*, 1999). There are other productions, which I shall mention in my conclusion, that make use of Shakespeare, but I want to limit my discussion to New York book musicals. (I take production information on all of these shows from the appendices of the annual Burns Mantle *Best Plays* series.)

Shakespearean musical comedies are infrequent, although more musicals draw on Shakespeare than on any other literary figure. Unlike opera, which often uses Shakespeare, book musicals use him relatively rarely. (The principal reason opera uses Shakespearean texts without much complication, I suspect, is its long-standing association with the legit and its firmly maintained distance from variety theater.) Among the many hundreds that have opened in New York, fewer than twenty musicals have been Shakespearean. The relationship each musical has to its Shakespearean base is crucial: the show employs Shakespeare for the sake of incongruity, prestige, or whatever, but simultaneously erases him to create enough aesthetic distance for success.

In the song "Brush Up Your Shakespeare"—and I shall argue in musical comedy generally—Shakespeare becomes a beard, a subterfuge that permits the show to get on with what it really wants to do (i.e., amuse and sanction naughtiness) by misdirection. I use "beard," a term associated with gay culture because I agree that "Long before its kind was manifestly endangered, the Broadway musical took on a protective coloration" (Miller 1998, 1). I would add that a musical's protective coloration is not limited to sexual preference: Shakespeare can also serve as a beard for transgressive desires about race or female independence. Musicals in Miller's reading (and John Clum would agree) serve as a beard for gay experience because they are "a somehow gay genre, the only one mass culture ever produced" (Miller 1998, 16). But the participation of gay writers and performers places them in a position analogous to that of African American performers in variety theater: they must seem to assent to stereotypes or values that they resist in their private lives. Just as minstrel shows depended on racist stereotypes, musicals have until recently depended upon a fiction of universal heterosexuality. If Miller is also correct in seeing "the Broadway musical [as] the unique genre of mass culture to be elaborated in the name of the mother" (Miller 1998, 83), what is one to make of Shakespearean musicals, invoking the literary father? Whatever else happens in a Shakespearean musical, he does not become a fabulous diva or a peculiar presence; he remains what he has always been in American theater, a mainstay of the legit stage. When a revue cites Shakespeare, it gets a laugh at the expense of legit plays, following the long tradition of burlesquing Shakespeare. An example of variety stage citation is "The Shakespeherian Rag," used in *The Ziegfield Follies of 1912* (Hawkes 1986, 73–91), or Lorenz Hart and Morrie Ryskind's vaudeville sketch *Shakespeares of 1922,* written for the comedian George Price (Hart 1986, 28–9). These numbers assume that Shakespeare's plays are innately serious, tragedies or histories, a point that becomes important when Broadway musicals move from mocking Shakespeare in occasional songs to using his work as the basis for a show's book. The whole point of a musical comedy was that it was different from the legitimate stage, epitomized by productions of Shakespeare. Such song references were not ignorant ones: Shakespeares of 1922 included King Lear's rendition of "April Showers":

> Though April showers may come my way
> They can't grow flowers in bales of hay.
> And when it's raining, I just reflect,
> Because it isn't raining rain at all,
> It's just a stage effect!
> I see a rainbow, and life's worthwhile,
> For I'm insane, bo, that's why I smile.
> I haven't even got a bathtub,
> So I hope the rain is strong
> Whenever April showers come along.

As Levine and Cartelli note, burlesques demonstrate that the audience knows Shakespeare. This song demands a knowledgeable audience to get the jokes about Lear ("I'm insane"), as well as the metatheatrical joke that rain is a stage effect. Yet the sketch is clearly not of the legit world: in other number's Price mocks Jews and bootleggers, and uses baseball jokes and Mammy songs, references not permitted in the legit. This song invites the audience to preen itself on cultural sophistication, while sneering at the stuffiness of high culture and the vulgarity of low. The audience laughs at Shakespeare's simultaneous presence and absence from the stage.

A Hit and a Flop

The first book musicals to use Shakespeare, *The Boys from Syracuse* (*Boys*) and *Swingin' the Dream* (*Swingin'*) opened in 1938 and 1939, the first a success and the second a failure. The contrast between them is instructive. According to Richard Rodgers,

> We [Rodgers and Hart] were on a train heading for Atlantic City, where we thought the fresh sea air might help to stimulate some new ideas. For some

reason we began discussing Shakespeare, which led to our discovery that no one had ever thought of using one of his plays as the basis of a musical comedy.

The mere fact that it had never been done before was reason enough for us to start thinking that it should be our next project. The problems of *I Married an Angel* were pushed aside as we began tossing around titles of plays. *Even eliminating the tragedies and histories,* we had a pretty large field to choose from. (Rodgers 1975, 190–91, my emphasis)

Burlesque treatments of Shakespeare focus on tragedies and histories because the point of a burlesque is to deflate a serious and prestigious work. Moreover, the serious plays were those most often produced on the legit stage, so audiences would more readily recognize and laugh at them. In 1938, however, a musical comedy required a light comedy book, hence Rodgers's caveat that they eliminated tragedies and comedies.

A show like *Boys* uses a Shakespearean play's shell, the plot line and central characters; dispenses with the language and structure; and makes a distinctively contemporary point, rather than mocking the original. The Shakespeare play becomes a beard, allowing the show to make its point without either the encumbrance of being faithful to or the aim of mocking a legit text. The musical borrows the respectability, but gets rid of the troublesome aspects.

Rodgers and Hart chose *Comedy of Errors,* because it let them link Hart's brother Teddy to the more successful comedian Jimmy Savo. As Rodgers tells it:

[O]ne play attracted us from the start, and for a very personal reason. Larry's younger brother, Teddy, was a clever comedian best known for such George Abbott farces as *Three Men on a Horse* and *Room Service.* He was short and dark, and though he looked a great deal like Larry, he was always being mistaken for another gifted comic, Jimmy Savo.

"Why don't we do *The Comedy of Errors?*" Larry said rubbing his hands together as he always did when a good idea hit him. "Teddy and Jimmy would be a natural for the twin Dromios." Nepotism notwithstanding, we both realized that it was an inspired casting idea . . . (Rodgers 1975, 191)

Hart recognized that a coincidence would help his brother's career. Dorothy Hart quotes him as saying, "Teddy had to be star [sic], and this was the first star part that ever fit him" (Hart 1986, 133). In this show, Rodgers and Hart had little interest in popularizing a giant of English literature or sharing their reverence for Shakespeare. They wanted to showcase a specific performer (Teddy Hart) to enjoy a substantial profit (the goal of any musical produced in such a competitive and commercial venue as Broadway), and to bend the conventions of musical comedy by writing a show substantially more risqué than any that they had written before.

While the plot line of *Boys* follows Shakespeare's play, the musical retains only two lines of Shakespeare's text: "The venom clamors of a jealous woman / Poisons more deadly than a mad dog's tooth" (5.1.69–70). When the line occurred, Savo popped his head out from behind the curtain to announce to the audience, "Shakespeare!" Using the Shakespearean plot line allowed the musical to take more chances with off-color materials than was conventional in 1938. Reading the lyrics today one finds the much discussed bawdiness tame. Antipholus of Syracuse sings:

> When a man is lonely it is good to know
> There's a red light burning in the patio.
> I wanna go back, go back
> To dear old Syracuse.
> Wives don't want divorces there,
> The men are strong as horses there,
> But should a man philander,
> The goose forgives the gander.

Antipholus of Ephesus sings "The shortest day of the year, / Has the longest night of the year." Adriana, Luciana, and Luce have a trio, "Sing for Your Supper," that compares a canary to a courtesan and concludes, "Songbirds always eat." Clum argues that Hart's lyrics also express closeted gay desire, a fascinating counternarrative (1999, 58–69) suggesting resistance to the heterosexuality mandated in musicals at this point. These instances are as racy as the lyrics get, although a performer can always convey licentiousness in performance, no matter how innocuous the material. But while this material seems harmless today, in 1938 it roused considerable attention from the reviewers.

Critic after critic points to the bawdiness of the show, proclaiming it as "coarse," "brash," "bawdy," and "ribald," producing "blushes of shame." Brooks Atkinson claims in his *Times* review: "Some one will have to call out the fire department to dampen down the classical ardors of this hilarious tale. . . . Let us pass over their bawdries with decorous reserve, pausing only to remark that they are vastly enjoyable." Yet by using Shakespeare's play, the creative team knew that their bawdiness was sanctioned by Shakespeare's reputation. How could anyone object to jokes about adultery, prostitutes, or near incest that originated in the high cultural institution of Shakespeare? Moreover, the show offered the respectable Shakespeare with its inheritance from the variety stage: risqu—songs, dances, and gags, sugar-coating the high cultural. The reviewers often comment on how the musical comedy improves on Shakespeare. Richard Watts, Jr., remarks, "If you have been wondering all these years just what was wrong with *The Comedy of Errors,* it is now possible to tell you. It has been waiting for a score by Rodgers and Hart and direction by George Abbott" (*Herald Tribune*). His enthusiasm is echoed by others, particularly Stark Young (*New Republic*), who pronounced that "In general, the whole production seemed to have gusto and a certain freshness along the ancient classic line. . . . [The] production is closer to the classic than the Elizabethan tradition could have been." Reviews combine self-congratulatory recognition of Shakespearean elements, with gleeful pleasure in the way that Shakespeare has been erased and the story spiced up. Taking over the legit text and abandoning it for the variety form means that critics find a musical version better (or more pleasurable) than a legit one.

Shakespeare exists as a beard, and nothing else. Hart himself best summed up the matter in a deliberately smart-ass way: "If it's good enough for Shakespeare, it's good enough for us." The second Shakespearean musical would prove Hart wrong, for using material that was "good enough for Shakespeare" led to a flop for *Swingin' the Dream*.

In 1939 Gilbert Seldes and Erik Charell wrote *Swingin'*, a musical comedy version of *A Midsummer Night's Dream*. It sounds like an extraordinary production. *Swingin'* reset the action to Louisiana around 1900, with white performers playing Theseus's court (Theseus becomes governor of Louisiana) and African American performers playing the mechanicals (New Orleans firemen) or fairies. The production of *Swingin'* employed an impressive group of theatrical artists. Jimmy Van Heusen based his swing version on Mendelssohn's score, writing music for such performers as Louis Armstrong, the Bud Freeman band, the Benny Goodman sextet (including Fletcher Henderson at piano and Lionel Hampton on vibes), with Don Voorhees conducting. Agnes de Mille did the production's choreography for such dancers as the Rhythmettes and Bill Bailey. Special effects were plentiful:

> The huge Center Theatre's stage [demolished in 1954] was exploited for various trick and interesting effects, with sets and costumes modelled after Walt Disney's cartoons. Titania made an entrance in a World's Fair "World of Tomorrow" electric wheelchair, a Murphy bed emerged from a tree in the forest; microphones (to help audibility in the cavernous playhouse) sprang up in the shape of caterpillars and snails; and there was a noteworthy scene of plantation life on the lawn of the governor's . . . mansion, with a cast of jitter-bugging celebrants. (Leiter 1989: 502)

The performers were outstanding: Louis Armstrong played Bottom, Bill Bailey played Cupid, the Dandridge sisters were attendant fairies, Juan Hernandez played Oberon, Moms Mabley played Quince. The young lovers were white (Dorothy McGuire played Helena, for example), but the fairies and mechanicals were African American: Butterfly McQueen played Puck,

Maxine Sullivan played Titania. These are important performers, either in the African American performance tradition (Moms Mabley never really broke through with a white audience, for example, but was enormously influential in African American clubs, performing until the 1970s), or in the broadest popular spectrum (Louis Armstrong and Butterfly McQueen are obvious examples). If prominent names and a lively design were all one needed for a play to succeed, *Swingin'* would have had a long and happy run. It failed. The production closed in less than two weeks.

Why did the play fail? The reviewers generally complained that it was too respectful toward the Shakespearean text. When the performers were allowed to cut loose from the original play, according to John Mason Brown or Brooks Atkinson, the popular performers were splendid, filling the stage with vigor and originality. Too often, however, the show focused "on the tedious story of the lovers," as Brown remarked (*Post*). In the *Times* Atkinson agreed:

> It would have been better to throw Shakespeare out the window. The pedestrian jest cracked in his name merely stands in the way of a lively raree-show. Every now and then a flare of dancing breaks through the professorial patter, and the Benny Goodman boys perform brilliantly on a piece of music. But the going is heavy through long stretches of the evening. "The Boys from Syracuse" did better by forgetting Shakespeare altogether.

Too much Shakespeare was a problem, yet a second factor cannot be ignored: race. The "tedious story of the young lovers," to use Brown's phrase, was carried out by white performers, while the singers and dancers were African American performers. Part of the pleasure in a show like *Boys* was that it claimed to be Shakespearean, even though it wasn't. Thus *Boys* could make sexual jokes that pushed past the conventions of the time because it simultaneously was and was not a Shakespearean work. Clearly the pleasure that the audience was intended to receive from *Swingin'* involved their recognition that African American performers who were important on the variety stage were doing Shakespeare, the epitome of the legit stage from which they were largely excluded. The show invoked race, but not enough; it threw away the play text, but only occasionally; it wavered. The audience was not invited to wink at what the play was getting away with or to collaborate in its naughty use of Shakespeare that was not-Shakespeare.

Errol Hill writes generously of *Swingin'*, suggesting that it was one of several projects in the 1930s that "proved to be a turning point in the relationship of Afro-Americans to Shakespeare's plays" (Hill 1984, 118). Until these 1930s productions, he argues, "Black folk attending his plays did so as much out of duty to their cultural uplift as in recognition of the fact that Afro-Americans were as talented as Caucasians and could achieve success in the highest form of dramatic production" (118). Whether one decides that *Swingin'* was a tricked up minstrel show or a subversive challenge to racism probably depends on whether one regards Shakespeare as an integral part of African American theater (as a work like *The African Company Performs Richard III* suggests) or as separate from African American culture and embodying white America's fundamental racism (as burlesques of *Othello*, common in variety theater, suggest). In any case, the show's failure moots the question. Later Shakespearean musicals returned to the two topics engaged by *Boys* and *Swingin'*: sex and race. Behind Shakespeare's beard, shows like *Kiss Me, Kate* and *Your Own Thing* pushed the boundaries of conventionality in their treatment of sexual independence and cross-dressing. The next musical version of Shakespeare to use "race" was *West Side Story* (1957) with its Puerto Rican Capulets. When Joseph Papp used performers of color in the musical version of *Two Gentlemen of Verona* (1971), the casting roused little controversy and great enthusiasm. For *Swingin'* the problem seems to have been too little race and too much Shakespeare: rather than erasing Shakespeare and then using the freedom to push boundaries, as *Boys* had done, *Swingin'* had been overcautious. Shakespeare's presence had restricted rather than liberated the show.

The Smash Shows

Once the precedent had been established, two shows, *Kiss Me, Kate* (*Kate*) and *West Side Story* (*West Side*), drew on Shakespeare with enormous success. In any analysis of Broadway musicals these two shows invariably appear as central achievements, both for the song writers (Cole Porter, Stephen Sondheim, and Leonard Bernstein) and for the musical comedy form. *Kate,* the first musical comedy to win the Tony for Best Play, had songs by Cole Porter, a book by Sam and Bella Spewack, and choreography by Hanya Holm. Indeed, the *Journal-American* review was headlined, "A Musical Comedy That Has Everything." *Kate* opened December 30, 1948, and the next day garnered raves about its excellence. Today *Kate* stands as one of the great musical comedies of American theater, a milestone from the Golden Age of Broadway. At the time, however, people expected a flop, for Porter had been in a slump.

Kate cited Shakespeare without using him much. It took fewer liberties with Shakespeare's text than *Boys* had, choosing rather to embed bits of Shakespeare in a frame story about a *Taming of the Shrew* production featuring two divorced stars who remain in love. After endless comic squabbling, Fred/Petruchio asserts himself and tames Lilli/Kate. By defeating a pair of itinerant gangsters who have wandered into the production, all live happily ever after. The Cole Porter songs remain delightful, the show had a gifted cast starring Alfred Drake and Patricia Morison, and no one can wonder at the show's success. Again the show depends on the joke of citing Shakespeare in an American idiom. *Boys* had shown appropriation could succeed, yet *Kate* was more cautious than its progenitor, insisting on its frame and doing some parts of the Shakespeare comedy straight. Swain has analyzed the sophistication and understanding of Porter's settings for Shakespearean texts in "Where Is the Life That Late I Led?" "I've Come to Wive It Wealthily," and "I Am Ashamed That Women Are So Simple" (Swain 1990, 129–52). Having cited Shakespeare, however, *Kate* largely ignores him, so that the play may do what it wants to do: interrogate sexual relationships.

Perhaps the most interesting aspect of that interrogation is its malleable vision of gender and sexuality. While critics agree on the show's interest in sexuality, they read its concerns individually. William McBrien and others argue that Porter's songs refer to his life as a gay man who enjoys cruising and rough trade (McBrien 1998, 313; see also Clum 1999, 72). Richard Burt offers a playfully queer reading of the movie version and its "series of double entendres focusing on Vancssi/Kate's ass and Graham/Petruchio's inadequate penis size" (Burt [1998]1999, 172). Yet the transgressive narrative may also be feminist. Barbara Hodgdon suggests that "If *Kate* vents sadomasochistic fantasies in soft-shoe routines to teach that fighting phallic power can be fun, it also suggests that managing monogamy's double-toil-and-trouble standards is strictly women's business." In conversation, Irene Dash has suggested to me that the show has many positive things to say about female independence. I myself think its gestures toward sexual freedom finally collapse into cynical conservatism. Lois/Bianca tells her lover that "I'm Always True to You, Darling, in My Fashion," despite her clear pleasure in seeing other men and trading her sexual favors for gifts. Lilli/Kate also enjoys her independence. Divorced (and thus free from sexual restrictions placed on unmarried women in 1948), she is a highly successful actress in both films and plays, courted by a powerful man. If Fred angers her, she can walk. The men too enjoy freedom. Whomever one desires is sexually knowledgeable and available; Fred has no qualms about having both Lois and Lilli. Marriage, the show implies, leads attractive people to bicker or smack one another around, cuts the opportunities for a woman to advance herself, forces women to put up with tyrants or scoundrels and men to put up with shrews or fools. As Petruchio sings of marriage, "Oh, what a bore at night!" The notion that marriage is dull, limiting, and potentially violent simply fades by the end when Lilli abruptly submits to Fred, both yielding independence for a respectable remarriage. Behind Shakespeare's beard, that show can say that marriage (or compulsory heterosexuality if one is gay, as Cole Porter was) is not ideal, but it then backs down for a safe conventionality, conducting that surrender in Shakespeare's language, via Porter's setting of "I Am Ashamed." Kate's songs remain standards, its performances were superb, and its book is remarkably conservative.

West Side (1957) is wholesomely progressive, an instance of liberal humanism. Today it seems inevitable that it should have succeeded with music by Leonard Bernstein, lyrics by Stephen Sondheim, book by Arthur Laurents, and staging and choreography by Jerome Robbins, although *Swingin'* shows that nothing is inevitable. The reviews for *West Side* comment repeatedly on the show's innovations: "an original project" with "a searching point of view," "an entirely new form," "a bold new kind of musical theater," praising Bernstein's music and Robbins's choreography. The point repeatedly made is that the show is serious. Based on *Romeo and Juliet*, *West Side* never cites it explicitly, so that Shakespeare's work is continually present and absent. Suddenly the comedic aspect of appropriation dropped out of the picture; the joke sustaining *Boys* and *Kate* is spurned as if putting Shakespeare into colloquial American terms no longer amused.

Shakespeare did, however, provide aesthetic guidance: the speed of the story, the tension of the warring factions, the poignance of the deaths all owe something to Shakespeare's original; while the earthiness of the street characters, like that of Mercutio in Shakespeare's play, provides a needed tartness to the lovers' sweetness. Shakespeare was kept safely offstage: no explicit reference was made to him or to his play, although most reviewers commented on it as a source. Unnamed, Shakespeare remains in evidence. Walter Kerr (*Herald Tribune*) even said, "Perhaps the echoes of another "Romeo and Juliet" are too firm: the people often seem to be behaving as they do because of arbitrary commands from a borrowed plot." Yet the show has important differences from the Shakespearean tragedy. Maria is alive as the curtain falls. Shakespeare's warring families are tragic in part because they are so much alike: in Shakespeare's Verona no one can distinguish a Capulet from a Montague, a plot device that gets Romeo to the ball where he meets Juliet. The infamous feud has no known basis. In *West Side* the feud is based on ethnicity, albeit a curiously pale imitation of life's tension: Poles and Puerto Ricans look, sound, and behave differently from one another in the musical.

The show was also, of course, of eminent social respectability in 1957: it stood for tolerance, assimilation, and an end to violence, all of which evoked a welter of sentimental response. Reviewers responded to this innovative show, and the brilliance (undeniable) of its music and dancing, with doting and even patriotic raves. One of the strongest was the closing paragraph of Frank Aston's review (*World-Telegraph*):

> [*West Side*] is far more than a Romeo meowing to a Juliet on a fire escape. It is a marvel peculiar to this country. Here we breed evil in our cities, but here we also parade a Bernstein and a Robbins so that a big part of this tortured

world may say, "America must be proud of boys like those." And theater-going Americans may reply, "You're darn tootin' we are."

Spectators received exceptional entertainment, impeccable cultural antecedents, and a dose of social uplift. Yet they avoided confronting Shakespeare directly (nor for that matter did they have to think very hard about race). Clearly the show was a bargain. *West Side* allowed middle-class whites to feel some identification with lower-class immigrants, but D. A. Miller would extend that process beyond the socioeconomic category. Miller suggests that gay men are Maria, celebrating themselves as "pretty, witty, and bright," reveling in both the pleasure of Tony's wooing and the pathos as the heterosexual union is destroyed. His queer reading is, finally, less peculiar than Aston's flag-waving "darn tootin'" response.

The catholicity of *West Side* and cynicism of *Kate* establish the boundaries for what musicals can do with Shakespeare. In *Kate,* you need only "Brush Up Your Shakespeare" and you can have any object of desire. In *West Side* you simply think of Shakespeare, never speaking of him, and you have the power to experience any class, race, or gender. Spoken, the word "Shakespeare" allows every act; unspoken, the word allows every identity. And the power of these musicals reaches beyond the characters who people them to transform the people who create the characters. Cole Porter's reputation is magically resuscitated. The Spewacks find a world of opportunities open to them. Jerome Robbins and Leonard Bernstein enter triumphantly into new kingdoms. Stephen Sondheim begins not at the bottom, but at the top of musical theater.

An Onslaught of Failures

After *West Side,* citing Shakespeare, initially an uncertain tactic to draw an easy laugh, might have seemed a proven strategy for making stars. But changes in America diminished musical comedy, for complex reasons centered on changes in economics, politics, and taste. (Clum, Mordden, and Steyn all consider why musical theater has faded.) In simple terms, Cole Porter's sophistication or Bernstein and Sondheim's progressivism sounded stale. The failure of vaudeville in the 1930s had ended the creative tension that existed between the variety stage and the elite, and the consequences of that shift were felt in subsequent decades. Instead of the musical stage laughing at the legit as a pretentiously elite form, the success of movies and television meant that musical shows were themselves elite and condescendingly (or nostalgically) mocked. In the 1960s and '70s, musicals based on Shakespeare boomed, but most failed. Where, after all, could a show based on Shakespeare go next? Earlier musicals had lifted a complete plot to amuse an audience or borrowed part of a plot to amuse or improve an audience. What remained to be done? Lack of opportunity did not, of course, stop anyone: Rick Simas reports failed musicals based on *As You Like It* (1964); *Midsummer Night's Dream* (*Babes in the Woods*, 1964); *Twelfth Night* (*Love and Let Love*, 1968, and *Music Is*, 1976); *Romeo and Juliet* (*Sensations*, 1970); *King Lear* (*Pop*, 1974); *Hamlet* (*Rockabye Hamlet*, 1976); and *Tempest* (*Dreamstuff*, 1976). *Catch My Soul*, 1973, based on *Othello*, was a rock film version. (Only history plays resisted musical treatment.) Two shows succeeded: the soft-rock musical, *Your Own Thing* was an off-Broadway hit in 1968, as was New York Shakespeare Festival's *Two Gentlemen of Verona* (*Two Gents*) in 1971.

Rock musicals offered a potentially new approach to Shakespeare, yet enjoyed little success. With the notable exception of *Hair*, the musical theater quickly moved away from rock and back to pop or on to Andrew Lloyd-Webber. Opening a few months after *Hair*, *Your Own Thing*, with book by Donald Driver and songs by Hal Hester and Danny Apolinar, combined good humor and topicality. Set in New York, it examined gender confusions, atypical love relationships, and pop culture. In it, Shakespeare was a beard for the 1960s sexual revolution. As in *Kate*, one reason for the play's commercial success was its careful defusing of any explosive topics. Thus a character realized he might be a homosexual, agonized comically over the prospect, defeated his own homophobia, and accepted himself as a fine human being, only to discover that he'd been a heterosexual all along. There are no risks in this sort of thing. As Robert Sandla comments, "The show spoke for what it was pleased to call 'the Now Generation,' but there was nothing in it to scare Grandma" (1999, 7)

Shakespeare was largely banished, although two of the songs kept his language ("Come Away, Death" and "She Never Told Her Love"). As usual, the reviewers praised this tactic of erasing Shakespeare, with both the *Post* and the *Daily News* claiming *Your Own Thing* was more enjoyable than Shakespeare's *Twelfth Night*. Shakespearean references were a pleasant cheekiness; an implicit tribute to the British Invasion was intended; and Shakespeare's sanctioning of cross-dressing allowed the production to use the device without shocking anyone. Today the work seems trite and the language painfully dated. Sandla quotes as a "pivotal line: 'Love is a gas! It's where it's at! And if your own thing is against Establishment's barf concepts, you can drop out and groove with it'" (1999, 8). *Your Own Thing* ran for 933 performances, but has no currency today. Its rock songs now just sound like commercial pop.

The New York Shakespeare Festival's *Two Gents* (1971) was adapted by John Guare and Mel Shapiro, with music by Galt MacDermot and lyrics by John Guare. *Two Gents* offered a politicized subtext about race and sex in America within a musical version of Shakespeare's text. With a denunciation of war and a celebration of interracial friendship and love,

"It was accessible Shakespeare, a wonderful show in the spirit of the time," recalled Bernard Gersten. "Never had any Shakespeare we had done engendered such a response." (Epstein 1994, 261)

Like most of the Festival's productions in this period, it cast performers of color and challenged the idea that Shakespeare was principally open to a white, upper-class audience. Yet its treatment of women is uncomfortable. Epstein quotes Elizabeth Swados's description of the festival's atmosphere:

"There was David and David Mamet and Tom Babe and they all seemed like Davids to me. They were good-looking, slightly sweaty straight guys—it always seemed like there were at least ten of them, and that they would close doors louder than the women and sit around and talk about war. . . ."
The 'Davids' cultivated an aggressively heterosexual style, which included tough language, hard drinking in Papp's office and at the nearby Cedar Tavern and a confrontational status toward society. (Epstein 1994, 317)

This style is reflected in *Two Gents*. The production eliminated scenes in Shakespeare's original text that allow women to talk to one another, and it was set in an "aggressively heterosexual" world that denied the misery of rape or violence against women.

Two Gents is not unmindful of the women in the play. Among its changes, it has Lucetta go with Julia to Milan to keep her company, not to help keep her safe. Shakespeare's Julia must travel alone and her fear of attack makes her travel in men's apparel, for her world is more dangerous. While Lucetta may join Julia in *Two Gents,* the touching scene between Julia and Sylvia in *Two Gentlemen* is missing completely. Indeed, save for the early scene between Julia and Lucetta, a woman never talks to another woman in *Two Gents;* women speak only to men. In *Two Gentlemen,* by contrast, women talking make up some of the play's most memorable scenes. Julia and Lucetta talk together in 1.2 and again in 2.7, Julia comments on what Silvia says in 4.3, and Julia and Silvia talk together in 4.4.

Silvia may seem stronger willed in *Two Gents* than in *Two Gentlemen.* When the Duke issues his order, "Go back to your tower, dear, she protests, "I don't want to go back to my tower. / No. No. Valentine! Valentine!" When Proteus woos her, she sings:

> Love me
> Not your idea of me
> Release me
> From your fantasy
> Love me
> Forget your fear of me

Don't tell me to keep my chin up
Stick a baby in my womb
I won't be nobody's pin up
In nobody's locker room

As this lyric indicates, *Two Gents* is plainspoken about sex. In one of the big musical numbers, celebrating love, the lyric belongs quintessentially to that age of Aquarius:

Boom chicka chicka chicka
Fuck fucka wucka wucka
Cock cocka wocka wocka
Puss pussa wussa wussa
Fuck fucka wucka wucka now

A stage direction during this number remarks that the "ensemble is down right as if at a revival meeting." Notably *Two Gents* caps off all its frankness by having Julia reveal that she is pregnant when she confronts the perfidious Proteus at the end.

Yet the sexual revolution had a way to go. Although speaking frankly in *Two Gents*, Silvia is less forceful in her actions. The Silvia of *Two Gentlemen* "woos" Valentine "by a figure" as Speed points out, quickly perceives that Proteus is fickle (2.4.90–94), helps plan her unsuccessful elopement with Valentine, and arranges her own escape with Eglamour as a protector against the world's dangers. In *Two Gents*, Silvia has Valentine write the letter to Eglamour, but quickly shifts her affection to Valentine; allows Valentine to make all the plans for their unsuccessful elopement; and simply calls to Eglamour to come and take her away, sure that he'll think of something. (Like Julia in the earlier scene, she faces little danger; the outlaws have gone.) She may sing that she's "nobody's pin up," but she's nobody's rocket scientist either.

The musical's sexual frankness, however, is the place where it is finally most dated by being least serious. When Proteus tries to rape Silvia, *Two Gents* retains some of Shakespeare's language, but adds business, a song, and stage directions that undercut the moment. Silvia and Eglamour are kissing passionately and about to make love. Proteus sees them and sings first of his frustration, "I want to kiss her mouth," and then, "Now I'm angry." He attacks them, and Eglamour runs away. Proteus attacks Silvia, with telling stage directions:

(Proteus forces Silvia to the ground)
SILVIA: O Heaven!
Proteus: I'll force thee. Yield to my desire.

(And he plops himself on top of her. Starts to kiss her. He removes his
glasses. Valentine enters left platform. Crosses down left of Proteus and
Silvia. Silvia giggles in delight. They become aware of Valentine. Proteus
puts on his glasses.)

The question of how a production of *Two Gentlemen* deals either with Proteus's attempted rape or with Valentine's preference for his friend over his
true love is clearly difficult. But to suggest that Silvia welcomes first Eglamour's kisses, "giggles in delight" at a rape by Proteus, and finally marries
Valentine with no qualms just increases the difficulties. This Silvia is a patriarchal fantasy figure like little Annie Fannie: to "fuck fucka wucka wucka"
is all that concerns her and the partner doesn't matter. Rape simply becomes
rough sex.

Most of the critics who reviewed the production praised its exuberance,
its joy, and its accessibility. Those critics who did complain about the production disliked the way it "at times degenerated into . . . musical-comedy
glitter and self-conscious ethnicity" (Brustein 1975, 186), but the implicit
dismissal of rape went unremarked. Peter Schjeldahl is the only reviewer I
have found who even mentions the change in the scene, and he thinks it is
an improvement:

> While streamlining it here and there, Guare and Shapiro have pretty much
> preserved the story of "Two Gentlemen." . . . [I]n a notoriously implausible
> scene, Proteus finds and tries to rape her. . . . [The] adaptors have hung not
> only a lot of zestful singing and dancing but, boldly, an up-to-date set of val-
> ues about love and sex and a number of up-to-the-minute theatrical sallies.
> Thus Silvia is no longer an upright, lovesick maiden; she has become an in-
> genuous swinger. (*New York Times,* August 8,1971)

Two Gents broke ground by using actors of different races, by integrating
rock music with Shakespeare's language, by including an antiwar message.
Yet what happens to the women is startling: Their roles are reduced, they
exist almost exclusively in relation to men, and they enjoy rape. By presenting the sexual attitudes of patriarchal folklore, the production had found a
way to persuade the public to sanction its break with other conservative social attitudes.

My perception of the show as misogynistic is possible only in hindsight:
when the show opened it was groundbreaking, and the version of "sexual
freedom" it presented seemed both an exhilarating possibility and an ethical
one. I saw and enjoyed the production then; now I wonder why it didn't
bother me. Today, the sexuality the show presents seems to creak with age,
as embarrassing as "fuck fucka wucka wucka now." When Shakespeare serves
as beard, he can permit the impermissible, but once the forbidden topic is

allowed—the cross-dressing of *Your Own Thing* or the heterosexual freedom of *Two Gents*—Shakespeare becomes largely irrelevant. As a result, the bawdiness of *Boys* is now invisible, the sexual revolution of *Your Own Thing* is silly, and the freedom of *Two Gents* turns sour.

Recent Shows

The transitional nature of *Your Own Thing* and *Two Gents* is perhaps also indicated by their identity as off-Broadway shows (although *Two Gents* did transfer successfully). In recent seasons three shows have been Shakespearean musicals—*The Lion King, Play On!,* and *Bombitty of Errors* (*Bombitty*). Two of these, *Play On!* and *Bombitty* play with gender roles, although neither breaks new ground. All three engage the topic of race, although only *Play On!* has a sustained or sustaining message.

Lion King (1997) is, of course, a Disney vehicle that has enjoyed great commercial success on Broadway; the plot is a loose analogue to *Hamlet.* The characters are the animals of the veldt, effectively presented via dance, masks, and puppetry. *Lion King* operates like *West Side,* as a story that expects to stand on its own, but retains a link to Shakespeare as a source of potential gravitas, held unmentioned and in reserve. It is also like *West Side* in its sentimentalizing of the Shakespeare plot: The prince, Simba, like Maria, lives at the end. This maneuver also offers a variation from the earlier show. The creators of *West Side* made it no secret that *Romeo and Juliet* was their starting place. Although the Disney Corporation acknowledges the link between *Lion King* and *Hamlet* once on their website, the connection goes largely unremarked, as if it were embarrassing. Perhaps the enterprise of adapting a children's cartoon into a live show that entertains families makes it necessary to disguise the unamusing source, a Shakespearean tragedy. A tourist who wants to see animals sing and dance to the music of Elton John is not likely to welcome the memory of a gloomy Danish prince speaking archaic English. Moreover, the show may have an implicit racial subtext in its evocation of Africa. Surely some awkwardness attends a work celebrating an African world that depends on a literary text central to the canon of European culture. One need only recall *The Song of the South* to realize that Disney has some experience of making a well-meant gesture that is regarded as patronizing and racist. Whatever the case, Shakespeare is firmly suppressed.

Bombitty is an off-Broadway show in which four white men rap *Comedy of Errors* in hip-hop style, taking on all of the roles, Betties and MCs. *Bombitty* is actually the closest of these recent shows to the Shakespearean original. Here the tactic is to retain the plot and jettison the language: The show makes a value claim for a mass culture form, in this case rap performance, by linking it to Shakespeare, a nice example of using Shakespeare as convenient beard. The potential citation of race, so strongly associated with rap in America, is modified in this show since the performers are white, and indeed all of the reviewers comment on that. Hip-hop in *Bombitty* resembles the rags that Hawkes has explored: the show offers a written version of largely unwritten form that "constitutes a bid . . . for genteel, white, European respectability" (Hawkes 1986, 89). The reviewers also echo the old claim that the musical improves on the original. Shakespeare's play is said to be "belabored," "tired," "dead," while Bombitty is "invigorating," "energetic," "a thrill." Thus the shift to musical comedy is claimed as an improvement on the Shakespearean original, a claim made regularly since 1938.

In some ways, *Play On!* operates like *Bombitty.* The show uses the storyline of *Twelfth Night,* resets it to the Harlem Renaissance, and adds songs by Duke Ellington. Occasionally a phrase from the play is used, but the language is largely colloquial American. The show is only incidentally concerned with Shakespeare: Ellington and his music matter far more, while the central issue is how an African American woman can fit herself into the masculine history of the Harlem Renaissance. What the show insists on is racial pride. It tells us repeatedly that African American history is important and inclusive (although it rewrites that history and Shakespeare's play as firmly heterosexual). *Play On!* handles the Malvolio subplot in a particularly interesting way. The Malvolio character, identified as a servant, plays the buffoon only briefly. He is shown as a sympathetic man, whom other characters pity despite their teasing. By eliminating any Sebastian character, the show allows the servant to become the master at the play's end when he marries Lady Liv, the Olivia character. *Play On!* is certainly no mockery of Shakespeare, nor does it suppress Shakespeare like *Lion King.* Both *Bombitty* and *Play On!* use Shakespeare to make a status claim for popular music, rap or Duke Ellington. The creators of *Bombitty* present the music aggressively, but retreat into Shakespeare's plot. The creators of *Play On!,* on the other hand, invade Shakespeare like a conqueror (to paraphrase another critic) and make him their own.

All of these shows continue to cite Shakespeare for their own ends, but to erase him after he has been cited. They gain the benefit of his authority without having to handle him as an actual presence, because he serves as a protective presence that allows them to consider gender and race without risk. Shakespeare is, and must be, respectable in American theatrical tradition, but on the musical stage he is permitted to be pleasurable as well, allowing performers to tell dirty jokes or the audience to consider racial crossings that were not considered in a legit setting. As cultural values have splintered, the need for such a device, Shakespeare as beard, has faded.

Yet there is far more to consider than what I have done in this chapter. The richness of the topic means that other scholars have opportunities to consider how Shakespeare intersects with American culture in musicals. I would have to cover too much were I to consider at length the predecessors to book musicals, the burleques and variety shows that cite Shakespeare, such as Eddie Foy's *Mr. Hamlet of Broadway* (1905), the earliest sustained use of Shakespeare in a musical that I have found and a show that has never been discussed. Nor can I explore the regional effect of Shakespearean musicals: how an Amherst production of *West Side Story,* a show initially praised for its consideration of Puerto Rican life, came under protest for its distortion of Puerto Rican life, for example, or the way that George Greanias, a Houston political figure notable for his respectability, first achieved public recognition for his musical, *Hello, Hamlet!* (the idea for which came to him, he claims, in a class taught by novelist Larry McMurtry). Nor is there room here for such shows as the British hit *Return to the Forbidden Planet,* which mixes Shakespeare with sci-fi and rock and roll in a perverse tribute to Americana; *The Donkey Show,* the ultimate disco experience that borrows from *Midsummer Night's Dream;* or the hip-hop dance piece, *Rome and Jewels.* These are topics for others to consider.

Notes

1. Cartelli is somewhat skeptical of this claim and refers to Levine's essay as "democratic nostalgia [rather] than an historically defensible position" and his conclusion as "too optimistic"; Thomas Cartelli 1999, 44, 185. For further assessment of Levine, see Alan Sinfield 1992 Michael Anderegg 1999, and William Warner 1990.

Works Cited

Anderegg, Michael. 1999. *Orson Welles, Shakespeare, and Popular Culture.* New York: Columbia Univ. Press.

Burt, Richard. [1998] 1999. *Unspeakable ShaXXXpeares: Queer Theory and American Kiddie Culture.* 2nd ed. New York: St. Martin's Press.

Brustein, Robert. 1975. *The Culture Watch: Essays on Theatre and Society, 1969–1974.* New York: Knopf.

Cartelli, Thomas. 1999. *Repositioning Shakespeare: National Formations, Postcolonial Appropriations.* London and New York: Routledge.

Clum, John M. 1999. *Something for the Boys: Musical Theater and Gay Culture.* New York: St. Martin's Press.

Driver, Donald with Hal Hester and Danny Apolinar. 1970. *Your Own Thing.* New York, Dell.

Epstein, Helen. 1994. *Joe Papp: An American Life.* Boston: Little, Brown and Company.

George-Graves, Nadine. 2000. *The Royalty of Negro Vaudeville: The Whitman Sisters and the Negotiation of Race, Gender and Class in African-American Theater, 1900–1940.* New York: St. Martin's Press.

Gilbert, Douglas. [1940]1963. *American Vaudeville: Its Life and Times.* 2nd Ed. New York: Dover Publications.

Guare, John and Mel Shapiro. 1973. *Two Gentlemen of Verona.* New York: Holt, Rinehart, and Winston.

Hart, Lorenz. 1986. *The Complete Lyrics of Lorenz Hart.* Ed. by Dorothy Hart and Robert Kimball. New York: Alfred A. Knopf.

Hawkes, Terence. 1986. *That Shakespeherian Rag: Essays on a Critical Process.* London: Methuen.

Hill, Errol. 1984. *Shakespeare in Sable: A History of Black Shakespearean Actors.* Amherst: Univ. of Massachusetts Press.

Hodgdon, Barbara. 1992. "Katherina Bound; or, Play (K)ating the Strictures of Everyday Life." *PMLA.* 107: 538–553.

Laurents, Arthur, Leonard Bernstein, and Stephen Sondheim. 1965. *West Side Story.* New York: Dell.

Leiter, Samuel. 1989. *Encyclopedia of the New York Stage 1930–40.* Westport, Conn.: Greenwood.

Levine, Lawrence. 1993. "William Shakespeare and the American People: A Study in Cultural Transformation." In *The Unpredictable Past: Explorations in American Cultural History.* New York: Oxford Univ. Press, 139–71.

McBrien, William. 1998. *Cole Porter: A Biography.* New York: Knopf.

Miller, D. A. 1998. *Place for Us: Essay on the Broadway Musical.* Cambridge, Mass. and London: Harvard Univ. Press.

Mordden, Ethan. 1983. *Broadway Babies: The People Who Made the American Musical.* New York: Oxford Univ. Press.

Rodgers, Richard. 1975. *Musical Stages: An Autobiography.* New York: Random House.

Sandla, Robert. 1999. *Liner Notes to Your Own Thing.* New York: RCA Victor.

Simas, Rick. 1987. *The Musicals No One Came to See: A Guidebook to Four Decades of Musical—Comedy Casualties on Broadway, Off-Broadway, and in Out-of-Town Try-Out, 1943 - 1983.* New York: Garland.

Sinfield, Alan. 1992. *Faultlines: Cultural Materialism and the Politics of Dissident Reading.* Berkeley: Univ. of California Press.

Spewack, Bella and Sam, with lyrics by Cole Porter. 1953. *Kiss Me, Kate.* New York: Knopf.

Steyn, Mark. 1997. *Broadway Babies Say Goodnight: Musicals Then and Now.* New York: Routledge.

Swain, Joseph P. 1990. *The Broadway Musical: A Critical and Musical Survey.* New York and Oxford: Oxford Univ. Press.

Warner, William. 1990. "The Resistance to Popular Culture." *American Literary History.* 2(4): 726–742.

CHAPTER 10

REVIVING JULIET, REPACKAGING ROMEO

Transformations of Character in Pop and Post-Pop Music

STEPHEN M. BUHLER

Romeo and Juliet are ubiquitous figures in popular and mass-market culture and have been for well over a century, perhaps for as long as marketing strategies have appropriated from works increasingly set as "high culture." Over the course of that century, references to "Juliet and her Romeo" (5.3.310)[1]—as the Prince names the couple and characterizes their story in his concluding couplet—changed as the play became more strongly identified with youth and with shifting societal attitudes toward the young. Adolescence, the period of development called to mind by the characters' chronological ages, came to be seen as a subculture with its own behavior patterns, tastes, and purchasing power. Many of this group's attributes were constructed and communicated in and through music.

In this essay, I will focus on how Romeo and Juliet have been depicted and transformed in mass-marketed pop music directed primarily at young audiences and, secondarily, at audiences who have identified themselves with youth culture. The characters' representation in "post-pop" music, much of which borrows from pop music idioms but deliberately distances itself from mass-market strategies, built—and continue to build—on earlier transformations. Such repackaging was not an isolated series of encounters between literature and the marketplace: it was part of a larger dynamic of exchange between competing and complementary sources of culture. The U.S. educational system, as well as the music industry, configured adolescents as an audience to be reached—as, in effect, consumers. What resulted in connection with *Romeo and Juliet* was a widespread reconsideration of the play's significance and of its leading characters. Marketing did not determine, but instead encouraged new interpretations. As my title suggests, the repackaging led to markedly different understandings of who Romeo and Juliet could be, of the qualities and behaviors with which they could instantly be associated. Romeo, at one time the embodiment of suave insincerity, was recast as passionate commitment personified; Juliet, formerly presented as merely reactive to her lover's blandishments, has shown signs of increased independence and agency. Many of these shifts in characterization have gained force not only by virtue of the music that drives the songs or of the societal attitudes that provide their context: they also gain force by virtue of engagements with the playtexts (and *Romeo and Juliet* has a vexed textual history[2]) that are the songs' direct and indirect inspiration. Perhaps most curiously and productively of all, economic factors that contributed to the transformations have also appeared overtly in song lyrics reflecting and shaping popular understandings of these two characters.

Songs invoking and constructing the characters of Romeo and Juliet comprise a group of mechanically-reproduced (or digitally-generated) artifacts that function both as popular culture and as mass media—which means that they cannot function exclusively as either. I have deliberately chosen the phrase *pop music*, as opposed to "popular music," in acknowledgment of its dual presence and absence in those totalizing categories. Youth culture, in these cases, and mass media are not merely unworthy scaffolds that hath dared to bring forth so great an object as the Bard—and occasionally succeed in spite of themselves. Several songs interact with Shakespearean materials in ways that openly engage with the processes of mediation (in all its senses) and with the interplay between varieties of aesthetic authority and understandings of audience acceptance—including commercial success.

The marketplace serves as a reminder that Romeo and Juliet are not stable, set personalities in the playtexts that have been brought back to life, thanks to pop music. Nevertheless, the characters and the playtexts from which they emerge have been seen as more lively, more vital after being reworked in pop musical culture: in this sense, they have been revived. Romeo as a young person is taken more seriously when young people take themselves more seriously and are encouraged to do so by the cultural productions in which they participate as consumers, audiences, and (at times) producers. He cannot be readily dismissed when his sincerity is not so easily questioned. Juliet, too, provides a mirror of social attitudes toward adolescent females. In this, she is similar to Ophelia, whose name has appeared—with but a single paragraph of justification (Pipher 20)—in the title of *Reviving Ophelia,* a bestselling book devoted to "Saving the Selves of

Adolescent Girls." Over the centuries, the character of Juliet has been rewritten in accordance with shifting notions of identity and propriety for very young women. Sometimes the language has been gutted, removing "all sexual innuendo and other subtleties from her speech, transforming her into a perfectly innocent heroine" acceptable to audiences of a given era (Levenson 22). Sometimes her age has been quietly adjusted upward, making the inclusion of such complexities less distasteful. Certainly critical views that stress the "purity" and "innocence" of Shakespeare's protagonists and their love participate in similarly mirroring processes. Representations of Juliet that acknowledge her agency in several spheres of action appeal (in both senses of the term) to shifting notions and self-images of girlhood and young womanhood.

Because of the intensity of young people's participation in pop musical culture, such self-reflection began to affect more general understandings of what it means to be young. Youth themselves—encouraged by sectors of the market who have benefited from their greater economic agency—have consequently taken a more active role in shaping the depiction of their representatives, not only in images, but also in song lyrics. Juliet and Romeo became emblematic of youth during the second half of the twentieth century; their depiction responds to cultural norms, cross-currents, and conflicts as understood by young people themselves. Eventually new understandings of their characters influenced professional representations of the play: how *Romeo and Juliet* is staged, taught, and interpreted allows for additional refractions and even resistances. So what follows goes far beyond an exploration of what could be called "trickle-down hermeneutics": it does not merely discover traces of critical, theatrical, and pedagogical understandings of Romeo's and Juliet's characters as they are reflected in pop music lyrics. Instead, it explores how elements of the youth subculture shaped more general understandings of Shakespeare—how, in effect, some readings can "bubble-up" from emergent discourses—and how those readings can eventually be authoritatively co-opted as well. Consumers can, to some degree, shape products: this includes the cultural variety.

Most of the songs that supply my examples are drawn from the relatively broad range of musical styles that represented youth-centered pop music from the 1950s on: doo-wop, rhythm-and-blues (including Motown), top–40 rock, the very mixed bag that "album-based" rock presents (including post-pop). A few songs venture into such offshoots of—and reactions against—pop music such as hip-hop and rock-tinged chamber music. Despite the variety, there are nevertheless shaping discourses, if not absolute limits, that help to define the range. Whether mainstream or alternative, pop musical culture until late in the twentieth century was usually framed by the perspectives of young, white males seeking definition both with and against the supposedly universal "middle class" of economic self-image in the United States. Within this perspective, both singer and song identified most strongly with Romeo and cast Juliet in the role of assistant or obstacle (or both) in the campaign toward personal and social definition. But the perspective is neither absolute or universal, and the exceptions which allow Juliet greater agency and vitality are frequent and compelling. Over time, concurrent with changing understandings of young women as economic agents, Juliet becomes more of a focal point and more her own person.

Before considering the songs directly, however, the history of *Romeo and Juliet* as a young persons' play warrants review. For some time, the play was considered to be fairly grown-up material, despite the palpable youth of its protagonists. As a result, pop music allusions to its characters usually assumed an "adult," sophisticated tone. Irving Berlin's "I'm Putting All My Eggs in One Basket," featured in the film *Follow the Fleet* (1936) as performed by Fred Astaire and Ginger Rogers, has its initial speaker confess: "I've been a roaming Romeo, my Juliets have been many." The 1945 hit for Johnny Mercer, "Personality," written by Johnny Burke and Jimmy Van Heusen, suggestively ponders the nature of Juliet's appeal—along with that of other famous beauties:

> And what did Romeo see in Juliet?
> She had a well-developed . . . personality!

Since other legendary ladies are described as having the "cutest" or "a perfect" personality, the listeners are encouraged to make anatomical substitutions in accordance with personal taste. If the letter of Shakespearean bawdry is missing from these lyrics, the spirit of it survives. (For examples of "naughty, knotty, not-He" Shakespeare in American musical comedy, see Fran Teague's essay.)

The stress in these examples is on Romeo as romantic admirer and erotic aggressor; the songs also share a subtext establishing the triviality and instability of Romeo's attentions. In addition, any hints of Juliet's own initiative in raising the emotional and physical stakes and, indeed, on taking steps to keep Romeo from roaming are, to present-day eyes, conspicuous in their absence—and would likely be to Elizabethan eyes, as well. But the absences would perhaps not be so glaring in their own immediate times. Standard readings in criticism and editing practices for performance have often elided, even for adult consumption, those lines that make it possible to establish Juliet's character as very much Romeo's match in assertiveness. A notable exception occurred when the actors playing those roles were noticeably no longer youths: in the 1936 MGM star-vehicle production of the play, featuring Leslie Howard and Norma Shearer in the title roles, Romeo is rebuffed by Rosalind (making his instantaneous devotion to Juliet much less problematic) and Juliet retains the majority of her lines explicitly anticipating the consummation of their marriage. Interestingly, the studio financed some 500,000 study guides to be distributed to U.S. high schools in order "to stress the educational features" of the film and, of course, to generate business. It is not known how many guides actually made their way into students' hands and, conversely, how many teachers resisted this attempt to reshape curriculum.

At the time, *Romeo and Juliet* was not regularly taught in secondary school classrooms; educators and anthologists alike were understandably hesitant to require their young charges to study, in effect, textbook examples of filial impiety and cultural indecorum. The young lovers defy parental wishes and societal norms, ranging from masculine honor to feminine reserve, with equal abandon. The bawdiness of Mercutio and the Nurse and the Capulet servants settled the matter: as late as 1966, Bertrand Evans could warn against the "indelicacy" and embarrassment that teaching the play inevitably involved (15–16) and could admit that he had avoided any detailed analysis of Mercutio's wit or Juliet's passion (231) without having to declare the reasons for his reticence. Soon, however, the play became enshrined in the pedagogical canon. By 1973, *Romeo and Juliet* was part of the Schools Project at the Folger Shakespeare Library (Williams 263). By 1976, Alice Griffin had included it in her dramatic anthology, *Rebels and Lovers: Shakespeare's Young Heroes and Heroines* (*A Midsummer Night's Dream, Henry IV, part one,* and *Hamlet* provide the other rebellious and/or amorous exemplars). Some of the reasons for this shift are evident in Griffin's implicit premise: Shakespeare could be presented as speaking directly to disaffected youth at the end of the Vietnam era and in its aftermath. Other, deeper premises are well worth exploring in their own right. Seeing Shakespeare as "relevant" especially to the concerns of young people and seeing *Romeo and Juliet* as perhaps the most relevant of all followed the emergence of a new conception of the adolescent—the teenager—as a widely accepted social category and followed a perceived need for teachers, among others, to "speak" to those so categorized. What is most important for the present discussion is that these developments led teachers to include the tragedy as a standard work in schools in the United States and also, if to a lesser extent, in Great Britain. *Romeo and Juliet* is now one of the works most students are likely to encounter in secondary school, if often—without acknowledgment—in expurgated form (see Andreas). Those pesky problems in language and decorum do persist.

The music industry also recognized—and helped to create—the need for products that spoke directly to a younger audience (marketing's appropriation of youth culture is the subject of Thomas Frank's disdainful *The Conquest of Cool;* far more acute analysis is provided by Dick Hebdige's

Subculture: The Meaning of Style, esp. pp. 92–96). During the late 1950s and continuing through the 60s and 70s, pop music increasingly became, depending on your point of view, either a young person's game or a game with young people as the targets or, most likely, both. As a result, song lyrics aimed at that market could more regularly invoke the story of the "starcross'd lovers" in ways that reflected changing ideas of how young women should behave and that reflected how the play that most famously presents the lovers was itself presented in the classroom, on the stage, and on screen. Several cultural factors led to the reconstruction of young people as a separate demographic category and market base: Grace Palladino (5–10) traces how this development was in part a response to the cumulative effects of progressive educational practice in U.S. high schools. The societal reaction and its consequences provide a vivid example of the "regulated restlessness" that cultural theorist Tony Bennett has seen at work in educational theories that mandate a "progressive relationship to the self" (158). As the dynamic came full circle, the youthful age of both Romeo and Juliet could be stressed more and more in the classroom and eventually on screen, partly as an invitation for young readers to "see themselves" in Shakespeare. During this first transitional period, through roughly the mid 1960s, Romeo becomes increasingly more sincere and Juliet (if more gradually) more proactive. In the next period, into the early 1980s, Juliet becomes more assertive—if, at times, at Romeo's expense. Finally, both characters begin to embody forms of cultural negotiation that recognize complicity in the political and economic institutions being resented or resisted. Complicity does not enforce assent, however: Romeo and Juliet are presented as characters that understand their ambiguous positions in society; they and the songs that reinterpret them have come to represent both subculture and "high culture" in the mass market.

One of the first examples of the once again ardent Romeo was provided by a recording that both co-opted the music increasingly admired by young audiences and also distanced itself from that music. The original R & B version of "Fever" was composed by Otis Blackwell, writing under the name of John Davenport, and Eddie Coolly; it was memorably recorded in 1956 by Little Willie John, whose rendition topped the R & B charts and enjoyed some crossover recognition in the pop charts. The song was covered, with far greater financial success, by Peggy Lee in 1958. Lee, who was a veteran of pop music before the development of youth-culture expression and marketing, aimed for an adult (and primarily white) listenership and added new lyrics. Many others have since reinterpreted the song and must choose which version to perform. The speaker in Lee's additions to "Fever" connects the fiery longing he or she currently experiences with the circumstances faced by famed historical lovers, including Shakespeare's:

> Romeo loved Juliet / Juliet she felt the same
> When he put his arms around her / He said Julie, baby, you're
>   my flame
> Thou givest fever / When we kisseth . . .

The entertaining approximation of Elizabethan language coincides with the new understanding of Romeo's and especially Juliet's age. While the focus remains on Romeo, his ardor is reciprocated by Juliet; Lee's delivery makes the reciprocity clearer. The sparse, bass-driven arrangement for Lee's recording underscores the importance of the words and the unquestioned sincerity of the emotional experience. Because of the song's hybrid qualities, this is not simply the earlier version of adult sophistication nor is it (as Paul Anka would similarly protest) "Puppy Love": the passion is a product of "flaming youth" in its emergent, increasingly distinctive glory. The verse later includes a direct borrowing from Shakespeare in the positive use of the phrase "flaming youth," as taken from Hamlet's indictment of Gertrude's alleged, middle-aged corruption (*Hamlet* 3.4.84). The phrase helps to make a parallel argument against a perceived lack of devotion at work in the older generation; at best, that generation is unable to acknowledge devotedness in the young.

By contrast, "Soft Summer Breeze" presents young lovers who openly fear being dismissed as too young to be taken seriously. The song was a 1956 success by the Diamonds (best known for the doo-wop tribute and travesty, "Little Darlin'"). Written by big-band and rhythm-and-blues veteran Eddie Heywood with Judy Spencer, its modern-day couple asserts the superiority of their love to the passion attributed to Shakespeare's "kids."

> Let folks talk about Romeo and Juliet
> Kid stuff can't compare
> To the day when they first met

The startling youth of Shakespeare's protagonists allows Heywood's and Spencer's (what evocatively Early Modern names!) couple to dismiss what has traditionally been thought the stuff of tragedy as mere kid stuff; by contrast, they have loved at first sight more maturely and meaningfully. Even here, however, there is little hint of adopting a "grown-up" approach to the materials, despite the maturity of the songwriters themselves: instead, especially in the Diamonds' heartfelt delivery, the song demands that the lovers' own experience not be viewed in that way.

Lee's lyrics shows that once Romeo's sincerity is established, Juliet's role in events can be taken more seriously as well. That seriousness could extend to latter-day equivalents to Juliet and could register as anything but somber. The speaker in "That's Why I Love You So," written by Berry Gordy and

Roquel "Billy" Davis (as Tyran Carlo) and recorded by Jackie Wilson in 1959, places emphasis on Juliet's agency, by comparing her response to Romeo with his beloved's devotion to him. The song's bridge proclaims that "If Shakespeare thought that Juliet / Really loved Romeo from the time they met," the playwright would be astonished—would "blow his top"—at the ardor demonstrated by the singer's lady love. After raising questions about how intensely Juliet at first responded to Romeo, the singer celebrates the amorous initiative of the lady he is addressing. Juliet *might* have loved at first sight and with immediate response—performance and editing practices have effectively muddied the waters. But there is no question in the speaker's mind about his own experience and Wilson's exuberant, near-falsetto vocal harbors no doubt at all.

All three of these transitional songs have some connection with the increased presence of African-Americans in mainstream music directed at young audiences, whether in composition or performance or both. The performance histories also connect with the appropriation of black music by white-owned companies and their artists—and, in Gordy's case, with black responses to that co-optation. Interestingly, none of the lyrics engage directly with the economics of youth-oriented music. The next (and last) example from the earliest transition period is a prime example of mainstream white pop-rock, written by young songwriters who specialized in the developing idiom for the burgeoning market. The song foregrounds some of the economics involved and projects them onto the story of Shakespeare's lovers. The Reflections' 1964 single, "(Just Like) Romeo and Juliet," was written by Freddie Gorman and Bob Hamilton. It offers an intriguing look at the market forces that were helping to shape youth culture, accepted notions of behavior, and accepted readings of texts like, for example, *Romeo and Juliet*. Here the speaker assures his girl, unmistakably marked as such, that "Our love's gonna be written down in history, just like" the love demonstrated by the couple in the title—if, that is, he is successful in finding a job, buying a car, going to the drive in, ordering gifts for her from a catalog. There is plenty of working class pride and anxiety expressed in the lines and no little concern over generational roles: to be a cool kid, to be worthy of his Juliet's love, he has to be the right kind of youthful consumer, which in his case requires gainful employment. As the speaker admits, he's

> Wonderin' what tomorrow's gonna really bring
> If I don't find work tomorrow
> There's gonna be heartaches and sorrow.

There is, thanks to the allusion to Shakespeare's play, a further hint of parental disapproval. The girl's father may be insisting that unless the speaker gets that job, the relationship has to end. Without work soon, we hear—"tomorrow," in fact—"Our love's gonna be destroyed like a tragedy, just like Romeo and Juliet."

The upbeat tempo offers hope—the tagline is cheerfully repeated over and over—and also obscures the desperation in the words. Here, a youthful Juliet is constructed as reassuringly demure: obedient to authority, receptive to her suitor's emotions and plans. The male speaker, while alert to social and economic pressures, is bent on conforming to them and seems intent on transforming his Juliet into a helpmate in this campaign. If he fails, however, she will be an enduring symbol of the system that has worked against him.

By the following year, a more assertive Juliet would mark a new stage in the development of pop musical culture presentations of the characters. A wonderfully ambiguous allusion in the Supremes' "Back in My Arms Again" gives Juliet her own voice, while commenting on the history of Romeo's reconfiguration. The song was written by Motown's superb production team of Brian Holland, Lamont Dozier, and Edward Holland, Jr. expressly for the Supremes and unmistakably for their lead vocalist, Diana Ross. Released in 1965, the song presents as its speaker a young woman who has decided to take back her temporarily unfaithful boyfriend. She is ecstatic at the immediate results of her choice: the song's refrain, "Yes, he's back in my arms again" both "right by my side" and "so satisfied," is delivered in full harmony over a rhythm track powered by the incomparable Benny Benjamin on drums. While the speaker is happy, her decision prompts sharp criticism from several of her friends, who one by one are deemed incapable of giving proper advice. Mary, who has "lost her love so true," cannot be of much help, while "Flo, she don't know / 'Cause the boy she loves is a Romeo." Flo becomes, unmistakably, a Juliet-figure—one that is strong-minded and unafraid to express her opinions, however unreliable they appear to the speaker. What is less certain is the nature of "the boy she loves": what kind of Romeo is he? At first glance, he seems a throwback to the "roaming Romeo" of Irving Berlin, but if that is the case then Flo might be eminently qualified to give advice. After all, the speaker's beloved has first strayed and now returned. The difference may be that the speaker has learned how to keep her young man, something that has eluded Flo. But this Romeo might be the newer model, youthful (a "boy," we're told) and utterly devoted. In that instance, Flo cannot understand the speaker's problems because she has never experienced them: her Romeo has remained faithful.

Pop music depictions of Juliet's character from the early 1960s on are often influenced by *West Side Story*. This Broadway musical adaptation of *Romeo and Juliet* debuted in 1957 with a book by Arthur Laurents, lyrics by Stephen Sondheim, and music by Leonard Bernstein. The impact of the musical intensified after the highly successful 1961 United Artists release of a film version, which received industry acclaim (including ten Academy Awards) along with critical and audience approval. *West Side Story* participates in the larger cultural trend linking the situations in Shakespeare's play with the circumstances faced by contemporary U.S. youth, but presciently marks youth as self-consciously marginalized and resistant. Adult society fades into the background in this version; its role in establishing and sustaining the deadly feud, so evident in the playtexts, is almost thoroughly suppressed. Flaming youth is personified here in the "juvenile delinquent" members of rival, ethnically-based gangs and even the surrogate father-figure of Friar Laurence is largely subsumed by a dress-maker's mannequin, which "officiates" at the exchange of vows between Tony and Maria. The importance of *West Side Story* in reinforcing views of these characters can be seen in Franco Zeffirelli's 1968 film version, which featured a daringly youthful cast and offered a distinctive "generation gap" reading of the play. As Kenneth Rothwell has observed, *Romeo and Juliet* "has always been a tale *about* but not necessarily *for* young people" and Zeffirelli, encouraged by Bernstein's musical and current trends of thought, made a film that was deeply connected to youth culture and therefore "palatable" to younger audiences (Rothwell 134–35). It proved so palatable that Nino Roti's music spawned several pop music hits: his song for the film, "What Is A Youth?," draws additional attention to generational factors while cleverly invoking Renaissance variations on the *carpe diem* theme; with new lyrics—and also as an instrumental—it appeared as "A Time for Us" and was widely covered by a range of artists. The new lyrics draw upon one of Bernstein's and Sondheim's most celebrated songs from *West Side Story,* "Somewhere," which begins "There's a place for us" and includes, in the next verse, "There's a time for us." The borrowing makes the musical's influence on Zeffirelli's film and on the film's reception still more obvious.

The pop songwriter who has, arguably, been the most haunted by these specific representations of *Romeo and Juliet* and similar reworkings of Shakespeare's characters is Bruce Springsteen, who rings provocative changes on the story and specifically on the depiction of Juliet. The romanticized view of adolescent street life that Bernstein, Laurents, and Sondheim helped to perpetuate in *West Side Story* also provides a more general framework for Springsteen, whose depictions of Atlantic Seaboard urban life aspire to lush tragedy or mythic resonance. Springsteen makes direct allusions to both Romeo and Juliet in at least three very different songs: "Incident on 57th Street," on his second album, *The Wild, the Innocent, and the E Street Shuffle* (1973); "Fire," recorded by the Pointer Sisters in 1979 and frequently performed by Springsteen himself in concert; and "Point Blank," on the 1980 album *The River.* All three songs suggest a Juliet that can choose not to participate in the tragic sequence of events and therefore reflect a Juliet that is an instrumental figure, rather than complementary one, in Shakespeare's rendering of the tale.

"Incident on 57th Street" presents its protagonist and the object of his desire in Shakespearean terms, as filtered through *West Side Story*. "Spanish Johnny" is distinguished from his peers ("Those romantic young boys, all they ever want to do is fight") by his love for "Puerto Rican Jane," who shares her ethnic identity with the Broadway musical's Sharks and with Maria, its Juliet figure:

> Well, like a cool Romeo, he made his moves;
> Oh, she looked so fine.
> Like a late Juliet, she knew he'd never be true,
> But then she really didn't mind.
> Upstairs a band was playin',
> The singer was singin' something about goin' home.
> She whispered, "Spanish Johnny, you can leave me tonight,
> But just don't leave me alone."

Unlike earlier songs that had found Shakespeare's characters possibly lacking in passion or commitment, "Incident on 57th Street" suggests that its own characters are aware both of their tragic precedents and of their inability or refusal to imitate them. Johnny, partly following Romeo's example, is inspired by his lady's beauty to act. He remains "cool," however, following the advice of Sondheim's Jets to be so ("Just play it cool, boy, real cool") and limited by his own era's conventions. Johnny apparently feels that he cannot directly invoke the extravagant expressions of desire that were available to Shakespeare's Romeo and that were open to Juliet's initial skepticism. The lateness of the late-twentieth century Juliet is also connected to a kind of coolness: she will not hurry into either a statement of trust or one of devotion. Shakespeare's Juliet, though mindful that the newfound love is "too rash, too unadvis'd, too sudden" (2.2.118), will still only delay until the exchange of solemn vows the very next day. Johnny's would-be lady love is no fool, neither rushing into things nor promising more than she cares to deliver. Despite the awareness of the difference, there is no direct confession of regret, although the "really didn't mind" can register as ironic and rueful, given the expression of need that follows.

The original speaker in "Fire" can come across as more of a "roaming Romeo" than the devoted variety, a throwback to the sophisticated vision of the character that dominated pop culture references before the advent of youth subculture. Springsteen's persona here has a number of come-on lines that expertly reject the lady's repeated refusals: this version of Puerto Rican Jane cannot have the last word. Once again, however, a change in the gender of the singer and of the implied speaker can deeply affect how the lyrics register on the listener. In the Pointer Sisters' presentation, the lady herself admits that her statements of rejection are false: "My words say, 'split!' But my words, they lie." The suggestion of duplicity becomes explicit in the lines,

> Romeo and Juliet, Samson and Delilah,
> Baby, you can bet their love they didn't deny.

The juxtapositioning of those two couples is striking. A male speaker may be obliquely asserting that if anyone has to be worried in this case, it's himself: why should she be reluctant when he has, supposedly, more to lose? A female speaker, in contrast, may be giving her addressee fair warning: don't presume on either her responsiveness or his security. In both cases, it isn't clear (as seen in "Fever") whether the couples are meant to be thought of as contrasts or complements. Juliet may be presented as Delilah's opposite; after all, Juliet goes against "her people" even as Delilah chooses to remain loyal to the Philistine tribe. But the lyrics also group all four lovers together, since none of them denied their initial attraction. Should Juliet be seen as a Delilah-figure, someone responsible for the downfall of her beloved?

The Pointer Sisters' playful eroticism (nearly growling the first syllable of Romeo's name) in performance matches the songwriter's lighter touch in the song. Springsteen's ambivalence toward Juliet comes across far more sharply in "Point Blank." Much of *The River,* the album on which the song appears, is devoted to disappointments and disillusionments, to what happens when youthful idealism is confronted with hard, especially economic reality. In this song, both Springsteen and his speaker draw contrasts between a present situation and two different renderings of the story of *Romeo and Juliet:*

> I was gonna be your Romeo
> You were gonna be my Juliet
> These days you don't wait for Romeos
> You wait on that welfare check
> And on all the pretty things that you can't ever have.

Springsteen here draws upon the consumerist heart of the Reflections' "(Just Like) Romeo and Juliet," as well as the precedent of the source play. He also expands upon the logic of a passive female protagonist, as assumed in the earlier song: this Juliet cannot take action, but can only wait for one form of rescue or another. She chooses to wait for basic subsistence and for (perhaps) the products held out as a promise to participants in the U.S. economic system; she, too, cannot wait for alternative and questionable values. Springsteen suggests, however, that this is a conscious choice: all Juliets, now, can be credited or blamed with some measure of autonomy.

A less optimistic—or humanist—view is offered by Tom Waits, another inheritor from *Romeo and Juliet* and from *West Side Story.* Waits' cityscapes reach beyond the Broadway-influenced pop culture view of the streets, back to the works of Beat Generation writers—who always looked a bit askance at their youthful successors. Waits' "Romeo Is Bleeding" (on his 1978 album *Blue Valentine*) neatly captures some of the differences between his approach and that of Springsteen: his song is more elusive than allusive in its relations to Shakespeare's play than any of Springsteen's evocations, and it yet more clearly offers a critique of *rom*anticized violence. The Romeo of Waits' song inspires rejoicing that "everything is cool" among the boys who "all try to stand like Romeo" and ape his every move. In songspiel delivery over a hipster-styled vamp, Waits notes that the boys are unaware of the fatal wound Romeo hides from them:

> and he sings along with the radio / with a bullet in his chest
> and he combs back his fenders / and they all agree it's clear
> that everything is cool now that romeo's here

Despite the admiration of his uncomprehending friends, Waits' protagonist experiences only futility as his life seeps away from him and he "feels the blood in his shoes." His impending death is a consequence of a path he did not unmistakably choose. The song's main point of departure may be the playtexts' meditations on fate and fatality, with Romeo's line, "He jests at scars that never felt a wound," and Mercutio's non-metaphoric experience of being wounded both making important contributions. It seems, too, that Zeffirelli's depiction of Mercutio's death—in which Romeo's friend jokingly hides the deathblow from everyone else—may well have shaped Waits' antiromantic reworking of Romeo. The attack on romanticism is well grounded, however: while Juliet does not appear in "Romeo is Bleeding," a heartfelt version of "Somewhere" from *West Side Story,* combining full orchestration with Waits' ravaged vocal, begins the album. Unlike Springsteen in the same period, Waits has positioned himself outside the mainstream of rock music and instead comments upon it.

In contrast, Lou Reed embraces rock while critiquing the romanticism of *West Side Story* in his searing "Romeo Had Juliette." The song appears on Reed's *New York* album (1989) and participates in its unflinching examination of the city Reed loves. His recontextualization of an interracial love-affair between Romeo Rodriguez (who, in imitation of Waits' Romeo and in distinction from him "Runs a comb through his black pony-tail") and

"lithesome Juliette Bell" is set amidst deadly turf battles between crack co-
caine dealers. The singer's persona notes that

> Manhattan's sinking like a rock / Into the filthy Hudson, what
> a shock—
> They wrote a book about it, / They said it was like ancient
> Rome.

The pun makes a connection between Romeo's name and the eternal, eter-
nally-decadent city, suggesting a parallel between the persistent allure of
New York and Romeo's and Juliette's mutual desire and fulfillment. They
"wanted" each other, then "had" each other—Reed echoes the play's final
phrase in "had *her* Romeo"—but the meanings of their shared possession
disappear in the songs final lines with the "something [that] flickered for a
minute," but "then it vanished and was gone." In Reed's view, what the woe-
ful story of Juliet and her Romeo could signify when set in 1950s New York
simply doesn't apply any more.

Another example of a Juliet whose renewed agency inspires an ambivalent depiction is provided by Mark Knopfler, guitarist and guiding light for
Dire Straits. That group's 1980 album *Making Movies* includes one of the
most sustained reworkings of the play and its cultural mutations, especially
(as the album's title indicates) in film: the reworking also factors economics
into these lovers' fates. Knopfler brings his best recovering-schoolteacher
sensibilities to bear in "Romeo and Juliet," which brings together *West Side
Story,* Zeffirelli's film version, and echoes of the original playtexts. The first
two verses set up the now-familiar scene: "a lovestruck Romeo sings a street-
suss serenade"—accompanied, at first, only by his own acoustic guitar
(which sounds like Knopfler's beloved National Steel) to an unreceptive
Juliet. For her part, she has been singing the Angels' 1963 single "My
Boyfriend's Back" and quickly cautions Romeo that he "shouldn't come
around here singing up at people like that." The rest of the song, starting
with a refrain (the lyrics of which will change), takes on Romeo's voice and
presents his side of the twentieth-century story. "I forget I forget the movie
song," he complains, but then refers to it in his confession that "it was just
that the time was wrong"—there will not be another Zeffirelli-style "Time
for Us" in their experience. In the second and third refrains, he insists that
Juliet knows another movie song: "There's a place for us," recalling the Hollywood version of *West Side Story.*

In the new refrain's lines, Knopler offers glimpses of Shakespeare's Juliet.
His Romeo reminds Juliet that she had said, "I love you like the stars above,
I'll love you till I die." The line does more than refer to the story of "star-
cross'd lovers"; by making these Juliet's own words, Knopfler insists on in-

cluding an often-excised, sometimes problematic scene from Shakespeare. After the exchange of vows in front of Friar Laurence and before the marriage's consummation, Juliet eagerly awaits her bridegroom's arrival. Impatient for nightfall, she exclaims

> Come, gentle night, come, loving, black-brow'd night,
> Give me my Romeo, and, when I shall die,
> Take him and cut him out in little stars,
> And he will make the face of heaven so fine
> That all the world will be in love with night,
> And pay no worship to the garish sun. (3.2.20–25)

The second line is often revised by editors to read "when he shall die," but Knopfler's song is grounded in the above version, which makes the Early Modern English pun on "die"—to achieve sexual climax—refer to Juliet personally.

Knopfler's Juliet may want to distance herself from all that, to rewrite the story—she has apparently found a different source for the material goods so desired in "Just Like Romeo and Juliet" and in Springsteen's reworking of these materials in "Point Blank." She has left the "dirty," "mean" streets the two of them once shared in *West Side Story* and Springsteen's "Incident on 57th Street." In this revision, Knopfler suggests that she has found economic stability with a latter-day Paris and wants to minimize her past with Romeo: not "O Romeo, Romeo, wherefore art thou Romeo?" but "Oh Romeo, yeah you know I used to have a scene with him." The famous Balcony Scene becomes merely a youthful fling in her account. But the language of Shakespeare's Juliet is used to indict her self-concerned 1980s counterpart: she could choose otherwise; she has done so.

Few constructions of Juliet and Romeo during the 1970s and 80s are as expansive in their engagement with the characters and their shifting cultural meanings. Many songs take pains to keep Juliet in a secondary role, making her far less active than the playtexts indicate or that other renderings suggest. In "Don't Fear the Reaper," for example, composed by Donald Roeser for his band Blue Oyster Cult (on the 1976 album *Agents of Fortune*), we hear ironic echoes of "Like Romeo and Juliet" (but not *just*) after being told that "Romeo and Juliet are together in eternity." We hear this, however, through the sensibilities of the figure who becomes the song's central character, a woman in mourning for her beloved. She contemplates following Juliet's example, when it seems "clear that she couldn't go on." Instead of allowing her to do so, the band summons up a variant on the "Demon Lover" motif and has her Romeo appear at the window, blow out the candles lit in his memory, take his grieving lover's hand, and lead her away into Death's realm. Both the neo-glam "hair band" Ratt (in 1984's "Round and Round" on the

Out of the Cellar album) and long-lived rockers Aerosmith take a somewhat Mercutio-like perspective on what went on between Romeo and Juliet, but differ on questions of agency and mutuality. Ratt's protagonist declares that "We're gonna prove it tonight / Like Romeo to Juliet," placing all the initiative on Shakespeare's hero and himself: Juliet is not called upon to reciprocate. In the latter instance, the song "Flesh" on *Get A Grip* (1993), the writing team of Steven Tyler and Joe Perry, with guest keyboardist Desmond Child (a journeyman composer who would later cowrite "Livin' La Vida Loca"), conjures up a provocative parallel in the lines "From the day that Eve did Adam / Down to Romeo and Juliet." Here, what exactly Eve did with/to Adam in connection with the flesh and what exactly resulted are both left ambiguous; as a result, who did what between Romeo and Juliet (and who bears responsibility between them) is also undecided.

The Aerosmith song shrewdly follows Springsteen's example of linking Shakespeare's lovers with a problematic biblical precedent. It would be worth listening to a woman vocalist's take on "Flesh" as a parallel to the Pointer Sisters' revision of Springsteen's "Fire." The problem of Juliet's identity and initiative often intensifies when women themselves not only sing but compose versions of Juliet. Alanis Morissette, on her eponymous and very early first album (1991), collaborated with Leslie Howe in asking for a "Superman" (one song's title) who could "make me feel / A serious love like Juliet's is real." All this Juliet can do is respond to the mastery of an all-capable Romeo-of-Steel; perhaps she has been listening to Ratt's "Round and Round." Madonna, a bit further along in her respective career, presented matters more interestingly in her song, written with Patrick Leonard, "Cherish" (on the 1989 album *Like A Prayer*). The speaker alternates between assertiveness and dependence, between

> Romeo and Juliet, they never felt this way I bet
> So don't underestimate my point of view

and "You got the power to make me feel good." Much like Shakespeare's Juliet, Madonna's persona demonstrates both autonomy and need, culminating in the line: "Who? You! Can't get away, I won't let you." Along with echoes of the 1964 song, performed by the Association, with the same title (and with its own repetitions of "Cherish is the word I use"), Madonna's "Cherish" may also offer a reminiscence of Juliet's language, near the end of the Balcony Scene:

> ROMEO: I would I were thy bird.
> JULIET: Sweet, so would I
> Yet I should kill thee with much cherishing. (2.2.182–83)

Whether this is an intentional allusion or not, its intertext reinforces the ideal that this Romeo "can't get away"—she won't let him, indeed.

The last stage of pop culture transformations I will discuss presents both Romeo and Juliet as self-aware participants, commentators, and (at times) malcontents in their cultural contexts and associations. When Elvis Costello made the first of his visits to the story of Romeo and Juliet, in the first verse of his seminal "Mystery Dance" (which appears on the 1977 album *My Aim Is True* but also one of the demos first played by Charlie Gillett on BBC Radio London's "Honky Tonk"), neither character is content to play out the script as Shakespeare's playtexts suggest:

> Romeo was restless, he was ready to kill
> Jumped out the window, 'cause he couldn't sit still
> Juliet was waiting with a safety net

Romeo welcomes his beloved's intervention: he's not to be buried or dismissed, because he's "not dead yet." On the album, supported by the Marin County, California band Clover, Costello commandeers the persona of his namesake, Elvis Presley, with a fierce assault on "Jailhouse Rock." The synthesis of proto-punk and country (so appropriate to either Elvis) extends the applicability of the characters beyond the street scene of *West Side Story:* the song may have unwittingly contributed to the unfortunate tendency in the tabloids to depict Sid Vicious (of the Sex Pistols) and Nancy Spungen as the debased punk version of R and J. Costello's song initially focuses on Romeo but leaves little doubt that Juliet too is deliberately disrupting the tragic chain of events. Little wonder, then, that his collaboration with the Brodsky Quartet, *The Juliet Letters* (1992), takes its primary inspiration from the actual correspondence addressed to Juliet, in Verona, in the present time, by lovers and the lovelorn alike. In "Expert Rites," Costello impersonates the Veronese academic who endeavors to answer some of these letters; the song concludes with the exhortation, "Don't despair, my would-be Juliet." By contrast, the speaker in "Romeo's Seance" imagines a young man trying to reach the loved one he has lost to death, only to discover that she has already reached him:

> An unplugged radio plays. She is close NOW . . .
> THIS IS the song SHE dictated this evening. / Romeo is call-
> ing you.

Costello deftly subverts the scenario of "Don't Fear the Reaper" by refusing to make Juliet either a woman wailing for her Demon Lover or a Demon Lover herself. Her Romeo remains, however wounded, in the land of the living. By this time, however, Costello has distanced himself from youth-centered pop culture and from mass-market appeal: a string quartet may have been acceptable for coloring the Beatles' "Yesterday" and "Eleanor Rigby," but even those Paul McCartney-penned hits harkened back to pop music before the advent of youth culture.

Rock is less and less the musical medium of expression for that culture. Romeo and Juliet remain appealing, however, to rock's successors. There have been several rap and hip-hop takes on the characters; despite the skepticism evinced by Lou Reed, *West Side Story* and its imitators and revisionists have succeeded in giving Shakespeare's play nearly unimpeachable street credentials. One of the more striking versions was produced by singer Sylk-E. Fyne, whose "Romeo and Juliet" appears on her 1998 album, *Raw Sylk*. Playing off her own public persona as a woman who can hold her own against any male rap artist, Fyne casts herself in the role of a very assertive Juliet, one who knows volumes about love, about music, and about the business of music. The Reflections' "(Just Like) Romeo and Juliet" is quoted, but not by the female speaker. Instead, the phrase is uttered by the Romeo-figure (voiced by Chill), a rapper/DJ with whom this Juliet falls in love at first sight and hearing: "It's like Romeo and Juliet / Hot sex on a platter just to make you sweat." The Capulets' ball, transformed into a youth-organization dance in *West Side Story*, here becomes a club. In response to her Romeo, Fyne's Juliet asserts that she will make him her man because she

> Ain't got no love for nobody else but you—
> Cuz you'z my boo / I prove to you / My love be true

and then sings, surprisingly, "Do You Know Where You're Going To?"—the line that supplies the title for one of Diana Ross's songs, the theme from her 1975 film *Mahagony*. As Fyne's song unfolds, elements of danger, institutional obstacles, and fate all emerge—provided by hints at deadly rivalries among factions, by references to the music industry's incomprehension concerning the rap genre, and by a brief allusion to Bonnie and Clyde. There are hopeful tones in the mix, however, supplied by the music which is sampled to provide the backing track: Rene and Angela's 1985 R & B hit, "You Don't Have to Cry." Fyne's Juliet is confident of her ability to answer and even to overmatch her Romeo's verbal skill, sexuality, and emotional ardor; at the same time, his voice is relegated to a refrain, which cannot fully answer her concern whether he will remain true to her, physically and otherwise. Such doubts are also voiced, with superb rhetorical impact, by the Juliet of Shakespeare's Balcony Scene. As a result, Romeo is prompted to assert his love, his honesty, and ultimately his resolve to marry. In the absence of similar reassurances, Fyne's Juliet will enlist the aid of her equally forceful girlfriends to prevent the object of her desire from reverting to the type of the "roaming Romeo."[3]

By the end of the twentieth century, the story of youth culture itself had been thoroughly mediated, with a sharp—if sometimes ahistorical—awareness of precedent and intertext characterizing young people's own postmodern sense(s) of themselves. Just as 1968 seemed the right time for Zeffirelli's generational interpretation of *Romeo and Juliet,* the 1990s offered the opportunity to participate in the marketing of a new version to young audiences and to comment upon the marketing at the same time. The cityscape of Baz Luhrmann's Verona Beach in his 1996 film of *William Shakespeare's "Romeo + Juliet"* is dominated by the competing skyscrapers that house the corporate gangs that the Capulets and Montagues have become (adding parental involvement to the street dynamics of *West Side Story*) but is also filled with scattered snippets and recollections from Shakespeare as appropriated for advertising slogans: Prospero Whiskey, one billboard proclaims, is "Such stuff as dreams are made on." Some of the songs selected—and sometimes commissioned—for the film's soundtrack similarly resonate with bits and pieces of text (One Inch Punch's "A Pretty Piece of Flesh" and Mundy's "To You I Bestow"); others engage with pervasive cultural associations with Shakespeare's lovers. (On the film's borrowings from the conventions of the "teen film"—including *West Side Story* and Zeffirelli's *Romeo and Juliet*—see Loehlin 122.) A vivid illustration of the second approach is Garbage's "#1 Crush" (the soundtrack album's first number one hit on Billboard Magazine's "Modern Rock" chart), which was originally composed and recorded before the band was asked to contribute the song to the film. This might disqualify the song from speaking for Juliet in particular, if Shirley Manson, the band's vocalist, had not rewritten the lyrics for the soundtrack version. In Nellee Hooper's fine remix, Manson changes one of the song's original lines about "drowning in fear":

> I've been dying just to feel you by my side
> To know that you're mine
> I would cry for you, I would cry for you
> I will wash away your pain with all my tears
> And drown your fear.

Accepting the link between the line as first written and the water imagery that abounds in Luhrmann's film, Manson goes a step further and ensures that the strong female voice in the song makes a simultaneously reassuring and unsettling promise to subsume utterly her Romeo's anxieties. The song's implicit Juliet will consciously try—with no guarantee of success—to rewrite the story; Manson herself enacts such revision. On the film's soundtrack, the song parodies, anatomizes, and reinscribes Petrarchan devotion with a distinctive female viewpoint—as, at least arguably, can Shakespeare's playtexts. Over the airwaves or on sound systems, the song's dense mixture of electronically-generated "industrial" sounds suggests aural equivalents to lush Romanticism (as Wagner's *liebestod* theme from *Tristan und Isolde* is heard after the film's depiction of Juliet's death) and possible alternatives to it.

Bob Dylan, once one of youth culture's icons and a profound influence on many of the singer-songwriters discussed here, has recently returned to the figure of Romeo and has engaged with the character of Juliet for the first time. A verse in "Desolation Row," on the 1965 album *Highway 61 Revisited,* imagines what would happen if Romeo stumbled into someone else's story—in this case, that of a modern-day Cinderella. Shakespeare's emblematic lover enters, "moaning 'You belong to me, I believe,'" and somebody already on the scene tells him he's "in the wrong place" and had "better leave." Romeo's response is not described, but merely suggested by its aftermath: "after the ambulances go," Cinderella is left to clean up the mess. Thirty-six years later, on the 2001 album *Love & Theft,* Dylan remains impatient with Romeo. This time, however, he chooses Juliet to voice frustration not only with her partner in tragedy but also with a generation's obsession with being, well, forever young. "Floater (Too Much to Ask)" is melodically related to the Tin Pan Alley compositions that Dylan helped to displace and is lyrically alert to the significances attached to youth. In the song, Romeo criticizes Juliet for her "poor complexion," which fails to give even the "appearance of a youthful touch." Juliet's memorable rejoinder is "'Why don't you just shove off / If it bothers you so much?'" The vehemence of her (and Dylan's) reaction stems from the strength of cultural associations between Shakespeare's characters and notions of adolescent identity.

In the last five decades of pop music, Juliet and her Romeo have emerged as all the more serious and self-aware for their youthfulness. Economic factors provide one sustaining motive for their emergence as such; the marketplace has been recognized as constituting one of the cultural landscapes on which the characters meet, separate, and perhaps conjoin. The characters and their story have not become more definable as a result: they respond to cultural and economic pressures in unpredictable ways, just as Shakespeare playtexts remain multiple and editorially negotiable. Nevertheless, a clearer sense of what is at stake in *Romeo and Juliet* may be most readily available in those songs that play with the words that variably constitute Shakespeare's "play"; in songs that acknowledge and address the cultural factors that affect our coming to terms with his characters; in songs that at least endeavor to improvise ways of letting them speak. Our sense of the characters may most depend on the conditions of performance and our awareness of immediate context, our ability to consider instances of what Lawrence Grossberg terms "context-specific appropriation" (70). It is a function of the singer as well as the song, the actor as well as the role. The characters take on a certain outline when Peggy Lee sings "Fever": the outline changes, subtly or drastically, when Elvis Presley or Madonna gives voice to it and its characters. When the Pointer Sisters sing "Fire," Romeo and Juliet—as individuals and as a phrase—register distinctively; the experience is different when Bruce Springsteen sings (albeit authoritatively) or when Babyface and Des'ree do. Connecting with the now nameless young actor who first performed the role of Juliet and with the nameless young student who plays Juliet in Joe Calarco's recent stage adaptation, *Shakespeare's R & J,* Amy Ray of the Indigo Girls has assumed the role of Mark Knopfler's Romeo on the album *Rites of Passage,* 1992. Her cover of the Dire Straits song offers a lesbian recoding of a central story of romance in Western society (Burt 2000, 157); as such, it can awaken audiences' awareness of the refiguring of gender and genre that Elizabethan theater, an emerging economic enterprise, made possible. Shakespeare's play takes advantage of that refiguring in order to invite challenges and reconsiderations of ideas of propriety. Pop music lyrics, both in the early days of youth culture marketing and in its aftermaths, have regularly accepted the playtexts' unsettling invitation. Characters, sources, and reworkings alike gain vitality—are, in effect, revived—in such acceptance, howsoever it is packaged. In addition, many of these versions have enjoyed surprising longevity. As the above list indicates, songs about Juliet and her Romeo continue to be re-recorded and re-envisioned; they complicate and compromise, at least for now, the defining evanescence that seems to be captured in the very word *pop.*

Notes

1. All citations from Shakespeare's plays are taken from *The Riverside Shakespeare,* second edition.
2. Reconsiderations of the varying texts' value are offered by Halio and Urkowitz.
3. I am grateful to Douglas Lanier, who is working on Shakespearean appropriations in rap and hip-hop music, for his advice on this example in particular and on my essay generally.

Works Cited

Andreas, James. 1992. "The Neutering of *Romeo and Juliet.*" In *Ideological Approaches to Shakespeare: The Practice of Theory.* Robert P. Merrix and Nicholas Ranson, eds. Lewiston, NY: Edwin Mellen Press.

Bennett, Tony. 1998. *Culture: A Reformer's Science.* London: Sage Publications.

Burt, Richard. 2000. "No Holes Bard: Homonormativity and the Gay and Lesbian Romance with *Romeo and Juliet.*" In *Shakespeare Without Class: Misappropriations of Cultural Capital.* Don Hedrick and Bryan Reynolds, eds. New York: St. Martin's Press.

Calarco, Joe. 1998. *Shakespeare's R & J.* New York: Dramatists Play Service.

Evans, Bertrand. 1996. *Teaching Shakespeare in the High School.* New York: Macmillan.

Frank, Thomas. 1997. *The Conquest of Cool: Business Culture, Counter Culture, and the Rise of Hip Consumerism.* Chicago: Univ. of Chicago Press.

Griffin, Alice. 1976. *Rebels and Lovers: Shakespeare's Young Heroes and Heroines.* New York: New York Univ. Press.

Grossberg, Lawrence. 1997. *Dancing in Spite of Myself: Essays on Popular Culture.* Durham, NC: Duke Univ. Press.

Halio, Jay. 1995. "Handy-Dandy: Q1/Q2 *Romeo and Juliet.*" In *Shakespeare's "Romeo and Juliet": Texts, Contexts, and Interpretation.* Jay Halio, ed. Newark: Univ. of Delaware Press.

Hebdige, Dick. 1979. *Subculture: The Meaning of Style.* London: Methuen.

Levenson, Jill L. 1987. *Romeo and Juliet.* Shakespeare in Performance series. Manchester: Manchester Univ. Press.

Loehlin, James N. 2000. "'These Violent Delights Have Violent Ends': Baz Luhrmann's Millenial Shakespeare." In *Shakespeare, Film, Fin de Siècle.* Mark Thornton Burnett and Ramona Wray, eds. London: Macmillan.

Palladino, Grace. 1996. *Teenagers: An American History.* New York: Basic Books.

Pipher, Mary. 1994. *Reviving Ophelia.* New York: Ballantine Books.

Romeo and Juliet: A Motion Picture Edition. 1936. [Including MGM production screenplay.] New York: Random House.

Rothwell, Kenneth. 1999. *A History of Shakespeare on Screen.* Cambridge: Cambridge Univ. Press.

Shakespeare, William. 1997. *The Riverside Shakespeare.* Second edition. G. Blakemore Evans, ed. Boston: Houghton Mifflin.

Urkowitz, Steven. 1996. "Two Versions of *Romeo and Juliet* 2.6 and *Merry Wives of Windsor* 5.5.215–45: An Invitation to the Pleasures of Textual/Sexual Di[Per]versity." In *Elizabethan Theater: Essays in Honor of S. Schoenbaum.* Ed. by R. B. Parker and S. P. Zitner. Newark: Univ. of Delaware Press.

Williams, Deborah A. 1974. "Shakespeare in the High School Classroom." *Shakespeare Quarterly* 25: 262–64.

CHAPTER II

THE MAKING OF AUTHORSHIPS

Transversal Navigation in the Wake of *Hamlet,*
Robert Wilson, Wolfgang Wiens, and Shakespace

D. J. HOPKINS
AND BRYAN REYNOLDS

Whence We Depart

Manhattan, July 7, 1995: On this hot, muggy evening, an audience rapidly
filled Lincoln Center's air-conditioned Alice Tully Hall. Whereas the majority probably hailed from New York City and its nearby environs, one member of the audience had driven down from Cambridge and another had
flown in from San Diego just to see this particular performance of William
Shakespeare's *Hamlet.* At the time, these two, the authors of this paper, did
not know each other.

The Cambridgian (Reynolds) and his date were taking their seats somewhere in the back of the auditorium (they were tardy), and the San Diegan
(Hopkins) was sitting comfortably, engrossed in his press pack, when a cig-
arette-roughened voice politely interjected: "Excuse me." Hopkins moved
his legs to allow the fashionably late audience member and his companion
to slide past to their seats beside him. Looking up as they passed, Hopkins
recognized that the man, wearing a purple crushed-velvet jacket, was rock
star Lou Reed, and that the woman with him, sporting her signature dan-
delion-gone-to-seed hairdo, was performance artist Laurie Anderson. They
too came to see this production of *Hamlet,* presumably for the same reasons
as Hopkins and Reynolds: not out of sheer devotion to Shakespeare or *Hamlet,* but because of the individual to whom ownership of this particular production was assigned—a "star," not unlike Reed and Anderson themselves.[1]

With a horizon of expectations informed by, among other related forces, our preconceptions about the theatrical magic of Robert Wilson, all of us had willfully sought an experience in what Donald Hedrick and Bryan Reynolds call "Shakespace."[2]

Shakespeare has inspired and inhabited innumerable commercial, political, social, and cultural spaces, both ideational and physical, like academic discourse and Lincoln Center's Alice Tully Hall, respectively. These Shakespearean or Shakespeare-affected spaces, however conventional, radical, or something in between, Hedrick and Reynolds refer to as Shakespace, a term that accounts for these specific spaces and the time-speed, the "pace," at which they pass from generation to generation and from era to era. Shakespace is a socially and historically determined playground on which cultural and class differences sometimes slip "transversally" into an equivocal space that allows for and in fact fosters alternative opportunities for thought, emotion, expression, and development.

The mode of Shakespearean production we discuss here offers just such a space of alternative opportunities, but unlike the majority of the material discussed in this collection, we're discussing a medium with which Shakespeare himself was engaged: theater. Although we are living in a culture that exists *after* mass media, our culture has not (necessarily) done away with those modes of production that existed *before* mass media. In other words, people still produce Shakespeare's plays on the stage. What we will be discussing here is the nature of the stage and theatrical modes of production after mass media. Though the mode of production we consider is not itself a mass medium, theater corresponds to Richard Burt's understanding of the other chapters in this collection in one particular way: it is surprisingly marginal. While Lincoln Center may seem like a privileged site of production, particularly within New York City, its cultural importance and influence pale in comparison to the relative importance and influence of other modes of production in our mass media age. The film, television, and publishing industries dwarf theater production in terms of financial clout and cultural saturation; tellingly, one cannot speak of a "theater industry."

Increasingly marginalized in academic contexts, as well, theater has evolved to meet many of the criteria Burt offers for his definition of "schlock." Theater is often regarded as an obsolete mode of production that lies, as Burt puts it, "beyond the usual academic purview," perhaps specifically because it is not one of the reproducible mass media. But theater is not schlock *per se,* nor can we see the abstract and obstruse theater works of Robert Wilson as adhering to Burt's other descriptions of schlock as popular and trivial. For better or worse, the subject matter under consideration here—theater, Wilson, *Hamlet*—is anchored in "high culture," elevated (or relegated) to the realm of the official canon.

According to Reynolds's "transversal theory,"[3] which accounts for the critical approach of the present analysis, Shakespace often manifests as "official territory," and has therefore promoted various organizational social and political structures that are discriminatory, hierarchical, and repressive. Yet it has most powerfully manifested as "transversal territory."

Transversal and official territories function in relation to what Reynolds terms "subjective territory." As Reynolds describes elsewhere,[4] subjective territory is the range of the conceptual and emotional experience of those subjectified by the "state machinery," which includes all indoctrinating mechanisms of a society's "official territory," such as the educational, juridical, religious, and familial structures that support the ideology of the dominant classes and the government. In agreement with its investment in cultural, social, political, and economic fluctuations and aspirations, the organizing state machinery operates over time and space, sometimes consciously and sometimes unintentionally, to consolidate social and state powers in order to construct a society of subjects and thus "the state": the totalized state machinery. Subjective territory is therefore delineated by the conceptual and emotional boundaries that are defined by the prevailing science, morality, and ideology of official territory. These boundaries create common ground for an aggregate of individuals, and work to maintain the coexistence of the social body that this aggregate becomes. "In short," as Reynolds writes, "subjective territory is the existential and experiential realm in and from which a given subject of a given hierarchical society perceives and relates to the universe and her or his place in it."[5]

Whereas the infinite possibilities of conceptual and emotional experience are powerfully constrained by the state machinery's subjectification of the individual, transversal theory insists that subjective territory is not capable of fully containing the subject. Beyond the limits of subjective territory, exist nonsubjectified regions of one's conceptual and emotional range, the open space of transversal territory. This uncertain, unpredictable space houses and is the gateway to all of the possibilities that official territory wants to preclude and exclude. Transversal territory can be reached by transgressing the boundaries that the state machinery enforces. This transgression of subjective territory's boundaries is made possible by "transversal power" and through "transversal movements." Transversal power, which can be found in anything from criminal acts to natural catastrophes to the daily practice of walking in a city, is a dynamic of change.[6] It is what spurs people to move transversally, consciously or not, out of their subjective territory, into transversal territory, and possibly into the subjective territory of others. When people expose themselves to alternative ideas, emotions, and experiences, such as in the theater or classroom, and engage with those alternative energies, such as through empathy or trauma, they move transversally, thereby altering and expanding their own subjective territory. Their subjective territory becomes existentially and experientially bigger and different, incorporating new associations, sensibilities, and perspectives. In this article, we move transversally, navigating in the wake of Wilson's *Hamlet: A Monologue*. In doing so, we engage with several important implications to the transversality we encountered in the remarkable Shakespace that encompasses both Wilson's production and this article.

Our aim here is to analyze the Shakespace in which *Hamlet: A Monologue* operates and to analyze, from within this Shakespace, the discourse on authorship, media, and performance that this Shakespace is so importantly informed by and informs. In the context of this discourse, it may be that this production becomes a kind of "antischlock," troubling the relationship between elitist and popular culture from the top down. As we will demonstrate, *Hamlet: A Monologue* relies in no small measure on the popular knowledge of the play *Hamlet*. Wilson's transversal performance works to exploit the audience's familiarity with this Shakespearean source text to create a theater product that cannot be reduced to a popular (schlocky) commodity.

Our transversal method of analysis—that we hope to promote with this application—is what Bryan Reynolds and James Intriligator call the "investigative-expansive mode," as opposed to what they call "the dissective-cohesive mode" that characterizes most research.[7] Like the dissective-cohesive mode, the investigative-expansive mode requires that the subject matter of interest be divided up and partitioned into variables in accordance with the selected parameters of the investigation. But unlike the dissective-cohesive mode, whose goal is ultimately to reconstruct the variables as a coherent whole, the investigative-expansive mode examines both the internal connectedness of the variables (among themselves) and the external connectedness of the variables (to other forces) in coordination with an ongoing readiness to reparameterizing as the analysis progresses. The investigative-expansive mode welcomes the emergence of unanticipated problems, information, and ideas. Thus, the purpose is not to assemble a fully accounted for totality, but to better our comprehension of the subject matter's changing relationships to its own parts as well as to the environments of which it is a part. The subject matters of the present analysis are *Hamlet: A Monologue* and its critical relationship to issues of authorship, media, and performance. The chosen variables include Wilson's and his dramaturg Wolfgang Wiens's respective contributions to the performance of *Hamlet: A Monologue*, the current "conceptual crisis in drama studies" (as W. B. Worthen describes it), the textual history of Shakespeare's *Hamlet*, and competing theories of authorship. And the particular greater environments of concern are both the Shakespace and the hermeneutic space in and through which *Hamlet: A Monologue* and the related discourses on authorship, media, and performance will continue to journey.

A Matter of Presence

The set for the July 7, 1995 performance of *Hamlet: A Monologue* consisted of a bare stage, except for the bold presence of a tiered stack of dark-gray rock slabs, a sort of stylized "sterile promontory," a lit backscreen that changed colors (from blue to yellow to many others), and a single actor, who was usually clad in black. The play began with a single prone actor, Robert Wilson, lying on top of the rock stack, where he then struck a hieratic pose and spoke:

—Had I but time . . .
—O, I could tell you—but let it be.
—Wretched queen, adieu!
—I follow thee . . .
—Follow my mother! Drink of this potion!
—Venom, to thy work!
—I can no more—the king, the king's to blame.
—Lo, here I lie, never to rise again.
—O villainy! ho! let the door be locked—
—The drink, the drink!
—No, no, the drink, the drink—
—How does the queen?
—Look to the queen there, ho!
—Nay, come again.
—Come on.
—Come for the third, Laertes.
—I dare not drink yet, madam—by and by.
—Good madam!
—A touch, a touch!
—Another hit!
—Give him the cup.
—A hit, a very palpable hit.
—No!
—One!
—Come, my lord.
—Come on, sir.
—Come, begin! (Wilson/Wiens 1995, 1)

This is the beginning of *Hamlet: A Monologue*, the first speech of scene one, of a total of fifteen scenes. The lone actor came to his feet, and punctuated his fragmentary, backwards-tending narrative by executing a series of complex gestures calculated to express abstractly death throes, collapse, pain, combat, and similar correlatives to the spoken text. The words quoted above, though recognizable as lines attributed to various characters in the last scene of Shakespeare's play, are all spoken by this actor playing the character of Hamlet. Indeed, all of the words in the performance are attributed to that character: Hamlet himself is the only character we see, though he in turn performed the personae of the Ghost, Claudius, Gertrude, Ophelia, and Polonius, as necessary. All of the "unnatural acts, accidental judgments, casual slaughters" that constitute the action of a conventional staging of *Hamlet* were here distilled and funneled into a solo performance, *Hamlet: A Monologue*. In addition to being the only actor, Robert Wilson was also the director, scenographer, and coadaptor responsible for this marathon condensation of Shakespeare's text.

Our introduction to this essay, with an emphasis on personal experience and a tourist's eye for rock stars and artists, is not an indulgent and anecdotal foray into pop culture. We introduce the individual personalities of Reed, Anderson, Wilson, and ourselves to stress that at a theatrical performance, as at a rock concert, *presence* is essential to the event. We want to show that this particular production responded to and exemplified a culturally activated shift in the textual authority of Shakespeare's plays. Under the present-tense conditions that governed what we experienced as a "transversal theater performance," *Hamlet: A Monologue* demonstrated a textual authority over the written text that would seem to be its requisite, citational predecessor: the written text of Shakespeare's *Hamlet*.

Wilson's performance of *Hamlet* is predicated on a single premise: that the recent events of Hamlet's life "flash before his eyes" at the moment of his death. *Hamlet: A Monologue* begins at this moment of death and moves backwards through the events that would have occurred already in a conventional, "textually obedient" version of *Hamlet*. Although this *precis* of *Hamlet: A Monologue* is factually true, its usefulness as a summation of the impact of the performance text is challenged on two points. First, it runs the risk of giving the impression that the performance was reductive and superficial, which it most definitely was not. The script of *Hamlet: A Monologue*, conceived and adapted by dramaturg Wolfgang Wiens, recreates Hamlet's world as though Denmark were indeed bound within the subjective territory of the Prince. As the synthetic fragments quoted above show, this adaptation is not simply the scenes in reverse order and characters walking backwards. Every character who had heretofore inhabited Elsinore and all the events that had transpired there, in Shakespeare's *Hamlet*, are portrayed in Wiens's written text and Wilson's performance text through the expressive medium of one character: the idiosyncratic half-mad, half-dead Hamlet. The second, more significant reason that our "reverse order" description of *Hamlet: A Monologue* is ultimately invalid, despite its relative validity for literary criticism, is that it gives the false impression that the "events" of Hamlet's "story," as told in Wilson's "play," are of principal importance to the performance text of *Hamlet: A Monologue*. They are not.

His Own Public Elsinore

In performing the role of Hamlet, Wilson became multiple, plural; he became a *many,* yet so did his Hamlet. Wilson's Hamlet defined both what we call a "subjective territory" and a "transversal territory." His Hamlet moved transversally through the subjective territories of the other characters depicted in Shakespeare's play, synthesizing their conceptional and emotional experiences, and reflecting them in his own burgeoning subjective territory. Hamlet's subjective territory became the transversal territory from which multiple characters emerged and across which they traveled throughout the course of the performance. In other words, Hamlet articulated the dynamic, permeable subjective territory that delineated the other characters that appeared in this version of Shakespeare's play. From within this multivalent, subjective territory the other characters moved transversally and reparameterized their own conditions of existence despite the seemingly univocal and singularly present character/medium who/which made their own identities possible. In effect, Wilson transformed himself into the media for the transversal movements of a field of characters. He functioned as the medium for the character Hamlet and, as Hamlet, as the medium for the others. As a complex signifier for multiple referents, including the actor Wilson himself, Wilson's performance asserted fantastic presence. The history of Shakespeare's *Hamlet*—its multifarious presence in Shakespace (its entrails, tentacles, and gases)—was transposed and disseminated by *Hamlet: A Monologue*.

To recapitulate, with an added philosophical rendering: in the move from a five act, multicharacter play to a fifteen-scene monologue, Wilson created the terms for a subjective territory: a subset of all conceptual and emotional space in which individual subjects are constructed and constrained by the shared paradigms of a community, be those paradigms social structures, government regulations, or, as in the case of Wilson's Prince of Denmark, the *(dramatis) personae* of a play, all of whom are assembled within a single character's shattered sense of self. Shakespeare's *Hamlet* becomes Wilson's *Hamlet: A Monologue* in the subjective territory of a Hamlet dancing transversally at his mortality's vanishing point. In this theatrical Shakespace where Hamlet's life flashed before his eyes, Wilson and Wiens evolved a philosophical discourse on death. The life that flashed before Hamlet's eyes in the moment of his death was a life that included simultaneously presences and traces of the subjective territories of other characters that influenced his life. Death, then, requires either the hallucinated or real participation of others; life's departure is fueled finally by a fracturing, transversal self (or selves) or a culminating, communal expression. Wilson's character Hamlet was in and of itself a transversal theory of subjectivity that begins with the miracle of death. Hamlet's death moment was infused with the consciousness of Shakespeare's other characters, of Wilson, of Wiens, of Shakespeare. From our own experience and from our conversations with other audience members, we discovered that this infusion inspired the audience either to relate to multiple characters and thus multiple perspectives or to become alienated from Hamlet, making identification impossible. Or, it inspired both. Insofar as we anticipate identification with Hamlet, inasmuch as we have been taught that we should identify with Shakespeare's Hamlet (because such famous critics as Coleridge, Lamb, and Hazlitt have), Wilson's Hamlet's identification or alienation effects stimulated transversal movements: the performance was an irresistible invocation. Recall that at a séance, the "medium" is the controlling, conjuring figure through whom others—no longer living—enter to be among those still alive and in attendance. In the Wilson/Wiens's discourse on death, Wilson performed the medium Hamlet; but it was not the dead who passed through the living. In *Hamlet: A Monologue,* the character on death's threshold became the transversal medium for those who are still alive.

Becoming Investigative-Expansive

At this point, we want to shift directions to a subject that our analysis points toward but has yet to address: *Hamlet: A Monologue* is a theater text with particular relevance to the current "conceptual crisis in drama studies" notably articulated by Shakespeare scholar W. B. Worthen (1998, 1093). In a tremendous study of the factional disputes among different academic disciplines, Worthen meticulously outlines the means by which "performance came to be defined in opposition to theater structures and conventions," and as well the means by which, in an academic context, the "different disciplinary investments of performance studies and literary studies" often bring those fields into conflict with the disciplinary investments of theater studies (1998, 1093). Worthen casts doubt on those who would claim a 'ministerial' or 'derivative' relation to the dramatic text," arguing that "although the sense of dramatic performance as a performance *of* a play is widespread, as John Rouse remarks, just 'what the word *of* means' in this context is 'far from clear'" (1998, 1094–95).

In the essay to which Worthen refers, Rouse explores the issues of "Textuality and Authority in Theater and Drama" using as his chief example a very different *Hamlet* adaptation: Heiner Müller's *Hamletmachine,* in a 1986 production at the Thalia Theater in Hamburg, also directed by Wilson.

It isn't hard to understand why audiences took nearly a decade to learn to "make sense" out of Wilson's performance texts. In the first place, he doesn't subordinate the visual score to the acoustic; all of his productions subvert narrative organization, even when they make use of traditional dramatic texts. Wilson also subverts normal rules for the internal structuring of each of his scores. He came to theater from art and architecture and tends to privilege codes from these disciplines when combining the signs of his visual scores. (Rouse 1992, 152)

Here, Rouse describes Wilson's production method as one that works in opposition to a conventional, illustrative mode of theater. Rather, within the defined performance space, "the production ostends two texts and gives the spectator control over writing the intertext" (Rouse 1992, 154). Wilson himself seconds this description of his theater: "We make theater so that the spectator can put it together in [her or] his own head" (quoted in Rouse 1992, 154).

Worthen stops short of prescribing the redefinition of "drama studies" which might be necessary for the solution of this contentious issue, perhaps even for the preservation of the field itself. The problem of definition may begin with the conventional nomenclature that Worthen has inherited: Worthen begins his essay by referring to the field in dispute as "drama studies" (1998, 1093). The persistent use of the word "drama" to describe an academic discipline vexed by issues of "citationality" is more than merely ironic; it is the very site of the interdisciplinary impasse that Worthen seeks to negotiate. If the text is, as Worthen rightly suggests, merely "material for labor, for the work of [theatrical] production," then the retention of the word "drama" in the name of this field is a counterproductive vestige of theater's fealty to a preexisting literary work (1998, 1098). To extend Worthen's argument, any performance that calls itself "dramatic" is by definition "a hollow, even etiolated, species of the literary" (1998, 1098). As a result of this conditioning of the word "dramatic," when Worthen argues that "one of the ways both literary studies and performance studies have misconceived *dramatic* performance is by taking it merely as a reiteration of texts, a citation that imports literary or textual authority into performance" (1998, 1098), he is harboring nomenclature within his own rebuttal that preserves the key concept of the opposition's position: the literary citationality of "drama." Perhaps by way of a corrective, one might take a cue from Terry Eagleton, who concludes his book-length survey *Literary Theory* by rejecting altogether his title phrase and the limited concept it embodies:

My own view is that it is most useful to see "literature" as a name which people give from time to time for different reasons to certain kinds of "discursive practices," and that if anything is to be an object of study it is this whole field of practices rather than just those sometimes rather obscurely labeled "litera-ture." I am countering the theories set out in this book not with a *literary* the-ory, but with a different kind of discourse—whether one calls it of "culture," "signifying practices," or whatever is not of first importance—which would include the objects ("literature") with which these other theories deal, but which would transform them by setting them in a wider context. (1983, 205)

Eagleton prohibits the word "literature" from its associations with "theory" in order to broaden the possibilities open to theoretical discourse. A similar pro-hibition in nomenclature might lead to a resolution to the "crisis in drama studies," a shift in language that would bring about a corresponding concep-tual shift in the definition of the field of study. Academic disciplines that focus on a study of "drama," whether that drama be read or performed, are rightly the province of literature studies. It is not useful to challenge claims of literary citationality by calling live theater "drama" or the study of live theater "drama studies." The study of theater is "theater studies," not "drama stud-ies." A live theater performance is "theater" not "drama." Many theater stud-ies programs emphasize the dramatic component of their study, and many works of theater art emphasize a dramatic component in performance. But not all do this.[8] And as Wilson's appropriation of Shakespeare's *Hamlet* demonstrates, one can even imagine a performance of a canonical work of dramatic literature that, in performance, does not emphasize a dramatic com-ponent. Though taking as its point of departure no less grand a literary mas-terpiece than *Hamlet, Hamlet: A Monologue* demonstrates the possibilities for theatrical texts to defy a ministerial relationship to a written text. Wilson's theater text works against premises of literary citationality, not by doing vio-lence to the written text of *Hamlet,* but by acknowledging that the conven-tionally "read" text of *Hamlet* is only one unstable part of the theater text.

We have been referring to the "written text" and the "theater text," re-spectively "Shakespeare's text" and "Wilson's theatrical text." These appella-tions are not arbitrary, but rather incited by the complex signifying conditions that surround *Hamlet: A Monologue.* These elements must be dis-tinguished from each other in order to pursue effectively questions concern-ing citationality, authority, and the nature of Rouse's performative "of." Equally important is the recognition that the history of "textual" issues is closely linked to issues of textuality.

The Eternal "Retext"

The "text" of *Hamlet* has been central to controversy over textual authority for hundreds of years. Moreover, the word "text" has evolved and now has two very different meanings of importance here, both meanings very much applicable to a consideration of *Hamlet*. Many of Shakespeare's plays, as is well known, exist in multiple forms. The traditional definition of "text" is used in Shakespeare studies to refer to specific different versions of Shakespeare's plays, the contents of which may differ from one degree to another although the different versions of the play may have the same or roughly the same title. "Textual scholarship" is the field of study that considers the history of these different versions: how different versions may have come into being, how editors over the years have responded to the versions and their differences, and even added to those differences. Yet the vast majority of Shakespeare scholars focus their attention on a different Shakespearean "text" altogether. Studies of the "textuality" of Shakespeare's works consider the relationships between the plays and the complex network of social, cultural, and political forces in which those plays were originally situated as well as the impact of those same forces over the hundreds of years since.

This latter meaning of "text" has evolved more recently and is defined by Roland Barthes as "a methodological field" (1977, 157). But Barthes's understated *precis* of "text" fails to capture the sense of far-reaching interconnectedness and conceptual referentiality that has come to be associated with his use of the word. The earlier use of the word text is closer in meaning to Barthes's term "work," which he uses to refer to the "concrete" item or object that might be found "occupying a portion of book-space (in a library, for example)" (1977, 157–58). The object of textual scholarship is those items, which occupy a portion of book-space, which could be called in Barthesian terms, Shakespeare's "works." To make matters more complicated, these works have had value judgments applied to them over the years: some are "good" and some "bad."

The popularly accepted distinction between "good" and "bad" Quarto versions of Shakespeare's plays was initiated by A. W. Pollard, writing at the beginning of this century (1909). Pollard identified initially five texts that seemed particularly deficient in their first Quarto (Q1) version and particularly at variance from their Folio versions: *Romeo and Juliet, Henry V, Merry Wives of Windsor, Hamlet,* and *Pericles*.

Pollard sought to justify his identification of these plays as "bad" by referring to the introduction to the first Folio, written by the Folio publishers Heminge & Condell, in which they denounce "frauds and stealths of injurious impostors" who had printed and sold "stolen and surreptitious copies" of Shakespeare's plays. Pollard concluded that this accusation was leveled at these Q1 versions. To this list of five were subsequently added *The Taming of a Shrew, Contention,* and *Richard Duke of York*. (These three "bad" quartos are better known by their folio titles, which are, respectively: *The Taming of The Shrew* and *Henry VI, Parts Two* and *Three*.) The list was brought to ten with Q1 *Richard II* and Q1 *King Lear*.

In 1910, W. W. Greg performed a close analysis of the "bad" quarto version of *The Merry Wives of Windsor.* He concluded that the lapses and deficiencies in that text could be explained if one were to presume that the actor playing the role of "Mine Host" had written down the text from memory. This theory inaugurated the "memorial reconstruction" hypothesis, which accounts for the origin of the "bad" quartos by hypothesizing an actor or shorthand thief in the audience who had written out (from memory or by shorthand) a version of the script and would subsequently sell the script to a printer. Based on Greg's tentative hypothesis, "memorial reconstruction was adopted as blanket classification for these ten Shakespearean texts, ossifying Greg's original tentative suggestion into textual orthodoxy" (Maguire 1996, 5).

The late 1970s and '80s brought a sustained challenge to the memorial reconstruction hypothesis, introducing the question of revision. Michael Warren argued in 1976 that both versions of *King Lear* are "good," the later version of the Folio being Shakespeare's own revision of that text. This approach to *Lear* resulted in a collection of essays edited by Warren and Gary Taylor, *The Division of the Kingdoms: Shakespeare's Two Versions of King Lear,* as well as prompting Taylor and Stanley Wells to include both versions of *King Lear* in the *Oxford Complete Shakespeare.* Yet the textual complexity of *Lear* is slight when compared to the situation surrounding the texts of *Hamlet.*

The text of *Hamlet* exists for us in three versions: Q1 of 1603, Q2 of 1604/5 and the First Folio of 1623. After the discovery of Q1 in 1823, most scholars regarded it as a rough draft which was subsequently revised in Q2. Early in the twentieth century, the memorial reconstruction hypothesis took hold and became the norm of opinion whereby the existence of Q1 was explained. Since the First Quarto version has been perennially relegated to second-class status, Q2 has most often served as the basis for contemporary printed editions. However, Wells and Taylor have adopted the Folio as the principal text for their Oxford editions on the grounds that the Folio version is Shakespeare's own revision.

In her assessment of the status of Q1, Leah Marcus makes the observation that Q1—however understood as revised, memorized, or otherwise—is "bad" by definition, "and will continue to be bad so long as we rank the early texts of the play on the basis of their adherence to culturally predetermined standards of literary excellence" (Marcus 1996, 135). Marcus argues that advocates of memorial reconstruction find memory (and the oral tradition implied by the use of memory in theater) to be inherently untrustworthy. She concludes:

> Over and over again in Shakespeare's plays, but particularly in *Hamlet,* bad taste is associated with an outmoded oral theatrical culture. Similarly for twentieth century adherents of the theory of memorial reconstruction, "bad" Shake-

speare is the product of defective memory and insufficient literacy. . . . [G]ood taste is associated with writing as opposed to orality; and "good" Shakespeare with the creation of a theater that is specifically literary. (1996, 137)

In her chapter, "Bad Taste and Bad Hamlet," Marcus presents a theatrical situation that illustrates the cultural conflict between "good" and "bad": "In a small theater, Hamlet nears his most famous soliloquy" (1996, 132). Marcus sets the stage for the audience's much anticipated reception of this famous character's most famous set of words. The physical tension is heightened, theatrical elements focused, the history of acting invoked, and then: "something goes radically *wrong*" (1996, 132). Instead of the words that the audience knows and are culturally conditioned to expect, they hear a very different Hamlet:

> To be or not to be; aye, there's the point.
> To die, to sleep; is that all? Aye, all.
> No; to sleep, to dream; aye, marry, there it goes. (1603, 58)

The sense of dissonance here lies in the antipathy for the mode of oral performance and the trend toward a literary measure of a theatrical "good." The blunt staccato language of Q1, quoted above, seems far removed from the blank verse and carefully articulated philosophical probing of Q2.

> To be, or not to be, that is the question,
> Whether tis nobler in the minde to suffer
> The slings and arrowes of outragious fortune,
> And by opposing, end them, to die to sleepe
> No more, and by a sleepe, to say we end
> The hart-ake, and the thousand naturall shocks
> That flesh is heire to; tis a consumation
> Devoutly to be wisht to die to sleepe,
> To sleepe, perchance to dreame, I there's the rub. (1604–5, G2)

By comparison to Q2, the Q1 version sounds like an actor struggling to remember a complicated and incompletely memorized part. Or, to give some measure of credit to the text of *Hamlet* most often dismissed, the Q1 passage can be read as a character struggling to comprehend a complicated set of issues and exploring these ideas out loud in what appears as an (intentionally) inarticulate oral expression of his inner turmoil. This is the question of Q1: intentional or unintentional? Author or pirate? The answer to these questions—however fascinating and cleverly formulated, as is Marcus's "hypothetical reconstruction"—is irrelevant (Marcus 1996, 133). The sole verifiable conclusion that we can make relates more to our contemporary assessment of these texts than it does to the texts themselves. Q1 represents a threat to the purity of Shakespeare's *literary* legacy. Simultaneously, however, it represents one of the clearest links to Shakespeare's legacy as a practitioner of live theater, to a performance tradition widely regarded as "more honourd in the breach, then the observance," but a tradition that nevertheless extends continuously from Shakespeare's time to ours (1604–5, D). Consider our own description of the opening of *Hamlet: A Monologue.* A Lincoln Center patron expecting Shakespeare but getting Wilson would feel much the same "culture shock" as that which Marcus suggests a playgoer would feel if, when culturally conditioned to expect Q2, the playgoer got Q1.

This brief review of the history of the different versions of Shakespeare's scripts is intended to provide a glimpse of the suspicion for any suggestion that a theatrical or oral medium might be given a privileged position over a literary one. With this sense of the "badness" attached to performance media, we would like to return to a consideration of Wilson's version(s) of *Hamlet.*

A New Medium for the Text of *Hamlet*

Wilson says of the monologue, "It's all in a sense in his mind," Hamlet's own "autobiographical" recounting of events (Kessel 1995, 1:28). But as we suggested earlier, the visual and theatrical means by which Wilson and his collaborators (re)present the events of the play on stage receives the focus of Wilson's efforts, not the events themselves. And these means correspondingly became the focus of audience's attention.

Earlier we provided a quote from the opening of *Hamlet: A Monologue.* Now we need to qualify that quotation by saying that it is a quote from the *written* text of the adaptation. Wilson's name appears on the title page of the unpublished "text" where Wilson even gets billing ahead of Wiens in the by-line.[9] But it is possible to identify the script principally with the work of the dramaturg, Wolfgang Wiens, and not with Wilson—largely because all the other artists on the project do. In an interview about the origins of the project, the German assistant director, Ann-Christin Rommen (an unusually active contributor, given the conventional limitations of the position of AD), had this to say: "We come together—Wolfgang Wiens, who wrote this adaptation, and Bob and I—and we were reading the text, and Wolfgang had made the decision already that it would be fifteen scenes" (Kessel 1995, 12:04). Here, it is clear from Rommen's unguarded statement that Wiens is regarded as the individual behind the script, responsible for both its structure and its content. However, while clarification of Wiens's significant role in this project may be interesting to dramaturgs and other theater professionals, it would be inappropriate to assign to Wiens definitive authorship of *Hamlet: A Monologue*. Wiens's written text, citational in its relationship to Shakespeare's written text(s), was ultimately only a navigational aid for Wilson's final project, a compass that assisted the progress toward the performance text but did not determine that text.

What happened on stage in *Hamlet: A Monologue* happened there alone, though the theatrical performance was supported by several (physical) texts. The second text, an unusual medium for a "dramatic text," is equally applicable to *Hamlet: A Monologue,* and is in fact more readily identifiable with Wilson and his body of work. The following pictorial quote from this script corresponds to the portion of the written adaptation that we quoted above:

Figure 11.1 The sleep of death

This, too, is scene one of *Hamlet: A Monologue*. A "script" of sorts, which is separate from the written adaptation that bears the same title, this visual text version of the fifteen-scene monologue is composed of seventeen charcoal sketches drawn by Wilson (two of the scenes are rendered in two panels).[10] In a production by another director, a series of sketches would not constitute a second script, certainly not one with an impact on the performance equal to that of the lengthy and complex English-language script composed by one of Germany's foremost dramaturgs. And for what production of *Hamlet* could a series of sketches—or a work in any media—be said to supercede Shakespeare's masterpiece as a guiding principle of the production?

The storyboard sketches are a kind of Quarto version, if you will, of the Wilson production. He conceived a visual script for the performance that privileges only visual elements and spatial volumes: "What the stage looks like . . . how dense it is or how dark it is or how light" (Kessel 1995, 8:36). Can a series of storyboard drawings graphically representing fifteen scenes be considered in a "version" of Shakespeare's *Hamlet?* The answer is: Yes, but only a "bad" version. Marcus cuts the Gordian knot that ties critical discussion of Shakespeare's texts to the distinctions "good" and "bad," and her conclusions are equally applicable in a critical discussion of Wilson's texts. The only "good" version of the "To be or not to be" soliloquy is the version in which that line ends with "that is the question." In fact, one might go so far as to say that the only "good" version of *Hamlet* is a literary one that exists only on a page: any deviation from the reading experience of the play inherently constitutes one degree or another of "badness." But given that Q1 *Hamlet* is dismissed as "bad" because of its associations with an "outmoded oral theatrical culture," it is possible to accept other text versions as equally *Hamlet,* though equally "bad" because of their shared relationship with a performative medium rather than a literary one (Marcus 1996, 137). By embracing "badness" as the site of orality and theatricality, it is in fact possible to admit Wilson's series of charcoal renderings as a postmodern "Qw" of *Hamlet.*

murder most foul   mad i call it   get thee to a nunnery

Figure 11.2 (Boyd 1995, 15–16)

Transversal Authorship

A series of questions surround any radical appropriation of a classic text. The main question here is: Who is the author of *Hamlet: A Monologue?* Is it Wolfgang Wiens, the dramaturg who conceived this adaptation of Shakespeare's *Hamlet,* divided it into fifteen scenes, and composed the script? Is it the distant figure of Shakespeare, more cultural construct than verifiable human? Or is it Wilson? Wilson is the clear nominee for what might be called the "auteur" of this production: director, scenographer, coadaptor, and solo performer, not to mention his status as the only living "famous" person whose name is listed in the program. Wilson himself is the medium for this theater event, but given the nature of his work and the number of different contributions he makes to the final product, might he be the *media* of the event? Is it because of Wilson's "star" status that his "authorship" is so easily accepted? This train of thought ends with another question: "Who is the author of *Hamlet* itself?"

In his essay "What Is an Author?" Michel Foucault writes,

In a civilization like our own there are a certain number of discourses that are endowed with the "author-function," while others are deprived of it. . . . The author-function is therefore characteristic of the mode of existence, circulation, and functioning of certain discourses within a society. (1979, 148)

Foucault offers Freud and Marx as two exemplars of the group "founders of discursivity." These are the authors who have "produced . . . the possibilities and the rules for the formation of other texts" (1979, 154). Foucault posits that those who engage the rules established by the author-function are themselves authors, engaged in a valid form of discourse, one that extends and mediates the discourse introduced by one of a select few founding authors. Albeit dependent upon preexisting writing, Foucault considers this engaging mode of discourse neither "ministerial" nor "citational" in nature, and he does not condemn it as "a hollow even etiolated species of the literary" (Worthen 1998, 1098). Why then is theater considered "a mode of production fully inscribed within a discourse of textual [literary] and cultural authority" (1094)? The medium of theater is capable of negotiating a field of discourse, such as that defined by the author-function "Shakespeare," just as is literature.[11] A performance of *Hamlet, any* performance of that play, moves into the field of discourse produced by Shakespeare and the Shakespace in which it circulates. Productions of *Hamlet* can be judged hollow or not hollow based on individual merit, but to dismiss all of theater as hollow negates all performative social semiotics that inform theater as well as theater's necessary interactions with the author-function.

Additionally, there are certain assumptions about the nature of an author that remain latent in Foucault's formulation. According to Foucault, the author-function developed "in the course of the nineteenth century" (1979, 153). Given that Foucault's definition of the author-function is associated with relatively contemporary texts—unlike his history of authorship which extends, say, from Homer through Saint Jerome to the present—it is not entirely clear why the author-function should emerge at one particular time. There must have been something about that historical moment that constituted a favorable mode of reception for these authors and the rules that they developed. In other words, it is not that Freud and Marx established revolutionary modes of discourse, but that they wrote during an era in which there existed (and exists to this day) a population of readers predisposed to enter into discourse with rule-generating authors, as perhaps the readers of Hippocrates and Saint Jerome were not. In other words, it is not with the individuals Freud and Marx that the author-function resides, but with the population at large willing to enter into discourse with them or, rather, with the methodological field of their texts. Some might call this population a readership, others an audience. Ultimately, this discursive and interpretive population is the medium of authorship.

By accepting that Shakespeare can constitute an author-function we begin to construct a theory of the theatrical text that inscribes, or *enacts,* textual authority in the present-tense of the theater text. The significant difference between the author-function of Shakespeare and that of Marx or Hippocrates is that, by virtue of being not merely literary but theatrical, there is more than one way to engage the discourse of the author-function: critical writing *about* and theatrical performance *of.* But now, in investigative-expansive fashion, we have crossed back over the conceptual and textual divide drawn by Rouse: we have used the phrase "performance of" to describe the theater text's relationship to the written text. How then to reconcile the authority of the written text of *Hamlet* with the notion of a performance text, one that lives its brief but wholly self-authorized existence only on the stage? The relationship between theater and writing must be scrutinized. Any quotation from the written text of *Hamlet* can only appear on the page. A purely literary reference, while convenient for the purposes of writing articles such as this one, produces the impression of a purely literary referent. While the status of *Hamlet* as a literary text cannot be denied, neither should its status as the object of past theatrical texts, nor its potential as the object of future theater texts. The text of *Hamlet: A Monologue* resists easy quotation. Although Wilson's adaptation has taken as its point of origin the written text of Shakespeare's *Hamlet,* the principal text of *Hamlet: A Monologue* is a theatrical one. A Wilson sketch should perhaps accompany any quote from the Wiens text. Wilson's storyboard sketches are as much a part of the "script" for *Hamlet: A Monologue* as Wiens's adaptation, and as a result, Wilson's set of images are as much the performed object of Rouse's "of" as is Wiens's deconstructed assemblage.

Or perhaps one cannot quote from a theater text at all. Just as the ephemeral event itself must end, leaving behind hardly a Derridean "trace" of its performance (or as Prospero would say: "Leaving not a rack behind"), so too after the theater event one has no easy point of reference for discussion. One can quote Shakespeare's play, the adaptation, some sketches, or some production photos, but these are hardly pieces of the media that is "theater." Simply quoting lyrics from a song by Lou Reed does not remotely constitute an adequate citation of a Lou Reed concert. Hopkins's excitement at seeing Reed take a seat nearby embodies the sense of authorship, the concert citationality, that Reed's presence implies: Reed is undeniably a major "author" of his own concert appearances, and his presence is a kind of quote from his performances. In the same way, scripts, sketches, and photos can only "refer" to *Hamlet: A Monologue* and the only adequate "quotation" of the theater event called *Hamlet: A Monologue* would be one that includes the performance of a portion of the event and the actual presence of Robert Wilson.

Had I But Time

The productive excursions that comprise this paper exemplify transversal theory's investigative-expansive mode of analysis, which has spurred our explorations down relevant lines of inquiry, all of which, as we will now show, intersect at the opening of *Hamlet: A Monologue*. Of his process of textual assemblage, Wiens has said, "Trying to find the first line, it was the heaviest thing to do" (Kessel 1995, 13:20). We quoted that first line earlier as "Had I but time. . . ." However, we took that quote from the first page of the adaptation (Wiens's written text version) not from the actual performance (Wilson's theater text version). In so doing, we have misrepresented the actual opening of *Hamlet: A Monologue,* especially given that we couched that quote in the context of a documentary of our attendance at this theater event. Here is a transcription of the actual "first line" of the performance that Wilson delivered in Alice Tully Hall on July 7, 1995:

> Had I but time . . .
> Had I but time . . .
> Had I but time . . . (Kessel 1995, 13:30)

The "heaviness" of Wiens's effort clearly paid off: Wilson liked the first line so much that—in typical Wilsonian fashion—he felt that it should be said not once but three times. This repetition represents in microcosm the kind of performative "badness" active throughout *Hamlet: A Monologue.* The strength of the version of *Hamlet* that Wilson performed on stage is demonstrated in the above quote: in the words of Gregory Boyd, artistic director of the Alley Theatre, there is no preexisting text that Wilson is not willing to use as "raw material, as grist for his own mill" in the service of "setting up a conversation with the play, and standing in a contentious relationship to the play" (Kessel 1995, 15:33). Ultimately, each of the preexisting texts that inform *Hamlet: A Monologue* is extended and mediated in the theater.

In this way, the theater text of *Hamlet: A Monologue* dispels the notion of a derivative relationship between the theatrical performance and any written text or script. Wiens's adaptation itself is already at a significant interpretive remove from any text that might be attributed to Shakespeare. Wilson's staging of this mediated adaptation only extends the distance between Shakespeare's source text and the theater text. *Hamlet: A Monologue* has a relationship with *Hamlet* inasmuch as the former presupposes the latter. But Wilson's performance text cannot be said to have been a performance "of" any preexisting text, not Shakespeare's, not even Wiens's. Wilson bypassed the contemptuous critical underestimation of theater as merely the reiteration of dramatic literature: he took the stage himself in order to embody the primary text of *Hamlet* in a theatrical mode, as the principal site of authority, disjunct from any preexisting text.

The authority of the theatrical text is established in performance. But who is the author of a theatrical text? This may be the wrong question. The inquiry should be not for a "who" but for a "where." Just as we have suggested that it is the receiving population, or audience, who determines the author-function, so too could it be said that authority for a radical appropriation of a classic text, like *Hamlet: A Monologue,* rests with the audience. The written text of *Hamlet* was invoked continuously throughout Wilson's performance. It was the specter that haunted the theater text at a genetic level before that text established its conceptual and authorial independence in performance. Additionally, Shakespeare's *Hamlet,* a knowledge of *Hamlet,* a memory of the experience of reading or even re-reading the written text of *Hamlet,* was presupposed as a condition of membership in the audience of *Hamlet: A Monologue.* Shakespeare's *Hamlet* was a discursive presence in the subjective territories of the audience of *Hamlet: A Monologue,* and it was within the space of this audience that the discursive circuit closed. Inevitably, the transversal power of the performance extended beyond the audience's effected subjective territories, beyond the Shakespace of which the audience was a part, and into all conceptual and emotional spaces that the audience henceforth inhabits.

Notes

1. In *Liveness,* Philip Auslander argues that live performance and mass media are inherently "rivals" in our "cultural economy" (1). The "televisual" has superceded other modes of discourse to become "the determining element of our current cultural formation" (2). Within the discursive framework of the televisual, theater may in fact be unable to effectively convey the "liveness" that would seem to be its hallmark and the trait that would distinguish live performance from the reproducible mass medias. One culturally demarcated site where even Auslander suggests that live performance may still retain a measure of unmediatized liveness is the rock concert. We find Reed's attendance at Wilson's theater event evidence of one possible point of intersection between the rock concert and the theater; we look to Wilson's *Hamlet* in search of the possibility of theatrical liveness despite the evidence of ubiquitous moribund televisuality.

2. For a detailed discussion of Shakespace, see Don Hedrick and Bryan Reynolds, 2000.

3. Transversal theory was introduced by Reynolds, 1997, where Reynolds discusses the subjective territory of Elizabethan London and the ways in which plays and players (including by association Shakespeare himself) pursued strategies of resistance in response to a restrictive political and social milieu.

The terms "transversal" and "transversality" are adapted from Félix Guattari and extended to include "conceptuality and its territories" (Reynolds 148). See also Hedrick and Reynolds, 2000; Reynolds and Fitzpatrick; and Reynolds 2001.

4. See Reynolds, 1997, 145–51.

5. Reynolds, 1997, 147.

6. See Reynolds and Fitzpatrick, 2000.

7. Bryan Reynolds and James Intriligator introduced this methodology in a paper entitled "Transversal Power," given at the Manifesto Conference at Harvard University on May 9, 1998.

8. One could argue that the issue would be made clearer by clarifying the division between the disciplines under discussion. If all "Drama Departments" would just change their names to "Theater Departments": problem solved. But the whole question of an interdisciplinary turf war is blown apart by Worthen's essay itself. How does one categorize an essay like this? It was published in *PMLA*, so it could be called "Literature Studies." But Worthen is on the faculty of a theater department: Does that make this article "Theater Studies"? And despite the fact that Worthen's goal in this article is to rehabilitate a notion of theater as a valid field of study, this article relies to a large degree on Worthen's extensive understanding of performance studies. In its persistent interdisciplinarity, Worthen's article is a work of cultural studies: an examination of conflicts among three different academic disciplines and the disciplines' differing notions of what should be valued as a subject of study.

9. Both the official program published by the Alley Theatre and the press release distributed by Lincoln Center use the phrase "adapted by Wolfgang Wiens and Robert Wilson" to attribute authorship for *Hamlet: A Monologue*. However, the cover of the script of the adaptation provided to the authors by the archive at Wilson's fund-raising organization, the Byrd Hoffman Foundation, explicitly reads "adapted by Robert Wilson and Wolfgang Wiens." It should also be noted that two of the documentary sources produced by the Alley Theatre, a program and a video, refer to the title as *Hamlet* rather than *Hamlet: A Monologue* for reasons that are far from clear.

10. The storyboard sketches that we refer to here were reprinted in the program for *Hamlet: A Monologue* (see note 8 above).

11. One might conclude that other art forms are capable of founding and expanding discursive fields of this sort: in music, for example, contemporary composers and performers must negotiate the author-functions "Mozart," "John Cage," and "Lou Reed."

Works Cited

Auslander, Philip. 1999. *Liveness: Performance in a Mediatized Culture.* New York: Routledge.

Barthes, Roland. 1977. "From Work To Text." In *Image-Music-Text*. Trans. by Stephen Heath. New York: Hill and Wang, 155–164.

Eagleton, Terry. 1983. *Literary Theory*. Minneapolis: Univ. of Minnesota Press.

Foucault, Michel. 1979. "What Is an Author?" In *Textual Strategies: Perspectives in Post-structuralist Criticism*. Ed. and Trans. by Josué V. Harari. Ithaca, NY: Cornell Univ. Press, 141–160.

Hamlet, Alley Theatre. 1995. Program. Ed. by Gregory Boyd and Valdemar Zialcita. Alley Theatre, Houston, TX. May.

Hamlet: A Monologue. 1995. Dir. Robert Wilson. Lincoln Center, New York City. 6–8 July.

Hamlet: A Monologue. 1995. Adapted by Robert Wilson and Wolfgang Wiens. Second version. Byrd Hoffman Foundation, New York City.

Hamlet, The First Quarto. [1603]1998. William Shakespeare. Ed. by Kathleen O. Irace. New York: Cambridge Univ. Press.

Hamlet, The Second Quarto [1604–1605]1964. William Shakespeare. Facsimile reproduction. Ed. by Charlton Hinman. Oxford: Clarendon Press.

Hedrick, Don and Bryan Reynolds. 2000. "Shakespace and Transversal Power." In *Shakespeare Without Class: Misappropriations of Cultural Capital*. New York: St. Martin's Press, 3–47.

Kessel, Marion, dir. *The Making of a Monologue: Robert Wilson's Hamlet*. 1995. Documentary video. Arts Alive!/Alley Theatre.

Maguire, Laurie E. 1996. *Shakespearean Suspect Texts*. New York: Cambridge Univ. Press.

The Making of a Monologue: Robert Wilson's Hamlet. 1995. Documentary video. Dir. Marion Kessel. Arts Alive!/Alley Theatre.

Marcus, Leah. 1996. *Unediting the Renaissance*. New York: Routledge.

Reynolds, Bryan. 1997. "The Devil's House, 'or worse': Transversal Power and Antitheatrical Discourse in Early Modern England." *Theatre Journal* 49, 142–67.

———. 2001. *Becoming Criminal: Transversal Theater and Cultural Dissidence in Early Modern England*. Baltimore: Johns Hopkins Univ. Press.

Reynolds, Bryan and Joseph Fitzpatrick. 1999. "The Transversality of Michel de Certeau: Foucault's Panoptic Discourse and the Cartographic Impulse." *Diacritics* 29:3, 63–80.

Rouse, John. 1992. "Textuality and Authority in Theater and Drama: Some Contemporary Possibilities." *Critical Theory and Performance*. Ed. by Janelle G. Reinelt and Joseph R. Roach. Ann Arbor: Univ. of Michigan Press, 146–157.

Worthen, W. B. 1998. "Drama, Performativity, and Performance." *PMLA* 113 (October): 1093–1107.

CHAPTER 12

BARTLETT'S EVOLVING SHAKESPEARE

HELEN M. WHALL

Long before digital media, long before the movies, television, and radio—let alone e-books and Madison Avenue—quotation books "appropriated" Shakespeare. At least since John Heywood's 1546 collection of proverbs, compendiums of famous and worthy sayings, played a significant role both in shaping and reflecting the popular cultures of English-speaking peoples. Shakespeare, whose plays demonstrate how well tuned his own ear was to the shapely phrases turned by others, ultimately became the core of the leading American book of sayings, *Bartlett's Familiar Quotations.* In the sixteenth edition of *Bartlett's,* released in the fall of 1992, there are over 1,900 quotations from Shakespeare. The Bible comes in second at 1,591 entries. Around the Shakespeare/Bible core, the complete *Bartlett's* itself has grown from a slim 258 page volume printed privately by bookseller John Bartlett in 1855 to the 1,405 page "best-seller" that American parents often buy high-school graduates (along with a dictionary—or the equivalent software) as they pack them off to college. That very equation of *Bartlett's,* a quintessentially nonacademic text, with a research tool itself speaks volumes of the ways mass marketing blurs rather than crosses the boundaries and barricades so often placed between the artist and the academy, the academy and "the people."

Over the near century and a half since Bartlett began his project, the collection has grown from source book to resource book, from a place where one could find out "who said that" to "what do I say under these circumstances." While that evolution initially accentuates a binary opposition which insists, as Richard Burt puts it in the introduction to the present book, that "popular culture is made by the people" while mass culture is "imposed on the people" (4), the *Bartlett's* project ultimately illustrates the impossibility of sustaining such a distinction. John Bartlett actually began his lifelong undertaking with the mixed motives of both a populist and an elitist, though not especially those of a capitalist. His first self-published volumes reflected both an American fan's devotion to European letters and, as in early modern books of "noble sentences," a humanist's desire to improve his reader's moral fiber. But once Bartlett's collection became a viable commercial venture for Little, Brown and Company, who purchased Bartlett's copyright in the 1860s, editors and editorial boards took over all responsibility for determining what it was we should be able to "look up." The Shakespeare section has kept growing and growing and growing. Indeed, so much so that when we review the evolution of Bartlett's Shakespeare, we learn much about the criteria that implicitly guided and continues to guide selections in less stable sections of the volume. Academic readers willing to cross the borders between art and "mass media" may see in that evolution how Shakespeare has been introduced to, and processed for, the masses.

In the preface to his first edition, John Bartlett set forth his mission: "The object of this book is to show, to some extent, the obligations our language owes to various authors for numerous phrases and familiar quotations that have become 'Household words.'" But by the time of his preface to the fourth edition in 1863 (the first printed by Boston publishers Little, Brown, though with John Bartlett still as editor), Bartlett demonstrates prescient awareness of how difficult it is to determine criteria for the popular: "The Compiler of this Collection of Familiar Quotations thinks it desirable to say, in introducing the work to the favor of the public, that it is not easy to determine in all cases the degree of familiarity that may belong to phrases and sentences which present themselves for admission; for what is familiar to one class of readers may be quite new to another."

Although Bartlett goes on to insist that he has attempted to be guided in his selection by familiarity to the "general reader" rather than by "merit alone," we can readily see his personal identification with Shakespeare played out not simply in the breadth and length of his Shakespearean quotations but in the very shaping of the Shakespeare unit. Following the custom of nineteenth-century American editors of Shakespeare, Bartlett chose to cite *The Tempest* as his first play, and placed as his first quotation Prospero's lines: "I, thus neglecting worldly ends, all dedicated / To closeness, and the bettering of my mind." Here, however, Bartlett made a decision that would certainly interest psychoanalysts: he cropped Prospero's speech, thereby absolving the Duke of responsibility in the usurpation of his kingdom much as Prospero himself does. In fact, all eighteen entries from *The Tempest* retain this idealized view of Prospero. My own favorite cropped passage takes on similar biographical dimensions when we learn that John Bartlett's second lifetime project was a very thorough concordance to Shakespeare: "My library / Was dukedom large enough." Is it, moreover, a "lack of familiarity" or psychological resistance that prevents editor John Bartlett from citing Prospero's acceptance of Caliban as his own or of referring to any of the Mage's farewell epilogue? Clearly, Bartlett saw *The Tempest* as a portal opening rather than closing on his project.

Indeed, though quotations from history plays and tragedies outweigh other citations in all editions of *Bartlett's*, tracing the fate of *The Tempest* provides a useful lens on the project as it passes from editor to editor, age to age. John Bartlett maintained control of his book through nine editions, assuming his life's work would end with his life. But in 1914, nine years after Bartlett's death at the age of eighty-five, Little, Brown brought out a tenth edition under the editorship of Nathaniel Haskel Dole. Dole notes, "In this new edition the main body of John Bartlett's compilation, up to the beginning of the 19th century, has been practically unchanged." Dole adds primarily American authors such as Poe, Whittier, Longfellow, and Lowell. He leaves Shakespeare untouched—except to add a few citations here and there. But in placing new, indeed more "familiar" lines before Bartlett's opening citations from *The Tempest* (e.g., "I would fain die a dry death"), Dole obscures Bartlett's very purpose in beginning with *The Tempest*. In so doing, however, Dole also makes clear the power an editor has to preserve or reject, to obscure or to popularize.

In 1936, Christopher Morley took over the eleventh edition. His edition pushes to the foreground an editor's (and a publisher's) power to *make* something popular. Whereas there is a kind of humility in John Bartlett's acknowledgment that he might be at fault in missing the needs of different "classes" of readers, no one ever has nor will accuse Christopher Morley of humility. In his preface he bows toward his assistant, associate editor Louella D. Everett, while assuring us that "one collaborator . . . knows acutely what readers want; and the other believes himself to know what they ought to want." We are left no doubt as to which of the two's work would be "caviar to the general." Morley considerably expands all Bartlett's entries, making "literary power the criterion rather than width and vulgarity of fame." In appointing a Rhodes Scholar who never recovered from his Anglophilia, Little, Brown cut John Bartlett's original link to the populace and marketed the new volume directly to an American public self-consciously eager to learn what they "ought to want."

Though he follows Bartlett's ordering, the more "scholarly" Morley does standardize the Shakespeare entries for the first time, citing W. J. Craig's recent Oxford edition; he also expands considerably the already lengthy citations from Shakespeare's history plays and tragedies. And Morley adds his own favorite little attitudinal lines from the comedies, such as these (from *Two Gentlemen of Verona*): "Since maids, in modesty, say 'no' to that / Which they would have the proferer construe 'Ay.'" He also expands entries from *The Tempest,* bringing the number of entries for that play from twenty-six in Dole's edition to thirty-seven in his own. Morley retains Prospero's cropped lines on "neglecting worldly ends," but increases many of the play's chastise-ments, such as "Lest too light winning / Make the prize light"; "Keep a good tongue in your head"; "Do not give dalliance too much rein."

Morley's preference for these admonishments seems consistent with the determinedly hierarchic views that guide many of his additions to the eleventh edition, but even given cultural values in 1936, we might well ques-tion either the moral *or* literary merits of lines like "With foreheads villain-ous low." In a world sunk in depression, Morley does find space for one line from the epilogue: "And my ending is despair." When he edits the 1948 twelfth edition, he is forced by the circumstances of a darkening world to look beyond literary merit and cite references that range from Hitler and Einstein to the UN Charter—as well as to Winston Churchill, who admit-ted to growing up reading *Bartlett's.*

The thirteenth centennial edition (1955) was prepared by "the editorial staff" of Little, Brown who invoke the father of their project in a manner that seems to effect a compromise between Morley's elitism and Bartlett's dedication to tracking down "household phrases." The editors write: "We have borne in mind the original basis of selection which John Bartlett, a partner at Little, Brown, determined as 'familiar or worthy of being familiar.'" That last phrase—"worthy of being familiar"—underscores how much, by mid-twentieth century, *Bartlett's* had become a repository not just of literary, but also of cultural values. At the same time, the volume had acquired new scholarly credentials, as once again reflected in the Shakespeare section. The editors abandon John Bartlett's romanticized arrangement of the plays in favor of "the dates and order, about which there is much conjecture [set by] Sir Edmund Chambers." But the edi-tors also continued to avoid academicians, preferring instead those who, like Morley, are trained by, but are not of, the academy.

By 1968, *The Tempest* was enjoying a stage revival, which may explain why the editor of the fourteenth edition, Emily Morrison Beck, increased her *Tempest* entries from thirty-seven to forty-three. Here, the blurring of lines between academic and popular subcultures as well as kinds of Shake-spearean appropriations becomes almost complete. But most interestingly, during an age that called leaders into accountability, Beck cut completely Prospero's misleading reference to "neglecting worldly ends." She does in-clude, for the first time, Caliban's potent lines:

> You taught me language; and my profit on it
> Is, I know how to curse: the red plague rid you,
> For learning me your language!

When Beck edited the fifteenth edition in 1980, she again added selections to the ever-growing Shakespeare entries, but she left *The Tempest* "set," leaving to the most recent editor, Justin Kaplan, the decision finally to add Prospero's crucial admission that "This thing of darkness I Acknowledge mine." Kaplan proved to be the perfect editor for the turbulent '90s. In his preface to the sixteenth, 1992, edition, Kaplan writes that he considers "A quotation book . . . both intellectual history and cultural montage." He is the first editor who also forthrightly admits that "Some quotations, of course, become 'familiar' simply because they appear in a 'book of familiar quotations.'" It is perhaps this late twentieth-century self-consciousness that led Kaplan to set forth more explicitly than any other editor (even Morley) his criteria for inclusion. Quotations have been chosen "as well for their literary power, intellectual and historical significance, originality, and timeliness." The last criteria may explain why the Shakespeare entries have undergone something of a subtle but radical transformation. Kaplan also chose to collapse rather than blur the boundaries between editorial staff and academic specialists, turning often to those in the academy for recommendations. As one of the Shakespeareans Kaplan consulted for suggestions on "what to cut, what to add," I can testify both to Kaplan's postmodern deference to "specialists" as well as his acute awareness that academicians often carry their own axes and often swing those axes at the very notion of Shakespeare as both "popular" and "popularist."

In many ways, Justin Kaplan sustains the Little, Brown affinity for editors with a scholarly air but without academic credentials. Kaplan dropped out of the Harvard doctoral program but won a Pulitzer for his biography of Mark Twain. Unlike Morley, however, Kaplan supports numerous liberal (one might even say leftist) causes and an outright appreciation for the masses, though the unwashed are unlikely to be found at his dinner table. Ultimately, Kaplan's decision to invite many experts to his table so that they might talk in quotation marks meant that he had to evaluate the evaluators. Consultants quickly saw—or heard—what wasn't there in the Shakespeare section. Lines like, "Macduff was from his mother's womb/Untimely ripped" and "Now, gods, stand up for bastards." Such omissions from earlier volumes seem to reflect the squeamishness (if not prudery) and righteousness of earlier editors. Their addition to the current volume points to Kaplan's corrective measures, each of which reflects his and his chosen academicians' biases: female characters are given greater voice, and the canon is somewhat deromanticized.

The *Wall Street Journal's* editorial board considered such "timeliness" a matter of political correctitude rather than one of political righteousness and perhaps the difference lies only in the eye of the beholder. The *Journal,* in reviewing the sixteenth edition *in toto,* lamented that Kaplan did not find

Ronald Reagan particularly quotable yet included lines Jimmy Carter delivered to the Women's Agenda Conference. But in fact, Kaplan, like all the editors before him, also reflects even as he shapes popular opinion, a phenomenon that itself shifts in time. By 1992, Reagan's teflon had largely worn off while a resurrected Carter was showing up at peace talks with an extended hand. In numerous photo layouts, that hand just as often held a Habitat hammer as an olive branch. It seems that any source book like *Bartlett's*, if it is to succeed in the mass market, must in fact capture the popular sentiment of its own era even while hoping to influence what must inevitably see print in the next edition.

Kaplan's recalibration of the Shakespeare section to reflect a 1990s sensibility is evident throughout, but especially in the *Antony and Cleopatra* entries. He adds seven significant quotations, almost all of which return to the Queen of Egypt her complexity and her prominence in the play. New entries range from Cleopatra's advice to Antony that he "play one scene / Of excellent dissembling, and let it look / Like perfect honor" to her exclamation "My man of men" to her crucial speech to her maids as she contemplates suicide:

> The quick comedians
> Extemporally will stage us, and present
> Our Alexandrian revels: Antony
> Shall be brought drunken forth, and I shall see
> Some squeaking Cleopatra boy my greatness
> I' the' posture of a whore.

Such additions, however, did not come without a price. In order to make space for these and other inclusions, Kaplan had to decide what lines might best die a quiet death. At my suggestion, he removed Morley's entry from *Two Gentlemen of Verona*. Yet in arguing that only an attorney defending against date-rape would miss such lines, was I not also trying to influence Kaplan's influence as he mediated Shakespeare's influence? As *Bartlett's* evolves, so too does the collaborative nature of John Bartlett's once singular project. Even dragging less provocative, quite obscure lines off-stage highlighted the temporal limitations of "universal genius." Will popular readers miss—or miss being edified—by lines such as, "Sir, he made a chimney in my father's house, and the bricks are alive to prove it" (from *Henry VI, Part Two*) or even, "Thus far into the bowels of the land / Have we marched on without impediment" (from *Richard III*)? The Shakespearean who winces at even these cuts points to a different kind of limitation; we would cite the entire text of every play.

Of course, to cite the entire text is to reproduce *The New Oxford Shakespeare*. To assure that the flavor of context be at least preserved in a quotation book is more difficult though perhaps even more important when presenting the equivalent of forensic evidence to the general reader. Generations of *Bartlett's* editors, for example, seem to have been committed to suppressing evidence in order to preserve an image of kings above fault (unless they were outright tyrants like Richard III or Macbeth). Bartlett initiated this process with his manipulation of Prospero's image. So too did careful editing change the nature of King Lear's epiphany on the moor. Until 1992, his speech ran thus:

> Poor naked wretches, wheresoe'er you are
> That bide the pelting of this pitiless storm
> How shall your houseless heads and unfed sides
> Your loop'd and window'd raggedness, defend you
> From seasons such as these?

"Blind" seems too kind a word to attribute to earlier editors who so cropped this passage; "unconscionable" seems more apt. Then again, ours has been a culture slow to assume responsibility for homelessness. Is the 1992 version truly more "popular" or does the present entry attempt to use its medium to make accountability itself more popular? Now the busy speechmaker who turns not to Shakespeare but to Bartlett for an apt passage on the poor will read:

> O I have taken
> Too little care of this! Take physic, pomp
> Expose thyself to feel what wretches feel,
> That thou mayst shake the superflux to them,
> And show the heavens more just.

What forces kept earlier editors from including such eminently quotable, such utterly poetic, and so morally sound lines? What responsibility should the masters of modern media—comic book author, movie producer, web master or source-book editor—assume when appropriating Shakespeare? Should we appropriate Shakespeare? How can we not? Would a "true Shakespeare" reflect his or our views on race, gender, social order, or divine justice? Surely the answer must always be, as it should always be in critical studies, "Both. Neither." Try reviewing the sonnets and plays in order to advise what should be added and what left out of the upcoming millennial edition of *Bartlett's Book of Familiar Quotations.* That activity should make clear the sheer burden of any interpretive task. The weight of choosing for others what might best represent Shakespeare thus led me to advise citing Prospero's epilogue more fully than did John Bartlett himself. Now the reader of

Bartlett's may at least learn that the editor, critic, director, reader's end need not be despair if it is

> relieved by prayer,
> Which pierces so that it assaults
> Mercy itself and frees all faults.

Works Cited

Bartlett, John. 1855. *A Collection of Familiar Quotations with Complete Indices of Authors and Subjects*. Cambridge, MA: Josiah Bartlett.

―――. 1858. *A Collection of Familiar Quotations with Complete Indices of Authors and Subjects*. 3d ed. Cambridge, MA: Josiah Bartlett.

―――. 1937. *Familiar Quotations: A Collection of Passages, Phrases, and Proverbs Traced to Their Sources in Ancient and Modern Literature*, 11th ed. Ed. by Christopher Morley. Boston: Little, Brown and Company.

―――. 1968. *Familiar Quotations: A Collection of Passages, Phrases, and Proverbs Traced to Their Sources in Ancient and Modern Literature*, 14th ed. Ed. by Emily Morison Beck. Boston: Little, Brown and Company.

―――. 1992. *Familiar Quotations*, 16th ed. Ed. by Justin Kaplan. Boston: Little, Brown and Company.

Burt, Richard. 2002. "To e- or not to e-? Disposing of Schlockespeare in the Age of Digital Media," in *Shakespeare After Mass Media*. Ed. by Richard Burt. New York: Palgrave, 1–32.

CHAPTER 13

SHAKESPEARE AND THE HOLOCAUST

Julie Taymor's *Titus* is Beautiful, or Shakesploi Meets (the) Camp

RICHARD BURT

"Il cinema è l'arma più forte"
("Cinema is the strongest weapon")

—Mussolini's motto

Every day I'll read something that is right out of *Titus Andronicus,* so when people think this is "over the top," they're absolutely wrong. What could be more "over the top" than the Holocaust?

—Julie Taymor

"Belsen Was a Gas."

—Johnny Rotten

Shakespeare nach Auschwitz?

One morning in the summer of 2000, I was channel surfing the trash talk shows to get my daily fix of mass media junk via the hype-o of my television set. After "Transsexual Love Secrets" on Springer got a bit boring, I lighted on the Maury Povich Show. The day's topic was "My Seven-Year-Old Child Drinks, Smokes, Swears, and Hits Me!" Father figure Povich's final solution, like Sally Jessie Raphael's with much older kids on similar episodes of her show, was to send the young offenders to boot camp. Footage rolled of the kids crying their eyes out in camp as they were being yelled at an inch from their faces by paramilitary guards. The live television audience hooted, laughed, and applauded the more the girls cried. "What is going on here?" I asked myself. Was the Povich show unforeseen confirmation of Giorgio Agamben's thesis in *Homo Sacer* that the concentration camp, not the prison, is the paradigm of modernity?[1] Here was Povich playing the role of father as fascist (the children were all girls, and no father was present, or even mentioned). The audience's hoots, laughter, and applause, I took it, functioned as a cathartic release from their roles as parents, and the audience were allowed to identify with the sadistic guards and fantasize hurting children, perhaps even their own. The show was a backlash against the child-centered generation that has come to dominate U.S. culture.

Or was the Povich episode, a sensationalistic use of a neofascistic boot camp for higher ratings, also some bizarre universalization of what Norman Finkelstein has caustically called "the holocaust industry" and what others before have called, along similar lines, the "Shoah-business" (as in, "there's no business like Shoah business")?[2] In the wake of holocaust comedies like *Life Is Beautiful* (dir. Roberto Benigni, 1997), *Train of Life* (dir. Radu Mihaileanu, 1998), *Jakob the Liar* (dir. Peter Kassovitz,1999) and the recently opened theme park "Stalin's World" in the Ukraine, was a Holocaust World theme park just around the corner, opening somewhere in Germany or California?[3] And how seriously was Povich's show meant to be taken? Was it really a fascistic *Kindergarten Cop* (dir. Ivan Reitman, 1990) development, with Vater/Fuhrer Povich taking on Arnold Schwarzenegger's role in the romantic comedy thriller as undercover cop turned kindergarten teacher? Or not? Do seven-year-olds really smoke, drink, swear, or were they simply being coached to top Linda Blair's performance in *The Exorcist* (dir. William Friedkin, 1974)? Is boot camp camp, I wondered. Is Agamben's concentration camp camp? Is nothing sacred?

It is in relation to the possibly parodic routinization of the concentration camp in mass media that I want to read the appearance of the holocaust in Shakespeare films and the appearance of Shakespeare in representations of the holocaust, with Julie Taymor's film *Titus* (1999) as my focus. Taymor pointedly invokes the holocaust in interviews, seeing the violence in the play as a model of the violence that ended in the death camps. In one interview, Taymor says, for example, "I keep using the Holocaust because it's the biggest event of our century—it can be twisted and manipulated" (de Luca and Lindroth 2000, 31). Unlike films set in concentration camps or on the verge of moving into them, however, *Titus* does not represent them, evoking the camps only in the barbed wire cage in which first the Goth prisoners are carted and later Martius and Quintus on their to way to being executed. The analogy between ancient Rome and the holocaust is made indirectly with references primarily to Italian fascism and to the horror-film genre. Benito Mussolini's Rome, particularly his E. U. R. government-center building, modeled on the Roman Colosseum, makes several dramatic appearances in the film, and Taymor intentionally alludes in an orgy scene at Saturninus's court to similar scenes from Luchino Visconti's film about Nazi Germany in the 1930s, *The Damned* (1969). Additionally, much of *Titus* was shot at Cinecitta, the film studio founded by Mussolini. Only one piece of music is not scored by the soundtrack composer Elliot Goldenthal, a traditional Italian song called "Vivere" sung by Carlo Butti on a recording during the banquet scene, and this song is meant to evoke Mussolini and 1930s Italy.[4] Taymor also invokes Nazi cinema at one point. Commenting on the opening sequence of the soldiers marching into the colosseum at night, she says, "if you're shooting military marches and you do it well, on some level it's going to look like the work of [German Third Reich filmmaker] Leni Riefenstahl" (Pizzello 2000).

If the holocaust is called up by references to Italian and German fascism in a Shakespeare film like *Titus*, it is perhaps unsurprising that Shakespeare also shows up in holocaust representations. Shakespeare's *King Lear* is mentioned and lines from it are cited in the holocaust comedy *Jakob the Liar*, a remake of Frank Beyer's DDR film, *Jacob the Liar* (1974).[5] (The lines from *Lear* in the remake are not cited in the DDR original, which makes no mention of Shakespeare.) Similarly, Jiri Weiss's 1960 film *Romeo, Julie e tma* (*Romeo, Juliet, and the Darkness*) adapts *Romeo and Juliet* in an Anne Frank-like Holocaust setting of Nazi occupied Chezoslovakia in 1942. And in *The Prince of West End Avenue*, a 1994 novel by Alan Isler, the octogenarian narrator is a holocaust survivor who acts in an amateur production of *Hamlet*, with three intermissions to accommodate the bladders of the aged cast members, in the Emma Lazarus retirement home. Erwin Sylvanus has characters mention Hamlet and Ophelia in his one-act play *Korczak and His Children* (1958) and George Tabori brings up the gravedigger's scene from *Hamlet* in his play *Jubilaum* (1983).[6] There was a production of *The Merchant of Venice* set in a concentration camp at the Deutsches Nationaltheater in Weimar, Germany in 1995, with Shylock as a camp prisoner forced to perform in the play. The director was an Israeli, Hanan Snir.[7]

This exchange between Shakespeare's plays and fictional accounts either of the holocaust or told by holocaust survivors may serve to solve shared problems in performances and representations of both. If a film of such an excessively violent and bloody play as *Titus Andronicus* risks being construed as a schlock horror film or as a black comedy, then indirect references to the holocaust via Italian and German fascism in Taymor's cinematic adaptation

help save her film as a serious engagement with a serious tragedy. Responding to an interviewer's question, "What is the function of combining violence with humor [in *Titus*]?" Taymor brings up the concentration camp: "I
think that when we're in our deepest, darkest circumstance, whether you're
a prisoner or in a concentration camp or something similarly awful, the only
way to survive is through humor" (de Luca and Lindroth 2000, 31).

Representations of the holocaust similarly gain support from Shakespeare. The holocaust is often represented as excessive, something beyond all
aesthetic representation, particularly tragedy. Aesthetics and the holocaust
are a contradiction in terms: Theodor Adorno's famous declaration "nach
Auschwitz ein Gedicht zu schreiben, ist barbarisch" (to write poetry after
Auschwitz is barbaric) might now be rewritten as "to write poetry *about*
Auschwitz is barbaric." And as Slavoj Žižek comments on the subgenre of
the holocaust comedy, this taboo on representing the holocaust may also
serve political purposes:

> Paradoxical as it might sound, the rise of the holocaust comedy is correlative
> to the elevation of the holocaust itself into *the* metaphysical, diabolical Evil—
> the ultimate traumatic point at which the objectifying of historical knowledge
> breaks down and even witnesses concede words fail. The holocaust cannot be
> explained, visualized, represented, or transmitted, since it marks the black
> hole, the implosion of the (narrative) universe. Any attempt to politicize
> equals an anti-Semitic negation of its uniqueness. However, this very de-
> politicization of the holocaust . . . can also be a cynically manipulative politi-
> cal strategy to manipulate certain practices and disqualify others. It fits
> perfectly today's culture of victimization: is the holocaust not the supreme
> proof that to be human is to be a victim, not an active political agent? (27)

Holocaust comedies are preferable to serious and false films like Stephen
Spielberg's *Schindler's List* (1993), Žižek maintains, because they "accept in
advance [their] failure to render the horror of the holocaust" (27). The turn
to Shakespearean tragedy in *Jakob the Liar* might be regarded as a means of
defending against a critique like Žižek's of the holocaust's depoliticization.
In *Jakob the Liar,* Shakespeare is represented as lost, no longer performed by
the actors confined to the Warsaw Ghetto. His sublime status, no longer per-
formable or readable, available only through memory, is a means by which
the holocaust may be indirectly given a sense of tragic grandeur even as the
genre of the film, namely, comedy, keeps in place the depoliticized idea that
all representations of the holocaust will fail to do it justice.

Yet this mutually supportive exchange between Shakespearean tragedy
and the holocaust did not prove to be especially successful. Indeed, both
Titus and *Jakob the Liar* bombed at the box office. I take the box office fail-
ures of *Titus* and *Jakob the Liar* and the posttheatrical release marketing of

Titus to be representative of a larger failure, namely, that Shakespeare cannot save the holocaust, nor can the holocaust save Shakespeare. This failure is not due to the aftermath of the holocaust, in which tragedy and poetry are no longer possible, but to the present desacralization of the aesthetic in mass culture. In his indictment of the holocaust industry, Norman Finkelstein has pointed to the proliferation of museums and memorials, which he incisively argues, have been used to support right-wing policies in Israel and in the United States. Equally crucial to the construction of memory in these institutions and their legitimation is their status as art, both in their architecture and exhibition displays, Adorno's view notwithstanding.[8] At the center of neoconservative criticism of Shakespeare on film and of the holocaust industry is what I call a neomodernist aesthetic through which adaptations and memorials may be saved as high culture even as they take the form of mass culture, either films like *Titus* or comic books like Art Spiegelman's *Maus*.[9] Artists who represent the holocaust face a similar problem to that of directors of *Titus Andronicus:* What Taymor refers to as the "over the top" status of the holocaust, outstripping even *Titus Andronicus* in horror, may also produce laughter at the grotesque inadequacy of a given representation.[10] Hence the controversy over a film like *Life Is Beautiful,* which might be said to allegorize this problem.

Shakespeare often plays a central role in such controversies. Shakespeare comes up in *Eichmann in Jerusalem,* for example, when Hannah Arendt characterizes Eichmann's evil by contrasting it with Shakespeare's villains: "Eichmann was not Iago and not Macbeth and nothing would have been further from his mind than to determine with Richard III to 'prove a villain'" (1963, 287). Whereas Shakespearean evil is dramatic, Nazi evil is banal. The former fails to represent the latter.

Jakob the Liar and *Titus* share another problem as well, namely, their emphasis on the child as survivor. The point of referring to *King Lear* in *Jakob the Liar* may in fact be to dismiss it, not only because the anti-heroic and anti-romantic nihilism it represents in Frankfurter's memory has to be replaced by the heroism of Heym, but because Lear does not manage to save the child he loves and who loves him. *Jakob the Liar* might even be regarded as a Nahum Tateish undoing of *Lear.* The remake revises the ending of the DDR *Jacob the Liar* so that, unlike Cordelia, the child, Lina, is saved by the Russians (in the original DDR film, Lina is almost certainly going to her death in the camps). The remake is thus in line, Sander Gilman insightfully argues, with 1990s representations of the Shoah: "The child must be rescued . . . is innocence itself and . . . must survive" (2000, 306). The remake's changes in a great DDR film result in an awful piece of Robin Williams *Good Morning in Poland* schlock. Taymor's *Titus* also makes a child central, enlarging the minor role of young Lucius into a central role. Lucius appears in the opening and closing interpolated frame and is omnipresent in the film. And Taymor chooses to have Lucius let Aaron's baby live rather than kill it. The result of this focus on the innocent (unless taught to be bad) child and baby survivors, as in *Jakob the Liar*, is schlock.

In this chapter, I argue that Taymor's *Titus* may not be saved by regarding it as an aftereffect of the holocaust any more than Shakespeare's *Titus Andronicus* can be saved by regarding it as an anticipation of the holocaust chiefly because of its reliance on the horror genre. Taymor casts Saturninus as a fascist leader, the Daddy of Sylvia Plath's poem in *Ariel* (1965) and Titus as antifascist, serial-killer father liberated from the obligations of paternity.[11] Yet Titus's antioedipal, antifascist violence only leads to the reinstallation at the end of the film of a fascist romanticization of the child in a closing shot straight out of Stephen Spielberg's *E. T* (1982).[12] The desacralization of human life that made possible the concentration camp and mass extermination, according to Agamben (1998), extends, I maintain, to the aesthetic, undermining neoconservative attempts both to save Shakespearean representations of violence from mere sensationalism and to save holocaust memorials from being condemned as part of a holocaust industry. This same process of desacralization has implications for avowedly progressive Shakespeare criticism as well, as I will show in the conclusion to this essay, since that process erodes distinctions between neoconservative and avowedly progressive Shakespeareans even as the two kinds of critics both ignore or dismiss schlock Shakespeare.

I'm Having Shakespeare For Dinner

Though both *Titus* and *Jakob the Liar* bombed, the two films differed markedly in terms of their posttheatrical-release marketing in the United States. While *Jakob the Liar* quickly disappeared from sight, a major blitz was undertaken to salvage Taymor's film. In what follows, my focus will exclusively be on *Titus*. Soon after Taymor's movie was released, a second edition of the lavishly illustrated, *Julie Taymor: Playing with Fire* (Blumenthal and Taymor) was released, complete with a new chapter on *Titus*. And just before the two-disc DVD edition of *Titus*, complete with director and actor commentaries and other extras was released, the screenplay (Taymor) was published, an equally lavishly illustrated, expensive and exclusively hardcover edition coffee-table book.[13] Moreover, both Clear Blue Sky Productions and Twentieth Century Fox put up elaborate websites, and Taymor gave interview after interview about both the film and the DVD edition for film magazines and websites.[14] In an interesting development, the neoconservative critic Jonathan Bate was enlisted to help save Taymor's film. In a nice piece of mutual backslapping, Bate's positive review in the *New York Times* was reprinted as an introduction to the screenplay, and a blurb saying

13.1. Lavinia after her rape and mutilation, in Lorn Richey's *Titus Andronicus* 1997.

"'A great edition of a great play,' Julie Taymor, Director of the major new motion picture starring Anthony Hopkins and Jessica Lange" was printed (in stick-on form) on the cover of Bate's Arden *Titus Andronicus*.[15] This marketing blitz appears aimed both at teachers and critics of Shakespeare and the serious, nonacademic connoisseur moviegoer, though that strategy is exactly the kind of thing mocked by a not-so-distant cousin of Hopkins's Titus, the serial killer, hyper-discriminating yuppie aesthete, Christian Bale, in *American Psycho* (dir. Mary Harron, 1999).

Taymor's *Titus* is one of four cinematic productions of Shakespeare's *Titus Andronicus* released in the late 1990s, including Lorn Richey's *Titus Andronicus* (1997), Christopher Dunne's *Titus Andronicus* (1999) and Richard Griffin's *William Shakespeare's Titus Andronicus* (2000).[16] Taymor's film differs from the other three not only in its much higher production values, star power, and acting abilities of its cast but in its relatively less graphic representation of the play's acts of violence. Richey's *Titus Andronicus* lets the blood flow, as the close-up of Lavinia and the shot of Titus killing Saturninus, below, evince.

Richey advertises his film as follows: "Low Budget meets High Art in this 'Shakes-ploitation' extravaganza! Seattle cult movie maker Lorn Richey has

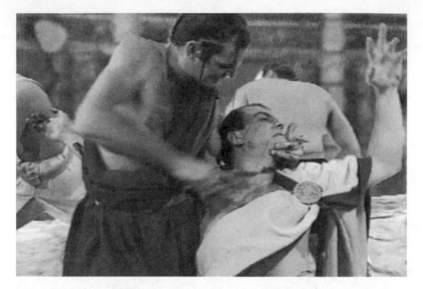

13.2. Titus killing Saturninus, in Lorn Richey's *Titus Andronicus* 1997.

created a blue-screen ancient Rome as the setting for William Shakespeare's bloodiest and most-muscular tragedy. Roman Generals and outlaw Goths clash in a drama of love, intrigue, brutality, adultery, murder, dismemberment, decapitation and cannibalism!"

Similarly, Christopher Dunne's film adaptation (1999) is advertised as follows: "This Cult/Horror motion picture is a wild but faithful adaptation of a classic hit. Set in early Rome, this is the saga of a man cruelly betrayed and brutally persecuted—ultimately to madness and murder by the 'wilderness of tigers' of the Roman court. This two hour and twenty-two minute feature tells the powerful tale as it was intended, focused on the simple truth: violence & revenge begets only more violence & revenge. A tale of relevance and depth, yet a bizarre and exotic indulgence in the imagery of humankind's inhumanity to itself. . . . MURDER, ODDBALL, CONSPIRACY, DEMENTIA, UNGLAMORIZED, HIGH CAMP, GENERAL WHACKY BEHAVIOR, CANNIBALISM, INFANTICIDE . . . and more!"

In contrast to these openly sensationalistic recodings of Shakespeare's *Titus Andronicus* as a horror cult film along the lines of schlockmeister Troma Films director Lloyd Kaufman's *Tromeo and Juliet* (1996), Taymor combines in *Titus* both performance traditions of the play: graphic realism and stylized artifice. In high modernist fashion, Taymor tries to elevate the violence in her film above sensationalistic, exploitative violence in films she eschews such as Quentin Tarantino's *Pulp Fiction* (1995).[17] On the one hand, Taymor departs

13.3. Schlock *Titus.*

from Peter Brooks's innovation of stylizing the violence by using red ribbons in place of stage blood. To give just a few examples, she shows Aaron cutting off Titus' hand, Aaron killing the nurse, blood drooling from Lavinia's mouth when Marcus discovers her after she has been raped and her hands cut off, and Titus cutting the throats of Chiron and Demetrius and later sticking a table knife through Tamora's neck. On the other hand, Taymor stops short of the gruesome explicitness of Dunne's and Richey's productions.[18] She does not provide graphic representations of Alarbus's execution, the beheadings of Quintus and Martius, nor of Lavinia's rape and mutilation; instead, Taymor represents the rape and mutilation as Lavinia's flashback, in the fourth of a series of what Taymor calls Penny Arcade Nightmares (P. A. N. s). Lavinia appears as a doe and her assailants as tigers.

Right after the rape itself, Taymor replaces Lavinia's severed hands with tree branches, as seen in the photo on the top of the next page, and later

13.4. Lavinia after she has been raped and mutilated, in Julie Taymor's *Titus* 1999.

wooden hands supplied by Lucius. Although Taymor has Lavinia carry Titus's hand in her mouth, Taymor does not have Lavinia kiss the heads of her brothers as Jonathan Bate has it in his Arden, (1995, 203), the edition Taymor used. Bate, incidentally, is the first editor, as he points out, to use the stage direction for this "macabre kiss" (1995, 48). And Lavinia almost places the walking stick in her mouth, as Marcus does when showing her how to write with it, but then withdraws it, as if it were too phallic, when writing the names of Chiron and Demetrius in the sand. Similarly, when Titus kills his son Mutius, we see Mutius from behind as Titus stabs him in the stomach. No blood is visible, just a reaction shot of Mutius's face. Even when Aaron cuts off Titus's hand, we don't see the cleaver cut into Titus's wrist.[19]

Along the same lines, Taymor does not represent the violence as camp. Like many directors of the play, she tries to prevent viewers from laughing at moments not meant to be funny by having the actors laugh as they commit various atrocities.[20] The assumption is that audiences will be horrified by both the laughter and the violence and so not want to laugh themselves. Taymor adopts several techniques from contemporary filmmaking. For example, she uses Mad Cow's Time Slice System, used notably in *The Matrix* (dir. Andy and Larry Wachowski, 1999), when Lucius shoots Saturninus after having already killed him by shoving a long spoon into his mouth and then into his head. And the Lavinia P. A. N. is edited like a music video and is meant to recall the video-arcade games played by Demetrius.[21]

Even with its relatively restrained representation of violence, *Titus* had great difficulty getting a distributor. An independent group called Overseas Film Group optioned Taymor's screenplay. Though the film's preview at

Cannes was a great success, no distributor would touch *Titus*. Despite Taymor's successful Broadway musical adaptation of the animated feature, *The Lion King*, Disney passed. Miramax then bailed. Eventually an independent studio, Clear Blue Sky Productions produced it for about seventeen million dollars, and finally Twentieth Century Fox distributed it and produced the DVD. Once released, *Titus* was frequently compared by reviewers to *Pulp Fiction*, and leading actor Anthony Hopkins's earlier role as cannibal serial killer Hannibal Lector in the horror film *Silence of the Lambs* (dir. Jonathan Demme, 1993) was also called up by reviewers as a gloss on Titus's cannibalistic feast prepared for his enemies, Tamora and Saturninus chief among them.[22] *Titus* also showed up with an announcement of its DVD release at a horror Internet site called Gorezone.[23]

The problems Taymor's film faced in production, distribution, and theatrical release were in large part due to bad timing. In the wake of the Columbine High School shootings and the lawsuit against Oliver Stone and *Natural Born Killers* (1994) in Alabama for inspiring a series of copycat murders based on those committed by the characters in Stone's, Hollywood executives got nervous. Even Shakespeare did not seem to be a legitimate cover. One of the Columbine murderers quoted Shakespeare's *The Tempest* ("Good wombs have born bad sons" [1.2.140]) in one of the last videotapes the killers made before their rampage (Janofsky 1999, A10).[24] A journalist writing about Taymor's difficulties finding a distributor commented that even Baz Luhrmann's *William Shakespeare's Romeo + Juliet* would have had a hard time getting a distributor had it been set for release in 1999.[25] Indeed, PBS Frontline broadcast an episode called *The Killer at Thurston High* (Michael Kelly, dir. 2000) about a high school student named Kip Kinkel who shot and killed both of his parents and who was deeply interested in the play *Romeo and Juliet* and the Luhrmann film and soundtrack CD. And Shakespeare did not save *Teaching Mrs. Tingle* (dir. Kevin Williamson, 1999). Williamson's script, about three high school students who kidnap a terrorizing high school teacher and then, in the original version, murder her, was botched and butchered so that the film could be released with an R-rating (Mrs. Tingle is merely fired in the final version). Ophelia, Romeo, and Juliet are all mentioned in the film, and leading actress Helen Mirren (Mrs. Tingle) has played many of Shakespeare's female characters on stage and on film. Shakespeare's cultural authority was not sufficient to prevent the film, even in its neutered form, from being assaulted in the press. Similarly, Miramax delayed the release of *O,* a modern-day adaptation of *Othello* set in a high school starring Julia Stiles as Desi, in 1999 because of the Columbine shootings (see Traister 2000) and again in March of 2001 because of the Santee high school shootings (see Waxman 2001). (The film was eventually bought by Lion Gates Films and released on August 24, 2001.) Ironically, Taymor's film was not spared the censor's scissors either, though for explicit sex rather than violence. Ten to twenty seconds of sexually explicit footage of male genitalia during the orgy scene were left on the cutting-room floor, and *Titus* managed to secure an R-rating.[26] Anything did not go, then, in the name of Shakespeare.

Beyond bad timing, however, Taymor's difficulties in distributing and releasing her film were due in part to what I am calling the desacralization of Shakespeare. Lawrence Levine (1988, 85–168) has described what he calls "the sacralization of culture" in the late nineteenth-century United States, and a reversal of that process is now taking place, though without the democratic, anti-elitist implications Levine associates with Shakespeare and American popular culture in general before it was sacralized.[27] The present desacralization of Shakespeare is due to a larger transformation in Shakespeare's reproduction, one in which visual culture has displaced literary culture and a modernist aesthetic has gone to the wayside. If, as Richard Halpern argues, at an earlier time Shakespeare's preeminence "depended on his sharing the stage with cultural 'trash'" (1997, 66), Shakespeare is now in many, if not most cases, indistinguishable from such trash in that Shakespeare is most widely accessible on film or other visual media.[28] And this displacement of the literary text by the movie, television, and computer screen involves another reversal. Most people, like the character Cher in *Clueless* (dir. Amy Heckerling, 1996), now come to Shakespeare first not through his texts but through some visual representation of them—a film, an advertisement, or a subgenre of fiction such as teen comedies, science fiction, or Harlequin romances.[29] It is not surprising that both Taymor and Jonathan Bate adopt the same cliché that Shakespeare would be a Hollywood screenwriter were he alive today.[30]

If we look for places where Shakespeare still has a sacred status, we find them in the romantic criticism of a Harold Bloom (1998) and in a romantic comedy like *Shakespeare in Love* (dir. John Madden Jr., 1998). Significantly, *Titus Andronicus* is mentioned in *Shakespeare in Love* in a way that disassociates it from the mature Shakespeare who emerges during the course of the film. When Shakespeare sees a boy outside the theater feeding mice to a cat, the boy tells him he admires a play in which heads are cut off and a daughter is mutilated with knives. The play is *Titus Andronicus,* and the boy says his name is John Webster. Shakespeare's bloody tragedy is associated with his juvenilia, and poor Webster is represented as an inferior playwright whose development was arrested at a very young age.

Before we may examine the impact of Shakespeare's desacralization as a writer of violent plays on Taymor's stylistic choices in *Titus,* I think it is necessary to consider not only why the film faced so many hurdles in its production and distribution but why there have been so many cinematic adaptations of *Titus Andronicus* in the late 1990s and into the millennium. In his analysis of the modernist investment in Shakespeare as a means of unifying the public sphere without erasing social distinctions and so preventing social disintegration, Richard Halpern has pointed out that "Shakespeare's Roman plays assume particular importance for modern political thought because it is there that something like an urban, public space emerges" (1997, 52). *Julius Caesar* was chief among the Roman plays, as Halpern documents: the first Vitagraph film production was of the play in 1908, as it was the play Orson Welles chose to open the Mercury Theater in 1937 (it ran for 157 performances) and the first released issue of *Classics Illustrated* in the 1950s (Halpern 1997, 67). And *Julius Caesar* was a fixture of the high school curriculum.[31] The link between Caesar and modern dictators, including Napoleon, Mussolini, Hitler, Mobutu, and Abeid Karume, was made as well in the program notes to a 1972 RSC production of *Julius Caesar*. During this time, *Titus Andronicus* was almost nowhere to be found in theatrical production or in mass culture other than in printed text. The reverse is now true, however, and Taymor even claims that younger audiences love her film. Whether or not they will be taught in high school, films of *Titus Andronicus* proliferate while, in the midst of an unprecedented glut of Shakespeare films over the last decade, no one has redone or announced his or her intention to redo *Julius Caesar*. And one would not expect a film of *Julius Caesar*, if one were now made, to be compared to a horror film.

Some critics might interpret this reversal as evidence of the further decline of the public sphere where horror movies have overtaken tragedy. Audiences are more bloodthirsty, more interested in film than theater, and film technology can deliver better special effects, more realistic violence. In the terms of this decline narrative, versions of which one can find in both left and right versions, one would argue that it is no accident that Taymor's *Titus* is set in a colosseum and that ancient Rome has reappeared in films such as Ridley Scott's *Gladiator* (2000) and Oliver Stone's *Any Given Sunday* (2000), which replays parts of the chariot scene in *Ben Hur* (William Wyler, 1959) to make a typically obvious equation between gladiators and football players.[32]

Departing from a moralistic and simplistic narrative of cultural decline, I would argue that so many cinematic versions of *Titus Andronicus* have recently been made both because of changes in Shakespeare's reproduction and reception and because of global political changes after the end of the Cold War. While *Julius Caesar* was at the center of the major conflicts of the twentieth century, (i.e., 1930's fascism, World War II, and the Cold War) films of *Titus Andronicus* preside at a moment of globalization lacking in major ideological conflicts such as capitalism versus communism, a moment in which the only real superpower left is the United States, but in which there are more wars being fought than ever, and with them more concentration camps. In the present world scene, it is harder to get one's political and cultural bearings, and divisions between left and right, it is commonly said, have shifted. In the 2000 U.S. Presidential campaign, for example, Ralph Nader and Pat Buchanan both wanted to see the end of the World Trade Organization. In this context, it should not be surprising that what one might call Paul Verhoeven's parafascist film, *Starship Troopers* (1997), was read by some critics as a glorification of fascism, imperialism, and militarism, by others as a critique (D'Amato and Rimanelli 2000). Given the universalization of the camp and the desacralization of the holocaust, it makes sense that the reading of *Julius Caesar* and *Coriolanus* as plays about a fascist leader and a fickle mob has become obsolete and that *Titus,* read as a play about fascist leader who cannot control the violence of his subjects becomes of widespread interest.[33]

Of the *Titus Andronicus* films that have been released in the late 1990s and the first year of the millennium, *Titus* is to my mind the most interesting not because of what it does with fascism, a problematic move I will explore shortly, but because of how it changes the meaning of antifascism, locating it not so much in political values—republican conspirators assassinating an imperial dictator, say, in *Julius Caesar*—as in psychotic violence. In the scene with Titus in a steaming bath that deliberately recalls Jacques-Louis David's famous painting of Marat, Taymor turns Titus into a kind of revolutionary journalist whose writings earlier literally pierced the court when tied to arrows shot by Titus and his allies. (The arrows puncture the floating mermaid and narrowly miss the people partying at court.)

As Revenge, Tamora becomes a failed counter-revolutionary Charlotte Corday. Even this association of Titus with revolutionary, republican values is compromised, however, by the fact that, unlike Marat, who has just been assassinated while reading Corday's letter in David's painting, Titus writes letters with his own blood in a literal bloodbath of his own making. The quotation of Marat's death calls up not so much the Declaration of the Rights of Man (1789) as it does the Reign of Terror (1793–94). Moreover, the revolutionary political coding of Titus, insofar as it is clear in this scene at all, is overridden by the dominant and more familiar coding of Titus that colors the entire film.

Because most audiences read backward from film to Shakespeare, Taymor's casting of Anthony Hopkins, given that Titus serves human flesh at his banquet, will inevitably call to the minds of many reviewers and other audiences the serial-killer cannibal, Hannibal Lector. The connection between Titus and Lector is underlined by Hopkins' quotation of his role in *Silence of the Lambs* when he sucks in his spit before slitting Chiron and Demetrius's throats. Perhaps Taymor had of necessity to cast Hopkins as the leading man because he was the only one with the star power and the ability willing to do it.[34] However she came to cast Hopkins, once she did and once she also decided on the fascist setting, Taymor's attempt to critique violence via fascism and the holocaust were inevitably in tension with her rein-scription of the horror genre.

The consequence for Taymor, in my view, is not that she compromises her critique of extreme violence represented by events such as the holocaust and unwittingly produces a horror film. The consequence is rather that in toning down the violence and making it a generational issue, Taymor reinscribes a fascist aesthetic and thus subverts her own critique of fascism and her re-demption of the play as a work of art rather than trash. Given the coding of Saturninus as a fascist politician, a Mussolini-like dictator, and Jessica Lange's appearance as Tamora, Shewolf of the SS Goths, the horror genre gives Titus's violence a new meaning. Titus becomes Lector/Titus, a serial killer who re-turns from one battle after another to do one sacrifice after another. He has come "five times / Bleeding to Rome" to do "sacrifice of expiation," making up for the deaths of his "valiant sons" by slaying "the noblest of the Goths" in previous battles, according to Marcus (1.1. 33–38). Taymor also changes the order of events in the first act, starting with Titus's return to Rome and putting the first 68 lines in which Saturninus and Bassinius vie for election after Alarbus's sacrifice. Changing the order of events this way highlights not only Alarbus's death and the dead Andronici that return with Titus but the fact that this violence has no origin and no apparent end. The scene in which Titus kills Mutius (Blake Ritson) is thus not really an aberration at all: hav-ing already lost twenty-one of his sons, what is the loss of another?

Resistance to fascism becomes in the film a kind of massive death-drive, and honor-killing in the play is transformed into psycho-killing in the film. Lector/Titus brings out the tendency already present in the play to produce an excessive amount of sadistic violence, an excess that lends itself to com-edy and parody. Lector/Titus's decision to side with Saturninus rather than Bassanius is not merely bad judgment but an act of psychotic destruction. Despite his support of primogeniture, Lector/Titus is not a traditionalist. Lector/Titus is deeply into entombing his twenty one out of twenty-five sons and sacrificing the prize Goth. Death for Lector/Titus is liberation:

> In peace and hour rest you here my sons;
> Rome's readiest champions, repose you here in rest,
> Secure from worldly chances and mishaps,
> Here lurks no treason, here no envy swells,
> Here grow no damned drugs, here are no storms,
> No noise, but silence and eternal sleep;
> In peace and honor rest you here, my sons. (1.1. 153–59)

Thus Lector/Titus is as willing to sacrifice his own sons as he is Alarbus. Lec-tor/Titus's psychotic violence is liberating and antifascist in that it contests the state's monopoly on violence, its capacity to say that some acts of violence are legitimate and sacred while others are not. Lector/Titus's freedom through violence extends to members of his own family, including Mutius, and Lavinia (Laura Fraser), whom he earlier suggested should commit suicide.

In addition to these sadistic acts of violence, Hopkins's Titus is revealed as a masochist. Hopkins has Titus smile before Saturninus kills him; his Lector/Titus does not raise a hand, much less put up a fight. Titus's death is continuous, then, with his own death drive, announced after he agrees to let Mutius be buried in the Andronici tomb ("Well, bury him, bury me the next." 1.1. 391). Hopkins also invites us to see Titus as a cannibal, further blurring the distinction between Tamora's family and his own. In two shots during the banquet, we see him chewing, but we can't be sure whether he really has pieces of the meat pies containing Chiron and Demetrius in his mouth or is merely imitating those who do. Antifascism in *Titus* is not collective rational resistance to a tyrannical state, but is located in the subjectivity of a hero who is both sadistic and masochistic and whose acts of violence do not respect distinctions between people who are in or out of his family.[35]

Rather than play up Titus as serial killer antifascist, however, Taymor tones him down and tends to play up children as relative innocents who have no legitimate access to violence. The P. A. N. s are meant to establish, according to Taymor, that the characters still have a conscience. In the case of Titus, the first two center on his killing of two children, Alarbus and Mutius. The first P. A. N. is a haunting of Titus and Tamora by Alarbus. Between the profiles of Tamora and Titus, we see marble-like body parts engulfed in flames flying toward the screen, then Alarbus's torso, breathing. Titus and Tamora both know that the reconciliation between Saturninus and Titus will not last. In the second arcade, this haunting is made an effect of Titus's conscience about his having killed Mutius. After Titus's aside in 3.1.16–22, angels appear and then a sacrificial lamb; the sacrificial sword that Titus had used to draw blood on Alarbus's chest then descends, and the head of the sheep turns into Mutius's head. Both Alarbus and Mutius are represented as innocent victims, and the effect is to humanize Titus as guilty father.

To sanctify the child survivor, Taymor not only introduces these P. A. N. s but moves away from the play's deconstruction of what Rene Girard (1991) would call good and bad violence toward an undeconstructed opposition between parents, who are violent, and children, who are less violent or nonviolent): the play, that is, deconstructs oppositions between violence enacted by the Goths and Romans, between Scythia and Rome ("Rome is but a wilderness of Tigers" [3.1. 54], "O cruel, irreligious piety" [1.1.133]; Titus's speech about the crypt and eternal sleep in 1.1.154–159 parallels Tamora's to Aaron about a golden slumber in 2.2.25–29; Lucius' twice-made remark that the Romans will "hew [Alarbus's] limbs" [1.1.110 and 132] is echoed by Marcus's description of the mutilated Lavinia, "lopped and hewed . . . of its two branches" [2.3.17–18]); and the barbed wire cage is used both for the Goth prisoners and for Titus's sons Martius and Quintus. To be sure, Taymor reinforces the play's deconstruction through a few visual parallels between Romans and Goths in *Titus* such as the cut from Saturninus reading in his court to Lucius reading in his tent between 4.4. and 5.1, and the echoing of Aaron's licking his tongue in the air at Lucius when Lucius beats him and Titus's licking his tongue in the air at Chiron when Chiron appears at Titus's house cross-dressed as Rape. Yet Taymor's central focus is on generational differences. Lucius looks better morally than Titus because of major cuts Taymor makes in the ending. And Taymor's Lucius lets Aaron's child survive as well. Taymor even turns Titus into a child. In the bath that recalls David's painting of the death of Marat, Titus is, Taymor says, a "naked baby."[36]

The sanctification of children registered in these P. A. N. s is present as well in the greatly expanded role of young Lucius (Osheen Jones) as a framing character at the beginning and the end, as in Jane Howell's 1985 BBC television production, and a witness throughout the film. The sanctification is clearest in the ending of *Titus,* which I believe to be its weakest part. Taymor cuts the grotesque moment in the play when Marcus, Lucius, and then young Lucius all successively kiss the lips of Titus's corpse. Instead, she has young Lucius open up the cage in which Aaron's infant has been placed and then pick the baby up and hold him. In the final, prolonged, and schlocky shot of the film, young Lucius walks with the baby out of the arena into a sunrise much as the boy Eliot carried the alien E.T. when they rode together on a bike off into the sky in Spielberg's *E. T.* Young Lucius, of course, cannot possibly know how to care for Aaron's baby. It's a moment worthy of a "Kids Raising Kids" episode of Rikki Lake.

To her credit, Taymor makes the difference between adults and children a nuanced one. Children are not inherently innocent, nor are all children innocent in the film. The redemptive force of the final scene is heightened by its contrast with earlier scenes in which Lucius appeared to be a violent successor to Titus (like grandfather, like son): in the opening frame, Taymor has the boy anticipate Titus in eating food as he stabs his toys and spills sugar and ketchup on them. Along similar lines, she has the young Lucius rather than Marcus kill the fly at dinner and speak the lines about doing so, and young Lucius accompanies Titus when Titus enlists other relatives to shoot arrows to the gods so that he may gain justice. This early violence, including the opening scene of the boy playing with his war toys, throws Lucius's later pacifism into bold relief.

Lucius is similarly contrasted with the Clown and little girl the age of young Lucius. Unlike Lucius, who becomes less violent as the film proceeds, the Clown, who rescues Lucius when his kitchen gets bombed, later is associated with violence, driving a truck much like the murderous strongman Zampano's in Fellini's *La Strada* (1954). The Clown turns out to be a man who uses violence as spectacle. A little girl arrives with him and initially seems to be innocent, setting up chairs for the smiling Lucius, Titus, Lavinia, and Marcus so they may watch an apparently innocuous entertainment. As it turns out, however, she is the bearer of horror, for the side of the truck flies up to reveal the decapitated and embalmed head of his son and his severed hand. She is perhaps a future Tamora. Nevertheless, by confining the horror genre to Lector/Titus and by playing up children as less violent, Taymor actually reinstalls a fascistic celebration of the child, as Kenneth Branagh did earlier in his *Henry V* (1989) when he interpolated a scene in which Henry V carries the boy Davy's corpse across the muddy battlefield after the English have won the battle of Agincourt as "Non nobis domine" (Not unto us, O Lord, not unto us, but unto thy name give glory) plays on the soundtrack. It is precisely the innocent child, dead or alive, who often legitimates violence against the Other in German and Italian fascist cinema.[37]

The sanctification of the pacific child is for Taymor a critique of media violence in the name of liveness. The film's opening, in which the boy plays with various kinds of toy soldiers and sci-fi figures before being taken into the colosseum, and the film's ending, in which we return to the colosseum before young Lucius leaves it, constitute a turn away from media violence (marked not only by the war toys but by the video arcade sequence with Chrion and Demetrius). Though framed in pointedly symmetrical terms, the turn back to the child does not exactly mirror the film's beginning but is preceded by the most mediatized, spectacular moment of the film; namely, when Lucius's killing of Saturninus by shoving a spoon into his mouth and brain is stopped by time splice editing and the spoon is replaced by a gun. Immediately after Lucius shoots Saturninus, Taymor cuts back into the colosseum staging the banquet as if it were a live performance, and, unlike the opening sequence, we get a number of shots of a silent, live audience. The movement from violent to pacific young Lucius is also, in short, a movement from mass media and digital film editing to live theater. Taymor's suggestion that there is quite literally a way out of the play rather naïvely misreads Shakespeare's own much darker and more self-conscious allegorization of aesthetic representation via the media of theater and print narrative (puns, Marcus's set speech upon discovering Lavinia after she is raped; Lavinia's disclosure of her rapists via a copy of Ovid's *Metamorphoses;* and so on) in which aesthetic excess destabilizes precisely the kinds of oppositions Taymor wants to affirm and correlate: between high art (film) and trash (blockbuster); Shakespeare and Shakesploitation; a critique of violence and an embrace of violence; modesty versus sexual perversion; and sacred and profane. Shakespeare suggests that the notion that closure has been achieved by Lucius's selection and his casting out of Aaron and Tamora is a deluded mystification achieved only by scapegoating, and the various lowbrow film and video Schlockspeare adaptations of the play mentioned arguably come much closer to Shakespeare's aesthetic excess than does Taymor's *Titus*.[38]

Springtime for Shakespeare in Italy

It is not a surprise that Taymor should have tuned into the fascism channel for her adaptation of Shakespeare's tragedy. In this respect, as in so many others, Taymor's film is quite derivative.[39] The analogy between *Titus Andronicus* and the holocaust has been around at least since 1955, when one reviewer faulted Peter Brooks's influential production for making the play too remote historically. "For post-Buchenwald generations," one reviewer wrote, "the play's profligate brutalities no longer seemed comfortably remote, or ridiculous." (Dessen 1989, 21) Douglas Seale mounted the first fascist *Titus* production at the Center Stage in Baltimore in 1967, with Saturninus looking like Mussolini and Titus as a Prussian officer. The Andronici were portrayed as Nazis and the Goths as Allied Forces (33–34). When the Clown is executed we see a Jewish star on his back. Trevor Nunn (1972) had the cast see Federico Fellini's *Satyricon* (1979) and supplied a stage orgy at the beginning of 4.2. (37). And *Titus Andronicus* was not the first Shakespeare play to be viewed in the light of 1930s fascism. In addition to the Orson Welles production I mentioned earlier, Joseph Mankiewicz filmed an antifascist production of *Julius Caesar*.[40] And some reviewers compared Taymor's film to the more recent stage production and film of Ian McKellen's interpretation of Shakespeare's *Richard III* as a 1930s English fascist leader.[41] Shakespeare has also been enlisted in the much earlier antifascist comedy *To Be or Not to Be* [dir. Ernest Lubitsch, 1942] with Jack Benny and Carole Lombard and then remade in 1983 by Alan Johnson with Mel Brooks and Anne Bancroft. The comedy is set in the Warsaw Ghetto just as Hitler invades Poland, with Benny/Brooks playing Hamlet and impersonating Hitler.

Yet, as in so many other areas, the Nazis' uses of Shakespeare complicate antifascist attempts to critique them by pinning the Nazis down on one side of a given binary opposition, either for or against Shakespeare. Shakespeare was the most produced playwright in Nazi Germany until World War II, and criticism produced pro-Hitler commentary. *Coriolanus* was compared favorably to Hitler by one critic, for example.[42] And Hitler expressly forbade the bombing of Stratford-upon-Avon because it was Shakespeare's birthplace. The Nazi Propaganda Ministry's protocols for the Jewish Kulturbund Theater, organized, sponsored, and protected, until 1941, by the Nazis, stated: "On principle, theater is allowed. There are no reservations about Shakespeare. All authors of German descent or those who belong to the Reich Theater Chamber are excluded from consideration" (Rovit and Goldfarb 1999, 77). Strikingly, Shakespeare was even approved by the Nazis in the camps. The SS encouraged productions of Shakespeare, among other dramatists. One prisoner translated *Measure for Measure* into Czech and another told précis of Shakespeare plays. Yet knowing how to act Shakespeare, we probably will not be surprised to learn, didn't save one's life in the camps. A planned production of *Twelfth Night* in Terezin, the "model" concentration camp just outside Prague, had to be abandoned after the actors were taken away in a new wave of transports (Rovit and Goldfarb 1999, 181; 243). The capacity of a Shakespeare actor named Gustaf Gruendgens to be on both Communist and Nazi sides was explored in *Mephisto* (dir. Istvan Szabo 1981; see also Hortmann 1998, 126–27; 156–61).

Taymor's shift of the fascist setting from Germany to Italy complicates her critique of fascism even further. Mussolini outflanked Hitler in architecture, painting, and the cinema, which he ranked as the most potent weapon, by combining the avant-garde with classicism instead of turning away from the avant-garde to embrace socialist realism.[43] Unlike Germany, Italy has made next to no attempt to own its fascist period and its own participation in the holocaust, and many of its major filmmakers' postwar work was compromised. Roberto Rossellini and Fellini had made fascist propaganda films, and Fellini made films soft on fascism such as *Amarcord* (1974). Even cinematic attacks on Italian fascism are problematic for their sexual politics, including Bernardo Bertolucci's *The Conformist* (1970) and *1900* (1976), Vittorio de Sica's *The Garden of the Finzi-Continis* (1970), Palo Pasolini's *Salo* (1975), Liliana Cavani's *The Night Porter* (1974), Lina Wertmuller's *The Seven Beauties* (1976), Luchino Visconti's *The Damned* (1969), and, most recently, Roberto Benigni's *Life Is Beautiful* (1998). The fascist appears in these films as the sexual pervert, notably in *The Damned,* which uses imagery taken from the gay cabaret scene to indict the upper classes as decadent. They deploy the same imagery and rhetorical strategies, as Kriss Ravetto (2001) argues, that the Fascists had deployed to attack the left.

Titus has several obvious flaws along these very lines. Taymor's film uses Shakespeare to make a critique of violence issuing ultimately in the mass exterminations of the holocaust, but ends up redeploying fascist iconography so that the fascists are also sexual perverts. Some critics might say that Julie Taymor's *Titus* should really have been called Julie Tamora's *Titus Androgynous.* Chiron is made to look gay as he dances like a go-go dancer in the pool room and later wears his hair in braided pigtails. The orgy scene begins with a shot of two men making love. Saturninus is also a sexual pervert, more like the son of Tamora than her husband, as we see her holding him when they are in bed in the nude. And the polymorphous, perverse Saturninus is not, of course, a father. Ironically, Alan Cumming had a haircut while filming *Titus* as a consequence of the fact that he was playing the flaming gay master of ceremonies in a Broadway revival *Cabaret,* the musical inspired by gay writer Christopher Isherwood's *Berlin Stories.*

The Andronici are desexualized, by contrast. Taymor's Tight-ass Andronicus, as it were, has no interest in sex. He strolls down the street with prostitutes on it, for example, lost in thought as he walks to the crypt. This desexualization produces a similar problem to the sexualization of Saturninus and the Goths when it comes to Lavinia's representation. Taymor adopts a right-wing feminism in which women and sex do not mix. Lavinia and Tamora are deliberately contrasted in terms of their sexuality. Tamora goes from unkempt Goth at the beginning of the film, pleading earnestly for her son's life, to a sexual monster with armor and massive hairpiece. Her sexualization is to be read as a sign of her moral corruption by her desire for revenge. By contrast, Lavinia's moral purity is represented by her lack of sexuality. In the P. A. N. of her rape, Lavinia is sexualized in the iconic moment in *The Seven Year Itch* (dir. Billy Wilder, 1955) where Marilyn Monroe stands over a grating without embarrassment while the air from the subway passing below blows up her dress. Taymor hyperbolically condemns this wonderful comic moment: "There's something about that image of Marilyn Monroe with the wind blowing up her dress which is an incredible rape. This woman has to hold her skirt down and there's the roar of the subway going underneath" (Wrathall 2000, 26). To stress Lavinia's purity, Taymor put her on a treestump pedestal like a ballerina of Edgar Degas. Sexuality, then, is made the equivalent of the violent act of rape, something that happens to (good) women rather than something that is a part of them. Only bad women like Tamora are in charge of their sexual pleasure. Finally, some critics may also fault the film for casting a light-skinned black man to play Aaron and for having a white child pick up the baby in a way that makes the exit from the colosseum appear to be the introduction of a new, racialized hierarchy, as if young Lucius were taking up the white boy's burden.

The film's indirect analogy between violence in the play and violence in the holocaust also produces an unsettling deconstruction of aggressor and victim. The ethnic group that risks extermination here—the imprisoned Goths—moves rapidly from being arbitrary and dehumanized sacrifices to having the run of the place and ruling the ruler. Aaron's status as a member of another marginalized group who comes totally, if briefly, to power and who is then tortured to death complicates things still further.

In addition to reproducing a fascist aesthetic and fascistic sexual and racial politics in the name of a child-centered antifascism, *Titus* is also open to an almost opposite critique, namely, that it is not political enough, that it depoliticizes violence. As Taymor comments in the epigraph to this chapter, she reads "every day" something significant about violence in the present and not too distant past out of *Titus Andronicus.*[44] The holocaust is one atrocity among others. And even the oft-drawn parallels between the holocaust and the concentration camps in Bosnia go without comment, as does Shakespeare's relation to the Bosnia conflict. Although the colosseum Taymor used in *Titus* is located in Pula, Croatia, and although the audience sitting in it at the end of the film are Croations, Taymor does not mention (nor does any other critic of the film), that Shakespeare's Sonnet 66 ("Tired with all these, for restful death I cry") has been extremely popular in Croatia as a protest song since the1950s. (Pfister forthcoming)[45]

Yet to dismiss *Titus* on the basis of these criticisms would be a mistake, I think. For one thing, to ask *Titus* or any other film to unmake fascism is to ask it to meet an impossible standard. Even if Taymor had played up Titus as serial killer more and played down the role of children, similar problems would have come up as the film took a turn toward camp. Mel Brooks acknowledged the unpredictability of representations of the Nazis in *The Producers,* in which a musical called *Springtime for Hitler* intended to be a flop instead becomes a smash hit, and Brooks alludes to the tasteless production in his remake of *To Be or Not to Be* in which the Jewish cast performs a number called *Naughty Nazis.*[46] And a deliberate turn toward a campy representation of the camp would not have saved *Titus* either. That strategy was already tried and adopted by the Sex Pistols in the late 1970s with "Belsen Was a Gas" and "Holiday in the Sun." In *Lipstick Traces,* Greil Marcus sees the Sex Pistols as the end of the avant-garde, their songs imploding in the band's short-lived career, and soon taken over by events such as a holocaust theme park proposed in 1980. A former English army sergeant came up with an idea for what he thought of as the ideal British vacation, namely, a trip to an imitation Nazi prison camp. "They'll have a horrible time and love every minute of it, or I'll want to know the reason why, " the sergeant was quoted as saying (Marcus 1988,122–23).

I would also want to defend *Titus* for the way it mixes historical periods. Taymor comments, "In productions in Shakespeare's day, they wore Elizabethan clothes and togas. Shakespeare was blending times and so am I, playing with reference points so you get a feeling about the 20th century—this imagery of totalitarianism" (Wrathall 2000, 25). In the opening sequence, children's toys are taken from different periods, and include Star Wars figures, G. I. Joes, and Goths and Romans. Similarly, in the colosseum, the soldiers drive tanks and ride motorcycles and horses, much as they do in the election parade. The costumes span periods, with the soldiers wearing Etruscan armor, Lavinia dressed as Grace Kelly in the 1950s, and Tamora as a woman from the 1930s. Rome itself is represented as "stratified."[47] Thus Rome is both Mussolini's, itself a mix of the ancient and the avant-garde, and Emperor Hadrian's (some of the scenes were shot in Hadrian's villa). Fake cobblestones were also placed on the ground to form ancient Roman-like roads in modern settings. Other temporal markers are mixed techno-logically, as with the use of the archaic penny arcade and MTV video and time-slicing editing.

Despite the intended use of P. A. N. s to construct internal memories for the characters through lyric interludes, they work against linear narrative, in my view, and defy the conventions by which a sequence is recognized as a character's flashback. They bear a relation less to realist cinema than to avant-garde and expressionist cinema. By mixing historical periods, Taymor disrupts, perhaps in spite of herself, any attempt to construct a narrative in which one could say either that the holocaust is foundational for Shake-spearean violence on film or that Shakespeare is foundational for our un-derstanding of the holocaust.

Even if one were to persist in saying that the problem with *Titus* is that it depoliticizes violence and universalizes the holocaust, the force of that cri-tique would be limited by the fact that it is not clear what a political read-ing of either the violence in *Titus* or in the holocaust would be. In his essay on holocaust comedies, Žižek makes an abrupt swerve in his final two para-graphs to Muslims and Bosnia camps:

> The Muslim is the zero point at which the opposition between tragedy and comedy, between the sublime, and the ridiculous, between dignity and deri-sion is suspended, the point at which one passes into its opposite. If we try to present their predicament as tragic, the result is comic; if we treat them as comic, tragedy emerges . . . Can one imagine a film rendering this? (2000, 29)

Žižek equates the Jewish concentration camp with the Muslim camp and re-produces the same claim for Muslim camps as the one that governed the Jewish holocaust, namely, that film cannot render it. So the Muslim be-comes a bigger victim than the Jew because not even comedy can represent (by knowing it fails to represent) the Muslim camp. Muslim suffering is thus legitimated on the model of the depoliticized holocaust Žižek critiques. If, as Agamben maintains, the camp is the paradigm of modernity, we might fault Taymor only for thinking it is possible to exit from it.

The Sub-lime Object of Shakespearology

I would like to close by considering some of the implications the exchange between Shakespeare and the holocaust has for Shakespeare criticism. In ad-dition to considering why so many directors want to make the film as we did earlier, we might also consider the resurgence of critical interest in the play, and not just in avowedly progressive critics. Why would a neoconservative like Jonathan Bate, we might wonder, want to redeem the play in his Arden edition and then defend Taymor's film, which, after all, takes many liberties with the play, not only rearranging scenes and adding material but cutting about an hour and a half of the script? By way of an answer, I would say that Bate, like any Shakespearean critic in the present, has to write in response to what I earlier called Shakespeare's trash, schlock status. Bate articulates a neomodernist aesthetic, defending what he anachronistically calls "Renaissance High Culture" (1995) through its reproduction in mass culture, especially film.

A fervent admirer of the reactionary film critic Michael Medved, Bate begins his introduction to the Arden edition by comparing the playgoer to the moviegoer: "Audiences may still be disturbed by the play's representations of bloody revenge, dismemberment, miscegenation, rape, and cannibalism, but theatergoers who are also moviegoers will be familiar with this kind of material" (Bate 1995, 1–2). Turning then to the BBC production, Bate mentions that the actress playing Lavinia, Anna Calder-Marshall, compared the play to a "video nasty." Following upon Calder-Marshall's comment that Titus learns about love by being maimed and by Lavinia's being maimed, Bate compares the play to *King Lear* and then elevates both plays above movies: "To understand *Titus Andronicus* thus is at once to perceive its proximity to *King Lear* and to apprehend the difference between a slasher movie and a tragedy" (2). Yet this distinction between tragedy and slasher films falls apart the moment one turns to cinematic productions of *King Lear*. Bate is able to elevate *Titus* above horror films only by forgetting that Shakespeare is most likely to be encountered today by television and moviegoers, not theatergoers. Moreover, Bate has to ignore the ways in which *Titus* is itself schlock, and hence not completely distinct from the trashier film versions of the play nor from slasher films. An archconservative like Harold Bloom asserts precisely this equivalence in terms of the play itself: *Titus Andronicus* is "the Shakespearean equivalent of what we now respond to in Stephen King and in much cinema" (1998, 78). And it is this very equivalence that leads Bloom to dismiss the play. While more conservative than Bate, Bloom too feels the need to engage with film and mass culture to provide a similar street credibility. Though Bloom denigrates performances of the plays and elevates reading them as literature, he went to see *Shakespeare in Love* and refers to media positively, despite his "Bloom brontosaurus" self-label, and his former student Camille Paglia does so even more. For example, having last seen *Titus Andronicus* in 1955, Bloom says "I don't think I would see the play again unless Mel Brooks directed it, with his company of zanies, or perhaps it could yet be made into a musical" (86). Like Bate, Bloom distinguishes between Shakespeare and schlock; he just draws the line between them in a different place.

More progressive critics might argue that Bate's reactionary neomodernism is a canny attempt to co-opt the potential for radical representation that film offers while Bloom's dismissal of the play is simply a more old-fashioned and funnier suppression of the play in the name of a more high-minded vision of Shakespeare's invention of what it means to be human. But their shared distinction between Shakespeare and schlock is drawn by more progressive critics as well, who are caught in a similar contradiction between elevating some Shakespeares as the bearers of aesthetic and cultural value and dismissing other ShaXXXspeares as trash. In one recent study of Shakespeare on film, for example, an avowedly progressive critic invokes films like *Clueless* to justify the study of Shakespeare on film but excludes any film that is not a canonical adaptation.[48]

In this reading of *Titus* and (the) camp and my discussion of the exchanges between representations of the holocaust and performances of Shakespeare, I have tried to suggest that it is in the cross-currents of schlock—sometimes in episodes of talk shows like *The Maury Povich Show*—that Shakespeare films (and holocaust memorials as well) must now necessarily be read if we are to grasp fully both their strengths and their limitations. We might consider what it means to address trashy Shakespeare by asking how we might deal with the openly schlocky cinematic productions of *Titus Andronicus?* Both (neo)cons and many progressives would no doubt separate out Taymor's *Titus* from the other slasher adaptation as an art-house film and as a pedagogical film. The child Lucius is set up as a witness to violence, like the audience who appears in the colosseum in the film's closing moments. In her preachy director's commentary, Taymor says she has Lucius kill Saturninus a second time because young Lucius has to understand "where the violence goes." Young Lucius learns a lesson about playing war with little toys, and the lesson is reinforced when we see bad boy Demetrius playing video-arcade games. As we have seen, however, this moralistic display of violence in order to abjure it foundered on its own excesses, and it is doubtful the film will be taught in high schools. Taymor participates in the present generational shift away from parent-centered child-rearing practices to child-centered child-rearing practices in a completely unselfconscious manner. And Shakespeare critics have yet to reflect on it, either in terms of what it means for the reception of "adult" Shakespeare adaptations or for the recent production of Shakespeare books and CD-ROMs for children.[49]

Yet inverting the hierarchy between art house and slasher adaptations in order to find some kind of subversion in the unspeakably trashy versions would seem to founder as well, though for the opposite reason, namely, that they are not excessive enough: they are much too low-tech in comparison with films like *Scream* (dir. Wes Craven, 1996) and its sequels, and the absence of special effects makes the violence represented in them seem laughable rather than gruesome and horrific. Perhaps a video-game version of *Titus Andronicus* will someday be released, the goal being to kill and cook as many Goths or as many Romans as you can. Whether that game would have enough to do with the play for critics to be able to interpret it or would be yet another post-hermeneutic, unspeakably schlocky ShaXXXspeare, however, remains to be seen.

Notes

I would like to thank Laurie Osborne and Judith Haber for their typically astute and insightful comments on earlier drafts of this chapter, and John Archer, Jonathan Bate, Don Hedrick, and Jennifer Stone for suggestions made in conversation about it.

1. See also Agamben, and De Vries and Weber. The Fox Network imitation *Survivor* reality television show entitled *Boot Camp*, aired in April 2001, offered further material for these speculations.

2. Former Israeli Foreign Secretary Abba Eban was the first, as far as I know, to observed that "There's no business like Shoah business." See also Kramer, 261, and Cole 2000 for a critique of the theme-parking of the holocaust as "Auschwitz-land." And see Bauman for a similar and very powerful critique of the sacralization of the holocaust.

3. On these films, see Žižek and Gilman. On holocaust laughter, see Viano. A gigantic Ferris wheel hung with deportation cars was proposed for the Holocaust memorial in Berlin. See Kramer, 285. And recently, one critic of the Berlin Jewish Museum has invoked Disneyland: "The Jewish Museum building is interesting, but to me it's a Holocaust sculpture, not a museum," said Julius Schoeps, the director of the Moses Mendelssohn Center, a Jewish research foundation, and a prominent member of the Berlin Jewish community. "And now there is an attempt to adorn it in a very American way, to make a museum of experiences with what I have called a Disneyland aesthetic" (Cohen).

4. See Taymor's commentary on the scene in the DVD edition.

5. *King Lear* comes up in the context of a marriage negotiation. Misha (Lev Schreiber), a boxer, asks for the hand of Rosa (Nina Siemaszko), from her father and mother, Mr. and Mrs. Frankfurter (Alan Arkin and Grazyna Barzsczweska). When Mr. Frankfurter opposes the marriage on the grounds that all of the Jews in the ghetto have no future, Misha replies that the war will end very soon because the Russians are at Bezonica. Misha asks Frankfurter "Do you know where Bezonica is?" and Frankfurter replies: "Do I know where Bezonica is? I played King Lear there three times. 'As flies to . . . ' (he pauses and tries to remember the rest of the line). Mrs. Frankfurter helps by adding 'As flies to wanton boys') and Frankfurter then remembers: 'As flies to wanton boys, they kill us for their sport.'" Misha supports his claim that he heard it from Jakob Heym (Robin Williams), who has a radio. Frankfurter consents to the marriage, but destroys his own

radio, which he fears will be found and will then result in his being shot and hung after the Nazis find out about Heym's radio and search the ghetto for radios. Coincidentally, the lines from *King Lear* cited in *Jakob the Liar* were meant to be suggested when young Lucius kills a fly in Deborah Warner's production of *Titus Andronicus*. See Bate, 67. Bate tries to link *Titus Andronicus* and *King Lear* throughout his Arden introduction. See Bate, 2 and 121, for examples. See also his introduction to the screenplay, 12. Some audience members of *Jakob the Liar* may also recall that Robin Williams, who stars in the remake, also played roles in films citing Shakespeare such as *Dead Poets Society* (dir. Peter Weir, 1989) and *What Dreams May Come* (dir. Vincent Ward, 1998), the title of which comes from Hamlet's "To be or not to be" soliloquy.

6. The reference to Hamlet and Ophelia is noted by Isser, 92 and the references to the gravedigger and the ghost are noted by Feinberg, 272.

7. There is a review of the production in *Shakespeare Jahrbuch*, 132 (1996), p. 174 ff.

8. Thus in the Berlin competition, there was "no aesthetic solution," but the jury was certain one would be found. See Kramer, 284.

9. See Young 2000 where "after images" and "art" exist in a vague and uneasy relation. See also Young 1999.

10. For one example, see the response to the Berlin competition in which a reviewer says he was repelled and that he was the only one not laughing. Kramer, 284–85.

11. For a brilliant reading of this poem and Plath and the holocaust, see Rose 1992.

12. Spielberg reportedly supported Taymor's film after viewing a test screening (Carver).

13. Bate's introduction is reprinted in a slightly revised form on pp. 8–13.

14. For interviews, see de Luca and Lindroth, and Schechner. For the Titus websites, go to http://www.clearblueskyfilms.com/featurefilms/titus and http://www.foxsearchlight.com/titus.

15. It was also included in an advertisement I received from Arden in July 2000.

16. For the websites for the films other than *Titus,* go to http://www.richeyproductions.com, http://home1.gte.net/titus98/, http://www.titusandronicus.8m.com/tituspage.html.

17. See Taymor's comments in two interviews: "I am so sick of stories like *Pulp Fiction* where you have a bunch of low-lifes being violent in a stereotypical low-life way. No real story" (Schechner, 45). "It's OK to have 'The Matrix' and blow everybody up and laugh at 'Pulp Fiction,' but, whoa, if you should do something that's beautiful like sex. It's so weird. It's so sick." Interview by Joel Snyder, National Endowment for the Arts, http://bayarea.citysearch.com/E/V/SFOCA/2024/75/38/.

18. In the Dunne production, all violence, including Lavinia's rape, is represented as graphically as possible, and additional acts of violence are interpolated in separate scenes or added to scenes whenever possible. Martius and

Quintus have their ears severed in a scene that recalls Quentin Tarentino's *Reservoir Dogs* (1993) and Aaron kills not only the nurse but the midwife as well. At the banquet, Titus stabs Aaron's child and Marcus smashes the child's head into a wall.

19. One interviewer comments, "She acknowledges that some people say there are specific scenes of beheadings or mutilations, but, she says, 'There's none of that stuff.' As an example, she refers to the depiction of violence against Lavinia, Titus's only daughter: 'You never see her hands being cut off, or her tongue, or any of that; that's off screen. But you do see the aftermath. Instead of stumps at her wrists, her arms end in twigs, and it's very surreal as she's left on a stump in the middle of a swamp.' Referring to one of the film's rare concrete and realistic scenes of violence, she notes 'There's a moment where, onscreen, Titus's hand is cut off in the kitchen. Again, you never see the cleaver go into the hand." Not seeing it, she agrees, is probably more effective. 'It's about violence, as opposed to being a violent movie.'" Interview with Joel Snyder, National Endowment for the Arts, http://bayarea.city-search.com/E/V/SFOCA/2024/75/38/.

20. The play is famous for moments of laughter or that produce laugher, including Titus's own laughter, "Ha, ha ha!" 3.1. 165 when his severed hand and the heads of Quintus and Martius are returned to him; Quintus falling in the pit with the slain Bassanius after Demetrius falls in the pit; Marcus, Lucius, Titus competing over whose hand should redeem Quintus and Martius; and Titus's severed hand in Lavinia's mouth. Taymor does use humor when she has Aaron place Titus's severed hand in a baggy and when she cuts from the killing of Chiron and Demetrius to the shot of steaming baked pies cooling on a window sill.

21. See the DVD commentary in the *Penny Arcade Nightmares* chapter on disc two.

22. See, for examples, Snead and Stone. In what is perhaps an intentional echo of the Titus as Hannibal connection in *Titus*, Rildey Scott has Hannibal Lecter play at being Titus by having Lecter cut off his left hand with a meat cleaver at the climax of *Hannibal* (2001).

23. http://www.horror.net/gorezone/anglais/june00.html

24. Janofsky writes: "And, as if to lift from their parents any sense of guilt, remorse or responsibility, Mr. Harris quietly quotes Shakespeare: 'Good wombs have born bad sons.'" Holden, B19 mentions the Columbine killings, though not the Shakespeare quotation, in his review of *Titus*.

25. See Thompson 2000 and Carver 1999.

26. AP, January 5, 2000. News; A11. See also AP, January 3, 2000.

27. See also Scholes, 1998. Scholes concludes that the "quasi-religious status once accorded English literature . . . is hardly viable any longer" (19).

28. See Burt 1999.

29. On *Clueless,* see Boose and Burt 1997 and Burt 1999.

30. Taymor says "Shakespeare's plays are screenplays" (Pizzerello), and Bate opens his introduction to the screenplay by saying, "If Shakespeare were alive today he would be writing and directing movies" (8).

31. *Coriolanus* was the second most important play, staged by the Nazis, Brecht, and Welles. It was not filmed then, nor has it been since. See Halpern 1997, 51–52; Habicht; and Reynolds. Two television adaptations have been made, however.

32. The chariot scene from *Ben Hur* was earlier updated in George Lucas's *Star Wars Episode 1: The Phantom Menace* (1999). Ancient Rome is called up in these films in a late imperial context. Unlike *Spartacus* (Stanley Kubrick, 1960), in which one can die a heroic martyr for a collective political good, embodied in the surviving wife and son, *Gladiator* narrowly limits the meaning of the hero's death to the fulfillment of a personal dream of reunion with his wife and son, who had been slain earlier by his enemies.

33. *Julius Caesar* has not entirely disappeared from view, of course. In the film *Free Enterprise* (dir. Robert Meyer Burnett, 1999), for example, William Shatner performs a rap version of Antony's funeral oration called "No Tears for Caesar." Originally, however, the script used *Titus Andronicus*. That play was rejected as too obscure to be recognized by the average filmgoer. See Director's commentary on the DVD edition. For a discussion of this film, see my introduction. *Julius Caesar* ("Let slip the dogs of war," in both cases) is also cited in *Army of Darkness* (dir. Sam Raimi, 1993) and *Star Trek VI* (dir. Nicholas Meyer, 1991). In a kind of throwback to Welles, a local production of *Julius Caesar* sponsored by the Green Party was performed in Amherst, Massachusetts the weekend before the November 7, 2000 U. S. Presidential Election.

34. The parallel was predictably noted by at least two reviewers. See Morrow and Baltake, *Titus* http://www.movieclub.com/reviews/archives/00titus/titus.html.

35. In contrast to Titus, Aaron kills the Nurse in order to defend his child.

36. DVD commentary.

37. To be sure, fascist cinema does not have a monopoly of images of innocent children. Bertolucci condemns a fascist in *1900* (1976) by having him brutally and horrifically kill a child by smashing his head in.

38. Deborah Warner's BBC production *Titus Andronicus* is very effective at unsettling both Marcus's and Lucius's claim to have achieved closure by showing close-ups of what looks like a casket with Aaron's (apparently dead) child inside, which young Lucius clutches, and by young Lucius's refusal to kiss Titus's corpse. Like Taymor, Warner distinguishes between the generations by suggesting that the younger is more human and more sensitive; unlike Taymor, however, Warner suggests that the younger generation has no power to effect political change by ending violence.

39. Jane Howell used the young Lucius to frame the play's action for her 1984 BBC television production. Peter Greenaway's representation of Caliban in *Prospero's Books* (1991) led one reviewer to compare Caliban to a concentration camp victim. See Adair.

40. On *Julius Caesar* and fascism, see Anderegg, 26–29 and Halperin, 51–113.

41. Joanne Akalitis set her 1989 New York production of Caroline dramatist John Ford's *'Tis Pity She's a Whore,* starring Val Kilmer, in Mussolini's Italy, and Ian McKellen and then Richard Loncarine set *Richard III* in an English fascist setting of the 1930s. See Greenblatt.

42. See Halpern 1997, 52, and on *Coriolanus,* Reynolds 2000.
43. On how Mussolini installed the cinema industry, defended against Hollywood product, and endowed Cinecittà, see Bondanella. On Italian fascism, see Nowell-Smith, and on the cult of ancient Rome in Italian fascism, see Duggan, 227–28. See also Landy; Sitney; and Mancini.
44. For similar remarks, see also Taymor's making of the film documentary on the DVD edition.
45. Pfister comments: "It has been translated at least five times in Tito's Yugoslavia and was sung on stage during a highly controversial production of *Macbeth* in 1973. Later it even became a hit, when one of our most popular singers, Ibriça Jusic, sung it in concerts and recorded it." Pfister also documents the circulation of Sonnet 66 in Nazi and post - World War II Germany.
46. There is an awkward moment that approaches the grimness of Lina Wertmueller's *Seven Beauties* near the end of Johnson's *To Be or Not to Be* when the gay dresser of Anna Bronski helps a frightened elderly couple dressed as clowns to make their escape from the theater full of Nazi officers in the audience. The dresser slaps Jewish stars on the couple, fires a toy gun at them from which a Nazi flag pops out, and then marches them out while shouting "Juden, Juden" as the officers laugh. On the Lubitsch original, see Tifft.
47. Taymor uses the word in her DVD commentary.
48. There is no mention of *Tromeo and Juliet,* for example, nor any of many other examples of what I have called "unspeakable ShaXXXspeares" (Burt 1999).
49. See the introduction to this book for some examples.

Works Cited

Adair, Gilbert. 1991. Review of *Prospero's Books. Guardian,* September 5, 26.
Adorno, Theodor. 1965. "Engagement." In *Notizen zur Literatur.* Vol. 3. Frankfurt: Suhrkamp Verlag, 125–27.
Agamben, Giorgio, 1998. *Homo Sacer: Sovereign Power and Bare Life.* Stanford, CA: Stanford Univ. Press.
———. 1999. *Remnants of Auschwitz: The Witness and the Archive.* Trans. by Daniel Heller. New York : Zone Books.
Anderegg, Michael. 1999. *Orson Welles, Shakespeare, and Popular Culture.* New York: Columbia Univ. Press.
Anon. 1999. "Lear Meets Hannibal Lector, OK?" *New York Times.* December 24, B1.
Associated Press. "Bard's *Titus* Too Hot for Censors: Director of 'Excess of Horrors' Forced to Slash Film to get R-rating." *Ottawa Citizen,* January 5, 2000, Wednesday, Final News; A11.
———. 2000. *Titus* Needs Violence To Make Point, Director Says," *The Toronto Star,* January 3, Edition 1.
Arendt, Hannah. 1963. *Eichmann in Jerusalem.* New York: Viking Press.
Bate. Jonathan. 1995. *Titus Andronicus.* New Arden. New York and London: Routledge.
Bauman, Zygmant. 1989. *Modernity and the Holocaust.* Cambridge, MA: MIT Press.

Bloom, Harold. 1998. *Shakespeare and the Invention of the Human.* New York: Riverhead Books.

Baltake, Joe. 2000. "*Titus*" http://www.movieclub.com/reviews/archives/00titus/titus.html.

Blumenthal, Eileen and Julie Taymor. 2000. *Julie Taymor, Playing with Fire: Theater, Opera, Film.* Updated and expanded ed. New York, Harry N. Abrams.

Bondanella, Peter. 1990. *Italian Cinema: From Neorealism to the Present.* New York: Continuum.

Boose, Lynda and Richard Burt. 1997. "Totally Clueless: Shakespeare Goes Hollywood in the 1990s." *Shakespeare, the Movie: Popularizing the Plays on Film, TV, and Video.* New York and London: Routledge.

Burt, Richard. 1999. *Unspeakable ShaXXXspeares: Queer Theory and American Kiddie Culture.* 2nd.ed. St. Martin's Press.

Cartmell, Deborah. 2000. *Interpreting Shakespeare on Screen.* New York: St. Martin's Press.

Carver, Benedict. 1999. "Tough Treading Ahead for Taymor's 'Titus.'" *Variety,* September 6.

Cohen, Roger. 2000. "A Jewish Museum Mired in Dissent Struggles to Be Born in Berlin." *New York Times,* August 15.

Cole, Tim. 2000. *Selling the Holocaust: From Auschwitz to Schindler; How History is Bought, Packaged and Sold.* New York and London: Routledge.

D'Amato, Brian and David Rimanelli. 2000. "Dutchman's Breaches." *Art Forum* Summer 38:10 (Summer) 150–155; 201.

De Vries, Hent and Samuel Weber et al., eds. 1997. *Violence, Identity and Self-Determination.* Stanford: Stanford Univ. Press.

de Luca, Maria and Mary Lindroth. 2000. "Mayhem, Madness, Method: An Interview with Julie Taymor." *Cineaste,* June 25 (3): 28–31.

Dessen, Alan C. *Titus Andronicus.* Manchester, New York, Manchester UP: 1989.

Duggan, Christopher. 1994. *A Concise History of Italy.* Cambridge: Cambridge Univ. Press.

Feinberg, Anat. 1998. "George Tabori's Mourning Work in *Jubilaum.*" In *Staging the Holocaust: The Shoah in Drama and Performance.* Ed. by Claude Schumacher. Cambridge, UK: Cambridge Univ. Press.

Finkelstein, Norman G. 2000. *The Holocaust Industry: Reflections on the Exploitation of Jewish Suffering.* London: Verso.

Gilman, Sander L. 2000. "Is Life Beautiful? Can the Shoah be Funny?" Some Thoughts on Recent and Older Films." *Critical Inquiry* 26: 2 (Winter): 279–308.

Girard, Rene. 1991. *A Theater of Envy: William Shakespeare.* New York: Oxford Univ. Press.

Greenblatt, Stephen. 2001. "Dreams of Kingship." In *Kulturtheorien.* Ed. by Helga Breuninger and Gerhart Schroeder. Frankfurt am Main Verlag.

Habicht, Werner. 1989. "Shakespeare and Theatre Politics in the Third Reich." In *The Play Out of Context: Transferring Plays from Culture to Culture.* Cambridge, UK: Cambridge Univ. Press, 110–20.

Halperin, Richard. 1997. "That Shakespeherian Mob: Mass Culture and the Literary Public Sphere." In *Shakespeare Among the Moderns.* Ithaca, NY: Cornell Univ. Press, 51–113.

Holden, Stephen. 1999. "It's Sort of a Family Dinner, Your Majesty." *New York Times,* Friday December 24, B19.

Hortmann, Wilhelm. 1998. *Shakespeare on the German Stage. Vol. 2, The Twentieth Century.* With a Section on Shakespeare on Stage in the German Democratic Republic by Maik Hamburger. Cambridge, UK: Cambridge Univ. Press.

Isler, Alan. 1994. *The Prince of West End Avenue.* Bridgehampton, NY: Bridge Works.

Isser, Edward R. 1997. *Stages of Annihilation: Theatrical Representations of the Holocaust.* Madison, NJ: Farleigh Dickinson Univ. Press; London; Cranbury, NJ: Associated Univ. Presses.

Janofsky, Michael. 1999. "Student Killers' Tapes Filled with Rage." *New York Times,* December 14, A10.

Kramer, Jane. 1996. *The Politics of Memory: Looking for Germany in the New Germany.* New York: Random House.

Landy, Marcia. 1998. *The Folklore of Consensus: Theatricality in the Italian Cinema, 1930–1943.* SUNY Series, Cultural Studies in Cinema/Video. Albany, NY: State Univ. of New York Press.

———. 1986. *Fascism in Film: The Italian Commercial Cinema, 1931–1943.* Princeton, NJ: Princeton Univ. Press.

Levine, Lawrence. 1988. "The Sacralization of Culture." In *Highbrow/Lowbrow: The Emergence of Cultural Hierarchy in America.* Cambridge, MA: Harvard Univ. Press, 85–168.

Mancini, Elaine. 1985. *Struggles of the Italian Film Industry during Fascism, 1930–1935.* Studies in Cinema, No 34. Ann Arbor, MI: UMI Research.

Marcus, Greil. 1989. *Lipstick Traces: A Secret History of the Twentieth Century.* Cambridge, MA: Harvard Univ. Press.

Morrow, Fiona. 2000. "Shakespeare Meets Hannibal Lecter," *London Independent,* August 4, 12.

Nowell-Smith, Geoffrey. 1996. *Companion to Italian Cinema.* London: British Film Institute.

Pfister, Manfred. Forthcoming. "Route 66: The Political Performance of Shakespeare's Sonnet 66 in Germany and Elsewhere." *Shakespeare Jahrbuch.*

Plath, Sylvia. 1965. *Ariel.* New York: Harper & Row.

Pizzello, Stephen. 2000. "From Stage to Screen: Theatrical Director Julie Taymor Reimagines Her Radical Stage Version of *Titus Andronicus* for the Screen." In Julie Taymor's *Titus* DVD edition, originally published in *American Cinematographer.*

Ravetto, Kriss. 2001. *The Unmaking of Fascist Aesthetics.* Minneapolis, MN: Univ. of Minnesota Press.

Reynolds, Bryan. 2000. "'What Is the City but the People?': Transversal Performance and Radical Politics in Shakespeare's *Coriolanus* and Brecht's *Coriolan.*" In *Shakespeare without Class: Misappropriations of Cultural Capital.* Ed. by Don Hedrick and Bryan Reynolds. New York: St. Martin's Press, 107–32.

Rose, Jacqueline. 1992. *The Haunting of Sylvia Plath.* Cambridge, MA: Harvard Univ. Press.

Rovit, Rebecca and Alvin Goldfarb, eds. 1999. *Theatrical Performance during the Holocaust: Texts, Documents, Memoirs.* Baltimore: Johns Hopkins Univ. Press.

Schechner, Richard. 1999. "Julie Taymor: From Jacques Lecoq to *The Lion King,*" *The Drama Review* 43: 3 (Fall), 36–53.

Sitney, P. Adams.1995. *Vital Crises in Italian Cinema: Iconography, Stylistics, Politics.* Austin: Univ. of Texas Press.

Snead, Elizabeth. 2000. "Julie Taymor's 'Pulp Shakespeare.'" *USA Today.* February 28. http://www.usatoday.com/life/enter/movies/movie245.htm.

Snyder, Joel. 2000. Interview with Julie Taymor, National Endowment for the Arts. http://bayarea.citysearch.com/E/V/SFOCA/2024/75/38/.

Stone, Alan A. 2000. "Shakespeare's Tarantino Play: Julie Taymor Resurrects the despised Titus Andronicus." April/May. http://bostonreview.mit.edu/BR25.2/stone.html.

Taymor, Julie. 2000. *Titus: The Illustrated Screenplay Adapted from the Play by William Shakespeare.* New York: Newmarket Press.

Thompson, Anne. 2000. "It's Savage. It's Subversive. Its Shakespeare." *Women in Hollywood 2000.* Premiere issue, 35–38.

Tifft, Stephen. 1991. "Miming the Führer: *To Be or Not to Be* and the Mechanisms of Outrage." *Yale Journal of Criticism* 5 (1): 1–40.

Traister, Rebecca. 2000. "The Story of *O,* Weinstein Style: High-School *Othello* Is Held Up." http://www.nyobserver.com/pages/story.asp?ID=3417. November 13.

Viano, Maurizio. 1999. "*Life is Beautiful:* Reception, Allegory, and Holocaust Laughter." *Film Quarterly* 53: 1 (Fall), 26–34.

Waxman, Sharon. 2001. "Studio Keeps a Lid on 'O' after School Shootings." March 10. http://www.washingtonpost.com/wp-dyn/articles/A49523-2001Mar9.html

Wrathall, John. 2000. "Bloody Arcades." *Sight and Sound* 10: 7 (July), 25–29.

Young, James E. 2000. *At Memory's Edge: After-Images of the Holocaust in Contemporary Art and Architecture.* New Haven: Yale Univ. Press.

———, ed. With contributions by Matthew Baigell, et al. 1994. *The Art of Memory: Holocaust Memorials in History.* New York: Prestel.

Žižek, Slavoj. 2000. "Camp Comedy," *Sight and Sound* 10: 4 (April) 2000: 26–29.

Websites Cited

http://www.clearblueskyfilms.com/featurefilms/titus
http://www.foxsearchlight.com/titus
http://www.richeyproductions.com
http://home1.gte.net/titus98
http://www.pbs.org/wgbh/pages/frontline/shows/kinkel/etc/script.html
http://www.titusandronicus.8m.com/tituspage.html

Films and Videos Cited

Allers, Roger and Robert Minkoff, dir. 1994. *The Lion King.* USA. Disney. Sound, col., 88 mins.

Benigni, Roberto, dir. 1998. *Life Is Beautiful.* Italy. Miramax. Sound, col., 116 mins.

Bertolucci, Bernardo, dir. 1970. *The Conformist.* Italy. Paramount. Sound, col., 108 mins.

———. 1976. *1900.* Italy. Sound, col., 255 mins.

Beyer, Frank, dir. 1977. *Jacob the Liar.* DDR. DEFA. Sound, col., 96 mins.

Branagh, Kenneth, dir. 1989. *Henry V.* UK. MGM. Sound, col., 138 mins.

Brooks, Mel, dir. 1969. *The Producers.* USA. MGM. Sound, col., 131 mins.

Cavani, Liliana, dir. 1974. *The Night Porter.* Italy. Janus Films. Sound, col., 118 mins.

Craven, Wes, dir. 1996. *Scream.* USA. Sound, col., 111 mins.

de Sica, Vittorio, dir. 1970. *The Garden of The Finzi Continis.* Italy. Sony. Sound, col., 94 mins.

Dunne, Christopher, dir. 1999. *Titus Andronicus.* USA. Joe Redner Productions. Sound, col., 140 mins.

Fellini, Federico, dir. 1974. *Amarcord.* Italy. Janus. Sound, col., 127 mins.

———. 1969. *Satyricon.* Italy. MGM. Sound, col., 130 mins.

———. 1954. *La Strada* Italy. Jamus Films. Sound, b/w., 107 mins.

Greenaway, Peter, 1991. *Prospero's Books.* Netherlands/France/Italy. Twentieth Century Fox. Sound, col., 126 mins.

Griffin, Richard, dir. 2000. *William Shakespeare's Titus Andronicus.* USA. South Main Street Productions. Sound, col., 207 mins.

Harron, Mary, dir. 1999. *American Psycho.* USA. Miramax. Sound, col., 103 mins.

Heckerling, Amy, dir. 1995. *Clueless.* USA. Paramount. Sound, col., 97 mins.

Howell, Jane, dir. 1985. *Titus Andronicus.* UK. BBC television. Sound, col.

Johnson, Alan, dir. 1983. *To Be or Not to Be.* USA. Twentieth Century Fox. Sound, col.,107 mins.

Kassovitz, Peter, dir. 1999. *Jakob the Liar.* USA. Columbia. Sound, col., 114 mins.

Kaufman, Loyd, dir. 1996. *Tromeo and Juliet.* USA. Troma Entertainment. Sound, col., 147 mins.

Kirk, Michael, dir. 2000. *The Killer at Thurston High.* PBS Frontline Airdate: January 18. 90 mins.

Kubrick, Stanley, dir. 1960. *Spartacus.* USA. Universal. Sound, col., 196 mins.

Loncarine, Richard, dir. 1996. *Richard III.* USA. MGM/UA. Sound, col., 104 mins.

Lubitsch, Ernest, dir. 1942. *To Be or Not to Be.* USA. United Artists. Sound, b/w., 99 mins.

Lucas. George, dir. 1999. *Star Wars Episode 1: The Phantom Menace.* USA. Lucas Films. Sound, col., 133 mins.

Luhrmann, Baz, dir. 1996. *William Shakespeare's Romeo + Juliet.* USA. Twentieth Century Fox. Sound, col., 129 mins.

Madden, II, John, dir. 1998 *Shakespeare in Love.* USA. Miramax. Sound, col., 122 mins.

Mankiwicz, Joseph, dir. 1953. *Julius Caesar.* USA. MGM. Sound, b/w, 122 mins.

Meyer, Nicholas. 1991. *Star Trek VI: The Undiscovered Country.* Paramount. USA. Sound, col., 113 mins.

Meyer, Robert Burnett, dir. 1998 *Free Enterprise.* USA. Mindfire. Sound, col., 116 mins.

Mihaileanu, Radu, dir. 1998. *Train of Life*. France. Sound, col., 102 mins.

Pasolini, Palo, dir. 1975. *Salo*. Italy. Sound, col., 114 mins.

Raimi, Sam. 1993. *Army of Darkness*. USA. MCA/Universal. Sound, col., 81 mins.

Reitman, Ivan, dir. 1990. *Kindergarten Cop*. USA. United Artists.Sound, col.,111 mins.

Richey, Lorn, dir. 1997. *Titus Andronicus*. USA. Richey Productions. Sound, col., 120 mins.

Scott, Ridley, dir. 2000. *Gladiator*. USA. Dreamworks. Sound, col., 154 mins.

————. 2001. *Hannibal*. USA. Metro Goldwyn Mayor / Universal. Sound, col., 131 mins.

Spielberg, Stephen, dir. 1982. *E.T.* USA. Universal. Sound, col., 115 mins.

————. 1993. *Schindler's List*. USA. Universal. Sound, b/w, 164 mins.

Stone, Oliver, dir. 1994 *Natural Born Killers*. USA. Vidmark. Sound, col., 182 mins.

Szabo Istvan, dir. 1981. *Mephisto*. MAFilm-Objektiv Studio. Sound, col., 132 mins.

Tarentino, Quentin, dir. 1993. *Reservoir Dogs*. USA. Miramax. Sound, col., 100 mins.

————. 1995. *Pulp Fiction*. USA. Miramax. Sound, col., 164 mins.

Taymor, Julie, dir. 1999. *Titus*. USA. Clear Blue Sky Productions/Twentieth Century Fox. Sound, col., 172 mins. DVD edition.

Verhoeven, Paul, dir. 1998. *Starship Troopers*. USA. Columbia Tristar. Sound, col., 130 mins.

Visconti, Luchino, dir. 1969. *The Damned*. Italy. Sound, col., 150 mins.

Wachowski, Andy and Larry, dir. 1999. *The Matrix*. USA. Warner Brothers. Sound, col., 136 mins.

Wiess, Jiri, dir. 1960. *Romeo, Julie a tma*. Czechoslovakia. Sound, b/w, 96 mins.

Wertmuller, Lina, dir. 1976. *The Seven Beauties*. Italy. Sound, col., 114 mins.

Williamson, Kevin, dir. 1999. *Teaching Mrs. Tingle*. USA. Miramax. Sound, col., 95 mins.

Wyler, William, dir. 1959. *Ben Hur*. USA. MGM. Sound, col., 211 mins.

INDEX

WITHDRAWN